Introd
Computation and
Programming Using Python
with Application to Understanding Data

Introduction to Computation and Programming Using Python
with Application to Understanding Data

Second Edition

John V. Guttag

PHI Learning Private Limited

Delhi-110092
2018

This Indian Reprint—₹ 695.00
(Original U.S. Edition—₹ 3155.00)

**INTRODUCTION TO COMPUTATION AND PROGRAMMING USING PYTHON
with Application to Understanding Data, Second Edition**
by John V. Guttag

© 2016 by Massachusetts Institute of Technology. All rights reserved. No part of this book may be reproduced in any form, by mimeograph or any other means, without permission in writing from the publisher.

ISBN-978-81-203-5292-6

Original edition published by the MIT Press, Cambridge, MA, U.S.A.

Reprinted in India by special arrangement with MIT Press, Cambridge, MA, U.S.A. Not for sale or shipment outside India, Bangladesh, Burma, Nepal, Sri Lanka, Bhutan, Pakistan and the Maldives.

Published by Asoke K. Ghosh, PHI Learning Private Limited, Rimjhim House, 111, Patparganj Industrial Estate, Delhi-110092 and Printed by Rajkamal Electric Press, Plot No. 2, Phase IV, HSIDC, Kundli-131028, Sonepat, Haryana.

To my family:

Olga
David
Andrea
Michael
Mark
Addie

CONTENTS

PREFACE xiii
ACKNOWLEDGMENTS xvii
1   GETTING STARTED 1
2   INTRODUCTION TO PYTHON 7
    2.1   The Basic Elements of Python 9
        2.1.1   Objects, Expressions, and Numerical Types 9
        2.1.2   Variables and Assignment 12
        2.1.3   Python IDE's 14
    2.2   Branching Programs 15
    2.3   Strings and Input 18
        2.3.1   Input 20
        2.3.2   A Digression About Character Encoding 21
    2.4   Iteration 22
3   SOME SIMPLE NUMERICAL PROGRAMS 25
    3.1   Exhaustive Enumeration 25
    3.2   For Loops 27
    3.3   Approximate Solutions and Bisection Search 30
    3.4   A Few Words About Using Floats 34
    3.5   Newton-Raphson 37
4   FUNCTIONS, SCOPING, AND ABSTRACTION 39
    4.1   Functions and Scoping 40
        4.1.1   Function Definitions 40
        4.1.2   Keyword Arguments and Default Values 42
        4.1.3   Scoping 43
    4.2   Specifications 47
    4.3   Recursion 50
        4.3.1   Fibonacci Numbers 52
        4.3.2   Palindromes 54
    4.4   Global Variables 57
    4.5   Modules 59
    4.6   Files 61

5 STRUCTURED TYPES, MUTABILITY, AND HIGHER-ORDER FUNCTIONS 65
- 5.1 Tuples 65
  - 5.1.1 Sequences and Multiple Assignment 67
- 5.2 Ranges 67
- 5.3 Lists and Mutability 68
  - 5.3.1 Cloning 73
  - 5.3.2 List Comprehension 74
- 5.4 Functions as Objects 75
- 5.5 Strings, Tuples, Ranges, and Lists 77
- 5.6 Dictionaries 79

6 TESTING AND DEBUGGING 85
- 6.1 Testing 86
  - 6.1.1 Black-Box Testing 87
  - 6.1.2 Glass-box Testing 88
  - 6.1.3 Conducting Tests 90
- 6.2 Debugging 92
  - 6.2.1 Learning to Debug 94
  - 6.2.2 Designing the Experiment 95
  - 6.2.3 When the Going Gets Tough 98
  - 6.2.4 When You Have Found "The" Bug 99

7 EXCEPTIONS AND ASSERTIONS 101
- 7.1 Handling Exceptions 101
- 7.2 Exceptions as a Control Flow Mechanism 105
- 7.3 Assertions 108

8 CLASSES AND OBJECT-ORIENTED PROGRAMMING 109
- 8.1 Abstract Data Types and Classes 109
  - 8.1.1 Designing Programs Using Abstract Data Types 114
  - 8.1.2 Using Classes to Keep Track of Students and Faculty 115
- 8.2 Inheritance 118
  - 8.2.1 Multiple Levels of Inheritance 121
  - 8.2.2 The Substitution Principle 123
- 8.3 Encapsulation and Information Hiding 123
  - 8.3.1 Generators 128
- 8.4 Mortgages, an Extended Example 130

9 A SIMPLISTIC INTRODUCTION TO ALGORITHMIC COMPLEXITY .. 135
- 9.1 Thinking About Computational Complexity 135
- 9.2 Asymptotic Notation 139

CONTENTS

- 9.3 Some Important Complexity Classes 141
  - 9.3.1 Constant Complexity 141
  - 9.3.2 Logarithmic Complexity 141
  - 9.3.3 Linear Complexity 142
  - 9.3.4 Log-Linear Complexity 144
  - 9.3.5 Polynomial Complexity 144
  - 9.3.6 Exponential Complexity 145
  - 9.3.7 Comparisons of Complexity Classes 147
- **10 SOME SIMPLE ALGORITHMS AND DATA STRUCTURES 151**
  - 10.1 Search Algorithms 152
    - 10.1.1 Linear Search and Using Indirection to Access Elements 153
    - 10.1.2 Binary Search and Exploiting Assumptions 154
  - 10.2 Sorting Algorithms 158
    - 10.2.1 Merge Sort 159
    - 10.2.2 Exploiting Functions as Parameters 162
    - 10.2.3 Sorting in Python 162
  - 10.3 Hash Tables 164
- **11 PLOTTING AND MORE ABOUT CLASSES 169**
  - 11.1 Plotting Using PyLab 169
  - 11.2 Plotting Mortgages, an Extended Example 175
- **12 KNAPSACK AND GRAPH OPTIMIZATION PROBLEMS 183**
  - 12.1 Knapsack Problems 184
    - 12.1.1 Greedy Algorithms 184
    - 12.1.2 An Optimal Solution to the 0/1 Knapsack Problem 188
  - 12.2 Graph Optimization Problems 190
    - 12.2.1 Some Classic Graph-Theoretic Problems 195
    - 12.2.2 Shortest Path: Depth-First Search and Breadth-First Search 196
- **13 DYNAMIC PROGRAMMING 203**
  - 13.1 Fibonacci Sequences, Revisited 203
  - 13.2 Dynamic Programming and the 0/1 Knapsack Problem 205
  - 13.3 Dynamic Programming and Divide-and-Conquer 213
- **14 RANDOM WALKS AND MORE ABOUT DATA VISUALIZATION 215**
  - 14.1 Random Walks 216
  - 14.2 The Drunkard's Walk 217
  - 14.3 Biased Random Walks 224
  - 14.4 Treacherous Fields 231

15 STOCHASTIC PROGRAMS, PROBABILITY, AND DISTRIBUTIONS 235
- 15.1 Stochastic Programs 236
- 15.2 Calculating Simple Probabilities 238
- 15.3 Inferential Statistics 239
- 15.4 Distributions 254
  - 15.4.1 Probability Distributions 256
  - 15.4.2 Normal Distributions 258
  - 15.4.3 Continuous and Discrete Uniform Distributions 263
  - 15.4.4 Binomial and Multinomial Distributions 264
  - 15.4.5 Exponential and Geometric Distributions 265
  - 15.4.6 Benford's Distribution 269
- 15.5 Hashing and Collisions 269
- 15.6 How Often Does the Better Team Win? 272

16 MONTE CARLO SIMULATION 275
- 16.1 Pascal's Problem 276
- 16.2 Pass or Don't Pass? 277
- 16.3 Using Table Lookup to Improve Performance 282
- 16.4 Finding π 283
- 16.5 Some Closing Remarks About Simulation Models 288

17 SAMPLING AND CONFIDENCE INTERVALS 291
- 17.1 Sampling the Boston Marathon 292
- 17.2 The Central Limit Theorem 298
- 17.3 Standard Error of the Mean 302

18 UNDERSTANDING EXPERIMENTAL DATA 305
- 18.1 The Behavior of Springs 305
  - 18.1.1 Using Linear Regression to Find a Fit 309
- 18.2 The Behavior of Projectiles 314
  - 18.2.1 Coefficient of Determination 317
  - 18.2.2 Using a Computational Model 319
- 18.3 Fitting Exponentially Distributed Data 320
- 18.4 When Theory Is Missing 324

19 RANDOMIZED TRIALS AND HYPOTHESIS CHECKING 327
- 19.1 Checking Significance 328
- 19.2 Beware of P-values 334
- 19.3 One-tail and One-sample Tests 336
- 19.4 Significant or Not? 338
- 19.5 Which N? 340

  19.6 Multiple Hypotheses...342
20 CONDITIONAL PROBABILITY AND BAYESIAN STATISTICS 345
  20.1 Conditional Probabilities..346
  20.2 Bayes' Theorem..348
  20.3 Bayesian Updating..350
21 LIES, DAMNED LIES, AND STATISTICS..355
  21.1 Garbage In Garbage Out (GIGO)...355
  21.2 Tests Are Imperfect...356
  21.3 Pictures Can Be Deceiving..357
  21.4 Cum Hoc Ergo Propter Hoc...359
  21.5 Statistical Measures Don't Tell the Whole Story 361
  21.6 Sampling Bias...362
  21.7 Context Matters 363
  21.8 Beware of Extrapolation...364
  21.9 The Texas Sharpshooter Fallacy...364
  21.10 Percentages Can Confuse..367
  21.11 Statistically Significant Differences Can Be Insignificant......368
  21.12 The Regressive Fallacy 369
  21.13 Just Beware 370
22 A QUICK LOOK AT MACHINE LEARNING...371
  22.1 Feature Vectors 374
  22.2 Distance Metrics 377
23 CLUSTERING 383
  23.1 Class Cluster..385
  23.2 K-means Clustering..387
  23.3 A Contrived Example...390
  23.4 A Less Contrived Example...395
24 CLASSIFICATION METHODS..403
  24.1 Evaluating Classifiers 403
  24.2 Predicting the Gender of Runners 408
  24.3 K-nearest Neighbors...408
  24.4 Regression-based Classifiers...415
  24.5 Surviving the Titanic 425
  24.6 Wrapping Up...430
PYTHON 3.5 QUICK REFERENCE..431
INDEX 435

PREFACE

This book is based on courses that have been offered at MIT since 2006, and as "Massive Online Open Courses" (MOOCs) through edX and MITx since 2012. The first edition of the book was based on a single one-semester course. However, over time I couldn't resist adding more material than could be fit into a semester. The current edition is suitable for a two-semester introductory computer science sequence.

When I started working on the second edition I thought that I would just add a few chapters, but I ended up doing far more. I reorganized the back half of the book, and converted the entire book from Python 2 to Python 3.

The book is aimed at students with little or no prior programming experience who have a desire to understand computational approaches to problem solving. For some of the students the material in this book will be a stepping stone to more advanced computer science courses. But for many of the students it will be their only formal exposure to computer science.

Because this will be the only formal exposure to computer science for many of the students, we emphasize breadth rather than depth. The goal is to provide students with a brief introduction to many topics, so that they will have an idea of what's possible when the time comes to think about how to use computation to accomplish a goal. That said, this is not a "computation appreciation" book. It is challenging and rigorous. Students who wish to really learn the material will have to spend a lot of time and effort learning to bend the computer to their will.

The main goal of this book is to help students become skillful at making productive use of computational techniques. They should learn to use computational modes of thoughts to frame problems and to guide the process of extracting information from data. The primary knowledge they will take away from this book is the art of computational problem solving.

This book is not easily slotted into a conventional computer science curriculum. Chapters 1-11 contain the kind of material typically included in a computer science course aimed at students with little or no programming experience. Chapters 12-14 contain slightly more advanced material, various subsets of which could be added to the introductory course if the students are more advanced. Chapters 15-24 are about using computation to help understand data.

They cover the material that we think should become the usual second course in a computer science curriculum (replacing the traditional data structures course).

In Chapters 1-11, we braid together four strands of material:

- The basics of programming,
- The Python 3 programming language,
- Computational problem solving techniques,
- Computational complexity, and
- Using plots to present information.

We cover most of Python's features, but the emphasis is on what one can do with a programming language, not on the language itself. For example, by the end of Chapter 3 the book has covered only a small fraction of Python, but it has already introduced the notions of exhaustive enumeration, guess-and-check algorithms, bisection search, and efficient approximation algorithms. We introduce features of Python throughout the book. Similarly, we introduce aspects of programming methods throughout the book. The idea is to help students learn Python and how to be a good programmer in the context of using computation to solve interesting problems.

The examples in this book have been tested using Python 3.5. Python 3 cleaned up many of the inconsistencies in the design of the various releases of Python 2 (often referred to as Python 2.x). However, it is not backward compatible. That meant that most programs written using Python 2 cannot be run using implementations of Python 3. For that reason, Python 2.x continues to be widely used. The first time we use features of Python 3 that differ from Python 2, we point out how the same thing could be accomplished in Python 2. All of the examples in this book are available online in both Python 3.5 and Python 2.7.

Chapters 12-13 provide an introduction to optimization, an important topic not usually covered in introductory courses. Chapters 14-16 provide an introduction to stochastic programs, another important topic not usually covered in introductory courses. Our experience at MIT is that we can can cover either Chapters 12-13 or Chapters 15-16, but not both, in our one-semester introductory course.

Chapters 15-24 are designed to provide a self-contained introduction to using computation to help understand data. They assume no knowledge of mathematics beyond high school algebra, but do assume that the reader is comfortable with rigorous thinking and is not intimidated by mathematical concepts. This part of the book is devoted to topics not found in most introductory texts: data visualization, simulation models, probabilistic and statistical thinking, and machine learning. We believe that this is a far more relevant body of material for most students than what is typically covered in the second computer science course.

We chose not to include problems at the end of chapters. Instead we inserted "finger exercises" at opportune points within the chapters. Some are quite short, and are intended to allow readers to confirm that they understood the material they just read. Some are a bit more challenging, and are suitable for exam questions. And others are challenging enough to be useful as homework assignments.

The book has three pervasive themes: systematic problem solving, the power of abstraction, and computation as a way of thinking about the world. When you have finished this book you should have:

- Learned a language, Python, for expressing computations,
- Learned a systematic approach to organizing, writing, and debugging medium-sized programs,
- Developed an informal understanding of computational complexity,
- Developed some insight into the process of moving from an ambiguous problem statement to a computational formulation of a method for solving the problem,
- Learned a useful set of algorithmic and problem reduction techniques,
- Learned how to use randomness and simulations to shed light on problems that don't easily succumb to closed-form solutions, and
- Learned how to use computational tools (including simple statistical, visualization, and machine learning tools) to model and understand data.

Programming is an intrinsically difficult activity. Just as "there is no royal road to geometry,"[1] there is no royal road to programming. If you really want to learn the material, reading the book will not be enough. At the very least you should try running some of the code in the book. Various versions of the courses from which this book has been derived have been available on MIT's OpenCourseWare (OCW) Web site since 2008. The site includes video recordings of lectures and a complete set of problem sets and exams. Since the fall of 2012, edX and MITx have offered online courses that cover much of the material in this book. We strongly recommend that you do the problem sets associated with one of the OCW or edX offerings.

---

[1] This was Euclid's purported response, circa 300 BCE, to King Ptolemy's request for an easier way to learn mathematics.

ACKNOWLEDGMENTS

The first edition of this book grew out of a set of lecture notes that I prepared while teaching an undergraduate course at MIT. The course, and therefore this book, benefited from suggestions from faculty colleagues (especially Ana Bell, Eric Grimson, Srinivas Devadas, Fredo Durand, Ron Rivest, and Chris Terman), teaching assistants, and the students who took the course. David Guttag overcame his aversion to computer science, and proofread multiple chapters.

Like all successful professors, I owe a great deal to my graduate students. The photo on the back cover of this book depicts me supporting some of my current students. In the lab, however, it is they who support me. In addition to doing great research (and letting me take some of the credit for it), Guha Balakrishnan, David Blalock, Joel Brooks, Ganeshapillai Gartheeban, Jen Gong, Yun Liu, Anima Singh, Jenna Wiens, and Amy Zhao all provided useful comments on various versions of this manuscript.

I owe a special debt of gratitude to Julie Sussman, P.P.A. Until I started working with Julie, I had no idea how much difference an editor could make. I had worked with capable copy editors on previous books, and thought that was what I needed for this book. I was wrong. I needed a collaborator who could read the book with the eyes of a student, and tell me what needed to be done, what should be done, and what could be done if I had the time and energy to do it. Julie buried me in "suggestions" that were too good to ignore. Her combined command of both the English language and programming is quite remarkable.

Finally, thanks to my wife, Olga, for pushing me to finish and for excusing me from various household duties so that I could work on the book.

1 GETTING STARTED

A computer does two things, and two things only: it performs calculations and it remembers the results of those calculations. But it does those two things extremely well. The typical computer that sits on a desk or in a briefcase performs a billion or so calculations a second. It's hard to image how truly fast that is. Think about holding a ball a meter above the floor, and letting it go. By the time it reaches the floor, your computer could have executed over a billion instructions. As for memory, a small computer might have hundreds of gigabytes of storage. How big is that? If a byte (the number of bits, typically eight, required to represent one character) weighed one gram (which it doesn't), 100 gigabytes would weigh 10,000 metric tons. For comparison, that's roughly the combined weight of 15,000 African elephants.

For most of human history, computation was limited by the speed of calculation of the human brain and the ability to record computational results with the human hand. This meant that only the smallest problems could be attacked computationally. Even with the speed of modern computers, there are still problems that are beyond modern computational models (e.g., understanding climate change), but more and more problems are proving amenable to computational solution. It is our hope that by the time you finish this book, you will feel comfortable bringing computational thinking to bear on solving many of the problems you encounter during your studies, work, and everyday life.

What do we mean by computational thinking?

All knowledge can be thought of as either declarative or imperative. **Declarative knowledge** is composed of statements of fact. For example, "the square root of x is a number y such that y*y = x." This is a statement of fact. Unfortunately, it doesn't tell us anything about how to find a square root.

Imperative knowledge is "how to" knowledge, or recipes for deducing information. Heron of Alexandria was the first to document a way to compute the square root of a number.[2] His method for finding the square root of a number, call it x, can be summarized as:

---

[2] Many believe that Heron was not the inventor of this method, and indeed there is some evidence that it was well known to the ancient Babylonians.

1. Start with a guess, g.
2. If g*g is close enough to x, stop and say that g is the answer.
3. Otherwise create a new guess by averaging g and x/g, i.e., (g + x/g)/2.
4. Using this new guess, which we again call g, repeat the process until g*g is close enough to x.

Consider, for example, finding the square root of 25.

1. Set g to some arbitrary value, e.g., 3.
2. We decide that 3*3 = 9 is not close enough to 25.
3. Set g to (3 + 25/3)/2 = 5.67.[3]
4. We decide that 5.67*5.67 = 32.15 is still not close enough to 25.
5. Set g to (5.67 + 25/5.67)/2 = 5.04
6. We decide that 5.04*5.04 = 25.4 is close enough, so we stop and declare 5.04 to be an adequate approximation to the square root of 25.

Note that the description of the method is a sequence of simple steps, together with a flow of control that specifies when each step is to be executed. Such a description is called an **algorithm**.[4] This algorithm is an example of a guess-and-check algorithm. It is based on the fact that it is easy to check whether or not a guess is a good one.

A bit more formally, an algorithm is a finite list of instructions that describe a **computation** that when executed on a set of inputs will proceed through a set of well-defined states and eventually produce an output.

An algorithm is a bit like a recipe from a cookbook:

1. Put custard mixture over heat.
2. Stir.
3. Dip spoon in custard.
4. Remove spoon and run finger across back of spoon.
5. If clear path is left, remove custard from heat and let cool.
6. Otherwise repeat.

It includes some tests for deciding when the process is complete, as well as instructions about the order in which to execute instructions, sometimes jumping to a specific instruction based on a test.

So how does one capture this idea of a recipe in a mechanical process? One way would be to design a machine specifically intended to compute square roots.

---

[3] For simplicity, we are rounding results.

[4] The word "algorithm" is derived from the name of the Persian mathematician Muhammad ibn Musa al-Khwarizmi.

Odd as this may sound, the earliest computing machines were, in fact, **fixed-program computers**, meaning they were designed to do very specific things, and were mostly tools to solve a specific mathematical problem, e.g., to compute the trajectory of an artillery shell. One of the first computers (built in 1941 by Atanasoff and Berry) solved systems of linear equations, but could do nothing else. Alan Turing's bombe machine, developed during World War II, was designed strictly for the purpose of breaking German Enigma codes. Some very simple computers still use this approach. For example, a simple handheld calculator[5] is a fixed-program computer. It can do basic arithmetic, but it cannot be used as a word processor or to run video games. To change the program of such a machine, one has to replace the circuitry.

The first truly modern computer was the Manchester Mark 1.[6] It was distinguished from its predecessors by the fact that it was a **stored-program computer**. Such a computer stores (and manipulates) a sequence of instructions, and has components that will execute any instruction in that sequence. By creating an instruction-set architecture and detailing the computation as a sequence of instructions (i.e., a program), we get a highly flexible machine. By treating those instructions in the same way as data, a stored-program machine can easily change the program, and can do so under program control. Indeed, the heart of the computer then becomes a program (called an **interpreter**) that can execute any legal set of instructions, and thus can be used to compute anything that one can describe using some basic set of instructions.

Both the program and the data it manipulates reside in memory. Typically, there is a program counter that points to a particular location in memory, and computation starts by executing the instruction at that point. Most often, the interpreter simply goes to the next instruction in the sequence, but not always. In some cases, it performs a test, and on the basis of that test, execution may jump to some other point in the sequence of instructions. This is called **flow of control,** and is essential to allowing us to write programs that perform complex tasks.

Returning to the recipe metaphor, given a fixed set of ingredients a good chef can make an unbounded number of tasty dishes by combining them in different ways. Similarly, given a small fixed set of primitive features a good programmer can produce an unbounded number of useful programs. This is what makes programming such an amazing endeavor.

---

[5] It's hard to believe, but once upon a time phones did not provide computational facilities. People actually used small devices that could be used only for calculation.

[6] This computer was built at the University of Manchester, and ran its first program in 1949. It implemented ideas previously described by John von Neumann and was anticipated by the theoretical concept of the Universal Turing Machine described by Alan Turing in 1936.

To create recipes, or sequences of instructions, we need a **programming language** in which to describe them, a way to give the computer its marching orders.

In 1936, the British mathematician Alan Turing described a hypothetical computing device that has come to be called a **Universal Turing Machine**. The machine had an unbounded memory in the form of "tape" on which one could write zeroes and ones, and some very simple primitive instructions for moving, reading, and writing to the tape. The **Church-Turing thesis** states that if a function is computable, a Turing Machine can be programmed to compute it.

The "if" in the Church-Turing thesis is important. Not all problems have computational solutions. Turing showed, for example, that it is impossible to write a program that given an arbitrary program, call it P, prints true if and only if P will run forever. This is known as the **halting problem**.

The Church-Turing thesis leads directly to the notion of **Turing completeness**. A programming language is said to be Turing complete if it can be used to simulate a universal Turing Machine. All modern programming languages are Turing complete. As a consequence, anything that can be programmed in one programming language (e.g., Python) can be programmed in any other programming language (e.g., Java). Of course, some things may be easier to program in a particular language, but all languages are fundamentally equal with respect to computational power.

Fortunately, no programmer has to build programs out of Turing's primitive instructions. Instead, modern programming languages offer a larger, more convenient set of primitives. However, the fundamental idea of programming as the process of assembling a sequence of operations remains central.

Whatever set of primitives one has, and whatever methods one has for using them, the best thing and the worst thing about programming are the same: the computer will do exactly what you tell it to do. This is a good thing because it means that you can make it do all sorts of fun and useful things. It is a bad thing because when it doesn't do what you want it to do, you usually have nobody to blame but yourself.

There are hundreds of programming languages in the world. There is no best language (though one could nominate some candidates for worst). Different languages are better or worse for different kinds of applications. MATLAB, for example, is a good language for manipulating vectors and matrices. C is a good language for writing programs that control data networks. PHP is a good language for building Web sites. And Python is a good general-purpose language.

Each programming language has a set of primitive constructs, a syntax, a static semantics, and a semantics. By analogy with a natural language, e.g., English, the primitive constructs are words, the syntax describes which strings of words constitute well-formed sentences, the static semantics defines which sentences are meaningful, and the semantics defines the meaning of those sentences. The primitive constructs in Python include **literals** (e.g., the number 3.2 and the string 'abc') and **infix operators** (e.g., + and /).

The **syntax** of a language defines which strings of characters and symbols are well formed. For example, in English the string "Cat dog boy." is not a syntactically valid sentence, because the syntax of English does not accept sentences of the form <noun> <noun> <noun>. In Python, the sequence of primitives 3.2 + 3.2 is syntactically well formed, but the sequence 3.2 3.2 is not.

The **static semantics** defines which syntactically valid strings have a meaning. In English, for example, the string "I runs fast," is of the form <pronoun> < verb> <adverb>, which is a syntactically acceptable sequence. Nevertheless, it is not valid English, because the noun "I" is singular and the verb "runs" is plural. This is an example of a static semantic error. In Python, the sequence 3.2/'abc' is syntactically well formed (<literal> <operator> <literal>), but produces a static semantic error since it is not meaningful to divide a number by a string of characters.

The **semantics** of a language associates a meaning with each syntactically correct string of symbols that has no static semantic errors. In natural languages, the semantics of a sentence can be ambiguous. For example, the sentence "I cannot praise this student too highly," can be either flattering or damning. Programming languages are designed so that each legal program has exactly one meaning.

Though syntax errors are the most common kind of error (especially for those learning a new programming language), they are the least dangerous kind of error. Every serious programming language does a complete job of detecting syntactic errors, and will not allow users to execute a program with even one syntactic error. Furthermore, in most cases the language system gives a sufficiently clear indication of the location of the error that it is obvious what needs to be done to fix it.

The situation with respect to static semantic errors is a bit more complex. Some programming languages, e.g., Java, do a lot of static semantic checking before allowing a program to be executed. Others, e.g., C and Python (alas), do relatively less static semantic checking before a program is executed. Python does do a considerable amount of semantic checking while running a program.

One doesn't usually speak of a program as having a semantic error. If a program has no syntactic errors and no static semantic errors, it has a meaning, i.e., it has semantics. Of course, that isn't to say that it has the semantics that its creator intended it to have. When a program means something other than what its creator thinks it means, bad things can happen.

What might happen if the program has an error, and behaves in an unintended way?

- It might crash, i.e., stop running and produce some sort of obvious indication that it has done so. In a properly designed computing system, when a program crashes it does not do damage to the overall system. Of course, some very popular computer systems don't have this nice property. Almost everyone who uses a personal computer has run a program that has managed to make it necessary to restart the whole computer.
- Or it might keep running, and running, and running, and never stop. If one has no idea of approximately how long the program is supposed to take to do its job, this situation can be hard to recognize.
- Or it might run to completion and produce an answer that might, or might not, be correct.

Each of these is bad, but the last of them is certainly the worst. When a program appears to be doing the right thing but isn't, bad things can follow: fortunes can be lost, patients can receive fatal doses of radiation therapy, airplanes can crash.

Whenever possible, programs should be written in such a way that when they don't work properly, it is self-evident. We will discuss how to do this throughout the book.

Finger exercise: Computers can be annoyingly literal. If you don't tell them exactly what you want them to do, they are likely to do the wrong thing. Try writing an algorithm for driving between two destinations. Write it the way you would for a person, and then imagine what would happen if that person were as stupid as a computer, and executed the algorithm exactly as written. How many traffic tickets might that person get?

2 INTRODUCTION TO PYTHON

Though each programming language is different (though not as different as their designers would have us believe), there are some dimensions along which they can be related.

- **Low-level versus high-level** refers to whether we program using instructions and data objects at the level of the machine (e.g., move 64 bits of data from this location to that location) or whether we program using more abstract operations (e.g., pop up a menu on the screen) that have been provided by the language designer.
- **General versus targeted to an application domain** refers to whether the primitive operations of the programming language are widely applicable or are finetuned to a domain. For example, SQL is designed to facilitate extracting information from relational databases, but you wouldn't want to use it build an operating system.
- **Interpreted versus compiled** refers to whether the sequence of instructions written by the programmer, called **source code**, is executed directly (by an interpreter) or whether it is first converted (by a compiler) into a sequence of machine-level primitive operations. (In the early days of computers, people had to write source code in a language that was very close to the **machine code** that could be directly interpreted by the computer hardware.) There are advantages to both approaches. It is often easier to debug programs written in languages that are designed to be interpreted, because the interpreter can produce error messages that are easy to correlate with the source code. Compiled languages usually produce programs that run more quickly and use less space.

In this book, we use **Python**. However, this book is not about Python. It will certainly help readers learn Python, and that's a good thing. What is much more important, however, is that careful readers will learn something about how to write programs that solve problems. This skill can be transferred to any programming language.

Python is a general-purpose programming language that can be used effectively to build almost any kind of program that does not need direct access to the computer's hardware. Python is not optimal for programs that have high reliability constraints (because of its weak static semantic checking) or that are built and maintained by many people or over a long period of time (again because of the weak static semantic checking).

However, Python does have several advantages over many other languages. It is a relatively simple language that is easy to learn. Because Python is designed to be interpreted, it can provide the kind of runtime feedback that is especially helpful to novice programmers. There are also a large number of freely available libraries that interface to Python and provide useful extended functionality. Several of those are used in this book.

Now we are ready to start learning some of the basic elements of Python. These are common to almost all programming languages in concept, though not necessarily in detail.

The reader should be forewarned that this book is by no means a comprehensive introduction to Python. We use Python as a vehicle to present concepts related to computational problem solving and thinking. The language is presented in dribs and drabs, as needed for this ulterior purpose. Python features that we don't need for that purpose are not presented at all. We feel comfortable about not covering the entire language because there are excellent online resources describing almost every aspect of the language. When we teach the course on which this book is based, we suggest to the students that they rely on these free online resources for Python reference material.

Python is a living language. Since its introduction by Guido von Rossum in 1990, it has undergone many changes. For the first decade of its life, Python was a little known and little used language. That changed with the arrival of Python 2.0 in 2000. In addition to incorporating a number of important improvements to the language itself, it marked a shift in the evolutionary path of the language. A large number of people began developing libraries that interfaced seamlessly with Python, and continuing support and development of the Python ecosystem became a community-based activity. Python 3.0 was released at the end of 2008. This version of Python cleaned up many of the inconsistencies in the design of the various releases of Python 2 (often referred to as Python 2.x). However, it was not backward compatible. That meant that most programs written for earlier versions of Python could not be run using implementations of Python 3.

Over the last few years, most of the important public domain Python libraries have been ported to Python 3 and thoroughly tested using Python 3.5—the version of Python we use in this book.

2.1 The Basic Elements of Python

A Python **program**, sometimes called a **script**, is a sequence of definitions and commands. These definitions are evaluated and the commands are executed by the Python interpreter in something called the **shell**. Typically, a new shell is created whenever execution of a program begins. Usually a window is associated with the shell.

We recommend that you start a Python shell now, and use it to try the examples contained in the remainder of this chapter. And, for that matter, later in the book as well.

A **command**, often called a **statement**, instructs the interpreter to do something. For example, the statement print('Yankees rule!') instructs the interpreter to call the function[7] print, which will output the string Yankees rule! to the window associated with the shell.

The sequence of commands

```
print('Yankees rule!')
print('But not in Boston!')
print('Yankees rule,', 'but not in Boston!')
```

causes the interpreter to produce the output

```
Yankees rule!
But not in Boston!
Yankees rule, but not in Boston!
```

Notice that two values were passed to print in the third statement. The print function takes a variable number of arguments separated by commas, and prints them, separated by a space character, in the order in which they appear.[8]

2.1.1 Objects, Expressions, and Numerical Types

Objects are the core things that Python programs manipulate. Every object has a **type** that defines the kinds of things that programs can do with that object.

Types are either scalar or non-scalar. **Scalar** objects are indivisible. Think of them as the atoms of the language.[9] **Non-scalar** objects, for example strings, have internal structure.

---

[7] Functions are discussed in Section 4.1.

[8] In Python 2, print is a command rather than a function. One would therefore write the line print 'Yankees rule!', 'but not in Boston'.

[9] Yes, atoms are not truly indivisible. However, splitting them is not easy, and doing so can have consequences that are not always desirable.

Many types of objects can be denoted by **literals** in the text of a program. For example, the text 2 is a literal representing a number and the text 'abc' a literal representing a string.

Python has four types of scalar objects:

- int is used to represent integers. Literals of type int are written in the way we typically denote integers (e.g., -3 or 5 or 10002).
- float is used to represent real numbers. Literals of type float always include a decimal point (e.g., 3.0 or 3.17 or -28.72). (It is also possible to write literals of type float using scientific notation. For example, the literal 1.6E3 stands for $1.6*10^3$, i.e., it is the same as 1600.0.) You might wonder why this type is not called real. Within the computer, values of type float are stored in the computer as **floating point numbers**. This representation, which is used by all modern programming languages, has many advantages. However, under some situations it causes floating point arithmetic to behave in ways that are slightly different from arithmetic on real numbers. We discuss this in Section 3.4.
- bool is used to represent the Boolean values True and False.
- None is a type with a single value. We will say more about this in Section 4.1.

Objects and **operators** can be combined to form **expressions**, each of which evaluates to an object of some type. We will refer to this as the **value** of the expression. For example, the expression 3 + 2 denotes the object 5 of type int, and the expression 3.0 + 2.0 denotes the object 5.0 of type float.

The == operator is used to test whether two expressions evaluate to the same value, and the != operator is used to test whether two expressions evaluate to different values. A single = means something quite different, as we will see in Section 2.1.2. Be forewarned, you will make the mistake of typing "=" when you meant to type "==". Keep an eye out for this error.

The symbol >>> is a **shell prompt** indicating that the interpreter is expecting the user to type some Python code into the shell. The line below the line with the prompt is produced when the interpreter evaluates the Python code entered at the prompt, as illustrated by the following interaction with the interpreter:

```
>>> 3 + 2
5
>>> 3.0 + 2.0
5.0
>>> 3 != 2
True
```

The built-in Python function type can be used to find out the type of an object:

```
>>> type(3)
<type 'int'>
>>> type(3.0)
<type 'float'>
```

Operators on objects of type int and float are listed in Figure 2.1.

---

i+j is the sum of i and j. If i and j are both of type int, the result is an int. If either of them is a float, the result is a float.

i-j is i minus j. If i and j are both of type int, the result is an int. If either of them is a float, the result is a float.

i*j is the product of i and j. If i and j are both of type int, the result is an int. If either of them is a float, the result is a float.

i//j is integer division. For example, the value of 6//2 is the int 3 and the value of 6//4 is the int 1. The value is 1 because integer division returns the quotient and ignores the remainder. If j == 0, an error occurs.

i/j is i divided by j. In Python 3, the / operator, performs floating point division. For example, the value of 6/4 is 1.5. If j == 0, an error occurs. (In Python 2, when i and j are both of type int, the / operator behaves the same way as // and returns an int. If either i or j is a float, it behaves like the Python 3 / operator.)

i%j is the remainder when the int i is divided by the int j. It is typically pronounced "i mod j," which is short for "i modulo j."

i**j is i raised to the power j. If i and j are both of type int, the result is an int. If either of them is a float, the result is a float.

The comparison operators are == (equal), != (not equal), > (greater), >= (at least), <, (less) and <= (at most).

Figure 2.1 Operators on types int and float

The arithmetic operators have the usual precedence. For example, * binds more tightly than +, so the expression x+y*2 is evaluated by first multiplying y by 2 and then adding the result to x. The order of evaluation can be changed by using parentheses to group subexpressions, e.g., (x+y)*2 first adds x and y, and then multiplies the result by 2.

The primitive operators on type bool are and, or, and not:

- **a and b** is True if both a and b are True, and False otherwise.
- **a or b** is True if at least one of a or b is True, and False otherwise.
- **not a** is True if a is False, and False if a is True.

2.1.2 Variables and Assignment

Variables provide a way to associate names with objects. Consider the code

```
pi = 3
radius = 11
area = pi * (radius**2)
radius = 14
```

It first **binds** the names pi and radius to different objects of type int.[10] It then binds the name area to a third object of type int. This is depicted in the left panel of Figure 2.2.

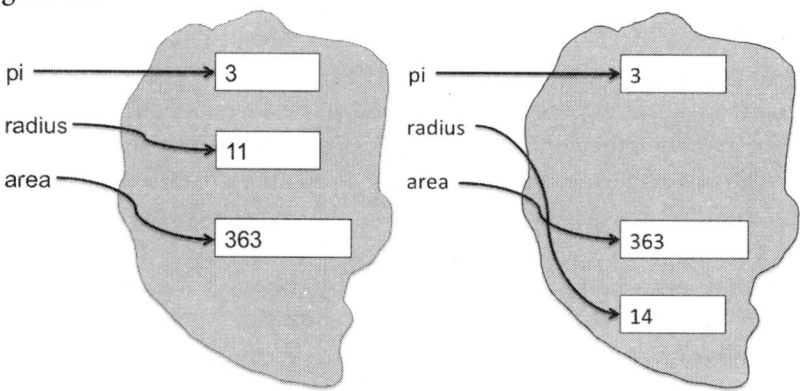

Figure 2.2 Binding of variables to objects

If the program then executes radius = 14, the name radius is rebound to a different object of type int, as shown in the right panel of Figure 2.2. Note that this assignment has no effect on the value to which area is bound. It is still bound to the object denoted by the expression 3*(11**2).

In Python, **a variable is just a name,** nothing more. Remember this—it is important. An **assignment** statement associates the name to the left of the = symbol with the object denoted by the expression to the right of the =. Remember this too. An object can have one, more than one, or no name associated with it.

---

[10] If you believe that the actual value of π is not 3, you're right. We even demonstrate that fact in Section 16.4.

Perhaps we shouldn't have said, "a variable is just a name." Despite what Juliet said,[11] names matter. Programming languages let us describe computations in a way that allows machines to execute them. This does not mean that only computers read programs.

As you will soon discover, it's not always easy to write programs that work correctly. Experienced programmers will confirm that they spend a great deal of time reading programs in an attempt to understand why they behave as they do. It is therefore of critical importance to write programs in such way that they are easy to read. Apt choice of variable names plays an important role in enhancing readability.

Consider the two code fragments

```
a = 3.14159              pi = 3.14159
b = 11.2                 diameter = 11.2
c = a*(b**2)             area = pi*(diameter**2)
```

As far as Python is concerned, they are not different. When executed, they will do the same thing. To a human reader, however, they are quite different. When we read the fragment on the left, there is no *a priori* reason to suspect that anything is amiss. However, a quick glance at the code on the right should prompt us to be suspicious that something is wrong. Either the variable should have been named radius rather than diameter, or diameter should have been divided by 2.0 in the calculation of the area.

In Python, variable names can contain uppercase and lowercase letters, digits (but they cannot start with a digit), and the special character _. Python variable names are case-sensitive e.g., Julie and julie are different names. Finally, there are a small number of **reserved words** (sometimes called **keywords**) in Python that have built-in meanings and cannot be used as variable names. Different versions of Python have slightly different lists of reserved words. The reserved words in Python 3 are and, as, assert, break, class, continue, def, del, elif, else, except, False, finally, for, from, global, if, import, in, is, lambda, nonlocal, None, not, or, pass, raise, return, True, try, while, with, and yield.

Another good way to enhance the readability of code is to add **comments**. Text following the symbol # is not interpreted by Python. For example, one might write

---

[11] "What's in a name? That which we call a rose by any other name would smell as sweet."

```
side = 1 #length of sides of a unit square
radius = 1 #radius of a unit circle
#subtract area of unit circle from area of unit square
areaC = pi*radius**2
areaS = side*side
difference = areaS - areaC
```

Python allows multiple assignment. The statement

```
x, y = 2, 3
```

binds x to 2 and y to 3. All of the expressions on the right-hand side of the assignment are evaluated before any bindings are changed. This is convenient since it allows you to use multiple assignment to swap the bindings of two variables.

For example, the code

```
x, y = 2, 3
x, y = y, x
print('x =', x)
print('y =', y)
```

will print

```
x = 3
y = 2
```

2.1.3 Python IDE's

Typing programs directly into the shell is highly inconvenient. Most programmers prefer to use some sort of text editor that is part of an **integrated development environment** (IDE).

One IDE, **IDLE**,[12] comes as part of the standard Python installation package. As Python has grown in popularity, other IDE's have sprung up. These newer IDE's often incorporate some of the more popular Python libraries and provide facilities not provided by IDLE. **Anaconda** and **Canopy** are among the more popular of these IDE's. The code appearing in this book was created and tested using Anaconda.

IDE's are applications, just like any other application on your computer. Start one the same way you would start any other application, e.g., by double-clicking on an icon.

---

[12] Allegedly, the name Python was chosen as a tribute to the British comedy troupe Monty Python. This leads one to think that the name IDLE is a pun on Eric Idle, a member of the troupe.

All of the Python IDE's provide
- A text editor with syntax highlighting, auto completion, and smart indentation,
- a shell with syntax highlighting, and
- an integrated debugger, which you can safely ignore for now.

When the IDE starts it will open a shell window into which you can type Python commands. It will also provide you with a file menu and an edit menu (as well as some other menus that make it convenient to do things such as printing your program).

The **file menu** includes commands to
- create a new editing window into which you can type a Python program,
- open a file containing an existing Python program, and
- save the contents of the current editing window into a file (with the file extension .py).

The **edit menu** includes standard text-editing commands (e.g., copy, paste, and find) plus some commands specifically designed to make it easy to edit Python code (e.g., indent region and comment out region).

For more information about some popular IDE's see

```
http://docs.python.org/library/idle.html/
https://store.continuum.io/cshop/anaconda/
https://www.enthought.com/products/canopy/
```

2.2 Branching Programs

The kinds of computations we have been looking at thus far are called **straight-line programs**. They execute one statement after another in the order in which they appear, and stop when they run out of statements. The kinds of computations we can describe with straight-line programs are not very interesting. In fact, they are downright boring.

Branching programs are more interesting. The simplest branching statement is a **conditional**. As shown in the boxed-in part of Figure 2.3, a conditional statement has three parts:
- a test, i.e., an expression that evaluates to either True or False;
- a block of code that is executed if the test evaluates to True; and
- an optional block of code that is executed if the test evaluates to False.

After a conditional statement is executed, execution resumes at the code following the statement.

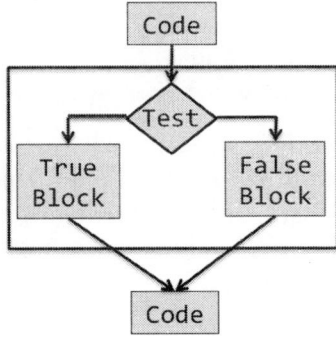

Figure 2.3 Flow chart for conditional statement

In Python, a conditional statement has the form

```
if Boolean expression:
    block of code
else:
    block of code
```

or

```
if Boolean expression:
    block of code
```

In describing the form of Python statements we use italics to describe the kinds of code that could occur at that point in a program. For example, *Boolean expression* indicates that any expression that evaluates to True or False can follow the reserved word if, and *block of code* indicates that any sequence of Python statements can follow else:.

Consider the following program that prints "Even" if the value of the variable x is even and "Odd" otherwise:

```
if x%2 == 0:
    print('Even')
else:
    print('Odd')
print('Done with conditional')
```

The expression x%2 == 0 evaluates to True when the remainder of x divided by 2 is 0, and False otherwise. Remember that == is used for comparison, since = is reserved for assignment.

Indentation is semantically meaningful in Python. For example, if the last statement in the above code were indented it would be part of the block of code

CHAPTER 2. INTRODUCTION TO PYTHON

associated with the else, rather than the block of code following the conditional statement.

Python is unusual in using indentation this way. Most other programming languages use some sort of bracketing symbols to delineate blocks of code, e.g., C encloses blocks in braces, { }. An advantage of the Python approach is that it ensures that the visual structure of a program is an accurate representation of the semantic structure of that program. Because indentation is semantically important, the notion of a line is important.

When either the true block or the false block of a conditional contains another conditional, the conditional statements are said to be **nested**. In the code below, there are nested conditionals in both branches of the top-level if statement.

```
if x%2 == 0:
    if x%3 == 0:
        print('Divisible by 2 and 3')
    else:
        print('Divisible by 2 and not by 3')
elif x%3 == 0:
    print('Divisible by 3 and not by 2')
```

The elif in the above code stands for "else if."

It is often convenient to use a **compound Boolean expression** in the test of a conditional, for example,

```
if x < y and x < z:
    print('x is least')
elif y < z:
    print('y is least')
else:
    print('z is least')
```

Conditionals allow us to write programs that are more interesting than straight-line programs, but the class of branching programs is still quite limited. One way to think about the power of a class of programs is in terms of how long they can take to run. Assume that each line of code takes one unit of time to execute. If a straight-line program has n lines of code, it will take n units of time to run. What about a branching program with n lines of code? It might take less than n units of time to run, but it cannot take more, since each line of code is executed at most once.

A program for which the maximum running time is bounded by the length of the program is said to run in **constant time**. This does not mean that each time it is run it executes the same number of steps. It means that there exists a constant, k, such that the program is guaranteed to take no more than k steps to run.

This implies that the running time does not grow with the size of the input to the program.

Constant-time programs are quite limited in what they can do. Consider, for example, writing a program to tally the votes in an election. It would be truly surprising if one could write a program that could do this in a time that was independent of the number of votes cast. In fact, one can prove that it is impossible to do so. The study of the intrinsic difficulty of problems is the topic of **computational complexity**. We will return to this topic several times in this book.

Fortunately, we need only one more programming language construct, iteration, to be able to write programs of arbitrary complexity. We get to that in Section 2.4.

Finger exercise: Write a program that examines three variables—x, y, and z—and prints the largest odd number among them. If none of them are odd, it should print a message to that effect.

2.3 Strings and Input

Objects of type str are used to represent strings of characters.[13] Literals of type str can be written using either single or double quotes, e.g., 'abc' or "abc". The literal '123' denotes a string of three characters, not the number one hundred twenty-three.

Try typing the following expressions in to the Python interpreter (remember that the >>> is a prompt, not something that you type):

```
>>> 'a'
>>> 3*4
>>> 3*'a'
>>> 3+4
>>> 'a'+'a'
```

The operator + is said to be **overloaded**: It has different meanings depending upon the types of the objects to which it is applied. For example, it means addition when applied to two numbers and concatenation when applied to two strings. The operator * is also overloaded. It means what you expect it to mean when its operands are both numbers. When applied to an int and a str, it a **repetition operator**—the expression n*s, where n is an int and s is a str, evaluates to a

---

[13] Unlike many programming languages, Python has no type corresponding to a character. Instead, it uses strings of length 1.

CHAPTER 2. INTRODUCTION TO PYTHON

str with n repeats of s. For example, the expression 2*'John' has the value 'JohnJohn'. There is a logic to this. Just as the mathematical expression 3*2 is equivalent to 2+2+2, the expression 3*'a' is equivalent to 'a'+'a'+'a'.

Now try typing

```
>>> a
>>> 'a'*'a'
```

Each of these lines generates an error message. The first line produces the message

```
NameError: name 'a' is not defined
```

Because a is not a literal of any type, the interpreter treats it as a name. However, since that name is not bound to any object, attempting to use it causes a runtime error. The code 'a'*'a' produces the error message

```
TypeError: can't multiply sequence by non-int of type 'str'
```

That **type checking** exists is a good thing. It turns careless (and sometimes subtle) mistakes into errors that stop execution, rather than errors that lead programs to behave in mysterious ways. The type checking in Python is not as strong as in some other programming languages (e.g., Java), but it is better in Python 3 than in Python 2. For example, it is pretty clear what < should mean when it is used to compare two strings or two numbers. But what should the value of '4' < 3 be? Rather arbitrarily, the designers of Python 2 decided that it should be False, because all numeric values should be less than all values of type str. The designers of Python 3 and most other modern languages decided that since such expressions don't have an obvious meaning, they should generate an error message.

Strings are one of several sequence types in Python. They share the following operations with all sequence types.

- The **length** of a string can be found using the len function. For example, the value of len('abc') is 3.
- **Indexing** can be used to extract individual characters from a string. In Python, all indexing is zero-based. For example, typing 'abc'[0] into the interpreter will cause it to display the string 'a'. Typing 'abc'[3] will produce the error message IndexError: string index out of range. Since Python uses 0 to indicate the first element of a string, the last element of a string of length 3 is accessed using the index 2. Negative numbers are used to index from the end of a string. For example, the value of 'abc'[-1] is 'c'.
- **Slicing** is used to extract substrings of arbitrary length. If s is a string, the expression s[start:end] denotes the substring of s that starts at index start and

ends at index end-1. For example, `'abc'[1:3] = 'bc'`. Why does it end at index end-1 rather than end? So that expressions such as `'abc'[0:len('abc')]` have the value one might expect. If the value before the colon is omitted, it defaults to 0. If the value after the colon is omitted, it defaults to the length of the string. Consequently, the expression `'abc'[:]` is semantically equivalent to the more verbose `'abc'[0:len('abc')]`.

2.3.1 Input

Python 3 has a function, input, that can be used to get input directly from a user.[14] It takes a string as an argument and displays it as a prompt in the shell. It then waits for the user to type something, followed by hitting the enter key. The line typed by the user is treated as a string and becomes the value returned by the function.

Consider the code

```
>>> name = input('Enter your name: ')
Enter your name: George Washington
>>> print('Are you really', name, '?')
Are you really George Washington ?
>>> print('Are you really ' + name + '?')
Are you really George Washington?
```

Notice that the first print statement introduces a blank before the "?". It does this because when print is given multiple arguments it places a blank space between the values associated with the arguments. The second print statement uses concatenation to produce a string that does not contain the superfluous blank and passes this as the only argument to print.

Now consider

```
>>> n = input('Enter an int: ')
Enter an int: 3
>>> print(type(n))
<type 'str'>
```

Notice that the variable n is bound to the str '3' not the int 3. So, for example, the value of the expression n*4 is '3333' rather than 12. The good news is that whenever a string is a valid literal of some type, a type conversion can be applied to it.

---

[14] Python 2 has two functions, input and raw_input, that are used to get input from users. Somewhat confusingly, raw_input in Python 2 has the same semantics as input in Python 3. The Python 2 function input treats the typed line as a Python expression and infers a type. Python 2 programmers would be well advised to use only raw_input.

Type conversions (also called **type casts**) are used often in Python code. We use the name of a type to convert values to that type. So, for example, the value of `int('3')*4` is 12. When a `float` is converted to an `int`, the number is truncated (not rounded), e.g., the value of `int(3.9)` is the `int` 3.

2.3.2 A Digression About Character Encoding

For many years most programming languages used a standard called ASCII for the internal representation of characters. This standard included 128 characters, plenty for representing the usual set of characters appearing in English-language text—but not enough to cover the characters and accents appearing in all the world's languages.

In recent years, there has been a shift to Unicode. The Unicode standard is a character coding system designed to support the digital processing and display of the written texts of all languages. The standard contains more than 120,000 different characters—covering 129 modern and historic scripts and multiple symbol sets. The Unicode standard can be implemented using different internal character encodings. You can tell Python which encoding to use by inserting a comment of the form

```
# -*- coding: encoding name -*-
```

as the first or second line of your program. For example,

```
# -*- coding: utf-8 -*-
```

instructs Python to use UTF-8, the most frequently used character encoding for World Wide Web pages.[15] If you don't have such a comment in your program, most Python implementations will default to UTF-8.

When using UTF-8, you can, text editor permitting, directly enter code like

```
print('Mluvíš anglicky?')
print('क्या आप अंग्रेज़ी बोलते हैं?')
```

which will print

```
Mluvíš anglicky?
क्या आप अंग्रेज़ी बोलते हैं?
```

You might be wondering how I managed to type the string `'क्या आप अंग्रेज़ी बोलते हैं?'`. I didn't. Because most the World Wide Web uses UTF-8, I was able to cut the string from a Web page and paste it directly into my program.

---

[15] In 2016, over 85% of the pages on the World Wide Web were encoded using UTF-8.

2.4 Iteration

We closed Section 2.2 with the observation that most computational tasks cannot be accomplished using branching programs. Consider, for example, writing a program that asks the user how many time he wants to print the letter X, and then prints a string with that number of X's. We might think about writing something like

```
numXs = int(input('How many times should I print the letter X? '))
toPrint = ''
if numXs == 1:
    toPrint = 'X'
elif numXs == 2:
    toPrint = 'XX'
elif numXs == 3:
    toPrint = 'XXX'
#...
print(toPrint)
```

But it would quickly become apparent that we would need as many conditionals as there are positive integers—and there are an infinite number of those. What we need is a program that looks like

```
numXs = int(input('How many times should I print the letter X? '))
toPrint = ''
concatenate X to toPrint numXs times
print(toPrint)
```

When we want a program to do the same thing many times, we can use **iteration**. A generic iteration (also called **looping**) mechanism is shown in the boxed-in part of Figure 2.4. Like a conditional statement, it begins with a test. If the test evaluates to True, the program executes the **loop** body once, and then goes back to reevaluate the test. This process is repeated until the test evaluates to False, after which control passes to the code following the iteration statement.

We can write the kind of loop depicted in Figure 2.4 using a **while** statement. Consider the following example:

```
# Square an integer, the hard way
x = 3
ans = 0
itersLeft = x
while (itersLeft != 0):
    ans = ans + x
    itersLeft = itersLeft - 1
print(str(x) + '*' + str(x) + ' = ' + str(ans))
```

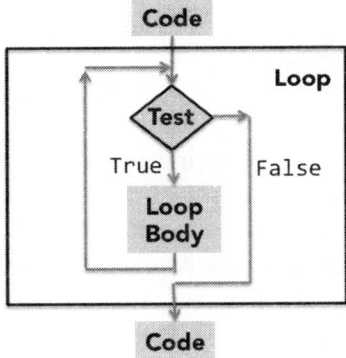

Figure 2.4 Flow chart for iteration

The code starts by binding the variable x to the integer 3. It then proceeds to square x by using repetitive addition. The table in Figure 2.5 shows the value associated with each variable each time the test at the start of the loop is reached. We constructed it by **hand-simulating** the code, i.e., we pretended to be a Python interpreter and executed the program using pencil and paper. Using pencil and paper might seem kind of quaint, but it is an excellent way to understand how a program behaves.[16]

Test #	x	ans	itersLeft
1	3	0	3
2	3	3	2
3	3	6	1
4	3	9	0

Figure 2.5 Hand simulation of a small program

The fourth time the test is reached, it evaluates to False and flow of control proceeds to the print statement following the loop. For what values of x will this program terminate? There are three cases to consider: x == 0, x > 0, and x < 0.

Suppose x == 0. The initial value of itersLeft will also be 0, and the loop body will never be executed.

Suppose x > 0. The initial value of itersLeft will be greater than 0, and the loop body will be executed at least once. Each time the loop body is executed, the value of itersLeft is decreased by exactly 1. This means that if itersLeft started out greater than 0, after some finite number of iterations of the loop, itersLeft

---

[16] It is also possible to hand-simulate a program using pen and paper, or even a text editor.

will equal 0. At this point the loop test evaluates to False, and control proceeds to the code following the while statement.

Suppose x < 0. Something very bad happens. Control will enter the loop, and each iteration will move itersLeft farther from 0 rather than closer to it. The program will therefore continue executing the loop forever (or until something else bad, e.g., an overflow error, occurs). How might we remove this flaw in the program? Initializing itersLeft to the absolute value of x almost works. The loop terminates, but it prints a negative value. If the assignment statement inside the loop is also changed, to ans = ans + abs(x), the code works properly.

Finger exercise: Replace the comment in the following code with a while loop.

```
numXs = int(input('How many times should I print the letter X? '))
toPrint = ''
#concatenate X to toPrint numXs times
print(toPrint)
```

It is sometimes convenient to exit a loop without testing the loop condition. Executing a **break** statement terminates the loop in which it is contained, and transfers control to the code immediately following the loop. For example, the code

```
#Find a positive integer that is divisible by both 11 and 12
x = 1
while True:
    if x%11 == 0 and x%12 == 0:
        break
    x = x + 1
print(x, 'is divisible by 11 and 12')
```

prints

```
132 is divisible by 11 and 12
```

If a break statement is executed inside a nested loop (a loop inside another loop), the break will terminate the inner loop.

We have now covered pretty much everything about Python that we need to know to start writing interesting programs that deal with numbers and strings. In the next chapter, we take a short break from learning Python, and use what we have already learned to solve some simple problems.

Finger exercise: Write a program that asks the user to input 10 integers, and then prints the largest odd number that was entered. If no odd number was entered, it should print a message to that effect.

3 SOME SIMPLE NUMERICAL PROGRAMS

Now that we have covered some basic Python constructs, it is time to start thinking about how we can combine those constructs to write some simple programs. Along the way, we'll sneak in a few more language constructs and some algorithmic techniques.

3.1 Exhaustive Enumeration

The code in Figure 3.1 prints the integer cube root, if it exists, of an integer. If the input is not a perfect cube, it prints a message to that effect.

```
#Find the cube root of a perfect cube
x = int(input('Enter an integer: '))
ans = 0
while ans**3 < abs(x):
    ans = ans + 1
if ans**3 != abs(x):
    print(x, 'is not a perfect cube')
else:
    if x < 0:
        ans = -ans
    print('Cube root of', x,'is', ans)
```

Figure 3.1 Using exhaustive enumeration to find the cube root

For what values of x will this program terminate? The answer is, "all integers." This can be argued quite simply.
- The value of the expression ans**3 starts at 0, and gets larger each time through the loop.
- When it reaches or exceeds abs(x), the loop terminates.
- Since abs(x) is always positive there are only a finite number of iterations before the loop must terminate.

Whenever you write a loop, you should think about an appropriate **decrementing function**. This is a function that has the following properties:

- It maps a set of program variables into an integer.
- When the loop is entered, its value is nonnegative.
- When its value is ≤ 0, the loop terminates.
- Its value is decreased every time through the loop.

What is the decrementing function for the while loop in Figure 3.1? It is abs(x) - ans**3.

Now, let's insert some errors and see what happens. First, try commenting out the statement ans = 0. The Python interpreter prints the error message

```
NameError: name 'ans' is not defined
```

because the interpreter attempts to find the value to which ans is bound before it has been bound to anything. Now, restore the initialization of ans, replace the statement ans = ans + 1 by ans = ans, and try finding the cube root of 8. After you get tired of waiting, enter "control c" (hold down the control key and the c key simultaneously). This will return you to the user prompt in the shell.

Now, add the statement

```
print('Value of the decrementing function abs(x) - ans**3 is',
      abs(x) - ans**3)
```

at the start of the loop, and try running it again. This time it will print

```
Value of the decrementing function abs(x) - ans**3 is 8
```

over and over again.

The program would have run forever because the loop body is no longer reducing the distance between ans**3 and abs(x). When confronted with a program that seems not to be terminating, experienced programmers often insert print statements, such as the one here, to test whether the decrementing function is indeed being decremented.

The algorithmic technique used in this program is a variant of **guess and check** called **exhaustive enumeration**. We enumerate all possibilities until we get to the right answer or exhaust the space of possibilities. At first blush, this may seem like an incredibly stupid way to solve a problem. Surprisingly, however, exhaustive enumeration algorithms are often the most practical way to solve a problem. They are typically easy to implement and easy to understand. And, in many cases, they run fast enough for all practical purposes. Make sure to remove or comment out the print statement that you inserted and to reinsert the statement ans = ans + 1, and then try finding the cube root of 1957816251. The program will finish almost instantaneously. Now, try 7406961012236344616.

CHAPTER 3. SOME SIMPLE NUMERICAL PROGRAMS

As you can see, even if millions of guesses are required, it's not usually a problem. Modern computers are amazingly fast. It takes on the order of one nanosecond—one billionth of a second—to execute an instruction. It's a bit hard to appreciate how fast that is. For perspective, it takes slightly more than a nanosecond for light to travel a single foot (0.3 meters). Another way to think about this is that in the time it takes for the sound of your voice to travel a hundred feet, a modern computer can execute millions of instructions.

Just for fun, try executing the code

```
maxVal = int(input('Enter a postive integer: '))
i = 0
while i < maxVal:
    i = i + 1
print(i)
```

See how large an integer you need to enter before there is a perceptible pause before the result is printed.

Finger exercise: Write a program that asks the user to enter an integer and prints two integers, root and pwr, such that 0 < pwr < 6 and root**pwr is equal to the integer entered by the user. If no such pair of integers exists, it should print a message to that effect.

3.2 For Loops

The while loops we have used so far are highly stylized. Each iterates over a sequence of integers. Python provides a language mechanism, the **for loop**, that can be used to simplify programs containing this kind of iteration.

The general form of a for statement is (recall that the words in italics are descriptions of what can appear, not actual code):

```
for variable in sequence:
    code block
```

The variable following for is bound to the first value in the sequence, and the code block is executed. The variable is then assigned the second value in the sequence, and the code block is executed again. The process continues until the sequence is exhausted or a break statement is executed within the code block.

The sequence of values bound to *variable* is most commonly generated using the built-in function **range**, which returns a series of integers. The range function takes three integer arguments: start, stop, and step. It produces the progression start, start + step, start + 2*step, etc. If step is positive, the last element is the largest integer start + i*step less than stop. If step is negative, the last element is the smallest integer start + i*step greater than stop. For example, the expression range(5, 40, 10) yields the sequence 5, 15, 25, 35, and range(40, 5, -10) yields the sequence 40, 30, 20, 10. If the first argument is omitted it defaults to 0, and if the last argument (the step size) is omitted it defaults to 1. For example, range(0, 3) and range(3) both produce the sequence 0, 1, 2. The numbers in the progression are generated on an "as needed" basis, so even expressions such as range(1000000) consume little memory.[17] We will discuss range in more depth in Section 5.2.

Less commonly, we specify the sequence to be iterated over in a for loop by using a literal, e.g., [0, 3, 2].

Consider the code

```
x = 4
for i in range(0, x):
    print(i)
```

It prints

```
0
1
2
3
```

Now, think about the code

```
x = 4
for i in range(0, x):
    print(i)
    x = 5
```

It raises the question of whether changing the value of x inside the loop affects the number of iterations. It does not. The arguments to the range function in the line with for are evaluated just before the first iteration of the loop, and not reevaluated for subsequent iterations.

To see how this works, consider

```
x = 4
for j in range(x):
    for i in range(x):
        print(i)
        x = 2
```

---

[17] In Python 2, range generates the entire sequence when invoked. Therefore, expressions such as range(1000000) use quite a lot of memory. In Python 2, xrange behaves the way range behaves in Python 3.

CHAPTER 3. SOME SIMPLE NUMERICAL PROGRAMS

which prints

```
0
1
2
3
0
1
0
1
0
1
```

because the range function in the outer loop is evaluated only once, but the range function in the inner loop is evaluated each time the inner for statement is reached.

The code in Figure 3.2 reimplements the exhaustive enumeration algorithm for finding cube roots. The break statement in the for loop causes the loop to terminate before it has been run on each element in the sequence over which it is iterating.

```
#Find the cube root of a perfect cube
x = int(input('Enter an integer: '))
for ans in range(0, abs(x)+1):
    if ans**3 >= abs(x):
        break
if ans**3 != abs(x):
    print(x, 'is not a perfect cube')
else:
    if x < 0:
        ans = -ans
    print('Cube root of', x,'is', ans)
```

Figure 3.2 Using for and break statements

The for statement can be used in conjunction with the **in operator** to conveniently iterate over characters of a string. For example,

```
total = 0
for c in '12345678':
    total = total + int(c)
print(total)
```

sums the digits in the string denoted by the literal '12345678' and prints the total.

Finger exercise: Let s be a string that contains a sequence of decimal numbers separated by commas, e.g., s = '1.23,2.4,3.123'. Write a program that prints the sum of the numbers in s.

3.3 Approximate Solutions and Bisection Search

Imagine that someone asks you to write a program that finds the square root of any nonnegative number. What should you do?

You should probably start by saying that you need a better problem statement. For example, what should the program do if asked to find the square root of 2? The square root of 2 is not a rational number. This means that there is no way to precisely represent its value as a finite string of digits (or as a float), so the problem as initially stated cannot be solved.

The right thing to have asked for is a program that finds an **approximation** to the square root—i.e., an answer that is close enough to the actual square root to be useful. We will return to this issue in considerable detail later in the book. But for now, let's think of "close enough" as an answer that lies within some constant, call it epsilon, of the actual answer.

The code in Figure 3.3 implements an algorithm that finds an approximation to a square root. It uses an operator, +=, that we have not previously used. The assignment statement ans += step is semantically equivalent to the more verbose code ans = ans+step. The operators -= and *= work similarly.

```
x = 25
epsilon = 0.01
step = epsilon**2
numGuesses = 0
ans = 0.0
while abs(ans**2 - x) >= epsilon and ans <= x:
    ans += step
    numGuesses += 1
print('numGuesses =', numGuesses)
if abs(ans**2 - x) >= epsilon:
    print('Failed on square root of', x)
else:
    print(ans, 'is close to square root of', x)
```

Figure 3.3 Approximating the square root using exhaustive enumeration

Once again, we are using exhaustive enumeration. Notice that this method for finding the square root has nothing in common with the way of finding square roots using a pencil that you might have learned in middle school. It is often the case that the best way to solve a problem with a computer is quite different from how one would approach the problem by hand.

When the code is run, it prints

```
numGuesses = 49990
4.999000000001688 is close to square root of 25
```

Should we be disappointed that the program didn't figure out that 25 is a perfect square and print 5? No. The program did what it was intended to do. Though it would have been OK to print 5, doing so is no better than printing any value close enough to 5.

What do you think will happen if we set x = 0.25? Will it find a root close to 0.5? Nope. It will report

```
numGuesses = 2501
Failed on square root of 0.25
```

Exhaustive enumeration is a search technique that works only if the set of values being searched includes the answer. In this case, we are enumerating the values between 0 and the value of x. When x is between 0 and 1, the square root of x does not lie in this interval. One way to fix this is to change the second operand of and in the first line of the while loop to get

```
while abs(ans**2 - x) >= epsilon and ans*ans <= x:
```

Now, let's think about how long the program will take to run. The number of iterations depends upon how close the answer is to 0 and on the size of the steps. Roughly speaking, the program will execute the while loop at most x/step times.

Let's try the code on something bigger, e.g., x = 123456. It will run for a bit, and then print

```
numGuesses = 3513631
Failed on square root of 123456
```

What do you think happened? Surely there exists a floating point number that approximates the square root of 123456 to within 0.01. Why didn't our program find it? The problem is that our step size was too large, and the program skipped over all the suitable answers. Try making step equal to epsilon**3 and running the program. It will eventually find a suitable answer, but you might not have the patience to wait for it to do so.

Roughly how many guesses will it have to make? The step size will be 0.000001 and the square root of 123456 is around 351.36. This means that the program will have to make in the neighborhood of 351,000,000 guesses to find a satisfactory answer. We could try to speed it up by starting closer to the answer, but that presumes that we know the answer.

The time has come to look for a different way to attack the problem. We need to choose a better algorithm rather than fine-tune the current one. But before doing so, let's look at a problem that, at first blush, appears to be completely different from root finding.

Consider the problem of discovering whether a word starting with a given sequence of letters appears in some hard-copy dictionary of the English language. Exhaustive enumeration would, in principle, work. You could start at the first word and examine each word until either you found a word starting with the sequence of letters or you ran out of words to examine. If the dictionary contained n words, it would, on average, take n/2 probes to find the word. If the word were not in the dictionary, it would take n probes. Of course, those who have had the pleasure of actually looking a word up in a physical (rather than online) dictionary would never proceed in this way.

Fortunately, the folks who publish hardcopy dictionaries go to the trouble of putting the words in lexicographical order. This allows us to open the book to a page where we think the word might lie (e.g., near the middle for words starting with the letter m). If the sequence of letters lexicographically precedes the first word on the page, we know to go backwards. If the sequence of letters follows the last word on the page, we know to go forwards. Otherwise, we check whether the sequence of letters matches a word on the page.

Now let's take the same idea and apply it the problem of finding the square root of x. Suppose we know that a good approximation to the square root of x lies somewhere between 0 and max. We can exploit the fact that numbers are **totally ordered**. That is, for any pair of distinct numbers, n1 and n2, either n1 < n2 or n1 > n2. So, we can think of the square root of x as lying somewhere on the line

0_____max

and start searching that interval. Since we don't necessarily know where to start searching, let's start in the middle.

0_____guess_____max

If that is not the right answer (and it won't be most of the time), ask whether it is too big or too small. If it is too big, we know that the answer must lie to the left. If it is too small, we know that the answer must lie to the right. We then repeat the process on the smaller interval. Figure 3.4 contains an implementation and test of this algorithm.

```
x = 25
epsilon = 0.01
numGuesses = 0
low = 0.0
high = max(1.0, x)
ans = (high + low)/2.0
while abs(ans**2 - x) >= epsilon:
    print('low =', low, 'high =', high, 'ans =', ans)
    numGuesses += 1
    if ans**2 < x:
        low = ans
    else:
        high = ans
    ans = (high + low)/2.0
print('numGuesses =', numGuesses)
print(ans, 'is close to square root of', x)
```

Figure 3.4 Using bisection search to approximate square root

When run, it prints

```
low = 0.0 high = 25 ans = 12.5
low = 0.0 high = 12.5 ans = 6.25
low = 0.0 high = 6.25 ans = 3.125
low = 3.125 high = 6.25 ans = 4.6875
low = 4.6875 high = 6.25 ans = 5.46875
low = 4.6875 high = 5.46875 ans = 5.078125
low = 4.6875 high = 5.078125 ans = 4.8828125
low = 4.8828125 high = 5.078125 ans = 4.98046875
low = 4.98046875 high = 5.078125 ans = 5.029296875
low = 4.98046875 high = 5.029296875 ans = 5.0048828125
low = 4.98046875 high = 5.0048828125 ans = 4.99267578125
low = 4.99267578125 high = 5.0048828125 ans = 4.998779296875
low = 4.998779296875 high = 5.0048828125 ans = 5.0018310546875
numGuesses = 13
5.00030517578125 is close to square root of 25
```

Notice that it finds a different answer than our earlier algorithm. That is perfectly fine, since it still meets the problem's specification.

More important, notice that at each iteration of the loop the size of the space to be searched is cut in half. Because it divides the search space in half at each step, it is called a **bisection search**. Bisection search is a huge improvement over our earlier algorithm, which reduced the search space by only a small amount at each iteration.

Let us try x = 123456 again. This time the program takes only thirty guesses to find an acceptable answer. How about x = 123456789 ? It takes only forty-five guesses.

There is nothing special about the fact that we are using this algorithm to find square roots. For example, by changing a couple of 2's to 3's, we can use it to approximate a cube root of a nonnegative number. In Chapter 4, we introduce a language mechanism that allows us to generalize this code to find any root.

Finger exercise: What would the code in Figure 3.4 do if the statement x = 25 were replaced by x = -25?

Finger exercise: What would have to be changed to make the code in Figure 3.4 work for finding an approximation to the cube root of both negative and positive numbers? (Hint: think about changing low to ensure that the answer lies within the region being searched.)

3.4 A Few Words About Using Floats

Most of the time, numbers of type float provide a reasonably good approximation to real numbers. But "most of the time" is not all of the time, and when they don't it can lead to surprising consequences. For example, try running the code

```
x = 0.0
for i in range(10):
    x = x + 0.1
if x == 1.0:
    print(x, '= 1.0')
else:
    print(x, 'is not 1.0')s
```

Perhaps you, like most people, find it surprising that it prints,

0.9999999999999999 is not 1.0

Why does it get to the else clause in the first place?

To understand why this happens, we need to understand how floating point numbers are represented in the computer during a computation. To understand that, we need to understand **binary numbers**.

When you first learned about decimal numbers—i.e., numbers base 10—you learned that any decimal number can be represented by a sequence of the digits 0123456789. The rightmost digit is the 10^0 place, the next digit towards the left the 10^1 place, etc. For example, the sequence of decimal digits 302 represents

CHAPTER 3. SOME SIMPLE NUMERICAL PROGRAMS

$3*100 + 0*10 + 2*1$. How many different numbers can be represented by a sequence of length n? A sequence of length 1 can represent any one of ten numbers (0-9); a sequence of length 2 can represent one hundred numbers (0-99). More generally, with a sequence of length n, one can represent 10^n different numbers.

Binary numbers—numbers base 2—work similarly. A binary number is represented by a sequence of digits each of which is either 0 or 1. These digits are often called **bits**. The rightmost digit is the 2^0 place, the next digit towards the left the 2^1 place, etc. For example, the sequence of binary digits 101 represents $1*4 + 0*2 + 1*1 = 5$. How many different numbers can be represented by a sequence of length n? 2^n.

Finger exercise: What is the decimal equivalent of the binary number 10011?

Perhaps because most people have ten fingers, we seem to like to use decimals to represent numbers. On the other hand, all modern computer systems represent numbers in binary. This is not because computers are born with two fingers. It is because it is easy to build hardware switches, i.e., devices that can be in only one of two states, on or off. That the computer uses a binary representation and people a decimal representation can lead to occasional cognitive dissonance.

In almost modern programming languages non-integer numbers are implemented using a representation called **floating point**. For the moment, let's pretend that the internal representation is in decimal. We would represent a number as a pair of integers—the **significant digits** of the number and an **exponent**. For example, the number 1.949 would be represented as the pair (1949, -3), which stands for the product $1949*10^{-3}$.

The number of significant digits determines the **precision** with which numbers can be represented. If for example, there were only two significant digits, the number 1.949 could not be represented exactly. It would have to be converted to some approximation of 1.949, in this case 1.9. That approximation is called the **rounded value**.

Modern computers use binary, not decimal, representations. We represent the significant digits and exponents in binary rather than decimal and raise 2 rather than 10 to the exponent. For example, the number 0.625 (5/8) would be represented as the pair (101, -11); because 5/8 is 0.101 in binary and -11 is the binary representation of -3, the pair (101, -11) stands for $5*2^{-3} = 5/8 = 0.625$.

What about the decimal fraction 1/10, which we write in Python as `0.1`? The best we can do with four significant binary digits is (0011, -101). This is equivalent to 3/32, i.e., 0.09375. If we had five significant binary digits, we would represent 0.1 as (11001, -1000), which is equivalent to 25/256, i.e., 0.09765625. How many significant digits would we need to get an exact floating point representation of 0.1? An infinite number of digits! There do not exist integers sig and exp such that sig * 2^{-exp} equals 0.1. So no matter how many bits Python (or any other language) chooses to use to represent floating point numbers, it will be able to represent only an approximation to 0.1. In most Python implementations, there are 53 bits of precision available for floating point numbers, so the significant digits stored for the decimal number 0.1 will be

11001100110011001100110011001100110011001100110011001

This is equivalent to the decimal number

0.1000000000000000055511151231257827021181583404541015625

Pretty close to 1/10, but not exactly 1/10.

Returning to the original mystery, why does

```
x = 0.0
for i in range(10):
    x = x + 0.1
if x == 1.0:
    print(x, '= 1.0')
else:
    print(x, 'is not 1.0')
```

print

```
0.9999999999999999 is not 1.0
```

We now see that the test `x == 1.0` produces the result False because the value to which x is bound is not exactly 1.0. What gets printed if we add to the end of the else clause the code `print x == 10.0*0.1`? It prints False because during at least one iteration of the loop Python ran out of significant digits and did some rounding. It's not what our elementary school teachers taught us, but adding 0.1 ten times does not produce the same value as multiplying 0.1 by 10.[18]

By the way, if you want to explicitly round a floating point number, use the round function. The expression `round(x, numDigits)` returns the floating point number equivalent to rounding the value of x to numDigits decimal digits following the decimal point. For example, print `round(2**0.5, 3)` will print 1.414 as an approximation to the square root of 2.

---

[18] In Python 2 another strange thing happens. Because the print statement does some automatic rounding, the else clause would print 1.0 is not 1.0.

Does the difference between real and floating point numbers really matter? Most of the time, mercifully, it does not. There are few situations where `1.0` is an acceptable answer and `0.9999999999999999` is not. However, one thing that is almost always worth worrying about is tests for equality. As we have seen, using `==` to compare two floating point values can produce a surprising result. It is almost always more appropriate to ask whether two floating point values are close enough to each other, not whether they are identical. So, for example, it is better to write `abs(x-y) < 0.0001` rather than `x == y`.

Another thing to worry about is the accumulation of rounding errors. Most of the time things work out OK, because sometimes the number stored in the computer is a little bigger than intended, and sometimes it is a little smaller than intended. However, in some programs, the errors will all be in the same direction and accumulate over time.

3.5 Newton-Raphson

The most commonly used approximation algorithm is usually attributed to Isaac Newton. It is typically called Newton's method, but is sometimes referred to as the Newton-Raphson method.[19] It can be used to find the real roots of many functions, but we shall look at it only in the context of finding the real roots of a polynomial with one variable. The generalization to polynomials with multiple variables is straightforward both mathematically and algorithmically.

A **polynomial** with one variable (by convention, we will write the variable as x) is either 0 or the sum of a finite number of nonzero terms, e.g., $3x^2 + 2x + 3$. Each term, e.g., $3x^2$, consists of a constant (the **coefficient** of the term, 3 in this case) multiplied by the variable (x in this case) raised to a nonnegative integer exponent (2 in this case). The exponent on a variable in a term is called the **degree** of that term. The degree of a polynomial is the largest degree of any single term. Some examples are, 3 (degree 0), 2.5x + 12 (degree 1), and $3x^2$ (degree 2). In contrast, 2/x and $x^{0.5}$ are not polynomials.

If p is a polynomial and r a real number, we will write p(r) to stand for the value of the polynomial when x = r. A **root** of the polynomial p is a solution to the equation p = 0, i.e., an r such that p(r) = 0. So, for example, the problem of finding an approximation to the square root of 24 can be formulated as finding an x such that $x^2 - 24 \approx 0$.

---

[19] Joseph Raphson published a similar method about the same time as Newton.

Newton proved a theorem that implies that if a value, call it guess, is an approximation to a root of a polynomial, then guess – p(guess)/p'(guess), where p' is the first derivative of p, is a better approximation.[20]

For any constant k and any coefficient c, the first derivative of the polynomial $cx^2 + k$ is $2cx$. For example, the first derivative of $x^2 - k$ is $2x$. Therefore, we know that we can improve on the current guess, call it y, by choosing as our next guess $y - (y^2 - k)/2y$. This is called **successive approximation**. Figure 3.5 contains code illustrating how to use this idea to quickly find an approximation to the square root.

```
#Newton-Raphson for square root
#Find x such that x**2 - 24 is within epsilon of 0
epsilon = 0.01
k = 24.0
guess = k/2.0
while abs(guess*guess - k) >= epsilon:
    guess = guess - (((guess**2) - k)/(2*guess))
print('Square root of', k, 'is about', guess)
```

Figure 3.5 Implementation of Newton-Raphson method

Finger exercise: Add some code to the implementation of Newton-Raphson that keeps track of the number of iterations used to find the root. Use that code as part of a program that compares the efficiency of Newton-Raphson and bisection search. (You should discover that Newton-Raphson is more efficient.)

---

[20] The first derivative of a function f(x) can be thought of as expressing how the value of f(x) changes with respect to changes in x. If you haven't previously encountered derivatives, don't worry. You don't need to understand them, or for that matter polynomials, to understand the implementation of Newton's method.

4 FUNCTIONS, SCOPING, AND ABSTRACTION

So far, we have introduced numbers, assignments, input/output, comparisons, and looping constructs. How powerful is this subset of Python? In a theoretical sense, it is as powerful as you will ever need, i.e., it is Turing complete. This means that if a problem can be solved via computation, it can be solved using only those statements you have already seen.

Which isn't to say that you should use only these statements. At this point we have covered a lot of language mechanisms, but the code has been a single sequence of instructions, all merged together. For example, in the last chapter we looked at the code in Figure 4.1.

```
x = 25
epsilon = 0.01
numGuesses = 0
low = 0.0
high = max(1.0, x)
ans = (high + low)/2.0
while abs(ans**2 - x) >= epsilon:
    numGuesses += 1
    if ans**2 < x:
        low = ans
    else:
        high = ans
    ans = (high + low)/2.0
print('numGuesses =', numGuesses)
print(ans, 'is close to square root of', x)
```

Figure 4.1 Using bisection search to approximate square root

This is a reasonable piece of code, but it lacks general utility. It works only for values denoted by the variables x and epsilon. This means that if we want to reuse it, we need to copy the code, possibly edit the variable names, and paste it where we want it. Because of this we cannot easily use this computation inside of some other, more complex, computation.

Furthermore, if we want to compute cube roots rather than square roots, we have to edit the code. If we want a program that computes both square and cube roots (or for that matter square roots in two different places), the program would contain multiple chunks of almost identical code. This is a very bad thing. The more code a program contains, the more chance there is for something to go wrong, and the harder the code is to maintain. Imagine, for example, that there was an error in the initial implementation of square root, and that the error came to light when testing the program. It would be all too easy to fix the implementation of square root in one place and forget that there was similar code elsewhere that was also in need of repair.

Python provides several linguistic features that make it relatively easy to generalize and reuse code. The most important is the function.

4.1 Functions and Scoping

We've already used a number of built-in functions, e.g., max and abs in Figure 4.1. The ability for programmers to define and then use their own functions, as if they were built-in, is a qualitative leap forward in convenience.

4.1.1 Function Definitions

In Python each **function definition** is of the form[21]

```
def name of function (list of formal parameters):
    body of function
```

For example, we could define the function maxVal[22] by the code

```
def maxVal(x, y):
    if x > y:
        return x
    else:
        return y
```

def is a reserved word that tells Python that a function is about to be defined. The function name (maxVal in this example) is simply a name that is used to refer to the function.

The sequence of names within the parentheses following the function name (x, y in this example) are the **formal parameters** of the function. When the function is used, the formal parameters are bound (as in an assignment statement) to

---

[21] Recall that italic is used to describe kinds of Python code.

[22] In practice, you would probably use the built-in function max, rather than define your own function.

CHAPTER 4. FUNCTIONS, SCOPING, AND ABSTRACTION   41

the **actual parameters** (often referred to as **arguments**) of the **function invocation** (also referred to as a **function call**). For example, the invocation

```
maxVal(3, 4)
```

binds x to 3 and y to 4.

The function body is any piece of Python code.[23] There is, however, a special statement, **return**, that can be used only within the body of a function.

A function call is an expression, and like all expressions it has a value. That value is the value returned by the invoked function. For example, the value of the expression maxVal(3,4)*maxVal(3,2) is 12, because the first invocation of maxVal returns the int 4 and the second returns the int 3. Note that execution of a return statement terminates an invocation of the function.

To recapitulate, when a function is called

1. The expressions that make up the actual parameters are evaluated, and the formal parameters of the function are bound to the resulting values. For example, the invocation maxVal(3+4, z) will bind the formal parameter x to 7 and the formal parameter y to whatever value the variable z has when the invocation is evaluated.
2. The **point of execution** (the next instruction to be executed) moves from the point of invocation to the first statement in the body of the function.
3. The code in the body of the function is executed until either a return statement is encountered, in which case the value of the expression following the return becomes the value of the function invocation, or there are no more statements to execute, in which case the function returns the value None. (If no expression follows the return, the value of the invocation is None.)
4. The value of the invocation is the returned value.
5. The point of execution is transferred back to the code immediately following the invocation.

Parameters provide something called **lambda abstraction**,[24] allowing programmers to write code that manipulates not specific objects, but instead whatever objects the caller of the function chooses to use as actual parameters.

---

[23] As we will see later, this notion of function is more general than what mathematicians call a function. It was first popularized by the programming language Fortran 2 in the late 1950s.

[24] The name "lambda abstraction" is derived from mathematics developed by Alonzo Church in the 1930s and 1940s.

Finger exercise: Write a function isIn that accepts two strings as arguments and returns True if either string occurs anywhere in the other, and False otherwise. Hint: you might want to use the built-in str operation in.

4.1.2 Keyword Arguments and Default Values

In Python, there are two ways that formal parameters get bound to actual parameters. The most common method, which is the only one we have used thus far, is called **positional**—the first formal parameter is bound to the first actual parameter, the second formal to the second actual, etc. Python also supports **keyword arguments**, in which formals are bound to actuals using the name of the formal parameter. Consider the function definition

```
def printName(firstName, lastName, reverse):
   if reverse:
      print(lastName + ', ' + firstName)
   else:
      print(firstName, lastName)
```

The function printName assumes that firstName and lastName are strings and that reverse is a Boolean. If reverse == True, it prints lastName, firstName, otherwise it prints firstName lastName.

Each of the following is an equivalent invocation of printName:

```
printName('Olga', 'Puchmajerova', False)
printName('Olga', 'Puchmajerova', reverse = False)
printName('Olga', lastName = 'Puchmajerova', reverse = False)
printName(lastName = 'Puchmajerova', firstName = ' Olga',
          reverse = False)
```

Though the keyword arguments can appear in any order in the list of actual parameters, it is not legal to follow a keyword argument with a non-keyword argument. Therefore, an error message would be produced by

```
printName('Olga', lastName = 'Puchmajerova', False)
```

Keyword arguments are commonly used in conjunction with **default parameter values**. We can, for example, write

```
def printName(firstName, lastName, reverse = False):
   if reverse:
      print(lastName + ', ' + firstName)
   else:
      print(firstName, lastName)
```

Default values allow programmers to call a function with fewer than the specified number of arguments. For example,

```
printName('Olga', 'Puchmajerova')
printName('Olga', 'Puchmajerova', True)
printName('Olga', 'Puchmajerova', reverse = True)
```

will print

```
Olga Puchmajerova
Puchmajerova, Olga
Puchmajerova, Olga
```

The last two invocations of printName are semantically equivalent. The last one has the advantage of providing some documentation for the perhaps mysterious argument True.

4.1.3 Scoping

Let's look at another small example,

```
def f(x): #name x used as formal parameter
    y = 1
    x = x + y
    print('x =', x)
    return x

x = 3
y = 2
z = f(x) #value of x used as actual parameter
print('z =', z)
print('x =', x)
print('y =', y)
```

When run, this code prints,

```
x = 4
z = 4
x = 3
y = 2
```

What is going on here? At the call of f, the formal parameter x is locally bound to the value of the actual parameter x. It is important to note that though the actual and formal parameters have the same name, they are not the same variable. Each function defines a new **name space**, also called a **scope**. The formal parameter x and the **local variable** y that are used in f exist only within the scope of the definition of f. The assignment statement x = x + y within the function body binds the local name x to the object 4. The assignments in f have no effect at all on the bindings of the names x and y that exist outside the scope of f.

Here's one way to think about this:

1. At top level, i.e., the level of the shell, a **symbol table** keeps track of all names defined at that level and their current bindings.
2. When a function is called, a new symbol table (often called a **stack frame**) is created. This table keeps track of all names defined within the function (including the formal parameters) and their current bindings. If a function is called from within the function body, yet another stack frame is created.
3. When the function completes, its stack frame goes away.

In Python, one can always determine the scope of a name by looking at the program text. This is called **static** or **lexical scoping**. Figure 4.2 contains an example illustrating Python's scope rules.

```
def f(x):
    def g():
        x = 'abc'
        print('x =', x)
    def h():
        z = x
        print('z =', z)
    x = x + 1
    print('x =', x)
    h()
    g()
    print('x =', x)
    return g

x = 3
z = f(x)
print('x =', x)
print('z =', z)
z()
```

Figure 4.2 Nested scopes

The history of the stack frames associated with the code is depicted in Figure 4.3. The first column contains the set of names known outside the body of the function f, i.e., the variables x and z, and the function name f. The first assignment statement binds x to 3.

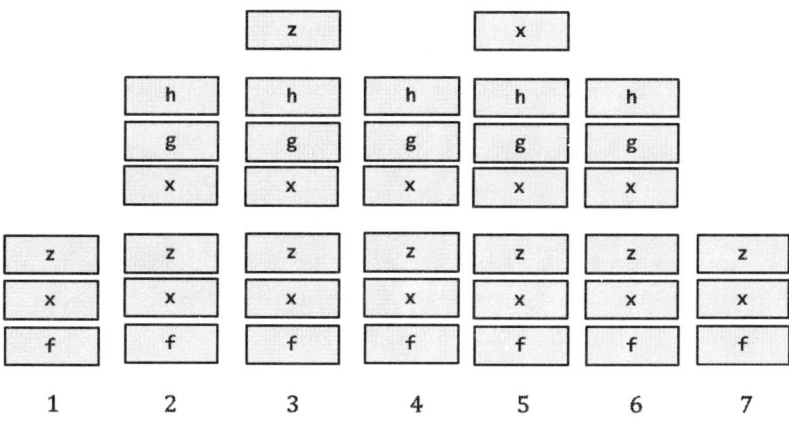

Figure 4.3 Stack frames

The assignment statement z = f(x) first evaluates the expression f(x) by invoking the function f with the value to which x is bound. When f is entered, a stack frame is created, as shown in column 2. The names in the stack frame are x (the formal parameter, not the x in the calling context), g and h. The variables g and h are bound to objects of type function. The properties of these functions are given by the function definitions within f.

When h is invoked from within f, yet another stack frame is created, as shown in column 3. This frame contains only the local variable z. Why does it not also contain x? A name is added to the scope associated with a function only if that name is either a formal parameter of the function or a variable that is bound to an object within the body of the function. In the body of h, x occurs only on the right-hand side of an assignment statement. The appearance of a name (x in this case) that is not bound to an object anywhere in the function body (the body of h) causes the interpreter to search the stack frame associated with the scope within which the function is defined (the stack frame associated with f). If the name is found (which it is in this case) the value to which it is bound (4) is used. If it is not found there, an error message is produced.

When h returns, the stack frame associated with the invocation of h goes away (it is **popped** off the top of the stack), as depicted in column 4. Note that we never remove frames from the middle of the stack, but only the most recently added frame. It is because it has this "last in first out" behavior that we refer to it as a **stack** (think of a stack of trays waiting to be taken in a cafeteria).

Next g is invoked, and a stack frame containing g's local variable x is added (column 5). When g returns, that frame is popped (column 6). When f returns, the stack frame containing the names associated with f is popped, getting us back to the original stack frame (column 7).

Notice that when f returns, even though the variable g no longer exists, the object of type function to which that name was once bound still exists. This is because functions are objects, and can be returned just like any other kind of object. So, z can be bound to the value returned by f, and the function call z() can be used to invoke the function that was bound to the name g within f—even though the name g is not known outside the context of f.

So, what does the code in Figure 4.2 print? It prints

```
x = 4
z = 4
x = abc
x = 4
x = 3
z = <function f.<locals>.g at 0x1092a7510>
x = abc
```

The order in which references to a name occur is not germane. If an object is bound to a name anywhere in the function body (even if it occurs in an expression before it appears as the left-hand side of an assignment), it is treated as local to that function.[25] Consider, for example, the code

```
def f():
    print(x)

def g():
    print(x)
    x = 1

x = 3
f()
x = 3
g()
```

It prints 3 when f is invoked, but the error message

```
UnboundLocalError: local variable 'x' referenced before assignment
```

is printed when the print statement in g is encountered. This happens because the assignment statement following the print statement causes x to be local to g. And because x is local to g, it has no value when the print statement is executed.

---

[25] The wisdom of this language design decision is debatable.

CHAPTER 4. FUNCTIONS, SCOPING, AND ABSTRACTION

Confused yet? It takes most people a bit of time to get their head around scope rules. Don't let this bother you. For now, charge ahead and start using functions. Most of the time you will find that you only want to use variables that are local to a function, and the subtleties of scoping will be irrelevant.

4.2 Specifications

Figure 4.4 defines a function, findRoot, that generalizes the bisection search we used to find square roots in Figure 4.1. It also contains a function, testFindRoot, that can be used to test whether or not findRoot works as intended.

```
def findRoot(x, power, epsilon):
    """Assumes x and epsilon int or float, power an int,
            epsilon > 0 & power >= 1
       Returns float y such that y**power is within epsilon of x.
            If such a float does not exist, it returns None"""
    if x < 0 and power%2 == 0: #Negative number has no even-powered
                               #roots
        return None
    low = min(-1.0, x)
    high = max(1.0, x)
    ans = (high + low)/2.0
    while abs(ans**power - x) >= epsilon:
        if ans**power < x:
            low = ans
        else:
            high = ans
        ans = (high + low)/2.0
    return ans

def testFindRoot():
    epsilon = 0.0001
    for x in [0.25, -0.25, 2, -2, 8, -8]:
        for power in range(1, 4):
            print('Testing x =', str(x), 'and power = ', power)
            result = findRoot(x, power, epsilon)
            if result == None:
                print('   No root')
            else:
                print('   ', result**power, '~=', x)
```

Figure 4.4 Finding an approximation to a root

The function testFindRoot is almost as long as findRoot itself. To inexperienced programmers, writing **test functions** such as this often seems to be a waste of effort. Experienced programmers know, however, that an investment in writing testing code often pays big dividends. It certainly beats typing test cases into the shell over and over again during **debugging** (the process of finding out why a program does not work, and then fixing it). It also forces us to think about which tests are likely to be most illuminating.

The text between the triple quotation marks is called a **docstring** in Python. By convention, Python programmers use docstrings to provide specifications of functions. These docstrings can be accessed using the built-in function **help**. For example, if we enter the shell and type help(abs), the system will display

```
Help on built-in function abs in module built-ins:

abs(x)
    Return the absolute value of the argument.
```

If the code in Figure 4.4 has been loaded into an IDE, typing help(findRoot) in the shell will display

```
findRoot(x, power, epsilon)
    Assumes x and epsilon int or float, power an int,
        epsilon > 0 & power >= 1
    Returns float y such that y**power is within epsilon of x.
        If such a float does not exist, it returns None
```

If we type findRoot(in the editor, the list of formal parameters will be displayed.

A **specification** of a function defines a contract between the implementer of a function and those who will be writing programs that use the function. We will refer to the users of a function as its **clients**. This contract can be thought of as containing two parts:

- **Assumptions**: These describe conditions that must be met by clients of the function. Typically, they describe constraints on the actual parameters. Almost always, they specify the acceptable set of types for each parameter, and not infrequently some constraints on the value of one or more of the parameters. For example, the first two lines of the docstring of findRoot describe the assumptions that must be satisfied by clients of findRoot.
- **Guarantees**: These describe conditions that must be met by the function, provided that it has been called in a way that satisfies the assumptions. The last two lines of the docstring of findRoot describe the guarantees that the implementation of the function must meet.

CHAPTER 4. FUNCTIONS, SCOPING, AND ABSTRACTION

Functions are a way of creating computational elements that we can think of as primitives. Just as we have the built-in functions max and abs, we would like to have the equivalent of a built-in function for finding roots and for many other complex operations. Functions facilitate this by providing decomposition and abstraction.

Decomposition creates structure. It allows us to break a program into parts that are reasonably self-contained, and that may be reused in different settings.

Abstraction hides detail. It allows us to use a piece of code as if it were a black box—that is, something whose interior details we cannot see, don't need to see, and shouldn't even want to see.[26] The essence of abstraction is preserving information that is relevant in a given context, and forgetting information that is irrelevant in that context. The key to using abstraction effectively in programming is finding a notion of relevance that is appropriate for both the builder of an abstraction and the potential clients of the abstraction. That is the true art of programming.

Abstraction is all about forgetting. There are lots of ways to model this, for example, the auditory apparatus of most teenagers.

Teenager says: *May I borrow the car tonight?*

Parent says: *Yes, but be back before midnight, and make sure that the gas tank is full.*

Teenager hears: *Yes.*

The teenager has ignored all of those pesky details that he or she considers irrelevant. Abstraction is a many-to-one process. Had the parent said Yes, but be back before 2:00 a.m., and make sure that the car is clean, it would also have been abstracted to Yes.

By way of analogy, imagine that you were asked to produce an introductory computer science course containing twenty-five lectures. One way to do this would be to recruit twenty-five professors and ask each of them to prepare a one-hour lecture on their favorite topic. Though you might get twenty-five wonderful hours, the whole thing is likely to feel like a dramatization of Pirandello's "Six Characters in Search of an Author" (or that political science course you took with fifteen guest lecturers). If each professor worked in isolation, they would have no idea how to relate the material in their lecture to the material covered in other lectures.

Somehow, one needs to let everyone know what everyone else is doing, without generating so much work that nobody is willing to participate. This is where

---

[26] "Where ignorance is bliss, 'tis folly to be wise."—Thomas Gray

abstraction comes in. You could write twenty-five specifications, each saying what material the students should learn in each lecture, but not giving any detail about how that material should be taught. What you got might not be pedagogically wonderful, but at least it might make sense.

This is the way organizations go about using teams of programmers to get things done. Given a specification of a module, a programmer can work on implementing that module without worrying unduly about what the other programmers on the team are doing. Moreover, the other programmers can use the specification to start writing code that uses that module without worrying unduly about how that module is to be implemented.

The specification of findRoot is an abstraction of all the possible implementations that meet the specification. Clients of findRoot can assume that the implementation meets the specification, but they should assume nothing more. For example, clients can assume that the call findRoot(4.0, 2, 0.01) returns some value whose square is between 3.99 and 4.01. The value returned could be positive or negative, and even though 4.0 is a perfect square, the value returned might not be 2.0 or -2.0.

4.3 Recursion

You may have heard of **recursion**, and in all likelihood think of it as a rather subtle programming technique. That's a charming urban legend spread by computer scientists to make people think that we are smarter than we really are. Recursion is a very important idea, but it's not so subtle, and it is more than a programming technique.

As a descriptive method recursion is widely used, even by people who would never dream of writing a program. Consider part of the legal code of the United States defining the notion of a "natural-born" citizen. Roughly speaking, the definition is as follows

- Any child born inside the United States,
- Any child born in wedlock outside the United States both of whose parents are citizens of the U.S., as long as one parent has lived in the U.S. prior to the birth of the child, and
- Any child born in wedlock outside the United States one of whose parents is a U.S. citizen who has lived at least five years in the U.S. prior to the birth of the child, provided that at least two of those years were after the citizen's fourteenth birthday.

The first part is simple; if you are born in the United States, you are a natural-born citizen (such as Barack Obama). If you are not born in the U.S., then one has to decide if your parents are U.S. citizens (either natural born or naturalized). To determine if your parents are U.S. citizens, you might have to look at your grandparents, and so on.

In general, a recursive definition is made up of two parts. There is at least one **base case** that directly specifies the result for a special case (case 1 in the example above), and there is at least one **recursive (inductive) case** (cases 2 and 3 in the example above) that defines the answer in terms of the answer to the question on some other input, typically a simpler version of the same problem.

The world's simplest recursive definition is probably the factorial function (typically written in mathematics using !) on natural numbers.[27] The classic **inductive definition** is

$$1! = 1$$
$$(n + 1)! = (n + 1) * n!$$

The first equation defines the base case. The second equation defines factorial for all natural numbers, except the base case, in terms of the factorial of the previous number.

Figure 4.5 contains both an iterative (factI) and a recursive (factR) implementation of factorial.

```
def factI(n):                          def factrR(n):
    """Assumes n an int > 0                """Assumes n an int > 0
    Returns n!"""                          Returns n!"""
    result = 1                             if n == 1:
    while n > 1:                               return n
        result = result * n                else:
        n -= 1                                 return n*factR(n - 1)
    return result
```

Figure 4.5 Iterative and recursive implementations of factorial

This function is sufficiently simple that neither implementation is hard to follow. Still, the second is a more obvious translation of the original recursive definition.

---

[27] The exact definition of "natural number" is subject to debate. Some define it as the positive integers and others as the nonnegative integers. That's why we were explicit about the possible values of n in the docstrings in Figure 4.5.

It almost seems like cheating to implement factR by calling factR from within the body of factR. It works for the same reason that the iterative implementation works. We know that the iteration in factI will terminate because n starts out positive and each time around the loop it is reduced by 1. This means that it cannot be greater than 1 forever. Similarly, if factR is called with 1, it returns a value without making a recursive call. When it does make a recursive call, it always does so with a value one less than the value with which it was called. Eventually, the recursion terminates with the call factR(1).

4.3.1 Fibonacci Numbers

The Fibonacci sequence is another common mathematical function that is usually defined recursively. "They breed like rabbits," is often used to describe a population that the speaker thinks is growing too quickly. In the year 1202, the Italian mathematician Leonardo of Pisa, also known as Fibonacci, developed a formula to quantify this notion, albeit with some not terribly realistic assumptions.[28]

Suppose a newly born pair of rabbits, one male and one female, are put in a pen (or worse, released in the wild). Suppose further that the rabbits are able to mate at the age of one month (which, astonishingly, some breeds can) and have a one-month gestation period (which, astonishingly, some breeds do). Finally, suppose that these mythical rabbits never die, and that the female always produces one new pair (one male, one female) every month from its second month on. How many female rabbits will there be at the end of six months?

On the last day of the first month (call it month 0), there will be one female (ready to conceive on the first day of the next month). On the last day of the second month, there will still be only one female (since she will not give birth until the first day of the next month). On the last day of the next month, there will be two females (one pregnant and one not). On the last day of the next month, there will be three females (two pregnant and one not). And so on. Let's look at this progression in tabular form, Figure 4.6.

Notice that for month n > 1, females(n) = females(n-1) + females(n-2). This is not an accident. Each female that was alive in month n-1 will still be alive in month n. In addition, each female that was alive in month n-2 will produce one new female in month n. The new females can be added to the females alive in month n-1 to get the number of females in month n.

---

[28] That we call this a Fibonacci sequence is an example of a Eurocentric interpretation of history. Fibonacci's great contribution to European mathematics was his book *Liber Abaci*, which introduced to European mathematicians many concepts already well known to Indian and Arabic scholars. These concepts included Hindu-Arabic numerals and the decimal system. What we today call the Fibonacci sequence was taken from the work of the Sanskrit mathematician Pingala.

CHAPTER 4. FUNCTIONS, SCOPING, AND ABSTRACTION

Month	Females
0	1
1	1
2	2
3	3
4	5
5	8
6	13

Figure 4.6 Growth in population of female rabbits

The growth in population is described naturally by the **recurrence**[29]

```
females(0) = 1
females(1) = 1
females(n + 2) = females(n+1) + females(n)
```

This definition is a little different from the recursive definition of factorial:

- It has two base cases, not just one. In general, you can have as many base cases as you need.
- In the recursive case, there are two recursive calls, not just one. Again, there can be as many as you need.

Figure 4.7 contains a straightforward implementation of the Fibonacci recurrence,[30] along with a function that can be used to test it.

```
def fib(n):
    """Assumes n int >= 0
       Returns Fibonacci of n"""
    if n == 0 or n == 1:
        return 1
    else:
        return fib(n-1) + fib(n-2)

def testFib(n):
    for i in range(n+1):
        print('fib of', i, '=', fib(i))
```

Figure 4.7 Recursive implementation of Fibonacci sequence

---

[29] This version of the Fibonacci sequence corresponds to the definition used in Fibonacci's *Liber Abaci*. Other definitions of the sequence start with 0 rather than 1.

[30] While obviously correct, this is a terribly inefficient implementation of the Fibonacci function. There is a simple iterative implementation that is much better.

Writing the code is the easy part of solving this problem. Once we went from the vague statement of a problem about bunnies to a set of recursive equations, the code almost wrote itself. Finding some kind of abstract way to express a solution to the problem at hand is very often the hardest step in building a useful program. We will talk much more about this later in the book.

As you might guess, this is not a perfect model for the growth of rabbit populations in the wild. In 1859, Thomas Austin, an Australian farmer, imported twenty-four rabbits from England, to be used as targets in hunts. Ten years later, approximately two million rabbits were shot or trapped each year in Australia, with no noticeable impact on the population. That's a lot of rabbits, but not anywhere close to the 120th Fibonacci number.[31]

Though the Fibonacci sequence does not actually provide a perfect model of the growth of rabbit populations, it does have many interesting mathematical properties. Fibonacci numbers are also quite common in nature.

Finger exercise: When the implementation of fib in Figure 4.7 is used to compute fib(5), how many times does it compute the value of fib(2) on the way to computing fib(5)?

4.3.2 Palindromes

Recursion is also useful for many problems that do not involve numbers. Figure 4.8 contains a function, isPalindrome, that checks whether a string reads the same way backwards and forwards.

The function isPalindrome contains two internal **helper functions**. This should be of no interest to clients of the function, who should care only that isPalindrome meets its specification. But you should care, because there are things to learn by examining the implementation.

The helper function toChars converts all letters to lowercase and removes all non-letters. It starts by using a built-in method on strings to generate a string that is identical to s, except that all uppercase letters have been converted to lowercase. We will talk a lot more about **method invocation** when we get to classes. For now, think of it as a peculiar syntax for a function call. Instead of putting the first (and in this case only) argument inside parentheses following the function name, we use **dot notation** to place that argument before the function name.

---

[31] The damage done by the descendants of those twenty-four cute bunnies has been estimated to be $600 million per year, and they are in the process of eating many native plants into extinction.

```
def isPalindrome(s):
    """Assumes s is a str
       Returns True if letters in s form a palindrome; False
         otherwise. Non-letters and capitalization are ignored."""

    def toChars(s):
        s = s.lower()
        letters = ''
        for c in s:
            if c in 'abcdefghijklmnopqrstuvwxyz':
                letters = letters + c
        return letters

    def isPal(s):
        if len(s) <= 1:
            return True
        else:
            return s[0] == s[-1] and isPal(s[1:-1])

    return isPal(toChars(s))
```

Figure 4.8 Palindrome testing

The helper function isPal uses recursion to do the real work. The two base cases are strings of length zero or one. This means that the recursive part of the implementation is reached only on strings of length two or more. The conjunction[32] in the else clause is evaluated from left to right. The code first checks whether the first and last characters are the same, and if they are goes on to check whether the string minus those two characters is a palindrome. That the second conjunct is not evaluated unless the first conjunct evaluates to True is semantically irrelevant in this example. However, later in the book we will see examples where this kind of **short-circuit evaluation** of Boolean expressions is semantically relevant.

This implementation of isPalindrome is an example of an important problem-solving principle known as **divide-and-conquer**. (This principle is related to but slightly different from divide-and-conquer algorithms, which are discussed in Chapter 10.) The problem-solving principle is to conquer a hard problem by breaking it into a set of subproblems with the properties that

- the subproblems are easier to solve than the original problem, and
- solutions of the subproblems can be combined to solve the original problem.

---

[32] When two Boolean-valued expressions are connected by "and," each expression is called a **conjunct**. If they are connected by "or," they are called **disjuncts**.

Divide-and-conquer is a very old idea. Julius Caesar practiced what the Romans referred to as *divide et impera* (divide and rule). The British practiced it brilliantly to control the Indian subcontinent. Benjamin Franklin was well aware of the British expertise in using this technique, prompting him to say at the signing of the U.S. Declaration of Independence, "We must all hang together, or assuredly we shall all hang separately."

In this case, we solve the problem by breaking the original problem into a simpler version of the same problem (checking whether a shorter string is a palindrome) and a simple thing we know how to do (comparing single characters), and then combine the solutions with and. Figure 4.9 contains some code that can be used to visualize how this works.

```python
def isPalindrome(s):
    """Assumes s is a str
       Returns True if s is a palindrome; False otherwise.
       Punctuation marks, blanks, and capitalization are ignored."""

    def toChars(s):
        s = s.lower()
        letters = ''
        for c in s:
            if c in 'abcdefghijklmnopqrstuvwxyz':
                letters = letters + c
        return letters

    def isPal(s):
        print('  isPal called with', s)
        if len(s) <= 1:
            print('  About to return True from base case')
            return True
        else:
            answer = s[0] == s[-1] and isPal(s[1:-1])
            print('  About to return', answer, 'for', s)
            return answer

    return isPal(toChars(s))

def testIsPalindrome():
    print('Try dogGod')
    print(isPalindrome('dogGod'))
    print('Try doGood')
    print(isPalindrome('doGood'))
```

Figure 4.9 Code to visualize palindrome testing

CHAPTER 4. FUNCTIONS, SCOPING, AND ABSTRACTION

When `testIsPalindrome` is run, it will print

```
Try dogGod
  isPal called with doggod
  isPal called with oggo
  isPal called with gg
  isPal called with
  About to return True from base case
  About to return True for gg
  About to return True for oggo
  About to return True for doggod
True
Try doGood
  isPal called with dogood
  isPal called with ogoo
  isPal called with go
  About to return False for go
  About to return False for ogoo
  About to return False for dogood
False
```

4.4 Global Variables

If you tried calling `fib` with a large number, you probably noticed that it took a very long time to run. Suppose we want to know how many recursive calls are made? We could do a careful analysis of the code and figure it out, and in Chapter 9 we will talk about how to do that. Another approach is to add some code that counts the number of calls. One way to do that uses **global variables**.

Until now, all of the functions we have written communicate with their environment solely through their parameters and return values. For the most part, this is exactly as it should be. It typically leads to programs that are relatively easy to read, test, and debug. Every once in a while, however, global variables come in handy. Consider the code in Figure 4.10.

In each function, the line of code `global numFibCalls` tells Python that the name `numCalls` should be defined at the outermost scope of the module (see Section 4.5) in which the line of code appears rather than within the scope of the function in which the line of code appears. Had we not included the code `global numFibCalls`, the name `numFibCalls` would have been local to each of the functions `fib` and `testFib`, because `numFibCalls` occurs on the left-hand side of an assignment statement in both `fib` and `testFib`. The functions `fib` and `testFib` both have unfettered access to the object referenced by the variable `numFibCalls`. The function testFib binds numFibCalls to 0 each time it calls fib, and fib increments the value of numFibCalls each time fib is entered.

```
def fib(x):
    """Assumes x an int >= 0
       Returns Fibonacci of x"""
    global numFibCalls
    numFibCalls += 1
    if x == 0 or x == 1:
        return 1
    else:
        return fib(x-1) + fib(x-2)

def testFib(n):
    for i in range(n+1):
        global numFibCalls
        numFibCalls = 0
        print('fib of', i, '=', fib(i))
        print('fib called', numFibCalls, 'times.')
```

Figure 4.10 Using a global variable

The call testFib(6) produces the output

```
fib of 0 = 1
fib called 1 times.
fib of 1 = 1
fib called 1 times.
fib of 2 = 2
fib called 3 times.
fib of 3 = 3
fib called 5 times.
fib of 4 = 5
fib called 9 times.
fib of 5 = 8
fib called 15 times.
fib of 6 = 13
fib called 25 times.
```

It is with some trepidation that we introduce the topic of global variables. Since the 1970s card-carrying computer scientists have inveighed against them. The indiscriminate use of global variables can lead to lots of problems. The key to making programs readable is locality. One reads a program a piece at a time, and the less context needed to understand each piece, the better. Since global variables can be modified or read in a wide variety of places, the sloppy use of them can destroy locality. Nevertheless, there are times when they are just what is needed.

4.5 Modules

So far, we have operated under the assumption that our entire program is stored in one file. This is perfectly reasonable as long as programs are small. As programs get larger, however, it is typically more convenient to store different parts of them in different files. Imagine, for example, that multiple people are working on the same program. It would be a nightmare if they were all trying to update the same file. Python modules allow us to easily construct a program from code in multiple files.

A **module** is a .py file containing Python definitions and statements. We could create, for example, a file circle.py containing the code in Figure 4.11.

```
pi = 3.14159

def area(radius):
    return pi*(radius**2)

def circumference(radius):
    return 2*pi*radius

def sphereSurface(radius):
    return 4.0*area(radius)

def sphereVolume(radius):
    return (4.0/3.0)*pi*(radius**3)
```

Figure 4.11 Some code related to circles and spheres

A program gets access to a module through an import statement. So, for example, the code

```
import circle
pi = 3
print(pi)
print(circle.pi)
print(circle.area(3))
print(circle.circumference(3))
print(circle.sphereSurface(3))
```

will print

```
3
3.14159
28.27431
18.849539999999998
113.09724
```

Modules are typically stored in individual files. Each module has its own private symbol table. Consequently, within circle.py we access objects (e.g., pi and area) in the usual way. Executing import M creates a binding for module M in the scope in which the import appears. Therefore, in the importing context we use dot notation to indicate that we are referring to a name defined in the imported module.[33] For example, outside of circle.py, the references pi and circle.pi can (and in this case do) refer to different objects.

At first glance, the use of dot notation may seem cumbersome. On the other hand, when one imports a module one often has no idea what local names might have been used in the implementation of that module. The use of dot notation to fully qualify names avoids the possibility of getting burned by an accidental name clash. For example, executing the assignment pi = 3 outside of the circle module does not change the value of pi used within the circle module.

There is a variant of the import statement that allows the importing program to omit the module name when accessing names defined inside the imported module. Executing the statement from M import * creates bindings in the current scope to all objects defined within M, but not to M itself. For example, the code

```
from circle import *
print(pi)
print(circle.pi)
```

will first print 3.14159, and then produce the error message

```
NameError: name 'circle' is not defined
```

Some Python programmers frown upon using this form of import because they believe that it makes code more difficult to read.

As we have seen, a module can contain executable statements as well as function definitions. Typically, these statements are used to initialize the module. For this reason, the statements in a module are executed only the first time a module is imported into a program. Moreover, a module is imported only once per interpreter session. If you start up a shell, import a module, and then change the contents of that module, the interpreter will still be using the original version of the

---

[33] Superficially, this may seem unrelated to the use of dot notation in method invocation. However, as we will see in Chapter 8, there is a deep connection.

module. This can lead to puzzling behavior when debugging. When in doubt, start a new shell.

There are lots of useful modules that come as part of the standard Python library. For example, it is rarely necessary to write your own implementations of common mathematical or string functions. A description of this library can be found at http://docs.python.org/2/library/.

4.6 Files

Every computer system uses **files** to save things from one computation to the next. Python provides many facilities for creating and accessing files. Here we illustrate some of the basic ones.

Each operating system (e.g., Windows and MAC OS) comes with its own file system for creating and accessing files. Python achieves operating-system independence by accessing files through something called a **file handle**. The code

```
nameHandle = open('kids', 'w')
```

instructs the operating system to create a file with the name kids, and return a file handle for that file. The argument `'w'` to open indicates that the file is to be opened for **writing**. The following code opens a file, uses the **write** method to write two lines, and then closes the file. It is important to remember to close the file when the program is finished using it. Otherwise there is a risk that some or all of the writes may not be saved.

```
nameHandle = open('kids', 'w')
for i in range(2):
    name = input('Enter name: ')
    nameHandle.write(name + '\n')
nameHandle.close()
```

In a Python string, the escape character "\" is used to indicate that the next character should be treated in a special way. In this example, the string '\n' indicates a newline character.

We can now open the file for **reading** (using the argument `'r'`), and print its contents. Since Python treats a file as a sequence of lines, we can use a for statement to iterate over the file's contents.

```
nameHandle = open('kids', 'r')
for line in nameHandle:
    print(line)
nameHandle.close()
```

If we had typed in the names David and Andrea, this will print

```
David
```

```
Andrea
```

The extra line between David and Andrea is there because print starts a new line each time it encounters the '\n' at the end of each line in the file. We could have avoided printing that by writing print line[:-1]. The code

```
nameHandle = open('kids', 'w')
nameHandle.write('Michael\n')
nameHandle.write('Mark\n')
nameHandle.close()
nameHandle = open('kids', 'r')
for line in nameHandle:
    print(line[:-1])
nameHandle.close()
```

will print

```
Michael
Mark
```

Notice that we have overwritten the previous contents of the file kids. If we don't want to do that we can open the file for **appending** (instead of writing) by using the argument 'a'. For example, if we now run the code

```
nameHandle = open('kids', 'a')
nameHandle.write('David\n')
nameHandle.write('Andrea\n')
nameHandle.close()
nameHandle = open('kids', 'r')
for line in nameHandle:
    print(line[:-1])
nameHandle.close()
```

it will print

```
Michael
Mark
David
Andrea
```

CHAPTER 4. FUNCTIONS, SCOPING, AND ABSTRACTION 63

Some of the common operations on files are summarized in Figure 4.12.

---

open(fn, 'w') fn is a string representing a file name. Creates a file for writing and returns a file handle.

open(fn, 'r') fn is a string representing a file name. Opens an existing file for reading and returns a file handle.

open(fn, 'a') fn is a string representing a file name. Opens an existing file for appending and returns a file handle.

fh.read() returns a string containing the contents of the file associated with the file handle fh.

fh.readline() returns the next line in the file associated with the file handle fh.

fh.readlines() returns a list each element of which is one line of the file associated with the file handle fh.

fh.write(s) writes the string s to the end of the file associated with the file handle fh.

fh.writeLines(S) S is a sequence of strings. Writes each element of S as a separate line to the file associated with the file handle fh.

fh.close() closes the file associated with the file handle fh.

Figure 4.12 Common functions for accessing files

5 STRUCTURED TYPES, MUTABILITY, AND HIGHER-ORDER FUNCTIONS

The programs we have looked at thus far have dealt with three types of objects: int, float, and str. The numeric types int and float are scalar types. That is to say, objects of these types have no accessible internal structure. In contrast, str can be thought of as a structured, or non-scalar, type. One can use indexing to extract individual characters from a string and slicing to extract substrings.

In this chapter, we introduce four additional structured types. One, tuple, is a rather simple generalization of str. The other three—list, range,[34] and dict—are more interesting. We also return to the topic of functions with some examples that illustrate the utility of being able to treat functions in the same way as other types of objects.

5.1 Tuples

Like strings, **tuples** are immutable ordered sequences of elements. The difference is that the elements of a tuple need not be characters. The individual elements can be of any type, and need not be of the same type as each other.

Literals of type tuple are written by enclosing a comma-separated list of elements within parentheses. For example, we can write

```
t1 = ()
t2 = (1, 'two', 3)
print(t1)
print(t2)
```

Unsurprisingly, the print statements produce the output

```
()
(1, 'two', 3)
```

Looking at this example, you might naturally be led to believe that the tuple containing the single value 1 would be written (1). But, to quote Richard Nixon, "that would be wrong." Since parentheses are used to group expressions, (1) is

---

[34] Type range does not exist in Python 2.

merely a verbose way to write the integer 1. To denote the singleton tuple containing this value, we write (1,). Almost everybody who uses Python has at one time or another accidentally omitted that annoying comma.

Repetition can be used on tuples. For example, the expression 3*('a', 2) evaluates to ('a', 2, 'a', 2, 'a', 2).

Like strings, tuples can be concatenated, indexed, and sliced. Consider

```
t1 = (1, 'two', 3)
t2 = (t1, 3.25)
print(t2)
print((t1 + t2))
print((t1 + t2)[3])
print((t1 + t2)[2:5])
```

The second assignment statement binds the name t2 to a tuple that contains the tuple to which t1 is bound and the floating point number 3.25. This is possible because a tuple, like everything else in Python, is an object, so tuples can contain tuples. Therefore, the first print statement produces the output,

`((1, 'two', 3), 3.25)`

The second print statement prints the value generated by concatenating the values bound to t1 and t2, which is a tuple with five elements. It produces the output

`(1, 'two', 3, (1, 'two', 3), 3.25)`

The next statement selects and prints the fourth element of the concatenated tuple (as always in Python, indexing starts at 0), and the statement after that creates and prints a slice of that tuple, producing the output

```
(1, 'two', 3)
(3, (1, 'two', 3), 3.25)
```

A for statement can be used to iterate over the elements of a tuple:

```
def intersect(t1, t2):
    """Assumes t1 and t2 are tuples
       Returns a tuple containing elements that are in
          both t1 and t2"""
    result = ()
    for e in t1:
        if e in t2:
            result += (e,)
    return result
```

5.1.1 Sequences and Multiple Assignment

If you know the length of a sequence (e.g., a tuple or a string), it can be convenient to use Python's multiple assignment statement to extract the individual elements. For example, after executing the statement x, y = (3, 4), x will be bound to 3 and y to 4. Similarly, the statement a, b, c = 'xyz' will bind a to 'x', b to 'y', and c to 'z'.

This mechanism is particularly convenient when used in conjunction with functions that return fixed-size sequences. Consider, for example the function definition

```
def findExtremeDivisors(n1, n2):
    """Assumes that n1 and n2 are positive ints
       Returns a tuple containing the smallest common divisor > 1 and
          the largest common divisor of n1 and n2. If no common divisor,
       returns (None, None)"""
    minVal, maxVal = None, None
    for i in range(2, min(n1, n2) + 1):
        if n1%i == 0 and n2%i == 0:
            if minVal == None:
                minVal = i
            maxVal = i
    return (minVal, maxVal)
```

The multiple assignment statement

```
minDivisor, maxDivisor = findExtremeDivisors(100, 200)
```

will bind `minDivisor` to 2 and `maxDivisor` to 100.

5.2 Ranges

Like strings and tuples, ranges are immutable. The range function returns an object of type range. As stated in Section 3.2, the range function takes three integer arguments: start, stop, and step, and returns the progression of integers start, start + step, start + 2*step, etc. If step is positive, the last element is the largest integer start + i*step less than stop. If step is negative, the last element is the smallest integer start + i*step greater than stop. If only two arguments are supplied, a step of 1 is used. If only one argument is supplied, that argument is the stop, start defaults to 0, and step defaults to 1.

All of the operations on tuples are also available for ranges, except for concatenation and repetition. For example, range(10)[2:6][2] evaluates to 4. When the == operator is used to compare objects of type range, it returns True if the two ranges represent the same sequence of integers. For example, range(0, 7, 2) == range(0, 8, 2) evaluates to True. However, range(0, 7, 2) == range(6, -1, -2) evaluates to False because though the two ranges contain the same integers, they occur in a different order.

Unlike objects of type tuple, the amount of space occupied by an object of type range is not proportional to its length. Because a range is fully defined by its start, stop, and step values; it can be stored in a small amount of space.

The most common use of range is in for loops, but objects of type range can be used anywhere a sequence of integers can be used.

5.3 Lists and Mutability

Like a tuple, a **list** is an ordered sequence of values, where each value is identified by an index. The syntax for expressing literals of type list is similar to that used for tuples; the difference is that we use square brackets rather than parentheses. The empty list is written as [], and singleton lists are written without that (oh so easy to forget) comma before the closing bracket. So, for example, the code,

```
L = ['I did it all', 4, 'love']
for i in range(len(L)):
    print(L[i])
```

produces the output,

```
I did it all
4
love
```

Occasionally, the fact that square brackets are used for literals of type list, indexing into lists, and slicing lists can lead to some visual confusion. For example, the expression [1,2,3,4][1:3][1], which evaluates to 3, uses the square brackets in three different ways. This is rarely a problem in practice, because most of the time lists are built incrementally rather than written as literals.

Lists differ from tuples in one hugely important way: lists are **mutable**. In contrast, tuples and strings are **immutable**. There are many operators that can be used to create objects of these immutable types, and variables can be bound to objects of these types. But objects of immutable types cannot be modified. On the other hand, objects of type list can be modified after they are created.

The distinction between mutating an object and assigning an object to a variable may, at first, appear subtle. However, if you keep repeating the mantra, "In Python a variable is merely a name, i.e., a label that can be attached to an object," it will bring you clarity.

CHAPTER 5. STRUCTURED TYPES, MUTABILITY, AND HIGHER-ORDER FUNCTIONS 69

When the statements
```
Techs = ['MIT', 'Caltech']
Ivys = ['Harvard', 'Yale', 'Brown']
```
are executed, the interpreter creates two new lists and binds the appropriate variables to them, as pictured in Figure 5.1.

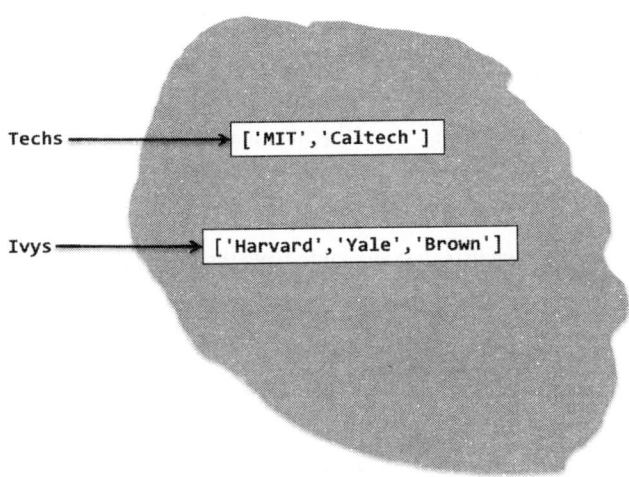

Figure 5.1 Two lists

The assignment statements
```
Univs = [Techs, Ivys]
Univs1 = [['MIT', 'Caltech'], ['Harvard', 'Yale', 'Brown']]
```
also create new lists and bind variables to them. The elements of these lists are themselves lists. The three print statements
```
print('Univs =', Univs)
print('Univs1 =', Univs1)
print(Univs == Univs1)
```
produce the output
```
Univs = [['MIT', 'Caltech'], ['Harvard', 'Yale', 'Brown']]
Univs1 = [['MIT', 'Caltech'], ['Harvard', 'Yale', 'Brown']]
True
```

It appears as if Univs and Univs1 are bound to the same value. But appearances can be deceiving. As Figure 5.2 illustrates, Univs and Univs1 are bound to quite different values.

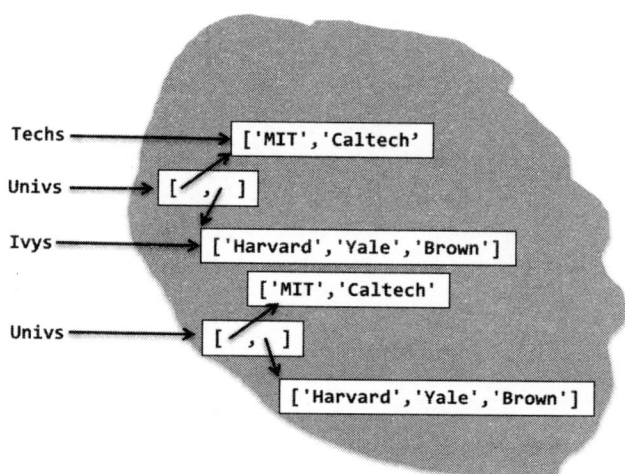

Figure 5.2 Two lists that appear to have the same value, but don't

That Univs and Univs1 are bound to different objects can be verified using the built-in Python function **id**, which returns a unique integer identifier for an object. This function allows us to test for **object equality**. When we run the code

```
print(Univs == Univs1) #test value equality
print(id(Univs) == id(Univs1)) #test object equality
print('Id of Univs =', id(Univs))
print('Id of Univs1 =', id(Univs1))
```

it prints

```
True
False
Id of Univs = 4447805768
Id of Univs1 = 4456134408
```

(Don't expect to see the same unique identifiers if you run this code. The semantics of Python says nothing about what identifier is associated with each object; it merely requires that no two objects have the same identifier.)

Notice that in Figure 5.2 the elements of Univs are not copies of the lists to which Techs and Ivys are bound, but are rather the lists themselves. The elements of Univs1 are lists that contain the same elements as the lists in Univs, but they are not the same lists. We can see this by running the code

```
print('Ids of Univs[0] and Univs[1]', id(Univs[0]), id(Univs[1]))
print('Ids of Univs1[0] and Univs1[1]', id(Univs1[0]), id(Univs1[1]))
```

CHAPTER 5. STRUCTURED TYPES, MUTABILITY, AND HIGHER-ORDER FUNCTIONS 71

which prints

```
Ids of Univs[0] and Univs[1] 4447807688 4456134664
Ids of Univs1[0] and Univs1[1] 4447805768 4447806728
```

Why does this matter? It matters because lists are mutable. Consider the code

```
Techs.append('RPI')
```

The append method has a **side effect**. Rather than create a new list, it mutates the existing list Techs by adding a new element, the string 'RPI', to the end of it. Figure 5.3 depicts the state of the computation after append is executed.

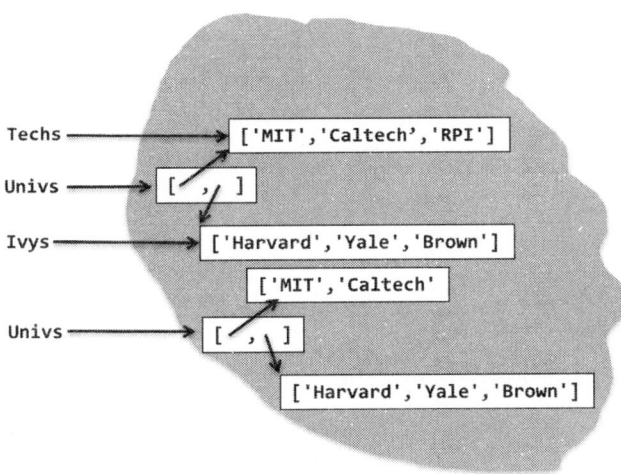

Figure 5.3 **Demonstration of mutability**

The object to which Univs is bound still contains the same two lists, but the contents of one of those lists has been changed. Consequently, the print statements

```
print('Univs =', Univs)
print('Univs1 =', Univs1)
```

now produce the output

```
Univs = [['MIT', 'Caltech', 'RPI'], ['Harvard', 'Yale', 'Brown']]
Univs1 = [['MIT', 'Caltech'], ['Harvard', 'Yale', 'Brown']]
```

What we have here is something called **aliasing**. There are two distinct paths to the same list object. One path is through the variable Techs and the other through the first element of the list object to which Univs is bound. One can mutate the object via either path, and the effect of the mutation will be visible through both paths. This can be convenient, but it can also be treacherous. Unintentional aliasing leads to programming errors that are often enormously hard to track down.

As with tuples, a `for` statement can be used to iterate over the elements of a list. For example,

```
for e in Univs:
    print('Univs contains', e)
    print('   which contains')
    for u in e:
        print('     ', u)
```

will print

```
Univs contains ['MIT', 'Caltech', 'RPI']
   which contains
      MIT
      Caltech
      RPI
Univs contains ['Harvard', 'Yale', 'Brown']
   which contains
      Harvard
      Yale
      Brown
```

When we append one list to another, e.g., `Techs.append(Ivys)`, the original structure is maintained. I.e., the result is a list that contains a list. Suppose we do not want to maintain this structure, but want to add the elements of one list into another list. We can do that by using list concatenation or the extend method, e.g.,

```
L1 = [1,2,3]
L2 = [4,5,6]
L3 = L1 + L2
print('L3 =', L3)
L1.extend(L2)
print('L1 =', L1)
L1.append(L2)
print('L1 =', L1)
```

will print

```
L3 = [1, 2, 3, 4, 5, 6]
L1 = [1, 2, 3, 4, 5, 6]
L1 = [1, 2, 3, 4, 5, 6, [4, 5, 6]]
```

Notice that the operator + does not have a side effect. It creates a new list and returns it. In contrast, extend and append each mutated L1.

Figure 5.4 contains short descriptions of some of the methods associated with lists. Note that all of these except `count` and `index` mutate the list.

CHAPTER 5. STRUCTURED TYPES, MUTABILITY, AND HIGHER-ORDER FUNCTIONS

> **L.append(e)** adds the object e to the end of L.
>
> **L.count(e)** returns the number of times that e occurs in L.
>
> **L.insert(i, e)** inserts the object e into L at index i.
>
> **L.extend(L1)** adds the items in list L1 to the end of L.
>
> **L.remove(e)** deletes the first occurrence of e from L.
>
> **L.index(e)** returns the index of the first occurrence of e in L, raises an exception (see Chapter 7) if e is not in L.
>
> **L.pop(i)** removes and returns the item at index i in L, raises an exception if L is empty. If i is omitted, it defaults to -1, to remove and return the last element of L.
>
> **L.sort()** sorts the elements of L in ascending order.
>
> **L.reverse()** reverses the order of the elements in L.

Figure 5.4 Methods associated with lists

5.3.1 Cloning

It is usually prudent to avoid mutating a list over which one is iterating. Consider, for example, the code

```
def removeDups(L1, L2):
    """Assumes that L1 and L2 are lists.
       Removes any element from L1 that also occurs in L2"""
    for e1 in L1:
        if e1 in L2:
            L1.remove(e1)
L1 = [1,2,3,4]
L2 = [1,2,5,6]
removeDups(L1, L2)
print('L1 =', L1)
```

You might be surprised to discover that this prints

```
L1 = [2, 3, 4]
```

During a for loop, the implementation of Python keeps track of where it is in the list using an internal counter that is incremented at the end of each iteration. When the value of the counter reaches the current length of the list, the loop terminates. This works as one might expect if the list is not mutated within the loop, but can have surprising consequences if the list is mutated. In this case, the hidden counter starts out at 0, discovers that L1[0] is in L2, and removes it—reducing the length of L1 to 3. The counter is then incremented to 1, and the code proceeds to check if the value of L1[1] is in L2. Notice that this is not the original value of L1[1] (i.e., 2), but rather the current value of L1[1] (i.e., 3). As you can see, it is possible to figure out what happens when the list is modified within the loop. However, it is not easy. And what happens is likely to be unintentional, as in this example.

One way to avoid this kind of problem is to use slicing to **clone**[35] (i.e., make a copy of) the list and write for e1 in L1[:]. Notice that writing

```
newL1 = L1
for e1 in newL1:
```

would not solve the problem. It would not create a copy of L1, but would merely introduce a new name for the existing list.

Slicing is not the only way to clone lists in Python. The expression list(L) returns a copy of the list L. If the list to be copied contains mutable objects that you want to copy as well, import the standard library module copy and use the function copy.deepcopy.

5.3.2 List Comprehension

List comprehension provides a concise way to apply an operation to the values in a sequence. It creates a new list in which each element is the result of applying a given operation to a value from a sequence (e.g., the elements in another list). For example,

```
L = [x**2 for x in range(1,7)]
print(L)
```

will print the list

```
[1, 4, 9, 16, 25, 36]
```

The for clause in a list comprehension can be followed by one or more if and for statements that are applied to the values produced by the for clause. These additional clauses modify the sequence of values generated by the first for clause and produce a new sequence of values, to which the operation associated with the comprehension is applied. For example, the code

```
mixed = [1, 2, 'a', 3, 4.0]
print([x**2 for x in mixed if type(x) == int])
```

squares the integers in mixed, and then prints [1, 4, 9].

---

[35] The cloning of animals, including humans, raises a host of technical, ethical, and spiritual conumdrums. Fortunately, the cloning of Python objects does not.

CHAPTER 5. STRUCTURED TYPES, MUTABILITY, AND HIGHER-ORDER FUNCTIONS

Some Python programmers use list comprehensions in marvelous and subtle ways. That is not always a great idea. Remember that somebody else may need to read your code, and "subtle" is not usually a desirable property.

5.4 Functions as Objects

In Python, functions are **first-class objects**. That means that they can be treated like objects of any other type, e.g., `int` or `list`. They have types, e.g., the expression `type(abs)` has the value `<type 'built-in_function_or_method'>`; they can appear in expressions, e.g., as the right-hand side of an assignment statement or as an argument to a function; they can be elements of lists; etc.

Using functions as arguments allows a style of coding called **higher-order programming**. It can be particularly convenient in conjunction with lists, as shown in Figure 5.5.

```
def applyToEach(L, f):
    """Assumes L is a list, f a function
       Mutates L by replacing each element, e, of L by f(e)"""
    for i in range(len(L)):
        L[i] = f(L[i])

L = [1, -2, 3.33]
print('L =', L)
print('Apply abs to each element of L.')
applyToEach(L, abs)
print('L =', L)
print('Apply int to each element of', L)
applyToEach(L, int)
print('L =', L)
print('Apply factorial to each element of', L)
applyToEach(L, factR)
print('L =', L)
print('Apply Fibonnaci to each element of', L)
applyToEach(L, fib)
print('L =', L)
```

Figure 5.5 Applying a function to elements of a list

The function `applyToEach` is called **higher-order** because it has an argument that is itself a function. The first time it is called, it mutates L by applying the unary built-in function `abs` to each element. The second time it is called, it applies a type conversion to each element. The third time it is called, it replaces each element by the result of applying the function factR (defined in Figure 4.5) to each element. And the fourth time it is called, it replaces each element by the result of applying the function fib (defined in Figure 4.7) to each element. It prints

```
L = [1, -2, 3.33]
Apply abs to each element of L.
L = [1, 2, 3.33]
Apply int to each element of [1, 2, 3.33]
L = [1, 2, 3]
Apply factorial to each element of [1, 2, 3]
L = [1, 2, 6]
Apply Fibonnaci to each element of [1, 2, 6]
L = [1, 2, 13]
```

Python has a built-in higher-order function, map, that is similar to, but more general than, the applyToEach function defined in Figure 5.5. it is designed to be used in conjunction with a for loop. In its simplest form the first argument to map is a unary function (i.e., a function that has only one parameter) and the second argument is any ordered collection of values suitable as arguments to the first argument.

When used in a for loop, map behaves like the range function in that it returns one value for each iteration of the loop.[36] These values are generated by applying the first argument to each element of the second argument. For example, the code

```
for i in map(fib, [2, 6, 4]):
    print(i)
```

prints

```
2
13
5
```

More generally, the first argument to map can be a function of n arguments, in which case it must be followed by n subsequent ordered collections (each of the same length). For example, the code

```
L1 = [1, 28, 36]
L2 = [2, 57, 9]
for i in map(min, L1, L2):
    print(i)
```

---

[36] In Python 2, map does not return values one at a time. Instead, it returns a list of values. That is to say, it behaves like the Python 2 range function rather than like the Python 2 xrange function.

prints

```
1
28
9
```

Python supports the creation of anonymous functions (i.e., functions that are not bound to a name), using the reserved word `lambda`. The general form of a **lambda expression** is

```
lambda <sequence of variable names>: <expression>
```

For example, the lambda expression `lambda x, y: x*y` returns a function that returns the product of its two arguments. Lambda expressions are frequently used as arguments to higher-order functions. For example, the code

```
L = []
for i in map(lambda x, y: x**y, [1 ,2 ,3, 4], [3, 2, 1, 0]):
    L.append(i)
print(L)
```

prints `[1, 4, 3, 1]`.

5.5 Strings, Tuples, Ranges, and Lists

We have looked at four different sequence types: str, tuple, range, and list. They are similar in that objects of of these types can be operated upon as described in Figure 5.6. Some of their other similarities and differences are summarized in Figure 5.7.

---

seq[i] returns the ith element in the sequence.

len(seq) returns the length of the sequence.

seq1 + seq2 returns the concatenation of the two sequences (not available for ranges).

n*seq returns a sequence that repeats seq n times (not available for ranges).

seq[start:end] returns a slice of the sequence.

e in seq is True if e is contained in the sequence and False otherwise.

e not in seq is True if e is not in the sequence and False otherwise.

for e in seq iterates over the elements of the sequence.

Figure 5.6 Common operations on sequence types

Type	Type of elements	Examples of literals	Mutable
str	characters	'', 'a', 'abc'	No
tuple	any type	(), (3,), ('abc', 4)	No
range	integers	range(10), range(1, 10, 2)	No
list	any type	[], [3], ['abc', 4]	Yes

Figure 5.7 Comparison of sequence types

Python programmers tend to use lists far more often than tuples. Since lists are mutable, they can be constructed incrementally during a computation. For example, the following code incrementally builds a list containing all of the even numbers in another list.

```
evenElems = []
for e in L:
    if e%2 == 0:
        evenElems.append(e)
```

One advantage of tuples is that because they are immutable, aliasing is never a worry. Another advantage of their being immutable is that tuples, unlike lists, can be used as keys in dictionaries, as we will see in the next section.

Since strings can contain only characters, they are considerably less versatile than tuples or lists. On the other hand, when you are working with a string of characters there are many built-in methods that make life easy. Figure 5.8 contains short descriptions of a few of them. Keep in mind that since strings are immutable these all return values and have no side effect.

One of the more useful built-in methods is split, which takes two strings as arguments. The second argument specifies a separator that is used to split the first argument into a sequence of substrings. For example,

```
print('My favorite professor--John G.--rocks'.split(' '))
print('My favorite professor--John G.--rocks'.split('-'))
print('My favorite professor--John G.--rocks'.split('--'))
```

prints

```
['My', 'favorite', 'professor--John', 'G.--rocks']
['My favorite professor', '', 'John G.', '', 'rocks']
['My favorite professor', 'John G.', 'rocks']
```

The second argument is optional. If that argument is omitted the first string is split using arbitrary strings of **whitespace characters** (space, tab, newline, return, and formfeed).

CHAPTER 5. STRUCTURED TYPES, MUTABILITY, AND HIGHER-ORDER FUNCTIONS

---

s.count(s1) counts how many times the string s1 occurs in s.

s.find(s1) returns the index of the first occurrence of the substring s1 in s, and -1 if s1 is not in s.

s.rfind(s1) same as find, but starts from the end of s (the "r" in rfind stands for reverse).

s.index(s1) same as find, but raises an exception (Chapter 7) if s1 is not in s.

s.rindex(s1) same as index, but starts from the end of s.

s.lower() converts all uppercase letters in s to lowercase.

s.replace(old, new) replaces all occurrences of the string old in s with the string new.

s.rstrip() removes trailing white space from s.

s.split(d) Splits s using d as a delimiter. Returns a list of substrings of s. For example, the value of 'David Guttag plays basketball'.split(' ') is ['David', 'Guttag', 'plays', 'basketball']. If d is omitted, the substrings are separated by arbitrary strings of whitespace characters.

Figure 5.8 Some methods on strings

5.6 Dictionaries

Objects of type **dict** (short for dictionary) are like lists except that we index them using **keys**. Think of a dictionary as a set of key/value pairs. Literals of type dict are enclosed in curly braces, and each element is written as a key followed by a colon followed by a value. For example, the code,

```
monthNumbers = {'Jan':1, 'Feb':2, 'Mar':3, 'Apr':4, 'May':5,
                1:'Jan', 2:'Feb', 3:'Mar', 4:'Apr', 5:'May'}
print('The third month is ' + monthNumbers[3])
dist = monthNumbers['Apr'] - monthNumbers['Jan']
print('Apr and Jan are', dist, 'months apart')
```

will print

```
The third month is Mar
Apr and Jan are 3 months apart
```

The entries in a dict are unordered and cannot be accessed with an index. That's why monthNumbers[1] unambiguously refers to the entry with the key 1 rather than the second entry.

Like lists, dictionaries are mutable. We can add an entry by writing

```
monthNumbers['June'] = 6
```

or change an entry by writing

```
monthNumbers['May'] = 'V'
```

Dictionaries are one of the great things about Python. They greatly reduce the difficulty of writing a variety of programs. For example, in Figure 5.9 we use dictionaries to write a (pretty horrible) program to translate between languages. Since one of the lines of code was too long to fit on the page, we used a backslash, \, to indicate that the next line of text is a continuation of the previous line.

The code in the figure prints,

```
Je bois "good" rouge vin, et mange pain.
I drink of wine red.
```

Remember that dictionaries are mutable. So one must be careful about side effects. For example,

```
FtoE['bois'] = 'wood'
Print(translate('Je bois du vin rouge.', dicts, 'French to English'))
```

will print

```
I wood of wine red
```

Most programming languages do not contain a built-in type that provides a mapping from keys to values. Instead, programmers use other types to provide similar functionality. It is, for example, relatively easy to implement a dictionary by using a list in which each element is a key/value pair. One can then write a simple function that does the associative retrieval, e.g.,

```
def keySearch(L, k):
    for elem in L:
        if elem[0] == k:
            return elem[1]
    return None
```

The problem with such an implementation is that it is computationally inefficient. In the worst case, a program might have to examine each element in the list to perform a single retrieval. In contrast, the built-in implementation is quite fast. It uses a technique called hashing, described in Chapter 10, to do the lookup in time that is nearly independent of the size of the dictionary.

```
EtoF = {'bread':'pain', 'wine':'vin', 'with':'avec', 'I':'Je',
        'eat':'mange', 'drink':'bois', 'John':'Jean',
        'friends':'amis', 'and': 'et', 'of':'du','red':'rouge'}
FtoE = {'pain':'bread', 'vin':'wine', 'avec':'with', 'Je':'I',
        'mange':'eat', 'bois':'drink', 'Jean':'John',
        'amis':'friends', 'et':'and', 'du':'of', 'rouge':'red'}
dicts = {'English to French':EtoF, 'French to English':FtoE}

def translateWord(word, dictionary):
    if word in dictionary.keys():
        return dictionary[word]
    elif word != '':
        return '"' + word + '"'
    return word

def translate(phrase, dicts, direction):
    UCLetters = 'ABCDEFGHIJKLMNOPQRSTUVWXYZ'
    LCLetters = 'abcdefghijklmnopqrstuvwxyz'
    letters = UCLetters + LCLetters
    dictionary = dicts[direction]
    translation = ''
    word = ''
    for c in phrase:
        if c in letters:
            word = word + c
        else:
            translation = translation\
                        + translateWord(word, dictionary) + c
            word = ''
    return translation + ' ' + translateWord(word, dictionary)

print(translate('I drink good red wine, and eat bread.',
                dicts,'English to French'))
print(translate('Je bois du vin rouge.',
                dicts, 'French to English'))
```

Figure 5.9 Translating text (badly)

A `for` statement can be used to iterate over the entries in a dictionary. However, the value assigned to the iteration variable is a key, not a key/value pair. The order in which the keys are seen in the iteration is not defined. For example, the code

```
monthNumbers = {'Jan':1, 'Feb':2, 'Mar':3, 'Apr':4, 'May':5,
                1:'Jan', 2:'Feb', 3:'Mar', 4:'Apr', 5:'May'}
keys = []
for e in monthNumbers:
    keys.append(str(e))
print(keys)
keys.sort()
print(keys)
```

might print

```
['Jan', 'Mar', '2', '3', '4', '5', '1', 'Feb', 'May', 'Apr']
['1', '2', '3', '4', '5', 'Apr', 'Feb', 'Jan', 'Mar', 'May']
```

The method keys returns an object of type dict_keys.[37] This is an example of a **view object**. The order in which the keys appear in the view is not defined. A view object is dynamic in that if the object with which it is associated changes, the change is visible through the view object. For example,

```
birthStones = {'Jan':'Garnet', 'Feb':'Amethyst', 'Mar':'Acquamarine',
               'Apr':'Diamond', 'May':'Emerald'}
months = birthStones.keys()
print(months)
birthStones['June'] = 'Pearl'
print(months)
```

might print

```
dict_keys(['Jan', 'Feb', 'May', 'Apr', 'Mar'])
dict_keys(['Jan', 'Mar', 'June', 'Feb', 'May', 'Apr'])
```

Objects of type dict_keys can be iterated over using for, and membership can be tested using in. An object of type dict_keys can easily be converted into a list, e.g., list(months).

Not all types of of objects can be used as keys: A key must be an object of a **hashable type**. A type is hashable if it has

- A __hash__ method that maps an object of the type to an int, and for every object the value returned by __hash__ does not change during the lifetime of the object, and
- An __eq__ method that is used to compare objects for equality.

All of Python's built-in immutable types are hashable, and none of Python's built-in mutable types are hashable. It is often convenient to use tuples as keys. Imagine, for example, using a tuple of the form (flightNumber, day) to represent

---

[37] In Python 2, keys returns a list containing the keys of the dictionary.

airline flights. It would then be easy to use such tuples as keys in a dictionary implementing a mapping from flights to arrival times.

As with lists, there are many useful methods associated with dictionaries, including some for removing elements. We do not enumerate all of them here, but will use them as convenient in examples later in the book. Figure 5.10 contains some of the more useful operations on dictionaries.[38]

---

len(d) returns the number of items in d.

d.keys() returns a view of the keys in d.

d.values() returns a view of the values in d.

k in d returns True if key k is in d.

d[k] returns the item in d with key k.

d.get(k, v) returns d[k] if k is in d, and v otherwise.

d[k] = v associates the value v with the key k in d. If there is already a value associated with k, that value is replaced.

del d[k] removes the key k from d.

for k in d iterates over the keys in d.

Figure 5.10 Some common operations on dicts

---

[38] All of the methods that return a view in Python 3 return a list in Python 2.

6 TESTING AND DEBUGGING

We hate to bring this up, but Dr. Pangloss was wrong. We do not live in "the best of all possible worlds." There are some places where it rains too little, and others where it rains too much. Some places are too cold, some too hot, and some too hot in the summer and too cold in the winter. Sometimes the stock market goes down—a lot. And, annoyingly, our programs don't always function properly the first time we run them.

Books have been written about how to deal with this last problem, and there is a lot to be learned from reading these books. However, in the interest of providing you with some hints that might help you get that next problem set in on time, this chapter provides a highly condensed discussion of the topic. While all of the programming examples are in Python, the general principles are applicable to getting any complex system to work.

Testing is the process of running a program to try and ascertain whether or not it works as intended. **Debugging** is the process of trying to fix a program that you already know does not work as intended.

Testing and debugging are not processes that you should begin to think about after a program has been built. Good programmers design their programs in ways that make them easier to test and debug. The key to doing this is breaking the program up into separate components that can be implemented, tested, and debugged independently of other components. At this point in the book, we have discussed only one mechanism for modularizing programs, the function. So, for now, all of our examples will be based around functions. When we get to other mechanisms, in particular classes, we will return to some of the topics covered in this chapter.

The first step in getting a program to work is getting the language system to agree to run it—that is, eliminating syntax errors and static semantic errors that can be detected without running the program. If you haven't gotten past that point in your programming, you're not ready for this chapter. Spend a bit more time working on small programs, and then come back.

6.1 Testing

The most important thing to say about testing is that its purpose is to show that bugs exist, not to show that a program is bug-free. To quote Edsger Dijkstra, "Program testing can be used to show the presence of bugs, but never to show their absence!"[39] Or, as Albert Einstein reputedly said, "No amount of experimentation can ever prove me right; a single experiment can prove me wrong."

Why is this so? Even the simplest of programs has billions of possible inputs. Consider, for example, a program that purports to meet the specification

```
def isBigger(x, y):
    """Assumes x and y are ints
       Returns True if x is less than y and False otherwise."""
```

Running it on all pairs of integers would be, to say the least, tedious. The best we can do is to run it on pairs of integers that have a reasonable probability of producing the wrong answer if there is a bug in the program.

The key to testing is finding a collection of inputs, called a **test suite**, that has a high likelihood of revealing bugs, yet does not take too long to run. The key to doing this is partitioning the space of all possible inputs into subsets that provide equivalent information about the correctness of the program, and then constructing a test suite that contains at least one input from each partition. (Usually, constructing such a test suite is not actually possible. Think of this as an unachievable ideal.)

A **partition** of a set divides that set into a collection of subsets such that each element of the original set belongs to exactly one of the subsets. Consider, for example, isBigger(x, y). The set of possible inputs is all pairwise combinations of integers. One way to partition this set is into these seven subsets:

x positive, y positive	x negative, y negative	
x positive, y negative	x negative, y positive	
x = 0, y = 0	x = 0, y ≠ 0	x ≠ 0, y = 0

If one tested the implementation on at least one value from each of these subsets, there would be reasonable probability (but no guarantee) of exposing a bug if one exists.

For most programs, finding a good partitioning of the inputs is far easier said than done. Typically, people rely on heuristics based on exploring different paths through some combination of the code and the specifications. Heuristics based

---

[39] "Notes On Structured Programming," Technical University Eindhoven, T.H. Report 70-WSK-03, April 1970.

on exploring paths through the code fall into a class called **glass-box testing**. Heuristics based on exploring paths through the specification fall into a class called **black-box testing**.

6.1.1 Black-Box Testing

In principle, black-box tests are constructed without looking at the code to be tested. Black-box testing allows testers and implementers to be drawn from separate populations. When those of us who teach programming courses generate test cases for the problem sets we assign students, we are developing black-box test suites. Developers of commercial software often have quality assurance groups that are largely independent of development groups.

This independence reduces the likelihood of generating test suites that exhibit mistakes that are correlated with mistakes in the code. Suppose, for example, that the author of a program made the implicit, but invalid, assumption that a function would never be called with a negative number. If the same person constructed the test suite for the program, he would likely repeat the mistake, and not test the function with a negative argument.

Another positive feature of black-box testing is that it is robust with respect to implementation changes. Since the test data is generated without knowledge of the implementation, the tests need not be changed when the implementation is changed.

As we said earlier, a good way to generate black-box test data is to explore paths through a specification. Consider, the specification

```
def sqrt(x, epsilon):
    """Assumes x, epsilon floats
            x >= 0
            epsilon > 0
       Returns result such that
            x-epsilon <= result*result <= x+epsilon"""
```

There seem to be only two distinct paths through this specification: one corresponding to `x = 0` and one corresponding to `x > 0`. However, common sense tells us that while it is necessary to test these two cases, it is hardly sufficient.

Boundary conditions should also be tested. When looking at lists, this often means looking at the empty list, a list with exactly one element, and a list containing lists. When dealing with numbers, it typically means looking at very small and very large values as well as "typical" values. For `sqrt`, for example, it might make sense to try values of `x` and `epsilon` similar to those in Figure 6.1.

The first four rows are intended to represent typical cases. Notice that the values for `x` include a perfect square, a number less than one, and a number with an irrational square root. If any of these tests fail, there is a bug in the program that needs to be fixed.

X	Epsilon
0.0	0.0001
25.0	0.0001
0.5	0.0001
2.0	0.0001
2.0	1.0/2.0**64.0
1.0/2.0**64	1.0/2.0**64.0
2.0**64.0	1.0/2.0**64.0
1.0/2.0**64.0	2.0**64.0
2.0**64.0	2.0**64.0

Figure 6.1 Testing boundary conditions

The remaining rows test extremely large and small values of x and epsilon. If any of these tests fail, something needs to be fixed. Perhaps there is a bug in the code that needs to be fixed, or perhaps the specification needs to be changed so that it is easier to meet. It might, for example, be unreasonable to expect to find an approximation of a square root when epsilon is ridiculously small.

Another important boundary condition to think about is aliasing. Consider, for example, the code

```
def copy(L1, L2):
    """Assumes L1, L2 are lists
       Mutates L2 to be a copy of L1"""
    while len(L2) > 0: #remove all elements from L2
        L2.pop() #remove last element of L2
    for e in L1: #append L1's elements to initially empty L2
        L2.append(e)
```

It will work most of the time, but not when L1 and L2 refer to the same list. Any test suite that did not include a call of the form copy(L, L), would not reveal the bug.

6.1.2 Glass-box Testing

Black-box testing should never be skipped, but it is rarely sufficient. Without looking at the internal structure of the code, it is impossible to know which test cases are likely to provide new information. Consider the trivial example:

```
def isPrime(x):
    """Assumes x is a nonnegative int
       Returns True if x is prime; False otherwise"""
    if x <= 2:
        return False
    for i in range(2, x):
        if x%i == 0:
            return False
    return True
```

Looking at the code, we can see that because of the test `if x <= 2`, the values 0, 1, and 2 are treated as special cases, and therefore need to be tested. Without looking at the code, one might not test `isPrime(2)`, and would therefore not discover that the function call `isPrime(2)` returns `False`, erroneously indicating that 2 is not a prime.

Glass-box test suites are usually much easier to construct than black-box test suites. Specifications are usually incomplete and often pretty sloppy, making it a challenge to estimate how thoroughly a black-box test suite explores the space of interesting inputs. In contrast, the notion of a path through code is well defined, and it is relatively easy to evaluate how thoroughly one is exploring the space. There are, in fact, commercial tools that can be used to objectively measure the completeness of glass-box tests.

A glass-box test suite is **path-complete** if it exercises every potential path through the program. This is typically impossible to achieve, because it depends upon the number of times each loop is executed and the depth of each recursion. For example, a recursive implementation of factorial follows a different path for each possible input (because the number of levels of recursion will differ).

Furthermore, even a path-complete test suite does not guarantee that all bugs will be exposed. Consider:

```
def abs(x):
    """Assumes x is an int
       Returns x if x>=0 and -x otherwise"""
    if x < -1:
        return -x
    else:
        return x
```

The specification suggests that there are two possible cases: x either is negative or it isn't. This suggests that the set of inputs {2, -2} is sufficient to explore all paths in the specification. This test suite has the additional nice property of forcing the program through all of its paths, so it looks like a complete glass-box suite as well. The only problem is that this test suite will not expose the fact that abs(-1) will return -1.

Despite the limitations of glass-box testing, there are a few rules of thumb that are usually worth following:

- Exercise both branches of all `if` statements.
- Make sure that each except clause (see Chapter 7) is executed.
- For each `for` loop, have test cases in which
  - The loop is not entered (e.g., if the loop is iterating over the elements of a list, make sure that it is tested on the empty list),
  - The body of the loop is executed exactly once, and
  - The body of the loop is executed more than once.
- For each `while` loop,
  - Look at the same kinds of cases as when dealing with `for` loops.
  - Include test cases corresponding to all possible ways of exiting the loop. For example, for a loop starting with
    ```
    while len(L) > 0 and not L[i] == e
    ```
    find cases where the loop exits because `len(L)` is greater than zero and cases where it exits because `L[i] == e`.
- For recursive functions, include test cases that cause the function to return with no recursive calls, exactly one recursive call, and more than one recursive call.

6.1.3 Conducting Tests

Testing is often thought of as occurring in two phases. One should always start with **unit testing**. During this phase testers construct and run tests designed to ascertain whether individual units of code (e.g., functions) work properly. This is followed by **integration testing**, which is designed to ascertain whether the program as a whole behaves as intended. In practice, testers cycle through these two phases, since failures during integration testing lead to making changes to individual units.

Integration testing is almost always more challenging than unit testing. One reason for this is that the intended behavior of an entire program is often considerably harder to characterize than the intended behavior of each of its parts. For example, characterizing the intended behavior of a word processor is considerably more challenging than characterizing the behavior of a function that counts the number of characters in a document. Problems of scale can also make integration testing difficult. It is not unusual for integration tests to take hours or even days to run.

Many industrial software development organizations have a **software quality assurance (SQA)** group that is separate from the group charged with implementing the software. The mission of this group is to ensure that before the software is released it is suitable for its intended purpose. In some organizations the development group is responsible for unit testing and the QA group for integration testing.

In industry, the testing process is often highly automated. Testers[40] do not sit at terminals typing inputs and checking outputs. Instead, they use **test drivers** that autonomously

- Set up the environment needed to invoke the program (or unit) to be tested,
- Invoke the program (or unit) to be tested with a predefined or automatically generated sequence of inputs,
- Save the results of these invocations,
- Check the acceptability of the results of the tests, and
- Prepare an appropriate report.

During unit testing, we often need to build **stubs** as well as drivers. Drivers simulate parts of the program that use the unit being tested, whereas stubs simulate parts of the program used by the unit being tested. Stubs are useful because they allow people to test units that depend upon software or sometimes even hardware that does not yet exist. This allows teams of programmers to simultaneously develop and test multiple parts of a system.

Ideally, a stub should

- Check the reasonableness of the environment and arguments supplied by the caller (calling a function with inappropriate arguments is a common error),
- Modify arguments and global variables in a manner consistent with the specification, and
- Return values consistent with the specification.

Building adequate stubs is often a challenge. If the unit the stub is replacing is intended to perform some complex task, building a stub that performs actions consistent with the specification may be tantamount to writing the program that the stub is designed to replace. One way to surmount this problem is to limit the

---

[40] Or, for that matter, those who grade problem sets in very large programming courses.

set of arguments accepted by the stub, and create a table that contains the values to be returned for each combination of arguments to be used in the test suite.

One attraction of automating the testing process is that it facilitates **regression testing**. As programmers attempt to debug a program, it is all too common to install a "fix" that breaks something that used to work. Whenever any change is made, no matter how small, you should check that the program still passes all of the tests that it used to pass.

6.2 Debugging

There is a charming urban legend about how the process of fixing flaws in software came to be known as debugging. The photo in Figure 6.2 is of a September 9, 1947, page in a laboratory book from the group working on the Mark II Aiken Relay Calculator at Harvard University.

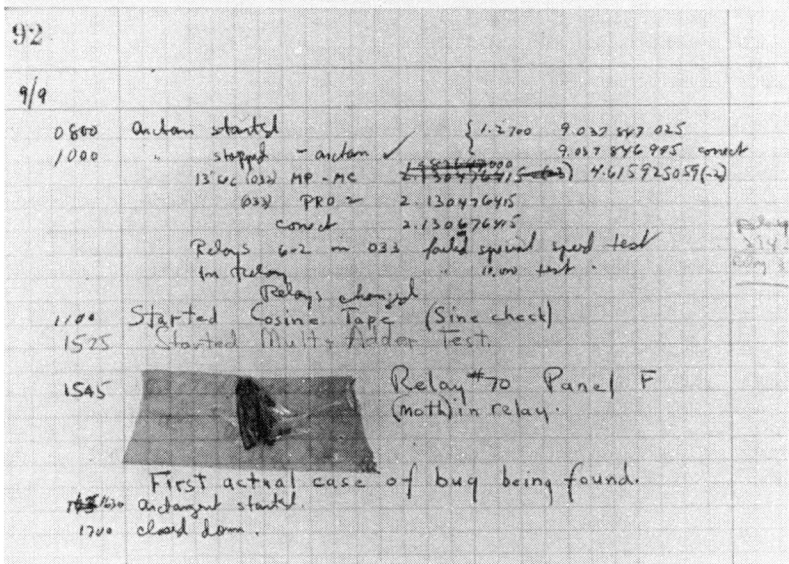

Figure 6.2 Not the first bug

Some have claimed that the discovery of that unfortunate moth trapped in the Mark II led to the use of the phrase debugging. However the wording, "First actual case of a bug being found," suggests that a less literal interpretation of the phrase was already common. Grace Murray Hopper, a leader of the Mark II pro-

CHAPTER 6. TESTING AND DEBUGGING

ject, made it clear that the term "bug" was already in wide use to describe problems with electronic systems during World War II. And well prior to that, *Hawkins' New Catechism of Electricity*, an 1896 electrical handbook, included the entry, "The term 'bug' is used to a limited extent to designate any fault or trouble in the connections or working of electric apparatus." In English usage the word "bugbear" means "anything causing seemingly needless or excessive fear or anxiety."[41] Shakespeare seems to have shortened this to "bug," when he had Hamlet kvetch about "bugs and goblins in my life."

The use of the word "bug" sometimes leads people to ignore the fundamental fact that if you wrote a program and it has a "bug," you messed up. Bugs do not crawl unbidden into flawless programs. If your program has a bug, it is because you put it there. Bugs do not breed in programs. If your program has multiple bugs, it is because you made multiple mistakes. Runtime bugs can be categorized along two dimensions:

- **Overt → covert**: An **overt bug** has an obvious manifestation, e.g., the program crashes or takes far longer (maybe forever) to run than it should. A **covert bug** has no obvious manifestation. The program may run to conclusion with no problem—other than providing an incorrect answer. Many bugs fall between the two extremes, and whether or not the bug is overt can depend upon how carefully one examines the behavior of the program.
- **Persistent → intermittent**: A **persistent bug** occurs every time the program is run with the same inputs. An **intermittent bug** occurs only some of the time, even when the program is run on the same inputs and seemingly under the same conditions. When we get to Chapter 14, we will start writing programs that model situations in which randomness plays a role. In programs of that of the kind, intermittent bugs are common.

The best kinds of bugs to have are overt and persistent. Developers can be under no illusion about the advisability of deploying the program. And if someone else is foolish enough to attempt to use it, they will quickly discover their folly. Perhaps the program will do something horrible before crashing, e.g., delete files, but at least the user will have reason to be worried (if not panicked). Good programmers try to write their programs in such a way that programming mistakes lead to bugs that are both overt and persistent. This is often called **defensive programming**.

The next step into the pit of undesirability is bugs that are overt but intermittent. An air traffic control system that computes the correct location for planes almost all of the time would be far more dangerous than one that makes obvious

---

[41] Webster's New World College Dictionary.

mistakes all the time. One can live in a fool's paradise for a period of time, and maybe get so far as deploying a system incorporating the flawed program, but sooner or later the bug will become manifest. If the conditions prompting the bug to become manifest are easily reproducible, it is often relatively easy to track down and repair the problem. If the conditions provoking the bug are not clear, life is much harder.

Programs that fail in covert ways are often highly dangerous. Since they are not apparently problematical, people use them and trust them to do the right thing. Increasingly, society relies on software to perform critical computations that are beyond the ability of humans to carry out or even check for correctness. Therefore, a program can provide undetected fallacious answer for long periods of time. Such programs can, and have, caused a lot of damage.[42] A program that evaluates the risk of a mortgage bond portfolio and confidently spits out the wrong answer can get a bank (and perhaps all of society) into a lot of trouble. A radiation therapy machine that delivers a little more or a little less radiation than intended can be the difference between life and death for a person with cancer. A program that makes a covert error only occasionally may or may not wreak less havoc than one that always commits such an error. Bugs that are both covert and intermittent are almost always the hardest to find and fix.

6.2.1 Learning to Debug

Debugging is a learned skill. Nobody does it well instinctively. The good news is that it's not hard to learn, and it is a transferable skill. The same skills used to debug software can be used to find out what is wrong with other complex systems, e.g., laboratory experiments or sick humans.

For at least four decades people have been building tools called debuggers, and there are debugging tools built into all of the popular Python IDE's. These are supposed to help people find bugs in their programs. They can help, but only a little. What's much more important is how you approach the problem. Many experienced programmers don't even bother with debugging tools. Most programmers say that the most important debugging tool is the print statement.

Debugging starts when testing has demonstrated that the program behaves in undesirable ways. Debugging is the process of searching for an explanation of

---

[42] On August 1, 2012, Knight Capital Group, Inc. deployed a new piece of stock-trading software. Within forty-five minutes a bug in that software lost the company $440,000,000. The next day, the CEO of Knight commented that the bug caused the software to enter "a ton of orders, all erroneous."

that behavior. The key to being consistently good at debugging is being systematic in conducting that search.

Start by studying the available data. This includes the test results and the program text. Study all of the test results. Examine not only the tests that revealed the presence of a problem, but also those tests that seemed to work perfectly. Trying to understand why one test worked and another did not is often illuminating. When looking at the program text, keep in mind that you don't completely understand it. If you did, there probably wouldn't be a bug.

Next, form a hypothesis that you believe to be consistent with all the data. The hypothesis could be as narrow as "if I change line 403 from x < y to x <= y, the problem will go away" or as broad as "my program is not terminating because I have the wrong exit condition in some while loop."

Next, design and run a repeatable experiment with the potential to refute the hypothesis. For example, you might put a print statement before and after each while loop. If these are always paired, then the hypothesis that a while loop is causing nontermination has been refuted. Decide before running the experiment how you would interpret various possible results. If you wait until after you run the experiment, you are more likely to fall prey to wishful thinking.

Finally, it's important to keep a record of what experiments you have tried. When you've spent many hours changing your code trying to track down an elusive bug, it's easy to forget what you have already tried. If you aren't careful, it is easy to waste way too many hours trying the same experiment (or more likely an experiment that looks different but will give you the same information) over and over again. Remember, as many have said, "insanity is doing the same thing, over and over again, but expecting different results."[43]

6.2.2 Designing the Experiment

Think of debugging as a search process, and each experiment as an attempt to reduce the size of the search space. One way to reduce the size of the search space is to design an experiment that can be used to decide whether a specific region of code is responsible for a problem uncovered during integration testing. Another way to reduce the search space is to reduce the amount of test data needed to provoke a manifestation of a bug.

Let's look at a contrived example to see how one might go about debugging it. Imagine that you wrote the palindrome-checking code in Figure 6.3.

---

[43] This line appears in Rita Mae Brown's, *Sudden Death*. However, it has been variously attributed to many other sources—including Albert Einstein.

```
def isPal(x):
    """Assumes x is a list
       Returns True if the list is a palindrome; False otherwise"""
    temp = x
    temp.reverse
    if temp == x:
        return True
    else:
        return False

def silly(n):
    """Assumes n is an int > 0
       Gets n inputs from user
       Prints 'Yes' if the sequence of inputs forms a palindrome;
          'No' otherwise"""
    for i in range(n):
        result = []
        elem = input('Enter element: ')
        result.append(elem)
    if isPal(result):
        print('Yes')
    else:
        print('No')
```

Figure 6.3 Program with bugs

Now, imagine that you are so confident of your programming skills that you put this code up on the Web—without testing it. Suppose further that you receive an email saying, "I tested your !!**! program on the following 1000-string input, and it printed Yes. Yet any fool can see that it is not a palindrome. Fix it!"

You could try and test it on the supplied 1000-string input. But it might be more sensible to begin by trying it on something smaller. In fact, it would make sense to test it on a minimal non-palindrome, e.g.,

```
>>> silly(2)
Enter element: a
Enter element: b
```

The good news is that it fails even this simple test, so you don't have to type in a thousand strings. The bad news is that you have no idea why it failed.

In this case, the code is small enough that you can probably stare at it and find the bug (or bugs). However, let's pretend that it is too large to do this, and start to systematically reduce the search space.

Often the best way to do this is to conduct a bisection search. Find some point about halfway through the code, and devise an experiment that will allow you to decide if there is a problem before that point that might be related to the symptom. (Of course, there may be problems after that point as well, but it is usually best to hunt down one problem at a time.) In choosing such a point, look for a place where there are some easily examined intermediate values that provide useful information. If an intermediate value is not what you expected, there is probably a problem that occurred prior to that point in the code. If the intermediate values all look fine, the bug probably lies somewhere later in the code. This process can be repeated until you have narrowed the region in which a problem is located to a few lines of code.

Looking at silly, the halfway point is around the line if isPal(result). The obvious thing to check is whether result has the expected value, ['a', 'b']. We check this by inserting the statement print(result) before the if statement in silly. When the experiment is run, the program prints ['b'], suggesting that something has already gone wrong. The next step is to print result roughly halfway through the loop. This quickly reveals that result is never more than one element long, suggesting that the initialization of result needs to be moved outside the for loop.

The "corrected" code for silly is

```
def silly(n):
    """Assumes n is an int > 0
       Gets n inputs from user
       Prints 'Yes' if the sequence of inputs forms a palindrome;
           'No' otherwise"""
    result = []
    for i in range(n):
        elem = input('Enter element: ')
        result.append(elem)
    print(result)
    if isPal(result):
        print('Yes')
    else:
        print('No')
```

Let's try that, and see if result has the correct value after the for loop. It does, but unfortunately the program still prints Yes. Now, we have reason to believe that a second bug lies below the print statement. So, let's look at isPal. The line of code if temp == x: is about halfway through that function. So, we insert the line

```
print(temp, x)
```

before that line. When we run the code, we see that temp has the expected value, but x does not. Moving up the code, we insert a print statement after the line of code temp = x, and discover that both temp and x have the value ['a', 'b']. A quick inspection of the code reveals that in `isPal` we wrote `temp.reverse` rather than `temp.reverse()`—the evaluation of `temp.reverse` returns the built-in reverse method for lists, but does not invoke it.[44]

We run the test again, and now it seems that both `temp` and `x` have the value `['b','a']`. We have now narrowed the bug to one line. It seems that `temp.reverse()` unexpectedly changed the value of `x`. An aliasing bug has bitten us: `temp` and `x` are names for the same list, both before and after the list gets reversed. One way to fix it is to replace the first assignment statement in `isPal` by `temp = x[:]`, which causes a copy of `x` to be made.

The corrected version of `isPal` is

```
def isPal(x):
    """Assumes x is a list
        Returns True if the list is a palindrome; False otherwise"""
    temp = x[:]
    temp.reverse()
    if temp == x:
        return True
    else:
        return False
```

6.2.3 When the Going Gets Tough

Joseph P. Kennedy, father of U.S. President John F. Kennedy, reputedly instructed his children, "When the going gets tough, the tough get going."[45] But he never debugged a piece of software. This subsection contains a few pragmatic hints about what do when the debugging gets tough.

- *Look for the usual suspects.* E.g., have you
    - Passed arguments to a function in the wrong order,
    - Misspelled a name, e.g., typed a lowercase letter when you should have typed an uppercase one,
    - Failed to reinitialize a variable,
    - Tested that two floating point values are equal (==) instead of nearly equal (remember that floating point arithmetic is not the same as the arithmetic you learned in school),
    - Tested for value equality (e.g., compared two lists by writing the expression L1 == L2) when you meant object equality (e.g., id(L1) == id(L2)),

---

[44] One might well wonder why there isn't a static checker that detected the fact that the line of code `temp.reverse` doesn't do any useful computatation, and is therefore likely to be an error.

[45] He also reputedly told JFK, "Don't buy a single vote more than necessary. I'll be damned if I'm going to pay for a landslide."

- o Forgotten that some built-in function has a side effect,
- o Forgotten the () that turns a reference to an object of type function into a function invocation,
- o Created an unintentional alias, or
- o Made any other mistake that is typical for you.
- *Stop asking yourself why the program isn't doing what you want it to. Instead, ask yourself why it is doing what it is.* That should be an easier question to answer, and will probably be a good first step in figuring out how to fix the program.
- *Keep in mind that the bug is probably not where you think it is.* If it were, you would probably have found it long ago. One practical way to go about deciding where to look is asking where the bug cannot be. As Sherlock Holmes said, "Eliminate all other factors, and the one which remains must be the truth."[46]
- *Try to explain the problem to somebody else.* We all develop blind spots. It is often the case that merely attempting to explain the problem to someone will lead you to see things you have missed. A good thing to try to explain is why the bug cannot be in certain places.
- *Don't believe everything you read.* In particular, don't believe the documentation. The code may not be doing what the comments suggest.
- *Stop debugging and start writing documentation.* This will help you approach the problem from a different perspective.
- *Walk away, and try again tomorrow.* This may mean that bug is fixed later in time than if you had stuck with it, but you will probably spend a lot less of your time looking for it. That is, it is possible to trade latency for efficiency. (Students, this is an excellent reason to start work on programming problem sets earlier rather than later!)

6.2.4 When You Have Found "The" Bug

When you think you have found a bug in your code, the temptation to start coding and testing a fix is almost irresistible. It is often better, however, to slow down a little. Remember that the goal is not to fix one bug, but to move rapidly and efficiently towards a bug-free program.

Ask yourself if this bug explains all the observed symptoms, or whether it is just the tip of the iceberg. If the latter, it may be better to think about taking care of this bug in concert with other changes. Suppose, for example, that you have discovered that the bug is the result of having accidentally mutated a list. You could circumvent the problem locally, perhaps by making a copy of the list. Al-

---

[46] Arthur Conan Doyle, "The Sign of the Four."

ternatively, you could consider using a tuple instead of a list (since tuples are immutable), perhaps eliminating similar bugs elsewhere in the code.

Before making any change, try and understand the ramification of the proposed "fix." Will it break something else? Does it introduce excessive complexity? Does it offer the opportunity to tidy up other parts of the code?

Always make sure that you can get back to where you are. There is nothing more frustrating than realizing that a long series of changes have left you farther from the goal than when you started, and having no way to get back to where you started. Disk space is usually plentiful. Use it to store old versions of your program.

Finally, if there are many unexplained errors, you might consider whether finding and fixing bugs one at a time is even the right approach. Maybe you would be better off thinking about whether there is some better way to organize your program or some simpler algorithm that will be easier to implement correctly.

7 EXCEPTIONS AND ASSERTIONS

An "exception" is usually defined as "something that does not conform to the norm," and is therefore somewhat rare. There is nothing rare about **exceptions** in Python. They are everywhere. Virtually every module in the standard Python library uses them, and Python itself will raise them in many different circumstances. You've already seen some of them.

Open a Python shell and enter

```
test = [1,2,3]
test[3]
```

and the interpreter will respond with something like

```
IndexError: list index out of range
```

IndexError is the type of exception that Python **raises** when a program tries to access an element that is outside the bounds of an indexable type. The string following IndexError provides additional information about what caused the exception to occur.

Most of the built-in exceptions of Python deal with situations in which a program has attempted to execute a statement with no appropriate semantics. (We will deal with the exceptional exceptions—those that do not deal with errors—later in this chapter.) Those readers (all of you, we hope) who have attempted to write and run Python programs will already have encountered many of these. Among the most commonly occurring types of exceptions are TypeError, IndexError, NameError, and ValueError.

7.1 Handling Exceptions

Up to now, we have treated exceptions as fatal events. When an exception is raised, the program terminates (crashes might be a more appropriate word in this case), and we go back to our code and attempt to figure out what went wrong. When an exception is raised that causes the program to terminate, we say that an **unhandled exception** has been raised.

An exception does not need to lead to program termination. Exceptions, when raised, can and should be **handled** by the program. Sometimes an exception is raised because there is a bug in the program (like accessing a variable that doesn't exist), but many times, an exception is something the programmer can and should anticipate. A program might try to open a file that does not exist. If an interactive program asks a user for input, the user might enter something inappropriate.

If you know that a line of code might raise an exception when executed, you should handle the exception. In a well-written program, unhandled exceptions should be the exception.

Consider the code

```
successFailureRatio = numSuccesses/numFailures
print('The success/failure ratio is', successFailureRatio)
print('Now here')
```

Most of the time, this code will work just fine, but it will fail if numFailures happens to be zero. The attempt to divide by zero will cause the Python runtime system to raise a ZeroDivisionError exception, and the print statements will never be reached.

It would have been better to have written something along the lines of

```
try:
    successFailureRatio = numSuccesses/numFailures
    print('The success/failure ratio is', successFailureRatio)
except ZeroDivisionError:
    print('No failures, so the success/failure ratio is undefined.')
print('Now here')
```

Upon entering the try block, the interpreter attempts to evaluate the expression numSuccesses/numFailures. If expression evaluation is successful, the program assigns the value of the expression to the variable successFailureRatio, executes the print statement at the end of the try block, and proceeds to the print statement following the try-except. If, however, a ZeroDivisionError exception is raised during the expression evaluation, control immediately jumps to the except block (skipping the assignment and the print statement in the try block), the print statement in the except block is executed, and then execution continues at the print statement following the try-except block.

Finger exercise: Implement a function that meets the specification below. Use a try-except block.

```
def sumDigits(s):
    """Assumes s is a string
       Returns the sum of the decimal digits in s
          For example, if s is 'a2b3c' it returns 5"""
```

Let's look at another example. Consider the code

```
val = int(input('Enter an integer: '))
print('The square of the number you entered is', val**2)
```

If the user obligingly types a string that can be converted to an integer, everything will be fine. But suppose the user types abc? Executing the line of code will cause the Python runtime system to raise a ValueError exception, and the print statement will never be reached.

What the programmer should have written would look something like

```
while True:
    val = input('Enter an integer: ')
    try:
        val = int(val)
        print('The square of the number you entered is', val**2)
        break #to exit the while loop
    except ValueError:
        print(val, 'is not an integer')
```

After entering the loop, the program will ask the user to enter an integer. Once the user has entered something, the program executes the try–except block. If neither of the first two statements in the try block causes a ValueError exception to be raised, the break statement is executed and the while loop is exited. However, if executing the code in the try block raises a ValueError exception, control is immediately transferred to the code in the except block. Therefore, if the user enters a string that does not represent an integer, the program will ask the user to try again. No matter what text the user enters, it will not cause an unhandled exception.

The downside of this change is that the program text has grown from two lines to eight. If there are many places where the user is asked to enter an integer, this can be problematical. Of course, this problem can be solved by introducing a function:

```
def readInt():
    while True:
        val = input('Enter an integer: ')
        try:
            return(int(val)) #convert str to int before returning
        except ValueError:
            print(val, 'is not an integer')
```

Better yet, this function can be generalized to ask for any type of input:

```
def readVal(valType, requestMsg, errorMsg):
    while True:
        val = input(requestMsg + ' ')
        try:
            return(valType(val)) #convert str to valType before returning
        except ValueError:
            print(val, errorMsg)
```

`readVal(int, 'Enter an integer:', 'is not an integer')`

The function `readVal` is **polymorphic**, i.e., it works for arguments of many different types. Such functions are easy to write in Python, since types are first-class objects. We can now ask for an integer using the code

`val = readVal(int, 'Enter an integer:', 'is not an integer')`

Exceptions may seem unfriendly (after all, if not handled, an exception will cause the program to crash), but consider the alternative. What should the type conversion `int` do, for example, when asked to convert the string `'abc'` to an object of type `int`? It could return an integer corresponding to the bits used to encode the string, but this is unlikely to have any relation to the intent of the programmer. Alternatively, it could return the special value `None`. If it did that, the programmer would need to insert code to check whether the type conversion had returned `None`. A programmer who forgot that check would run the risk of getting some strange error during program execution.

With exceptions, the programmer still needs to include code dealing with the exception. However, if the programmer forgets to include such code and the exception is raised, the program will halt immediately. This is a good thing. It alerts the user of the program to the fact that something troublesome has happened. (And, as we discussed in Chapter 6, overt bugs are much better than covert bugs.) Moreover, it gives someone debugging the program a clear indication of where things went awry.

If it is possible for a block of program code to raise more than one kind of exception, the reserved word `except` can be followed by a tuple of exceptions, e.g.,

`except (ValueError, TypeError):`

in which case the except block will be entered if any of the listed exceptions is raised within the try block.

CHAPTER 7. EXCEPTIONS AND ASSERTIONS

Alternatively, we can write a separate except block for each kind of exception, which allows the program to choose an action based upon which exception was raised. If the programmer writes

```
except:
```

the except block will be entered if any kind of exception is raised within the try block. These features are shown in Figure 7.1.

7.2 Exceptions as a Control Flow Mechanism

Don't think of exceptions as purely for errors. They are a convenient flow-of-control mechanism that can be used to simplify programs.

In many programming languages, the standard approach to dealing with errors is to have functions return a value (often something analogous to Python's None) indicating that something has gone amiss. Each function invocation has to check whether that value has been returned. In Python, it is more usual to have a function raise an exception when it cannot produce a result that is consistent with the function's specification.

The Python **raise** statement forces a specified exception to occur. The form of a raise statement is

```
raise exceptionName(arguments)
```

The *exceptionName* is usually one of the built-in exceptions, e.g., ValueError. However, programmers can define new exceptions by creating a subclass (see Chapter 8) of the built-in class Exception. Different types of exceptions can have different types of arguments, but most of the time the argument is a single string, which is used to describe the reason the exception is being raised.

Finger Exercise: Implement a function that satisfies the specification

```
def findAnEven(L):
    """Assumes L is a list of integers
       Returns the first even number in L
       Raises ValueError if L does not contain an even number"""
```

Consider the function definition in Figure 7.1.

```
def getRatios(vect1, vect2):
    """Assumes: vect1 and vect2 are equal length lists of numbers
       Returns: a list containing the meaningful values of
            vect1[i]/vect2[i]"""
    ratios = []
    for index in range(len(vect1)):
        try:
            ratios.append(vect1[index]/vect2[index])
        except ZeroDivisionError:
            ratios.append(float('nan')) #nan = Not a Number
        except:
            raise ValueError('getRatios called with bad arguments')
    return ratios
```

Figure 7.1 Using exceptions for control flow

There are two except blocks associated with the try block. If an exception is raised within the try block, Python first checks to see if it is a ZeroDivisionError. If so, it appends a special value, nan, of type float to ratios. (The value nan stands for "not a number." There is no literal for it, but it can be denoted by converting the string 'nan' or the string 'NaN' to type float. When nan is used as an operand in an expression of type float, the value of that expression is also nan.) If the exception is anything other than a ZeroDivisionError, the code executes the second except block, which raises a ValueError exception with an associated string.

In principle, the second except block should never be entered, because the code invoking getRatios should respect the assumptions in the specification of getRatios. However, since checking these assumptions imposes only an insignificant computational burden, it is probably worth practicing defensive programming and checking anyway.

The following code illustrates how a program might use getRatios. The name msg in the line except ValueError as msg: is bound to the argument (a string in this case) associated with ValueError when it was raised.[47] When the code

```
try:
    print(getRatios([1.0,2.0,7.0,6.0], [1.0,2.0,0.0,3.0]))
    print(getRatios([], []))
    print(getRatios([1.0, 2.0], [3.0]))
except ValueError as msg:
    print(msg)
```

---

[47] In Python 2 one writes except ValueError, msg rather than except ValueError as msg.

is executed it prints

```
[1.0, 1.0, nan, 2.0]
[]
getRatios called with bad arguments
```

For comparison, Figure 7.2 contains an implementation of the same specification, but without using a try-except.

```
def getRatios(vect1, vect2):
    """Assumes: vect1 and vect2 are lists of equal length of numbers
       Returns: a list containing the meaningful values of
              vect1[i]/vect2[i]"""
    ratios = []
    if len(vect1) != len(vect2):
        raise ValueError('getRatios called with bad arguments')
    for index in range(len(vect1)):
        vect1Elem = vect1[index]
        vect2Elem = vect2[index]
        if (type(vect1Elem) not in (int, float))\
           or (type(vect2Elem) not in (int, float)):
            raise ValueError('getRatios called with bad arguments')
        if vect2Elem == 0.0:
            ratios.append(float('NaN')) #NaN = Not a Number
        else:
            ratios.append(vect1Elem/vect2Elem)
    return ratios
```

Figure 7.2 Control flow without a try-except

The code in Figure 7.2 is longer and more difficult to read than the code in Figure 7.1. It is also less efficient. (The code in Figure 7.2 could be slightly shortened by eliminating the local variables vect1Elem and vect2Elem, but only at the cost of introducing yet more inefficiency by indexing into the lists repeatedly.)

Let us look at one more example, Figure 7.3. The function getGrades either returns a value or raises an exception with which it has associated a value. It raises a ValueError exception if the call to open raises an IOError. It could have ignored the IOError and let the part of the program calling getGrades deal with it, but that would have provided less information to the calling code about what went wrong. The code that uses getGrades either uses the returned value to compute another value or handles the exception and prints an informative error message.

```
def getGrades(fname):
    try:
        gradesFile = open(fname, 'r') #open file for reading
    except IOError:
        raise ValueError('getGrades could not open ' + fname)
    grades = []
    for line in gradesFile:
        try:
            grades.append(float(line))
        except:
            raise ValueError('Unable to convert line to float')
    return grades

try:
    grades = getGrades('quiz1grades.txt')
    grades.sort()
    median = grades[len(grades)//2]
    print('Median grade is', median)
except ValueError as errorMsg:
    print('Whoops.', errorMsg)
```

Figure 7.3 Get grades

7.3 Assertions

The Python assert statement provides programmers with a simple way to confirm that the state of a computation is as expected. An assert statement can take one of two forms:

assert *Boolean expression*

or

assert *Boolean expression, argument*

When an assert statement is encountered, the Boolean expression is evaluated. If it evaluates to True, execution proceeds on its merry way. If it evaluates to False, an AssertionError exception is raised.

Assertions are a useful defensive programming tool. They can be used to confirm that the arguments to a function are of appropriate types. They are also a useful debugging tool. The can be used, for example, to confirm that intermediate values have the expected values or that a function returns an acceptable value.

8 CLASSES AND OBJECT-ORIENTED PROGRAMMING

We now turn our attention to our last major topic related to programming in Python: using classes to organize programs around modules and data abstractions.

Classes can be used in many different ways. In this book we emphasize using them in the context of **object-oriented programming**. The key to object-oriented programming is thinking about objects as collections of both data and the methods that operate on that data.

The ideas underlying object-oriented programming are more than forty years old, and have been widely accepted and practiced over the last twenty-five years or so. In the mid-1970s people began to write articles explaining the benefits of this approach to programming. About the same time, the programming languages SmallTalk (at Xerox PARC) and CLU (at MIT) provided linguistic support for the ideas. But it wasn't until the arrival of C++ and Java that it really took off in practice.

We have been implicitly relying on object-oriented programming throughout most of this book. Back in Section 2.1.1 we said "Objects are the core things that Python programs manipulate. Every object has a **type** that defines the kinds of things that programs can do with that object." Since Chapter 2, we have relied upon built-in types such as list and dict and the methods associated with those types. But just as the designers of a programming language can build in only a small fraction of the useful functions, they can build in only a small fraction of the useful types. We have already looked at a mechanism that allows programmers to define new functions; we now look at a mechanism that allows programmers to define new types.

8.1 Abstract Data Types and Classes

The notion of an abstract data type is quite simple. An **abstract data type** is a set of objects and the operations on those objects. These are bound together so that one can pass an object from one part of a program to another, and in doing so provide access not only to the data attributes of the object but also to operations that make it easy to manipulate that data.

The specifications of those operations define an **interface** between the abstract data type and the rest of the program. The interface defines the behavior of the operations—what they do, but not how they do it. The interface thus provides an **abstraction barrier** that isolates the rest of the program from the data structures, algorithms, and code involved in providing a realization of the type abstraction.

Programming is about managing complexity in a way that facilitates change. There are two powerful mechanisms available for accomplishing this: decomposition and abstraction. Decomposition creates structure in a program, and abstraction suppresses detail. The key is to suppress the appropriate details. This is where data abstraction hits the mark. One can create domain-specific types that provide a convenient abstraction. Ideally, these types capture concepts that will be relevant over the lifetime of a program. If one starts the programming process by devising types that will be relevant months and even decades later, one has a great leg up in maintaining that software.

We have been using abstract data types (without calling them that) throughout this book. We have written programs using integers, lists, floats, strings, and dictionaries without giving any thought to how these types might be implemented. To paraphrase Molière's *Bourgeois Gentilhomme*, *"Par ma foi, il y a plus de cent pages que nous avons utilisé ADTs, sans que nous le sachions."*[48]

In Python, one implements data abstractions using **classes**. Figure 8.1 contains a **class definition** that provides a straightforward implementation of a set-of-integers abstraction called `IntSet`.

A class definition creates an object of type `type` and associates with that class object a set of objects of type `instancemethod`. For example, the expression `IntSet.insert` refers to the method `insert` defined in the definition of the class `IntSet`. And the code

```
print(type(IntSet), type(IntSet.insert))
```

will print

```
<class 'type'> <class 'function'>
```

Notice that the docstring (the comment enclosed in """) at the top of the class definition describes the abstraction provided by the class, not information about how the class is implemented. In contrast, the comments below the docstring contain information about the implementation. That information is aimed at programmers who might want to modify the implementation or build sub-

---

[48] "Good heavens, for more than one hundred pages we have been using ADTs without knowing it."

classes (see Section 8.2) of the class, not at programmers who might want to use the abstraction.

```python
class IntSet(object):
    """An intSet is a set of integers"""
    #Information about the implementation (not the abstraction)
    #Value of the set is represented by a list of ints, self.vals.
    #Each int in the set occurs in self.vals exactly once.

    def __init__(self):
        """Create an empty set of integers"""
        self.vals = []

    def insert(self, e):
        """Assumes e is an integer and inserts e into self"""
        if e not in self.vals:
            self.vals.append(e)

    def member(self, e):
        """Assumes e is an integer
           Returns True if e is in self, and False otherwise"""
        return e in self.vals

    def remove(self, e):
        """Assumes e is an integer and removes e from self
           Raises ValueError if e is not in self"""
        try:
            self.vals.remove(e)
        except:
            raise ValueError(str(e) + ' not found')

    def getMembers(self):
        """Returns a list containing the elements of self.
           Nothing can be assumed about the order of the elements"""
        return self.vals[:]

    def __str__(self):
        """Returns a string representation of self"""
        self.vals.sort()
        result = ''
        for e in self.vals:
            result = result + str(e) + ','
        return '{' + result[:-1] + '}' #-1 omits trailing comma
```

Figure 8.1 Class IntSet

When a function definition occurs within a class definition, the defined function is called a **method** and is associated with the class. These methods are sometimes referred to as **method attributes** of the class. If this seems confusing at the moment, don't worry about it. We will have lots more to say about this topic later in this chapter.

Classes support two kinds of operations:

- **Instantiation** is used to create instances of the class. For example, the statement s = IntSet() creates a new object of type IntSet. This object is called an **instance** of IntSet.
- **Attribute references** use dot notation to access attributes associated with the class. For example, s.member refers to the method member associated with the instance s of type IntSet.

Each class definition begins with the reserved word class followed by the name of the class and some information about how it relates to other classes. In this case, the first line indicates that IntSet is a subclass of object. For now, ignore what it means to be a subclass. We will get to that shortly.

As we will see, Python has a number of special method names that start and end with two underscores. The first of these we will look at is __init__. Whenever a class is instantiated, a call is made to the __init__ method defined in that class. When the line of code

```
s = IntSet()
```

is executed, the interpreter will create a new instance of type IntSet, and then call IntSet.__init__ with the newly created object as the actual parameter that is bound to the formal parameter self. When invoked, IntSet.__init__ creates vals, an object of type list, which becomes part of the newly created instance of type IntSet. (The list is created using the by now familiar notation [], which is simply an abbreviation for list().) This list is called a **data attribute** of the instance of IntSet. Notice that each object of type IntSet will have a different vals list, as one would expect.

As we have seen, methods associated with an instance of a class can be invoked using dot notation. For example, the code,

```
s = IntSet()
s.insert(3)
print(s.member(3))
```

creates a new instance of IntSet, inserts the integer 3 into that IntSet, and then prints True.

At first blush there appears to be something inconsistent here. It looks as if each method is being called with one argument too few. For example, `member` has two formal parameters, but we appear to be calling it with only one actual parameter. This is an artifact of the dot notation. The object associated with the expression preceding the dot is implicitly passed as the first parameter to the method. Throughout this book, we follow the convention of using `self` as the name of the formal parameter to which this actual parameter is bound. Python programmers observe this convention almost universally, and we strongly suggest that you use it as well.

A class should not be confused with instances of that class, just as an object of type `list` should not be confused with the `list` type. Attributes can be associated either with a class itself or with instances of a class:

- Method attributes are defined in a class definition, for example `IntSet.member` is an attribute of the class `IntSet`. When the class is instantiated, e.g., by the statement `s = IntSet()`, instance attributes, e.g., `s.member`, are created. Keep in mind that `IntSet.member` and `s.member` are different objects. While `s.member` is initially bound to the `member` method defined in the class `IntSet`, that binding can be changed during the course of a computation. For example, you could (but shouldn't!) write `s.member = IntSet.insert`.
- When data attributes are associated with a class we call them **class variables**. When they are associated with an instance we call them **instance variables**. For example, `vals` is an instance variable because for each instance of class `IntSet`, `vals` is bound to a different list. So far, we haven't seen a class variable. We will use one in Figure 8.3.

Data abstraction achieves representation-independence. Think of the implementation of an abstract type as having several components:

- Implementations of the methods of the type,
- Data structures that together encode values of the type, and
- Conventions about how the implementations of the methods are to use the data structures. A key convention is captured by the representation invariant.

The **representation invariant** defines which values of the data attributes correspond to valid representations of class instances. The representation invariant for `IntSet` is that `vals` contains no duplicates. The implementation of `__init__` is responsible for establishing the invariant (which holds on the empty list), and the other methods are responsible for maintaining that invariant. That is why `insert` appends e only if it is not already in `self.vals`.

The implementation of `remove` exploits the assumption that the representation invariant is satisfied when `remove` is entered. It calls `list.remove` only once, since the representation invariant guarantees that there is at most one occurrence of e in self.vals.

The last method defined in the class, __str__, is another one of those special __ methods. When the print command is used, the __str__ function associated with the object to be printed is automatically invoked. For example, the code

```
s = IntSet()
s.insert(3)
s.insert(4)
print(s)
```

will print

```
{3,4}
```

(If no __str__ method were defined, executing print(s) would cause something like <__main__.IntSet object at 0x1663510> to be printed.) We could also print the value of s by writing print s.__str__() or even print IntSet.__str__(s), but using those forms is less convenient. The __str__ method of a class is also invoked when a program converts an instance of that class to a string by calling str.

All instances of user-defined classes are hashable, and therefore can be used as dictionary keys. If no __hash__ method is provided, the hash value of the object is derived from the function id (see Section 5.3). If no __eq__ method is provided, all objects are considered unequal (except to themselves). If a user-defined __hash__ is provided, it should ensure that the hash value of an object is constant throughout the lifetime of that object.

8.1.1 Designing Programs Using Abstract Data Types

Abstract data types are a big deal. They lead to a different way of thinking about organizing large programs. When we think about the world, we rely on abstractions. In the world of finance people talk about stocks and bonds. In the world of biology people talk about proteins and residues. When trying to understand concepts such as these, we mentally gather together some of the relevant data and features of these kinds of objects into one intellectual package. For example, we think of bonds as having an interest rate and a maturity date as data attributes. We also think of bonds as having operations such as "set price" and "calculate yield to maturity." Abstract data types allow us to incorporate this kind of organization into the design of programs.

Data abstraction encourages program designers to focus on the centrality of data objects rather than functions. Thinking about a program more as a collection of types than as a collection of functions leads to a profoundly different organizing principle. Among other things, it encourages one to think about programming as a process of combining relatively large chunks, since data abstractions typically encompass more functionality than do individual functions. This, in turn, leads us to think of the essence of programming as a process not of writing individual lines of code, but of composing abstractions.

The availability of reusable abstractions not only reduces development time, but also usually leads to more reliable programs, because mature software is usually more reliable than new software. For many years, the only program libraries in common use were statistical or scientific. Today, however, there is a great range of available program libraries (especially for Python), often based on a rich set of data abstractions, as we shall see later in this book.

8.1.2 Using Classes to Keep Track of Students and Faculty

As an example use of classes, imagine that you are designing a program to help keep track of all the students and faculty at a university. It is certainly possible to write such a program without using data abstraction. Each student would have a family name, a given name, a home address, a year, some grades, etc. This could all be kept in some combination of lists and dictionaries. Keeping track of faculty and staff would require some similar data structures and some different data structures, e.g., data structures to keep track of things like salary history.

Before rushing in to design a bunch of data structures, let's think about some abstractions that might prove useful. Is there an abstraction that covers the common attributes of students, professors, and staff? Some would argue that they are all human. Figure 8.2 contains a class that incorporates some of the common attributes (name and birthday) of humans. It makes use of the standard Python library module datetime, which provides many convenient methods for creating and manipulating dates.

```
import datetime

class Person(object):

    def __init__(self, name):
        """Create a person"""
        self.name = name
        try:
            lastBlank = name.rindex(' ')
            self.lastName = name[lastBlank+1:]
        except:
            self.lastName = name
        self.birthday = None

    def getName(self):
        """Returns self's full name"""
        return self.name

    def getLastName(self):
        """Returns self's last name"""
        return self.lastName

    def setBirthday(self, birthdate):
        """Assumes birthdate is of type datetime.date
           Sets self's birthday to birthdate"""
        self.birthday = birthdate

    def getAge(self):
        """Returns self's current age in days"""
        if self.birthday == None:
            raise ValueError
        return (datetime.date.today() - self.birthday).days

    def __lt__(self, other):
        """Returns True if self precedes other in alphabetical
           order, and False otherwise. Comparison is based on last
           names, but if these are the same full names are
           compared."""
        if self.lastName == other.lastName:
            return self.name < other.name
        return self.lastName < other.lastName

    def __str__(self):
        """Returns self's name"""
        return self.name
```

Figure 8.2 Class Person

The following code makes use of Person.

```
me = Person('Michael Guttag')
him = Person('Barack Hussein Obama')
her = Person('Madonna')
print(him.getLastName())
him.setBirthday(datetime.date(1961, 8, 4))
her.setBirthday(datetime.date(1958, 8, 16))
print(him.getName(), 'is', him.getAge(), 'days old')
```

Notice that whenever `Person` is instantiated an argument is supplied to the `__init__` function. In general, when instantiating a class we need to look at the specification of the `__init__` function for that class to know what arguments to supply and what properties those arguments should have.

After the above code is executed, there will be three instances of class `Person`. One can then access information about these instances using the methods associated with them. For example, `him.getLastName()` will return `'Obama'`. The expression `him.lastName` will also return `'Obama'`; however, for reasons discussed later in this chapter, writing expressions that directly access instance variables is considered poor form, and should be avoided. Similarly, there is no appropriate way for a user of the `Person` abstraction to extract a person's birthday, despite the fact that the implementation contains an attribute with that value. (Of course, it would be easy to add a `getBirthday` method to the class.) There is, however, a way to extract information that depends upon the person's birthday, as illustrated by the last `print` statement in the above code.

Class `Person` defines yet another specially named method, `__lt__`. This method overloads the < operator. The method `Person__lt__` gets called whenever the first argument to the < operator is of type `Person`. The `__lt__` method in class `Person` is implemented using the binary < operator of type `str`. The expression `self.name < other.name` is shorthand for `self.name.__lt__(other.name)`. Since `self.name` is of type `str`, this `__lt__` method is the one associated with type `str`.

In addition to providing the syntactic convenience of writing infix expressions that use <, this overloading provides automatic access to any polymorphic method defined using `__lt__`. The built-in method `sort` is one such method. So, for example, if `pList` is a list composed of elements of type `Person`, the call `pList.sort()` will sort that list using the `__lt__` method defined in class `Person`.

The code

```
pList = [me, him, her]
for p in pList:
    print(p)
pList.sort()
for p in pList:
    print(p)
```

will first print

```
Michael Guttag
Barack Hussein Obama
Madonna
```

and then print

```
Michael Guttag
Madonna
Barack Hussein Obama
```

8.2 Inheritance

Many types have properties in common with other types. For example, types list and str each have len functions that mean the same thing. **Inheritance** provides a convenient mechanism for building groups of related abstractions. It allows programmers to create a type hierarchy in which each type inherits attributes from the types above it in the hierarchy.

The class object is at the top of the hierarchy. This makes sense, since in Python everything that exists at run time is an object. Because Person inherits all of the properties of objects, programs can bind a variable to a Person, append a Person to a list, etc.

The class MITPerson in Figure 8.3 inherits attributes from its parent class, Person, including all of the attributes that Person inherited from its parent class, object. In the jargon of object-oriented programming, MITPerson is a **subclass** of Person, and therefore **inherits** the attributes of its **superclass**. In addition to what it inherits, the subclass can:

- Add new attributes. For example, the subclass MITPerson has added the class variable nextIdNum, the instance variable idNum, and the method getIdNum.
- **Override**, i.e., replace, attributes of the superclass. For example, MITPerson has overridden __init__ and __lt__. When a method has been overridden, the version of the method that is executed is based on the object that is used to invoke the method. If the type of the object is the subclass, the version defined in

the subclass will be used. If the type of the object is the superclass, the version in the superclass will be used.

The method `MITPerson.__init__` first invokes `Person.__init__` to initialize the inherited instance variable `self.name`. It then initializes `self.idNum`, an instance variable that instances of `MITPerson` have but instances of `Person` do not.

The instance variable `self.idNum` is initialized using a **class variable**, `nextIdNum`, that belongs to the class `MITPerson`, rather than to instances of the class. When an instance of `MITPerson` is created, a new instance of `nextIdNum` is not created. This allows `__init__` to ensure that each instance of `MITPerson` has a unique `idNum`.

```
class MITPerson(Person):

    nextIdNum = 0 #identification number

    def __init__(self, name):
        Person.__init__(self, name)
        self.idNum = MITPerson.nextIdNum
        MITPerson.nextIdNum += 1

    def getIdNum(self):
        return self.idNum

    def __lt__(self, other):
        return self.idNum < other.idNum
```

Figure 8.3 Class `MITPerson`

Consider the code

```
p1 = MITPerson('Barbara Beaver')
print(str(p1) + '\'s id number is ' + str(p1.getIdNum()))
```

The first line creates a new `MITPerson`. The second line is a bit more complicated. When it attempts to evaluate the expression `str(p1)`, the runtime system first checks to see if there is an `__str__` method associated with class `MITPerson`. Since there is not, it next checks to see if there is an `__str__` method associated with the superclass, `Person`, of `MITPerson`. There is, so it uses that. When the runtime system attempts to evaluate the expression `p1.getidNum()`, it first checks to see if there is a `getIdNum` method associated with class `MITPerson`. There is, so it invokes that method and prints

```
Barbara Beaver's id number is 0
```

(Recall that in a string, the character "\" is an escape character used to indicate that the next character should be treated in a special way. In the string

```
'\'s id number is '
```

the "\" indicates that the apostrophe is part of the string, not a delimiter terminating the string.)

Now consider the code

```
p1 = MITPerson('Mark Guttag')
p2 = MITPerson('Billy Bob Beaver')
p3 = MITPerson('Billy Bob Beaver')
p4 = Person('Billy Bob Beaver')
```

We have created four virtual people, three of whom are named Billy Bob Beaver. Two of the Billy Bobs are of type MITPerson, and one merely a Person. If we execute the lines of code

```
print('p1 < p2 =', p1 < p2)
print('p3 < p2 =', p3 < p2)
print('p4 < p1 =', p4 < p1)
```

the interpreter will print

```
p1 < p2 = True
p3 < p2 = False
p4 < p1 = True
```

Since p1, p2, and p3 are all of type MITPerson, the interpreter will use the __lt__ method defined in class MITPerson when evaluating the first two comparisons, so the ordering will be based on identification numbers. In the third comparison, the < operator is applied to operands of different types. Since the first argument of the expression is used to determine which __lt__ method to invoke, p4 < p1 is shorthand for p4.__lt__(p1). Therefore, the interpreter uses the __lt__ method associated with the type of p4, Person, and the "people" will be ordered by name.

What happens if we try

```
Print('p1 < p4 =', p1 < p4)
```

The runtime system will invoke the __lt__ operator associated with the type of p1, i.e., the one defined in class MITPerson. This will lead to the exception

```
AttributeError: 'Person' object has no attribute 'idNum'
```

because the object to which p4 is bound does not have an attribute idNum.

CHAPTER 8. CLASSES AND OBJECT-ORIENTED PROGRAMMING

8.2.1 Multiple Levels of Inheritance

Figure 8.4 adds another couple of levels of inheritance to the class hierarchy.

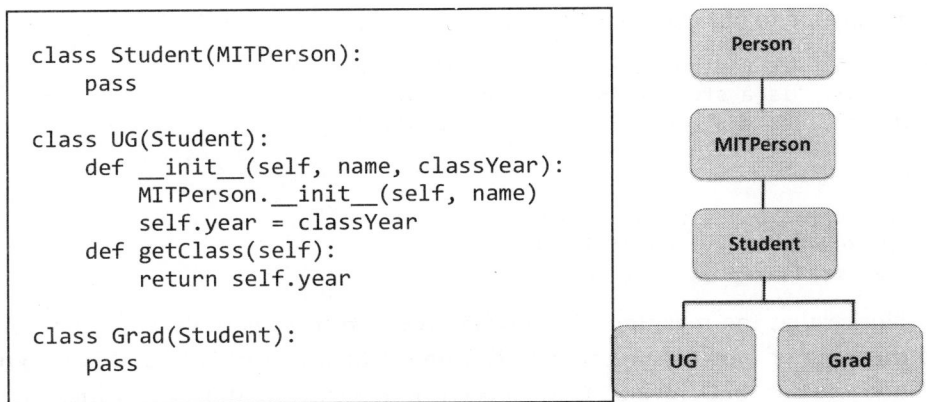

```
class Student(MITPerson):
    pass

class UG(Student):
    def __init__(self, name, classYear):
        MITPerson.__init__(self, name)
        self.year = classYear
    def getClass(self):
        return self.year

class Grad(Student):
    pass
```

Figure 8.4 Two kinds of students

Adding UG seems logical, because we want to associate a year of graduation (or perhaps anticipated graduation) with each undergraduate. But what is going on with the classes Student and Grad? By using the Python reserved word **pass** as the body, we indicate that the class has no attributes other than those inherited from its superclass. Why would one ever want to create a class with no new attributes?

By introducing the class Grad, we gain the ability to create two different kinds of students and use their types to distinguish one kind of object from another. For example, the code

```
p5 = Grad('Buzz Aldrin')
p6 = UG('Billy Beaver', 1984)
print(p5, 'is a graduate student is', type(p5) == Grad)
print(p5, 'is an undergraduate student is', type(p5) == UG)
```

will print

```
Buzz Aldrin is a graduate student is True
Buzz Aldrin is an undergraduate student is False
```

The utility of the intermediate type Student is a bit subtler. Consider going back to class MITPerson and adding the method

```
def isStudent(self):
    return isinstance(self, Student)
```

The function isinstance is built into Python. The first argument of isinstance can be any object, but the second argument must be an object of type type. The function returns True if and only if the first argument is an instance of the second argument. For example, the value of isinstance([1,2], list) is True.

Returning to our example, the code

```
print(p5, 'is a student is', p5.isStudent())
print(p6, 'is a student is', p6.isStudent())
print(p3, 'is a student is', p3.isStudent())
```

prints

```
Buzz Aldrin is a student is True
Billy Beaver is a student is True
Billy Bob Beaver is a student is False
```

Notice that the meaning of isinstance(p6, Student) is quite different from the meaning of type(p6) == Student. The object to which p6 is bound is of type UG, not student, but since UG is a subclass of Student, the object to which p6 is bound is considered to be an instance of class Student (as well as an instance of MITPerson and Person).

Since there are only two kinds of students, we could have implemented isStudent as,

```
def isStudent(self):
    return type(self) == Grad or type(self) == UG
```

However, if a new type of student were introduced at some later point it would be necessary to go back and edit the code implementing isStudent. By introducing the intermediate class Student and using isinstance we avoid this problem. For example, if we were to add

```
class TransferStudent(Student):

    def __init__(self, name, fromSchool):
        MITPerson.__init__(self, name)
        self.fromSchool = fromSchool

    def getOldSchool(self):
        return self.fromSchool
```

no change needs to be made to isStudent.

It is not unusual during the creation and later maintenance of a program to go back and add new classes or new attributes to old classes. Good programmers design their programs so as to minimize the amount of code that might need to be changed when that is done.

8.2.2 The Substitution Principle

When subclassing is used to define a type hierarchy, the subclasses should be thought of as extending the behavior of their superclasses. We do this by adding new attributes or overriding attributes inherited from a superclass. For example, TransferStudent extends Student by introducing a former school.

Sometimes, the subclass overrides methods from the superclass, but this must be done with care. In particular, important behaviors of the supertype must be supported by each of its subtypes. If client code works correctly using an instance of the supertype, it should also work correctly when an instance of the subtype is substituted for the instance of the supertype. For example, it should be possible to write client code using the specification of Student and have it work correctly on a TransferStudent.[49]

Conversely, there is no reason to expect that code written to work for TransferStudent should work for arbitrary types of Student.

8.3 Encapsulation and Information Hiding

As long as we are dealing with students, it would be a shame not to make them suffer through taking classes and getting grades.

Figure 8.5 contains a class that can be used to keep track of the grades of a collection of students. Instances of class Grades are implemented using a list and a dictionary. The list keeps track of the students in the class. The dictionary maps a student's identification number to a list of grades.

Notice that getGrades returns a copy of the list of grades associated with a student, and getStudents returns a copy of the list of students. The computational cost of copying the lists could have been avoided by simply returning the instance variables themselves. Doing so, however, is likely to lead to problems. Consider the code

```
allStudents = course1.getStudents()
allStudents.extend(course2.getStudents())
```

If getStudents returned self.students, the second line of code would have the (probably unexpected) side effect of changing the set of students in course1.

---

[49] This **substitution principle** was clearly enunciated by Barbara Liskov and Jeannette Wing in their 1994 paper, "A behavioral notion of subtyping."

The instance variable `isSorted` is used to keep track of whether or not the list of students has been sorted since the last time a student was added to it. This allows the implementation of `getStudents` to avoid sorting an already sorted list.

```python
class Grades(object):

    def __init__(self):
        """Create empty grade book"""
        self.students = []
        self.grades = {}
        self.isSorted = True

    def addStudent(self, student):
        """Assumes: student is of type Student
           Add student to the grade book"""
        if student in self.students:
            raise ValueError('Duplicate student')
        self.students.append(student)
        self.grades[student.getIdNum()] = []
        self.isSorted = False

    def addGrade(self, student, grade):
        """Assumes: grade is a float
           Add grade to the list of grades for student"""
        try:
            self.grades[student.getIdNum()].append(grade)
        except:
            raise ValueError('Student not in mapping')

    def getGrades(self, student):
        """Return a list of grades for student"""
        try: #return copy of list of student's grades
            return self.grades[student.getIdNum()][:]
        except:
            raise ValueError('Student not in mapping')

    def getStudents(self):
        """Return a sorted list of the students in the grade book"""
        if not self.isSorted:
            self.students.sort()
            self.isSorted = True
        return self.students[:] #return copy of list of students
```

Figure 8.5 Class Grades

Figure 8.6 contains a function that uses class Grades to produce a grade report for some students taking a course named sixHundred.

```
def gradeReport(course):
    """Assumes course is of type Grades"""
    report = ''
    for s in course.getStudents():
        tot = 0.0
        numGrades = 0
        for g in course.getGrades(s):
            tot += g
            numGrades += 1
        try:
            average = tot/numGrades
            report = report + '\n'\
                  + str(s) + '\'s mean grade is ' + str(average)
        except ZeroDivisionError:
            report = report + '\n'\
                  + str(s) + ' has no grades'
    return report

ug1 = UG('Jane Doe', 2014)
ug2 = UG('John Doe', 2015)
ug3 = UG('David Henry', 2003)
g1 = Grad('Billy Buckner')
g2 = Grad('Bucky F. Dent')
sixHundred = Grades()
sixHundred.addStudent(ug1)
sixHundred.addStudent(ug2)
sixHundred.addStudent(g1)
sixHundred.addStudent(g2)
for s in sixHundred.getStudents():
    sixHundred.addGrade(s, 75)
sixHundred.addGrade(g1, 25)
sixHundred.addGrade(g2, 100)
sixHundred.addStudent(ug3)
print(gradeReport(sixHundred))
```

Figure 8.6 Generating a grade report

When run, the code in the figure prints

```
Jane Doe's mean grade is 75.0
John Doe's mean grade is 75.0
David Henry has no grades
Billy Buckner's mean grade is 50.0
Bucky F. Dent's mean grade is 87.5
```

There are two important concepts at the heart of object-oriented programming. The first is the idea of **encapsulation**. By this we mean the bundling together of data attributes and the methods for operating on them. For example, if we write

```
Rafael = MITPerson('Rafael Reif')
```

we can use dot notation to access attributes such as Rafael's name and identification number.

The second important concept is **information hiding**. This is one of the keys to modularity. If those parts of the program that use a class (i.e., the clients of the class) rely only on the specifications of the methods in the class, a programmer implementing the class is free to change the implementation of the class (e.g., to improve efficiency) without worrying that the change will break code that uses the class.

Some programming languages (Java and C++, for example) provide mechanisms for enforcing information hiding. Programmers can make the attributes of a class **private**, so that clients of the class can access the data only through the object's methods. Python 3 uses a naming convention to make attributes invisible outside the class. When the name of an attribute starts with __ but does not end with __, that attribute is not visible outside the class. Consider the class in Figure 8.7.

```
class infoHiding(object):
    def __init__(self):
        self.visible = 'Look at me'
        self.__alsoVisible__ = 'Look at me too'
        self.__invisible = 'Don\'t look at me directly'

    def printVisible(self):
        print(self.visible)

    def printInvisible(self):
        print(self.__invisible)

    def __printInvisible(self):
        print(self.__invisible)

    def __printInvisible__(self):
        print(self.__invisible)
```

Figure 8.7 Information Hiding in Classes

CHAPTER 8. CLASSES AND OBJECT-ORIENTED PROGRAMMING 127

When we run the code

```
test = infoHiding()
print(test.visible)
print(test.__alsoVisible__)
print(test.__invisible)
```

it prints

```
Look at me
Look at me too
Error: 'infoHiding' object has no attribute '__invisible'
```

The code

```
test = infoHiding()
test.printInvisible()
test.__printInvisible__()
test.__printInvisible()
```

prints

```
Don't look at me directly
Don't look at me directly
Error: 'infoHiding' object has no attribute '__printInvisible'
```

And the code

```
class subClass(infoHiding):
    def __init__(self):
        print('from subclass', self.__invisible)

testSub = subClass()
```

prints

```
Error: 'subClass' object has no attribute '_subClass__invisible'
```

Notice that when a subclass attempts to use a hidden attribute of its superclass an AttributeError occurs. This can make using information hiding in Python a bit cumbersome.

Because it can be cumbersome, many Python programmers do not take advantage of the __ mechanism for hiding attributes—as we don't in this book. So, for example, a client of Person can write the expression Rafael.lastName rather than Rafael.getLastName().

This is unfortunate because it allows the client code to rely upon something that is not part of the specification of Person, and is therefore subject to change. If the implementation of Person were changed, for example to extract the last name whenever it is requested rather than store it in an instance variable, then the client code would no longer work.

Not only does Python let programs read instance and class variables from outside the class definition, it also lets programs write these variables. So, for example, the code `Rafael.birthday = '8/21/50'` is perfectly legal. This would lead to a runtime type error, were `Rafael.getAge` invoked later in the computation. It is even possible to create instance variables from outside the class definition. For example, Python will not complain if the assignment statement

```
me.age = Rafael.getIdNum()
```

occurs outside the class definition.

While this relatively weak static semantic checking is a flaw in Python, it is not a fatal flaw. A disciplined programmer can simply follow the sensible rule of not directly accessing data attributes from outside the class in which they are defined, as we do in this book.

8.3.1 Generators

A perceived risk of information hiding is that preventing client programs from directly accessing critical data structures leads to an unacceptable loss of efficiency. In the early days of data abstraction, many were concerned about the cost of introducing extraneous function/method calls. Modern compilation technology makes this concern moot. A more serious issue is that client programs will be forced to use inefficient algorithms.

Consider the implementation of `gradeReport` in Figure 8.6. The invocation of `course.getStudents` creates and returns a list of size n, where n is the number of students. This is probably not a problem for a grade book for a single class, but imagine keeping track of the grades of 1.7 million high school students taking the SATs. Creating a new list of that size when the list already exists is a significant inefficiency. One solution is to abandon the abstraction and allow `gradeReport` to directly access the instance variable `course.students`, but that would violate information hiding. Fortunately, there is a better solution.

The code in Figure 8.8, replaces the `getStudents` function in class Grades with a function that uses a kind of statement we have not yet used: a `yield` statement.

Any function definition containing a `yield` statement is treated in a special way. The presence of `yield` tells the Python system that the function is a **generator**. Generators are typically used in conjunction with `for` statements, as in

```
for s in course.getStudents():
```

in Figure 8.6.

```
def getStudents(self):
    """Return the students in the grade book one at a time
       in alphabetical order"""
    if not self.isSorted:
        self.students.sort()
        self.isSorted = True
    for s in self.students:
        yield s
```

Figure 8.8 New version of getStudents

At the start of the first iteration of a for loop that uses a generator, the generator is invoked and runs until the first time a yield statement is executed, at which point it returns the value of the expression in the yield statement. On the next iteration, the generator resumes execution immediately following the yield, with all local variables bound to the objects to which they were bound when the yield statement was executed, and again runs until a yield statement is executed. It continues to do this until it runs out of code to execute or executes a return statement, at which point the loop is exited.[50]

The version of getStudents in Figure 8.8 allows programmers to use a for loop to iterate over the students in objects of type Grades in the same way they can use a for loop to iterate over elements of built-in types such as list. For example, the code

```
book = Grades()
book.addStudent(Grad('Julie'))
book.addStudent(Grad('Charlie'))
for s in book.getStudents():
    print(s)
```

prints

```
Julie
Charlie
```

Thus the loop in Figure 8.6 that starts with

```
for s in course.getStudents():
```

does not have to be altered to take advantage of the version of class Grades that contains the new implementation of getStudents. (Of course, most code that depended upon getStudents returning a list would no longer work.) The same for

---

[50] This explanation of generators is a bit simplistic. To fully understand generators, you need to understand how built-in iterators are implemented in Python, which is not covered in this book.

loop can iterate over the values provided by getStudents regardless of whether getStudents returns a list of values or generates one value at a time. Generating one value at a time will be more efficient, because a new list containing the students will not be created.

8.4 Mortgages, an Extended Example

A collapse in U.S. housing prices helped trigger a severe economic meltdown in the fall of 2008. One of the contributing factors was that many homeowners had taken on mortgages that ended up having unexpected consequences.[51]

In the beginning, mortgages were relatively simple beasts. One borrowed money from a bank and made a fixed-size payment each month for the life of the mortgage, which typically ranged from fifteen to thirty years. At the end of that period, the bank had been paid back the initial loan (the principal) plus interest, and the homeowner owned the house "free and clear."

Towards the end of the twentieth century, mortgages started getting a lot more complicated. People could get lower interest rates by paying "points" to the lender at the time they took on the mortgage. A point is a cash payment of 1% of the value of the loan. People could take mortgages that were "interest-only" for a period of time. That is to say, for some number of months at the start of the loan the borrower paid only the accrued interest and none of the principal. Other loans involved multiple rates. Typically the initial rate (called a "teaser rate") was low, and then it went up over time. Many of these loans were variable-rate—the rate to be paid after the initial period would vary depending upon some index intended to reflect the cost to the lender of borrowing on the wholesale credit market.[52]

In principle, giving consumers a variety of options is a good thing. However, unscrupulous loan purveyors were not always careful to fully explain the possible long-term implications of the various options, and some borrowers made choices that proved to have dire consequences.

Let's build a program that examines the costs of three kinds of loans:

- A fixed-rate mortgage with no points,
- A fixed-rate mortgage with points, and

---

[51] In this context, it is worth recalling the etymology of the word mortgage. *The American Heritage Dictionary of the English Language* traces the word back to the old French words for dead (*mort*) and pledge (*gage*). (This derivation also explains why the "t" in the middle of mortgage is silent.)

[52] The London Interbank Offered Rate (LIBOR) is probably the most commonly used index.

CHAPTER 8. CLASSES AND OBJECT-ORIENTED PROGRAMMING

- A mortgage with an initial teaser rate followed by a higher rate for the duration.

The point of this exercise is to provide some experience in the incremental development of a set of related classes, not to make you an expert on mortgages.

We will structure our code to include a Mortgage class, and subclasses corresponding to each of the three kinds of mortgages listed above. Figure 8.9 contains the **abstract class** Mortgage. This class contains methods that are shared by each of its subclasses, but it is not intended to be instantiated directly. That is, no objects of type Mortgage will be created.

The function findPayment at the top of the figure computes the size of the fixed monthly payment needed to pay off the loan, including interest, by the end of its term. It does this using a well-known closed-form expression. This expression is not hard to derive, but it is a lot easier to just look it up and more likely to be correct than one derived on the spot.

Keep in mind that not everything you discover on the Web (or even in textbooks) is correct. When your code incorporates a formula that you have looked up, make sure that:

- You have taken the formula from a reputable source. We looked at multiple reputable sources, all of which contained equivalent formulas.
- You fully understand the meaning of all the variables in the formula.
- You test your implementation against examples taken from reputable sources. After implementing this function, we tested it by comparing our results to the results supplied by a calculator available on the Web.

Looking at __init__, we see that all Mortgage instances will have instance variables corresponding to the initial loan amount, the monthly interest rate, the duration of the loan in months, a list of payments that have been made at the start of each month (the list starts with 0.0, since no payments have been made at the start of the first month), a list with the balance of the loan that is outstanding at the start of each month, the amount of money to be paid each month (initialized using the value returned by the function findPayment), and a description of the mortgage (which initially has a value of None). The __init__ operation of each subclass of Mortgage is expected to start by calling Mortgage.__init__, and then to initialize self.legend to an appropriate description of that subclass.

```
def findPayment(loan, r, m):
    """Assumes: loan and r are floats, m an int
       Returns the monthly payment for a mortgage of size
       loan at a monthly rate of r for m months"""
    return loan*((r*(1+r)**m)/((1+r)**m - 1))

class Mortgage(object):
    """Abstract class for building different kinds of mortgages"""
    def __init__(self, loan, annRate, months):
        """Assumes: loan and annRate are floats, months an int
           Creates a new mortgage of size loan, duration months, and
           annual rate annRate"""
        self.loan = loan
        self.rate = annRate/12
        self.months = months
        self.paid = [0.0]
        self.outstanding = [loan]
        self.payment = findPayment(loan, self.rate, months)
        self.legend = None #description of mortgage

    def makePayment(self):
        """Make a payment"""
        self.paid.append(self.payment)
        reduction = self.payment - self.outstanding[-1]*self.rate
        self.outstanding.append(self.outstanding[-1] - reduction)

    def getTotalPaid(self):
        """Return the total amount paid so far"""
        return sum(self.paid)

    def __str__(self):
        return self.legend
```

Figure 8.9 Mortgage base class

The method makePayment is used to record mortgage payments. Part of each payment covers the amount of interest due on the outstanding loan balance, and the remainder of the payment is used to reduce the loan balance. That is why makePayment updates both self.paid and self.outstanding.

The method getTotalPaid uses the built-in Python function sum, which returns the sum of a sequence of numbers. If the sequence contains a non-number, an exception is raised.

```
class Fixed(Mortgage):
    def __init__(self, loan, r, months):
        Mortgage.__init__(self, loan, r, months)
        self.legend = 'Fixed, ' + str(round(r*100, 2)) + '%'

class FixedWithPts(Mortgage):
    def __init__(self, loan, r, months, pts):
        Mortgage.__init__(self, loan, r, months)
        self.pts = pts
        self.paid = [loan*(pts/100)]
        self.legend = 'Fixed, ' + str(round(r*100, 2)) + '%, '\
                      + str(pts) + ' points'

class TwoRate(Mortgage):
    def __init__(self, loan, r, months, teaserRate, teaserMonths):
        Mortgage.__init__(self, loan, teaserRate, months)
        self.teaserMonths = teaserMonths
        self.teaserRate = teaserRate
        self.nextRate = r/12
        self.legend = str(teaserRate*100)\
                      + '% for ' + str(self.teaserMonths)\
                      + ' months, then ' + str(round(r*100, 2)) + '%'
    def makePayment(self):
        if len(self.paid) == self.teaserMonths + 1:
            self.rate = self.nextRate
            self.payment = findPayment(self.outstanding[-1],
                                       self.rate,
                                       self.months - self.teaserMonths)
        Mortgage.makePayment(self)
```

Figure 8.10 Mortgage subclasses

Figure 8.10 contains classes implementing three types of mortgages. The classes Fixed and FixedWithPts override __init__ and inherit the other three methods from Mortgage. The class TwoRate treats a mortgage as the concatenation of two loans, each at a different interest rate. (Since self.paid is initialized to a list with one element, it contains one more element than the number of payments that have been made. That's why the method makePayment compares len(self.paid) to self.teaserMonths + 1.)

Figure 8.11 contains a function that computes and prints the total cost of each kind of mortgage for a sample set of parameters. It begins by creating one mortgage of each kind. It then makes a monthly payment on each for a given number of years. Finally, it prints the total amount of the payments made for each loan.

Notice that we used keyword rather than positional arguments in the invocation of compareMortgages. We did this because compareMortgages has a large number of formal parameters and using keyword arguments makes it easier to ensure that we are supplying the intended actual values to each of the formals.

```
def compareMortgages(amt, years, fixedRate, pts, ptsRate,
                     varRate1, varRate2, varMonths):
    totMonths = years*12
    fixed1 = Fixed(amt, fixedRate, totMonths)
    fixed2 = FixedWithPts(amt, ptsRate, totMonths, pts)
    twoRate = TwoRate(amt, varRate2, totMonths, varRate1, varMonths)
    morts = [fixed1, fixed2, twoRate]
    for m in range(totMonths):
        for mort in morts:
            mort.makePayment()
    for m in morts:
        print(m)
        print(' Total payments = $' + str(int(m.getTotalPaid())))

compareMortgages(amt=200000, years=30, fixedRate=0.07,
                 pts = 3.25, ptsRate=0.05, varRate1=0.045,
                 varRate2=0.095, varMonths=48)
```

Figure 8.11 Evaluate mortgages

When the code in Figure 8.11 is run, it prints

```
Fixed, 7.0%
 Total payments = $479017
Fixed, 5.0%, 3.25 points
 Total payments = $393011
4.5% for 48 months, then 9.5%
 Total payments = $551444
```

At first glance, the results look pretty conclusive. The variable-rate loan is a bad idea (for the borrower, not the lender) and the fixed-rate loan with points costs the least. It's important to note, however, that total cost is not the only metric by which mortgages should be judged. For example, a borrower who expects to have a higher income in the future may be willing to pay more in the later years to lessen the burden of payments in the beginning.

This suggests that rather than looking at a single number, we should look at payments over time. This in turn suggests that our program should be producing plots designed to show how the mortgage behaves over time. We will do that in Section 11.2.

9 A SIMPLISTIC INTRODUCTION TO ALGORITHMIC COMPLEXITY

The most important thing to think about when designing and implementing a program is that it should produce results that can be relied upon. We want our bank balances to be calculated correctly. We want the fuel injectors in our automobiles to inject appropriate amounts of fuel. We would prefer that neither airplanes nor operating systems crash.

Sometimes performance is an important aspect of correctness. This is most obvious for programs that need to run in real time. A program that warns airplanes of potential obstructions needs to issue the warning before the obstructions are encountered. Performance can also affect the utility of many non-real-time programs. The number of transactions completed per minute is an important metric when evaluating the utility of database systems. Users care about the time required to start an application on their phone. Biologists care about how long their phylogenetic inference calculations take.

Writing efficient programs is not easy. The most straightforward solution is often not the most efficient. Computationally efficient algorithms often employ subtle tricks that can make them difficult to understand. Consequently, programmers often increase the **conceptual complexity** of a program in an effort to reduce its **computational complexity**. To do this in a sensible way, we need to understand how to go about estimating the computational complexity of a program. That is the topic of this chapter.

9.1 Thinking About Computational Complexity

How should one go about answering the question "How long will the following function take to run?"

```
def f(i):
    """Assumes i is an int and i >= 0"""
    answer = 1
    while i >= 1:
        answer *= i
        i -= 1
    return answer
```

We could run the program on some input and time it. But that wouldn't be particularly informative because the result would depend upon

- the speed of the computer on which it is run,
- the efficiency of the Python implementation on that machine, and
- the value of the input.

We get around the first two issues by using a more abstract measure of time. Instead of measuring time in milliseconds, we measure time in terms of the number of basic steps executed by the program.

For simplicity, we will use a **random access machine** as our model of computation. In a random access machine, steps are executed sequentially, one at a time.[53] A **step** is an operation that takes a fixed amount of time, such as binding a variable to an object, making a comparison, executing an arithmetic operation, or accessing an object in memory.

Now that we have a more abstract way to think about the meaning of time, we turn to the question of dependence on the value of the input. We deal with that by moving away from expressing time complexity as a single number and instead relating it to the sizes of the inputs. This allows us to compare the efficiency of two algorithms by talking about how the running time of each grows with respect to the sizes of the inputs.

Of course, the actual running time of an algorithm depends not only upon the sizes of the inputs but also upon their values. Consider, for example, the linear search algorithm implemented by

```
def linearSearch(L, x):
    for e in L:
        if e == x:
            return True
    return False
```

Suppose that L is a list containing a million elements, and consider the call linearSearch(L, 3). If the first element in L is 3, linearSearch will return True almost immediately. On the other hand, if 3 is not in L, linearSearch will have to examine all one million elements before returning False.

In general, there are three broad cases to think about:

The best-case running time is the running time of the algorithm when the inputs are as favorable as possible. I.e., the **best-case** running time is the mini-

---

[53] A more accurate model for today's computers might be a parallel random access machine. However, that adds considerable complexity to the algorithmic analysis, and often doesn't make an important qualitative difference in the answer.

mum running time over all the possible inputs of a given size. For linearSearch, the best-case running time is independent of the size of L.
- Similarly, the **worst-case** running time is the maximum running time over all the possible inputs of a given size. For linearSearch, the worst-case running time is linear in the size of L.
- By analogy with the definitions of the best-case and worst-case running time, the **average-case** (also called **expected-case**) running time is the average running time over all possible inputs of a given size. Alternatively, if one has some *a priori* information about the distribution of input values (e.g., that 90% of the time x is in L), one can take that into account.

People usually focus on the worst case. All engineers share a common article of faith, Murphy's Law: If something can go wrong, it will go wrong. The worst-case provides an **upper bound** on the running time. This is critical in situations where there is a time constraint on how long a computation can take. It is not good enough to know that "most of the time" the air traffic control system warns of impending collisions before they occur.

Let's look at the worst-case running time of an iterative implementation of the factorial function:

```
def fact(n):
    """Assumes n is a natural number
       Returns n!"""
    answer = 1
    while n > 1:
        answer *= n
        n -= 1
    return answer
```

The number of steps required to run this program is something like 2 (1 for the initial assignment statement and 1 for the return) + 5n (counting 1 step for the test in the while, 2 steps for the first assignment statement in the while loop, and 2 steps for the second assignment statement in the loop). So, for example, if n is 1000, the function will execute roughly 5002 steps.

It should be immediately obvious that as n gets large, worrying about the difference between 5n and 5n+2 is kind of silly. For this reason, we typically ignore additive constants when reasoning about running time. Multiplicative constants are more problematical. Should we care whether the computation takes 1000 steps or 5000 steps? Multiplicative factors can be important. Whether a search engine takes a half second or 2.5 seconds to service a query can be the difference between whether people use that search engine or go to a competitor.

On the other hand, when one is comparing two different algorithms, it is often the case that even multiplicative constants are irrelevant. Recall that in Chapter 3 we looked at two algorithms, exhaustive enumeration and bisection search, for finding an approximation to the square root of a floating point number. Functions based on these algorithms are shown in Figure 9.1 and Figure 9.2.

```
def squareRootExhaustive(x, epsilon):
    """Assumes x and epsilon are positive floats & epsilon < 1
       Returns a y such that y*y is within epsilon of x"""
    step = epsilon**2
    ans = 0.0
    while abs(ans**2 - x) >= epsilon and ans*ans <= x:
        ans += step
    if ans*ans > x:
        raise ValueError
    return ans
```

Figure 9.1 Using exhaustive enumeration to approximate square root

```
def squareRootBi(x, epsilon):
    """Assumes x and epsilon are positive floats & epsilon < 1
       Returns a y such that y*y is within epsilon of x"""
    low = 0.0
    high = max(1.0, x)
    ans = (high + low)/2.0
    while abs(ans**2 - x) >= epsilon:
        if ans**2 < x:
            low = ans
        else:
            high = ans
        ans = (high + low)/2.0
    return ans
```

Figure 9.2 Using bisection search to approximate square root

We saw that exhaustive enumeration was so slow as to be impractical for many combinations of x and epsilon. For example, evaluating squareRootExhaustive(100, 0.0001) requires roughly one billion iterations of the while loop. In contrast, evaluating squareRootBi(100, 0.0001) takes roughly twenty iterations of a slightly more complex while loop. When the difference in the number of iterations is this large, it doesn't really matter how many instructions are in the loop. I.e., the multiplicative constants are irrelevant.

9.2 Asymptotic Notation

We use something called **asymptotic notation** to provide a formal way to talk about the relationship between the running time of an algorithm and the size of its inputs. The underlying motivation is that almost any algorithm is sufficiently efficient when run on small inputs. What we typically need to worry about is the efficiency of the algorithm when run on very large inputs. As a proxy for "very large," asymptotic notation describes the complexity of an algorithm as the size of its inputs approaches infinity.

Consider, for example, the code in Figure 9.3.

```
def f(x):
    """Assume x is an int > 0"""
    ans = 0
    #Loop that takes constant time
    for i in range(1000):
        ans += 1
    print('Number of additions so far', ans)
    #Loop that takes time x
    for i in range(x):
        ans += 1
    print('Number of additions so far', ans)
    #Nested loops take time x**2
    for i in range(x):
        for j in range(x):
            ans += 1
            ans += 1
    print('Number of additions so far', ans)
    return ans
```

Figure 9.3 Asymptotic complexity

If one assumes that each line of code takes one unit of time to execute, the running time of this function can be described as $1000 + x + 2x^2$. The constant 1000 corresponds to the number of times the first loop is executed. The term x corresponds to the number of times the second loop is executed. Finally, the term $2x^2$ corresponds to the time spent executing the two statements in the nested for loop. Consequently, the call f(10) will print

```
Number of additions so far 1000
Number of additions so far 1010
Number of additions so far 1210
```

and the call f(1000) will print

```
Number of additions so far 1000
Number of additions so far 2000
Number of additions so far 2002000
```

For small values of x the constant term dominates. If x is 10, over 80% of the steps are accounted for by the first loop. On the other hand, if x is 1000, each of the first two loops accounts for only about 0.05% of the steps. When x is 1,000,000, the first loop takes about 0.00000005% of the total time and the second loop about 0.00005%. A full 2,000,000,000,000 of the 2,000,001,001,000 steps are in the body of the inner for loop.

Clearly, we can get a meaningful notion of how long this code will take to run on very large inputs by considering only the inner loop, i.e., the quadratic component. Should we care about the fact that this loop takes $2x^2$ steps rather than x^2 steps? If your computer executes roughly 100 million steps per second, evaluating f will take about 5.5 hours. If we could reduce the complexity to x^2 steps, it would take about 2.25 hours. In either case, the moral is the same: we should probably look for a more efficient algorithm.

This kind of analysis leads us to use the following rules of thumb in describing the asymptotic complexity of an algorithm:

- If the running time is the sum of multiple terms, keep the one with the largest growth rate, and drop the others.
- If the remaining term is a product, drop any constants.

The most commonly used asymptotic notation is called "**Big O**" notation.[54] Big O notation is used to give an **upper bound** on the asymptotic growth (often called the **order of growth**) of a function. For example, the formula $f(x) \in O(x^2)$ means that the function f grows no faster than the quadratic polynomial x^2, in an asymptotic sense.

We, like many computer scientists, will often abuse Big O notation by making statements like, "the complexity of f(x) is $O(x^2)$." By this we mean that in the worst case f will take $O(x^2)$ steps to run. The difference between a function being "in $O(x^2)$" and "being $O(x^2)$" is subtle but important. Saying that $f(x) \in O(x^2)$ does

---

[54] The phrase "Big O" was introduced in this context by the computer scientist Donald Knuth in the 1970s. He chose the Greek letter Omicron because number theorists had used that letter since the late 19th century to denote a related concept.

not preclude the worst-case running time of f from being considerably less than $O(x^2)$.

When we say that f(x) is $O(x^2)$, we are implying that x^2 is both an upper and a **lower bound** on the asymptotic worst-case running time. This is called a **tight bound**.[55]

9.3 Some Important Complexity Classes

Some of the most common instances of Big O are listed below. In each case, n is a measure of the size of the inputs to the function.

- $O(1)$ denotes **constant** running time.
- $O(\log n)$ denotes **logarithmic** running time.
- $O(n)$ denotes **linear** running time.
- $O(n \log n)$ denotes **log-linear** running time.
- $O(n^k)$ denotes **polynomial** running time. Notice that k is a constant.
- $O(c^n)$ denotes **exponential** running time. Here a constant is being raised to a power based on the size of the input.

9.3.1 Constant Complexity

This indicates that the asymptotic complexity is independent of the size of the inputs. There are very few interesting programs in this class, but all programs have pieces (for example finding out the length of a Python list or multiplying two floating point numbers) that fit into this class. Constant running time does not imply that there are no loops or recursive calls in the code, but it does imply that the number of iterations or recursive calls is independent of the size of the inputs.

9.3.2 Logarithmic Complexity

Such functions have a complexity that grows as the log of at least one of the inputs. Binary search, for example, is logarithmic in the length of the list being searched. (We will look at binary search and analyze its complexity in Chapter 10.) By the way, we don't care about the base of the log, since the difference between using one base and another is merely a constant multiplicative factor. For

---

[55] The more pedantic members of the computer science community use Big Theta, Θ, rather than Big O for this.

example, $O(\log_2(x)) = O(\log_2(10)*\log_{10}(x))$. There are lots of interesting functions with logarithmic complexity. Consider

```
def intToStr(i):
    """Assumes i is a nonnegative int
       Returns a decimal string representation of i"""
    digits = '0123456789'
    if i == 0:
        return '0'
    result = ''
    while i > 0:
        result = digits[i%10] + result
        i = i//10
    return result
```

Since there are no function or method calls in this code, we know that we only have to look at the loops to determine the complexity class. There is only one loop, so the only thing that we need to do is characterize the number of iterations. That boils down to the number of times we can use integer division to divide i by 10 before getting a result of 0. So, the complexity of intToStr is $O(\log(i))$.

What about the complexity of

```
def addDigits(n):
    """Assumes n is a nonnegative int
       Returns the sum of the digits in n"""
    stringRep = intToStr(n)
    val = 0
    for c in stringRep:
        val += int(c)
    return val
```

The complexity of converting n to a string using intToStr is $O(\log(n))$, and intToStr returns a string of length $O(\log(n))$. The for loop will be executed $O(\text{len}(stringRep))$ times, i.e., $O(\log(n))$ times. Putting it all together, and assuming that a character representing a digit can be converted to an integer in constant time, the program will run in time proportional to $O(\log(n)) + O(\log(n))$, which makes it $O(\log(n))$.

9.3.3 Linear Complexity

Many algorithms that deal with lists or other kinds of sequences are linear because they touch each element of the sequence a constant (greater than 0) number of times.

Consider, for example,

```
def addDigits(s):
    """Assumes s is a str each character of which is a
       decimal digit.
       Returns an int that is the sum of the digits in s"""
    val = 0
    for c in s:
        val += int(c)
    return val
```

This function is linear in the length of s, i.e., $O(len(s))$—again assuming that a character representing a digit can be converted to an integer in constant time.

Of course, a program does not need to have a loop to have linear complexity. Consider

```
def factorial(x):
    """Assumes that x is a positive int
       Returns x!"""
    if x == 1:
        return 1
    else:
        return x*factorial(x-1)
```

There are no loops in this code, so in order to analyze the complexity we need to figure out how many recursive calls get made. The series of calls is simply

factorial(x), factorial(x-1), factorial(x-2), ... , factorial(1)

The length of this series, and thus the complexity of the function, is $O(x)$.

Thus far in this chapter we have looked only at the time complexity of our code. This is fine for algorithms that use a constant amount of space, but this implementation of factorial does not have that property. As we discussed in Chapter 4, each recursive call of factorial causes a new stack frame to be allocated, and that frame continues to occupy memory until the call returns. At the maximum depth of recursion, this code will have allocated x stack frames, so the space complexity is also $O(x)$.

The impact of space complexity is harder to appreciate than the impact of time complexity. Whether a program takes one minute or two minutes to complete is quite visible to its user, but whether it uses one megabyte or two megabytes of memory is largely invisible to users. This is why people typically give more attention to time complexity than to space complexity. The exception occurs when a program needs more space than is available in the fast memory of the machine on which it is run.

9.3.4 Log-Linear Complexity

This is slightly more complicated than the complexity classes we have looked at thus far. It involves the product of two terms, each of which depends upon the size of the inputs. It is an important class, because many practical algorithms are log-linear. The most commonly used log-linear algorithm is probably merge sort, which is $O(n \log(n))$, where n is the length of the list being sorted. We will look at that algorithm and analyze its complexity in Chapter 10.

9.3.5 Polynomial Complexity

The most commonly used polynomial algorithms are **quadratic**, i.e., their complexity grows as the square of the size of their input. Consider, for example, the function in Figure 9.4, which implements a subset test.

```
def isSubset(L1, L2):
    """Assumes L1 and L2 are lists.
       Returns True if each element in L1 is also in L2
       and False otherwise."""
    for e1 in L1:
        matched = False
        for e2 in L2:
            if e1 == e2:
                matched = True
                break
        if not matched:
            return False
    return True
```

Figure 9.4 Implementation of subset test

Each time the inner loop is reached it is executed O(len(L2)) times. The function isSubset will execute the outer loop O(len(L1)) times, so the inner loop will be reached O(len(L1)) times. Therefore, the complexity of the function isSubset is O(len(L1)*len(L2)).

Now consider the function intersect in Figure 9.5. The running time for the part building the list that might contain duplicates is clearly O(len(L1)*len(L2)). At first glance, it appears that the part of the code that builds the duplicate-free list is linear in the length of tmp, but it is not. The test e not in result potentially involves looking at each element in result, and is therefore O(len(result)); consequently the second part of the implementation is O(len(tmp)*len(result)). However, since the lengths of result and tmp are bounded by the length of the smaller

of L1 and L2, and since we ignore additive terms, the complexity of intersect is
O(len(L1)*len(L2)).

```
def intersect(L1, L2):
    """Assumes: L1 and L2 are lists
        Returns a list without duplicates that is the intersection of
        L1 and L2"""
    #Build a list containing common elements
    tmp = []
    for e1 in L1:
        for e2 in L2:
            if e1 == e2:
                tmp.append(e1)
                break
    #Build a list without duplicates
    result = []
    for e in tmp:
        if e not in result:
            result.append(e)
    return result
```

Figure 9.5 Implementation of list intersection

The running time for the part building the list that might contain duplicates is clearly O(len(L1)*len(L2)). At first glance, it appears that the part of the code that builds the duplicate-free list is linear in the length of tmp, but it is not. The test e not in result potentially involves looking at each element in result, and is therefore O(len(result)); consequently the second part of the implementation is O(len(tmp)*len(result)). However, since the lengths of result and tmp are bounded by the length of the smaller of L1 and L2, and since we ignore additive terms, the complexity of intersect is O(len(L1)*len(L2)).

9.3.6 Exponential Complexity

As we will see later in this book, many important problems are inherently exponential, i.e., solving them completely can require time that is exponential in the size of the input. This is unfortunate, since it rarely pays to write a program that has a reasonably high probability of taking exponential time to run. Consider, for example, the code in Figure 9.6.

```python
def getBinaryRep(n, numDigits):
    """Assumes n and numDigits are non-negative ints
       Returns a str of length numDigits that is a binary
       representation of n"""
    result = ''
    while n > 0:
        result = str(n%2) + result
        n = n//2
    if len(result) > numDigits:
        raise ValueError('not enough digits')
    for i in range(numDigits - len(result)):
        result = '0' + result
    return result

def genPowerset(L):
    """Assumes L is a list
       Returns a list of lists that contains all possible
       combinations of the elements of L. E.g., if
       L is [1, 2] it will return a list with elements
       [], [1], [2], and [1,2]."""
    powerset = []
    for i in range(0, 2**len(L)):
        binStr = getBinaryRep(i, len(L))
        subset = []
        for j in range(len(L)):
            if binStr[j] == '1':
                subset.append(L[j])
        powerset.append(subset)
    return powerset
```

Figure 9.6 Generating the power set

The function genPowerset(L) returns a list of lists that contains all possible combinations of the elements of L. For example, if L is ['x', 'y'], the powerset of L will be a list containing the lists [], ['x'], ['y'], and ['x', 'y'].

The algorithm is a bit subtle. Consider a list of n elements. We can represent any combination of elements by a string of n 0's and 1's, where a 1 represents the presence of an element and a 0 its absence. The combination containing no items is represented by a string of all 0's, the combination containing all of the items is represented by a string of all 1's, the combination containing only the first and last elements is represented by 100...001, etc.

Generating all sublists of a list L of length n can be done as follows:
- Generate all n-bit binary numbers. These are the numbers from 0 to 2^n.
- For each of these 2^n +1 binary numbers, b, generate a list by selecting those elements of L that have an index corresponding to a 1 in b. For example, if L is ['x', 'y'] and b is 01, generate the list ['y'].

Try running genPowerset on a list containing the first ten letters of the alphabet. It will finish quite quickly and produce a list with 1024 elements. Next, try running genPowerset on the first twenty letters of the alphabet. It will take more than a bit of time to run, and return a list with about a million elements. If you try running genPowerset on all twenty-six letters, you will probably get tired of waiting for it to complete, unless your computer runs out of memory trying to build a list with tens of millions of elements. Don't even think about trying to run genPowerset on a list containing all uppercase and lowercase letters. Step 1 of the algorithm generates $O(2^{len(L)})$ binary numbers, so the algorithm is exponential in len(L).

Does this mean that we cannot use computation to tackle exponentially hard problems? Absolutely not. It means that we have to find algorithms that provide approximate solutions to these problems or that find perfect solutions on some instances of the problem. But that is a subject for later chapters.

9.3.7 Comparisons of Complexity Classes

The plots in this section are intended to convey an impression of the implications of an algorithm being in one or another of these complexity classes.

The plot on the left in Figure 9.7 compares the growth of a constant-time algorithm to that of a logarithmic algorithm. Note that the size of the input has to reach about a million for the two of them to cross, even for the very small constant of twenty. When the size of the input is five million, the time required by a logarithmic algorithm is still quite small. The moral is that logarithmic algorithms are almost as good as constant-time ones.

The plot on the right of Figure 9.7 illustrates the dramatic difference between logarithmic algorithms and linear algorithms. Notice that the x-axis only goes as high as 1000. While we needed to look at large inputs to appreciate the difference between constant-time and logarithmic-time algorithms, the difference between logarithmic-time and linear-time algorithms is apparent even on small inputs. The dramatic difference in the relative performance of logarithmic and linear algorithms does not mean that linear algorithms are bad. In fact, most of the time a linear algorithm is acceptably efficient.

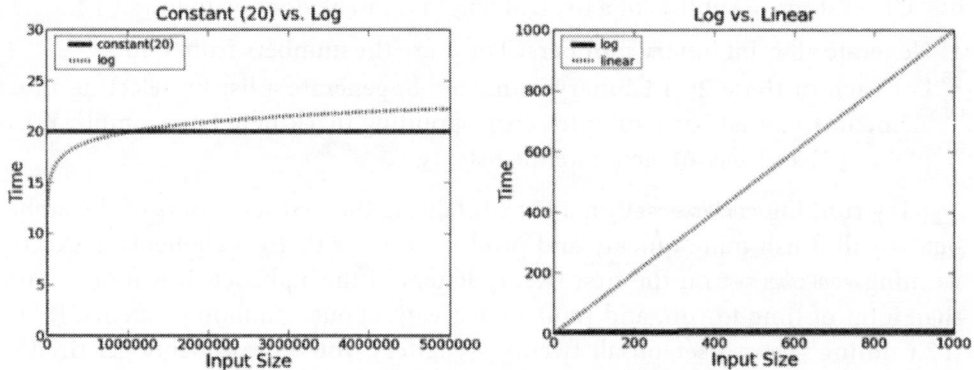

Figure 9.7 Constant, logarithmic, and linear growth

The plot on the left in Figure 9.8 shows that there is a significant difference between O(n) and O(n log(n)). Given how slowly log(n) grows, this may seem a bit surprising, but keep in mind that it is a multiplicative factor. Also keep in mind that in many practical situations, O(n log(n)) is fast enough to be useful. On the other hand, as the plot on the right in Figure 9.8 suggests, there are many situations in which a quadratic rate of growth is prohibitive.

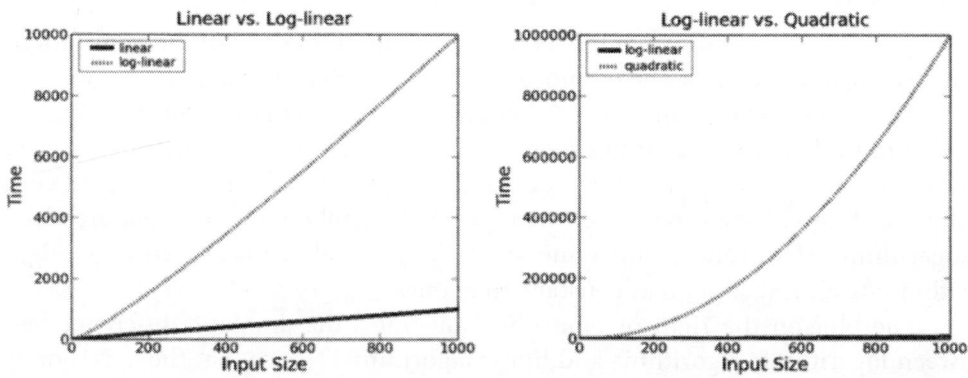

Figure 9.8 Linear, log-linear, and quadratic growth

The plots in Figure 9.9 are about exponential complexity. In the plot on the left of Figure 9.9, the numbers to the left of the y-axis run from 0.0 to 1.2. However, the notation x1e301 on the top left means that each tick on the y-axis should be multiplied by 10^{301}. So, the plotted y-values range from 0 to roughly $1.1*10^{301}$.

But it looks almost as if there are no curves in the plot on the left in Figure 9.9. That's because an exponential function grows so quickly that relative to the y value of the highest point (which determines the scale of the y-axis), the y values of earlier points on the exponential curve (and all points on the quadratic curve) are almost indistinguishable from 0.

The plot on the right in Figure 9.9 addresses this issue by using a logarithmic scale on the y-axis. One can readily see that exponential algorithms are impractical for all but the smallest of inputs.

Notice that when plotted on a logarithmic scale, an exponential curve appears as a straight line. We will have more to say about this in later chapters.

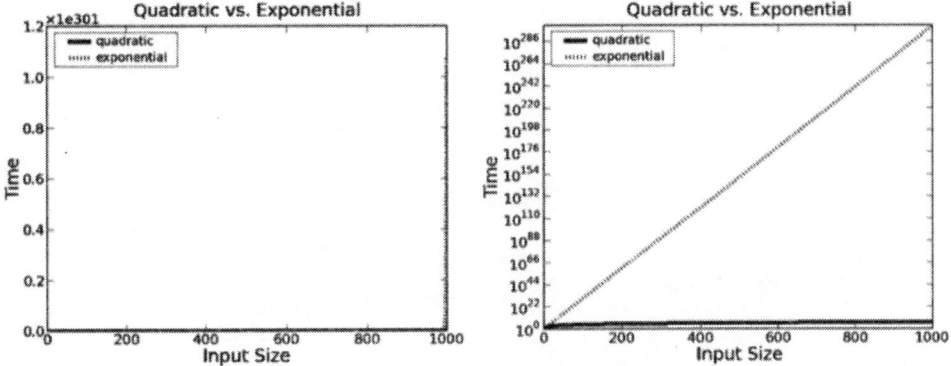

Figure 9.9 Quadratic and exponential growth

10 SOME SIMPLE ALGORITHMS AND DATA STRUCTURES

Though we expend a fair number of pages in this book talking about efficiency, the goal is not to make you expert in designing efficient programs. There are many long books (and even some good long books) devoted exclusively to that topic.[56] In Chapter 9, we introduced some of the basic concepts underlying complexity analysis. In this chapter we use those concepts to look at the complexity of a few classic algorithms. The goal of this chapter is to help you develop some general intuitions about how to approach questions of efficiency. By the time you get through this chapter you should understand why some programs complete in the blink of an eye, why some need to run overnight, and why some wouldn't complete in your lifetime.

The first algorithms we looked at in this book were based on brute-force exhaustive enumeration. We argued that modern computers are so fast that it is often the case that employing clever algorithms is a waste of time. Writing code that is simple and obviously correct, is often the right way to go.

We then looked at some problems (e.g., finding an approximation to the roots of a polynomial) where the search space was too large to make brute force practical. This led us to consider more efficient algorithms such as bisection search and Newton-Raphson. The major point was that the key to efficiency is a good algorithm, not clever coding tricks.

In the sciences (physical, life, and social), programmers often start by quickly coding up a simple algorithm to test the plausibility of a hypothesis about a data set, and then run it on a small amount of data. If this yields encouraging results, the hard work of producing an implementation that can be run (perhaps over and over again) on large data sets begins. Such implementations need to be based on efficient algorithms.

Efficient algorithms are hard to invent. Successful professional computer scientists might invent one algorithm during their whole career—if they are lucky. Most of us never invent a novel algorithm. What we do instead is learn to reduce the most complex aspects of the problems we are faced with to previously solved problems.

---

[56] *Introduction to Algorithms*, by Cormen, Leiserson, Rivest, and Stein, is an excellent source for those of you not intimidated by a fair amount of mathematics.

More specifically, we

- Develop an understanding of the inherent complexity of the problem,
- Think about how to break that problem up into subproblems, and
- Relate those subproblems to other problems for which efficient algorithms already exist.

This chapter contains a few examples intended to give you some intuition about algorithm design. Many other algorithms appear elsewhere in the book.

Keep in mind that the most efficient algorithm is not always the algorithm of choice. A program that does everything in the most efficient possible way is often needlessly difficult to understand. It is often a good strategy to start by solving the problem at hand in the most straightforward manner possible, instrument it to find any computational bottlenecks, and then look for ways to improve the computational complexity of those parts of the program contributing to the bottlenecks.

10.1 Search Algorithms

A **search algorithm** is a method for finding an item or group of items with specific properties within a collection of items. We refer to the collection of items as a **search space**. The search space might be something concrete, such as a set of electronic medical records, or something abstract, such as the set of all integers. A large number of problems that occur in practice can be formulated as search problems.

Many of the algorithms presented earlier in this book can be viewed as search algorithms. In Chapter 3, we formulated finding an approximation to the roots of a polynomial as a search problem, and looked at three algorithms—exhaustive enumeration, bisection search, and Newton-Raphson—for searching the space of possible answers.

In this section, we will examine two algorithms for searching a list. Each meets the specification

```
def search(L, e):
    """Assumes L is a list.
       Returns True if e is in L and False otherwise"""
```

The astute reader might wonder if this is not semantically equivalent to the Python expression e in L. The answer is yes, it is. And if one is unconcerned about the efficiency of discovering whether e is in L, one should simply write that expression.

10.1.1 Linear Search and Using Indirection to Access Elements

Python uses the following algorithm to determine if an element is in a list:

```
for i in range(len(L)):
    if L[i] == e:
        return True
return False
```

If the element e is not in the list the algorithm will perform O(len(L)) tests, i.e., the complexity is at best linear in the length of L. Why "at best" linear? It will be linear only if each operation inside the loop can be done in constant time. That raises the question of whether Python retrieves the ith element of a list in constant time. Since our model of computation assumes that fetching the contents of an address is a constant-time operation, the question becomes whether we can compute the address of the ith element of a list in constant time.

Let's start by considering the simple case where each element of the list is an integer. This implies that each element of the list is the same size, e.g., four units of memory (four eight-bit bytes[57]). Assuming that the elements of the list are stored contiguously, the address in memory of the ith element of the list is simply start + 4*i, where start is the address of the start of the list. Therefore we can assume that Python could compute the address of the ith element of a list of integers in constant time.

Of course, we know that Python lists can contain objects of types other than int, and that the same list can contain objects of many different types and sizes. You might think that this would present a problem, but it does not.

In Python, a list is represented as a length (the number of objects in the list) and a sequence of fixed-size pointers[58] to objects. Figure 10.1 illustrates the use of these pointers. The shaded region represents a list containing four elements. The leftmost shaded box contains a pointer to an integer indicating the length of the list. Each of the other shaded boxes contains a pointer to an object in the list.

---

[57] The number of bits used to store an integer, often called the word size, is typically dictated by the hardware of the computer.

[58] Of size 32 bits in some implementations and 64 bits in others.

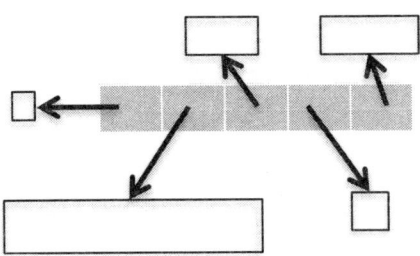

Figure 10.1 Implementing lists

If the length field occupies four units of memory, and each pointer (address) occupies four units of memory, the address of the ith element of the list is stored at the address start + 4 + 4*i. Again, this address can be found in constant time, and then the value stored at that address can be used to access the ith element. This access too is a constant-time operation.

This example illustrates one of the most important implementation techniques used in computing: **indirection**.[59] Generally speaking, indirection involves accessing something by first accessing something else that contains a reference to the thing initially sought. This is what happens each time we use a variable to refer to the object to which that variable is bound. When we use a variable to access a list and then a reference stored in that list to access another object, we are going through two levels of indirection.[60]

10.1.2 Binary Search and Exploiting Assumptions

Getting back to the problem of implementing search(L, e), is O(len(L)) the best we can do? Yes, if we know nothing about the relationship of the values of the elements in the list and the order in which they are stored. In the worst case, we have to look at each element in L to determine whether L contains e.

But suppose we know something about the order in which elements are stored, e.g., suppose we know that we have a list of integers stored in ascending order. We could change the implementation so that the search stops when it

---

[59] My dictionary defines the noun "indirection" as "lack of straightforwardness and openness: deceitfulness." In fact, the word generally had a pejorative implication until about 1950, when computer scientists realized that it was the solution to many problems.

[60] It has often been said that "any problem in computing can be solved by adding another level of indirection." Following three levels of indirection, we attribute this observation to David J. Wheeler. The paper "Authentication in Distributed Systems: Theory and Practice," by Butler Lampson *et al.*, contains the observation. It also contains a footnote saying that "Roger Needham attributes this observation to David Wheeler of Cambridge University."

reaches a number larger than the number for which it is searching, as in Figure 10.2.

```
def search(L, e):
    """Assumes L is a list, the elements of which are in
          ascending order.
       Returns True if e is in L and False otherwise"""
    for i in range(len(L)):
        if L[i] == e:
            return True
        if L[i] > e:
            return False
    return False
```

Figure 10.2 Linear search of a sorted list

This would improve the average running time. However, it would not change the worst-case complexity of the algorithm, since in the worst case each element of L is examined.

We can, however, get a considerable improvement in the worst-case complexity by using an algorithm, **binary search**, that is similar to the bisection search algorithm used in Chapter 3 to find an approximation to the square root of a floating point number. There we relied upon the fact that there is an intrinsic total ordering on floating point numbers. Here we rely on the assumption that the list is ordered.

The idea is simple:
1. Pick an index, i, that divides the list L roughly in half.
2. Ask if L[i] == e.
3. If not, ask whether L[i] is larger or smaller than e.
4. Depending upon the answer, search either the left or right half of L for e.

Given the structure of this algorithm, it is not surprising that the most straightforward implementation of binary search uses recursion, as shown in Figure 10.3.

The outer function in Figure 10.3, search(L, e), has the same arguments and specification as the function defined in Figure 10.2. The specification says that the implementation may assume that L is sorted in ascending order. The burden of making sure that this assumption is satisfied lies with the caller of search. If the assumption is not satisfied, the implementation has no obligation to behave well. It could work, but it could also crash or return an incorrect answer. Should search be modified to check that the assumption is satisfied? This might eliminate a source of errors, but it would defeat the purpose of using binary search, since checking the assumption would itself take O(len(L)) time.

```
def search(L, e):
    """Assumes L is a list, the elements of which are in
          ascending order.
       Returns True if e is in L and False otherwise"""

    def bSearch(L, e, low, high):
        #Decrements high - low
        if high == low:
            return L[low] == e
        mid = (low + high)//2
        if L[mid] == e:
            return True
        elif L[mid] > e:
            if low == mid: #nothing left to search
                return False
            else:
                return bSearch(L, e, low, mid - 1)
        else:
            return bSearch(L, e, mid + 1, high)

    if len(L) == 0:
        return False
    else:
        return bSearch(L, e, 0, len(L) - 1)
```

Figure 10.3 Recursive binary search

Functions such as search are often called **wrapper functions**. The function provides a nice interface for client code, but is essentially a pass-through that does no serious computation. Instead, it calls the helper function bSearch with appropriate arguments. This raises the question of why not eliminate search and have clients call bSearch directly? The reason is that the parameters low and high have nothing to do with the abstraction of searching a list for an element. They are implementation details that should be hidden from those writing programs that call search.

Let us now analyze the complexity of bSearch. We showed in the last section that list access takes constant time. Therefore, we can see that excluding the recursive call, each instance of bSearch is O(1). Therefore, the complexity of bSearch depends only upon the number of recursive calls.

If this were a book about algorithms, we would now dive into a careful analysis using something called a recurrence relation. But since it isn't, we will take a much less formal approach that starts with the question "How do we know that the program terminates?" Recall that in Chapter 3 we asked the same question about a while loop. We answered the question by providing a decrementing function for the loop. We do the same thing here. In this context, the decrementing function has the properties:

- It maps the values to which the formal parameters are bound to a nonnegative integer.
- When its value is 0, the recursion terminates.
- For each recursive call, the value of the decrementing function is less than the value of the decrementing function on entry to the instance of the function making the call.

The decrementing function for bSearch is high−low. The if statement in search ensures that the value of this decrementing function is at least 0 the first time bSearch is called (decrementing function property 1).

When bSearch is entered, if high−low is exactly 0, the function makes no recursive call—simply returning the value L[low] == e (satisfying decrementing function property 2).

The function bSearch contains two recursive calls. One call uses arguments that cover all the elements to the left of mid, and the other call uses arguments that cover all the elements to the right of mid. In either case, the value of high−low is cut in half (satisfying decrementing function property 3).

We now understand why the recursion terminates. The next question is how many times can the value of high−low be cut in half before high−low == 0? Recall that $\log_y(x)$ is the number of times that y has to be multiplied by itself to reach x. Conversely, if x is divided by y $\log_y(x)$ times, the result is 1. This implies that high−low can be cut in half using integer division at most $\log_2$(high−low) times before it reaches 0.

Finally, we can answer the question, what is the algorithmic complexity of binary search? Since when search calls bSearch the value of high−low is equal to len(L)-1, the complexity of search is O(log(len(L))).[61]

Finger exercise: Why does the code use mid+1 rather than mid in the second recursive call?

---

[61] Recall that when looking at orders of growth the base of the logarithm is irrelevant.

10.2 Sorting Algorithms

We have just seen that if we happen to know that a list is sorted, we can exploit that information to greatly reduce the time needed to search a list. Does this mean that when asked to search a list one should first sort it and then perform the search?

Let O(sortComplexity(L)) be the complexity of sorting a list. Since we know that we can always search a list in O(len(L)) time, the question of whether we should first sort and then search boils down to the question, is sortComplexity(L) + log(len(L)) less than len(L)? The answer, sadly, is no. One cannot sort a list without looking at each element in the list at least once, so it is not possible to sort a list in sub-linear time.

Does this mean that binary search is an intellectual curiosity of no practical import? Happily, no. Suppose that one expects to search the same list many times. It might well make sense to pay the overhead of sorting the list once, and then **amortize** the cost of the sort over many searches. If we expect to search the list k times, the relevant question becomes, is sortComplexity(L) + k*log(len(L)) less than k*len(L)?

As k becomes large, the time required to sort the list becomes increasingly irrelevant. How big k needs to be depends upon how long it takes to sort a list. If, for example, sorting were exponential in the size of the list, k would have to be quite large.

Fortunately, sorting can be done rather efficiently. For example, the standard implementation of sorting in most Python implementations runs in roughly O(n*log(n)) time, where n is the length of the list. In practice, you will rarely need to implement your own sort function. In most cases, the right thing to do is to use either Python's built-in sort method (L.sort() sorts the list L) or its built-in function sorted (sorted(L) returns a list with the same elements as L, but does not mutate L). We present sorting algorithms here primarily to provide some practice in thinking about algorithm design and complexity analysis.

We begin with a simple but inefficient algorithm, **selection sort**. Selection sort, Figure 10.4, works by maintaining the **loop invariant** that, given a partitioning of the list into a prefix (L[0:i]) and a suffix (L[i+1:len(L)]), the prefix is sorted and no element in the prefix is larger than the smallest element in the suffix.

We use induction to reason about loop invariants.

- Base case: At the start of the first iteration, the prefix is empty, i.e., the suffix is the entire list. Therefore, the invariant is (trivially) true.

CHAPTER 10. SOME SIMPLE ALGORITHMS AND DATA STRUCTURES

- Induction step: At each step of the algorithm, we move one element from the suffix to the prefix. We do this by appending a minimum element of the suffix to the end of the prefix. Because the invariant held before we moved the element, we know that after we append the element the prefix is still sorted. We also know that since we removed the smallest element in the suffix, no element in the prefix is larger than the smallest element in the suffix.
- Termination: When the loop is exited, the prefix includes the entire list, and the suffix is empty. Therefore, the entire list is now sorted in ascending order.

```
def selSort(L):
    """Assumes that L is a list of elements that can be
          compared using >.
       Sorts L in ascending order"""
    suffixStart = 0
    while suffixStart != len(L):
        #look at each element in suffix
        for i in range(suffixStart, len(L)):
            if L[i] < L[suffixStart]:
                #swap position of elements
                L[suffixStart], L[i] = L[i], L[suffixStart]
        suffixStart += 1
```

Figure 10.4 Selection sort

It's hard to imagine a simpler or more obviously correct sorting algorithm. Unfortunately, it is rather inefficient.[62] The complexity of the inner loop is $O(len(L))$. The complexity of the outer loop is also $O(len(L))$. So, the complexity of the entire function is $O(len(L)^2)$. I.e., it is quadratic in the length of L.

10.2.1 Merge Sort

Fortunately, we can do a lot better than quadratic time using a **divide-and-conquer algorithm**. The basic idea is to combine solutions of simpler instances of the original problem. In general, a divide-and-conquer algorithm is characterized by

- A threshold input size, below which the problem is not subdivided,
- The size and number of sub-instances into which an instance is split, and
- The algorithm used to combine sub-solutions.

---

[62] But not the most inefficient of sorting algorithms, as suggested by a successful candidate for the U.S. Presidency. See http://www.youtube.com/watch?v=k4RRi_ntQc8.

The threshold is sometimes called the **recursive base**. For item 2 it is usual to consider the ratio of initial problem size to the sub-instance size. In most of the examples we've seen so far, the ratio was 2.

Merge sort is a prototypical divide-and-conquer algorithm. It was invented in 1945, by John von Neumann, and is still widely used. Like many divide-and-conquer algorithms it is most easily described recursively:

1. If the list is of length 0 or 1, it is already sorted.
2. If the list has more than one element, split the list into two lists, and use merge sort to sort each of them.
3. Merge the results.

The key observation made by von Neumann is that two sorted lists can be efficiently merged into a single sorted list. The idea is to look at the first element of each list, and move the smaller of the two to the end of the result list. When one of the lists is empty, all that remains is to copy the remaining items from the other list. Consider, for example, merging the two lists [1,5,12,18,19,20] and [2,3,4,17]:

Remaining in list 1	Remaining in list 2	Result
[1,5,12,18,19,20]	[2,3,4,17]	[ ]
[5,12,18,19,20]	[2,3,4,17]	[1]
[5,12,18,19,20]	[3,4,17]	[1,2]
[5,12,18,19,20]	[4,17]	[1,2,3]
[5,12,18,19,20]	[17]	[1,2,3,4]
[12,18,19,20]	[17]	[1,2,3,4,5]
[18,19,20]	[17]	[1,2,3,4,5,12]
[18,19,20]	[ ]	[1,2,3,4,5,12,17]
[ ]	[ ]	[1,2,3,4,5,12,17,18,19,20]

What is the complexity of the merge process? It involves two constant-time operations, comparing the values of elements and copying elements from one list to another. The number of comparisons is O(len(L)), where L is the longer of the two lists. The number of copy operations is O(len(L1) + len(L2)), because each element gets copied exactly once. (The time to copy an element will depend on the size of the element. However, this does not affect the order of the growth of sort as a function of the number of elements in the list.) Therefore, merging two sorted lists is linear in the length of the lists.

Figure 10.5 contains an implementation of the merge sort algorithm.

```
def merge(left, right, compare):
    """Assumes left and right are sorted lists and
         compare defines an ordering on the elements.
       Returns a new sorted (by compare) list containing the
         same elements as (left + right) would contain."""
    result = []
    i,j = 0, 0
    while i < len(left) and j < len(right):
        if compare(left[i], right[j]):
            result.append(left[i])
            i += 1
        else:
            result.append(right[j])
            j += 1
    while (i < len(left)):
        result.append(left[i])
        i += 1
    while (j < len(right)):
        result.append(right[j])
        j += 1
    return result

def mergeSort(L, compare = lambda x, y: x < y):
    """Assumes L is a list, compare defines an ordering
         on elements of L
       Returns a new sorted list with the same elements as L"""
    if len(L) < 2:
        return L[:]
    else:
        middle = len(L)//2
        left = mergeSort(L[:middle], compare)
        right = mergeSort(L[middle:], compare)
        return merge(left, right, compare)
```

Figure 10.5 Merge sort

Notice that we have made the comparison operator a parameter of the mergeSort function, and written a lambda expression to supply a default value. So, for example, the code

```
L = [2,1,4,5,3]
print(mergeSort(L), mergeSort(L, lambda x, y: x > y))
```

prints

[1, 2, 3, 4, 5] [5, 4, 3, 2, 1]

Let's analyze the complexity of `mergeSort`. We already know that the time complexity of `merge` is O(len(L)). At each level of recursion the total number of elements to be merged is len(L). Therefore, the time complexity of `mergeSort` is O(len(L)) multiplied by the number of levels of recursion. Since `mergeSort` divides the list in half each time, we know that the number of levels of recursion is O(log(len(L)). Therefore, the time complexity of `mergeSort` is O(n*log(n)), where n is len(L).

This is a lot better than selection sort's O(len(L)^2). For example, if L has 10,000 elements, len(L)^2 is 100 million but len(L)*log$_2$(len(L)) is about 130,000.

This improvement in time complexity comes with a price. Selection sort is an example of an **in-place** sorting algorithm. Because it works by swapping the place of elements within the list, it uses only a constant amount of extra storage (one element in our implementation). In contrast, the merge sort algorithm involves making copies of the list. This means that its space complexity is O(len(L)). This can be an issue for large lists.[63]

10.2.2 Exploiting Functions as Parameters

Suppose we want to sort a list of names written as firstName lastName, e.g., the list ['Chris Terman', 'Tom Brady', 'Eric Grimson', 'Gisele Bundchen']. Figure 10.6 defines two ordering functions, and then uses these to sort a list in two different ways. Each function uses the `split` method of type `str`.

When the code in Figure 10.6 is run, it prints

```
Sorted by last name = ['Tom Brady', 'Gisele Bundchen', 'Eric Grimson']
Sorted by first name = ['Eric Grimson', 'Gisele Bundchen', 'Tom Brady']
```

10.2.3 Sorting in Python

The sorting algorithm used in most Python implementations is called **timsort**.[64] The key idea is to take advantage of the fact that in a lot of data sets the data is already partially sorted. Timsort's worst-case performance is the same as merge sort's, but on average it performs considerably better.

---

[63] **Quicksort**, which was invented by C.A.R. Hoare in 1960, is conceptually similar to merge sort, but considerably more complex. It has the advantage of needing only log(n) additional space. Unlike merge sort, its running time depends upon the way the elements in the list to be sorted are ordered relative to each other. Though its worst-case running time is O(n^2), its expected running time is only O(n*log(n)).

[64] Timsort was invented by Tim Peters in 2002 because he was unhappy with the previous algorithm used in Python.

```
def lastNameFirstName(name1, name2):
    arg1 = name1.split(' ')
    arg2 = name2.split(' ')
    if arg1[1] != arg2[1]:
        return arg1[1] < arg2[1]
    else: #last names the same, sort by first name
        return arg1[0] < arg2[0]

def firstNameLastName(name1, name2):
    arg1 = name1.split(' ')
    arg2 = name2.split(' ')
    if arg1[0] != arg2[0]:
        return arg1[0] < arg2[0]
    else: #first names the same, sort by last name
        return arg1[1] < arg2[1]

L = ['Tom Brady', 'Eric Grimson', 'Gisele Bundchen']
newL = mergeSort(L, lastNameFirstName)
print('Sorted by last name =', newL)
newL = mergeSort(L, firstNameLastName)
print('Sorted by first name =', newL)
```

Figure 10.6 Sorting a list of names

As mentioned earlier, the Python method list.sort takes a list as its first argument and modifies that list. In contrast, the Python function sorted takes an iterable object (e.g., a list or a view) as its first argument and returns a new sorted list. For example, the code

```
L = [3,5,2]
D = {'a':12, 'c':5, 'b':'dog'}
print(sorted(L))
print(L)
L.sort()
print(L)
print(sorted(D))
D.sort()
```

will print

```
[2, 3, 5]
[3, 5, 2]
[2, 3, 5]
['a', 'b', 'c']
AttributeError: 'dict' object has no attribute 'sort'
```

Notice that when the `sorted` function is applied to a dictionary, it returns a sorted list of the keys of the dictionary. In contrast, when the `sort` method is applied to a dictionary, it causes an exception to be raised since there is no method `dict.sort`.

Both the `list.sort` method and the `sorted` function can have two additional parameters. The `key` parameter plays the same role as `compare` in our implementation of merge sort: it supplies the comparison function to be used. The `reverse` parameter specifies whether the list is to be sorted in ascending or descending order relative to the comparison function. For example, the code

```
L = [[1,2,3], (3,2,1,0), 'abc']
print(sorted(L, key = len, reverse = True))
```

sorts the elements of L in reverse order of length and prints

```
[(3, 2, 1, 0), [1, 2, 3], 'abc']
```

Both the `list.sort` method and the `sorted` function provide **stable sorts**. This means that if two elements are equal with respect to the comparison (`len` in this example) used in the sort, their relative ordering in the original list (or other iterable object) is preserved in the final list. (Since no key can occur more than once in a `dict`, the question of whether `sorted` is stable when applied to a `dict` is moot.)

10.3 Hash Tables

If we put merge sort together with binary search, we have a nice way to search lists. We use merge sort to preprocess the list in O(n∗log(n)) time, and then we use binary search to test whether elements are in the list in O(log(n)) time. If we search the list k times, the overall time complexity is O(n∗log(n) + k∗log(n)).

This is good, but we can still ask, is logarithmic the best that we can do for search when we are willing to do some preprocessing?

When we introduced the type `dict` in Chapter 5, we said that dictionaries use a technique called hashing to do the lookup in time that is nearly independent of the size of the dictionary. The basic idea behind a **hash table** is simple. We convert the key to an integer, and then use that integer to index into a list, which can be done in constant time. In principle, values of any type can be easily converted to an integer. After all, we know that the internal representation of each object is a sequence of bits, and any sequence of bits can be viewed as representing an integer. For example, the internal representation of the string `'abc'` is the sequence of bits 0110000101100010011000011, which can be viewed as a representation of the decimal integer 6,382,179. Of course, if we want to use the internal representation of strings as indices into a list, the list is going to have to be pretty darn long.

What about situations where the keys are already integers? Imagine, for the moment, that we are implementing a dictionary all of whose keys are U.S. Social Security numbers, which are nine-digit integers. If we represented the dictionary by a list with 10^9 elements and used Social Security numbers to index into the list, we could do lookups in constant time. Of course, if the dictionary contained entries for only ten thousand (10^4) people, this would waste quite a lot of space.

Which gets us to the subject of hash functions. A **hash function** maps a large space of inputs (e.g., all natural numbers) to a smaller space of outputs (e.g., the natural numbers between 0 and 5000). Hash functions can be used to convert a large space of keys to a smaller space of integer indices.

Since the space of possible outputs is smaller than the space of possible inputs, a hash function is a **many-to-one mapping**, i.e., multiple different inputs may be mapped to the same output. When two inputs are mapped to the same output, it is called a **collision**—a topic we will return to shortly. A good hash function produces a **uniform distribution**; i.e., every output in the range is equally probable, which minimizes the probability of collisions.

Figure 10.7 uses a simple hash function (recall that i%j returns the remainder when the integer i is divided by the integer j) to implement a dictionary with integers as keys.

The basic idea is to represent an instance of class intDict by a list of **hash buckets**, where each bucket is a list of key/value pairs implemented as tuples. By making each bucket a list, we handle collisions by storing all of the values that hash to the same bucket in the list.

The hash table works as follows: The instance variable buckets is initialized to a list of numBuckets empty lists. To store or look up an entry with key dictKey, we use the hash function % to convert dictKey into an integer, and use that integer to index into buckets to find the hash bucket associated with dictKey. We then search that bucket (which is a list) linearly to see if there is an entry with the key dictKey. If we are doing a lookup and there is an entry with the key, we simply return the value stored with that key. If there is no entry with that key, we return None. If a value is to be stored, we first check if there is already an entry with that key in the hash bucket. If so, we replace the entry with a new tuple, otherwise we append a new entry to the bucket.

```python
class intDict(object):
    """A dictionary with integer keys"""

    def __init__(self, numBuckets):
        """Create an empty dictionary"""
        self.buckets = []
        self.numBuckets = numBuckets
        for i in range(numBuckets):
            self.buckets.append([])

    def addEntry(self, key, dictVal):
        """Assumes key an int. Adds an entry."""
        hashBucket = self.buckets[key%self.numBuckets]
        for i in range(len(hashBucket)):
            if hashBucket[i][0] == key:
                hashBucket[i] = (key, dictVal)
                return
        hashBucket.append((key, dictVal))

    def getValue(self, key):
        """Assumes key an int.
           Returns value associated with key"""
        hashBucket = self.buckets[key%self.numBuckets]
        for e in hashBucket:
            if e[0] == key:
                return e[1]
        return None

    def __str__(self):
        result = '{'
        for b in self.buckets:
            for e in b:
                result = result + str(e[0]) + ':' + str(e[1]) + ','
        return result[:-1] + '}' #result[:-1] omits the last comma
```

Figure 10.7 Implementing dictionaries using hashing

There are many other ways to handle collisions, some considerably more efficient than using lists. But this is probably the simplest mechanism, and it works fine if the hash table is large enough relative to the number of elements stored in it, and the hash function provides a good enough approximation to a uniform distribution.

Notice that the __str__ method produces a representation of a dictionary that is unrelated to the order in which elements were added to it, but is instead ordered by the values to which the keys happen to hash. This explains why we can't predict the order of the keys in an object of type dict.

The following code first constructs an intDict with seventeen buckets and twenty entries. The values of the entries are the integers 0 to 19. The keys are chosen at random, using random.choice, from integers in the range 0 to 10^5 - 1. (We discuss the random module in Chapters 14 and 15.) The code then prints the intDict using the __str__ method defined in the class. Finally, it prints the individual hash buckets by iterating over D.buckets. (This is a terrible violation of information hiding, but pedagogically useful.)

```
import random
D = intDict(17)
for i in range(20):
    #choose a random int in the range 0 to 10**5 - 1
    key = random.choice(range(10**5))
    D.addEntry(key, i)
print('The value of the intDict is:')
print(D)
print('\n', 'The buckets are:')
for hashBucket in D.buckets: #violates abstraction barrier
    print('  ', hashBucket)
```

When we ran this code it printed[65]

```
The value of the intDict is:
{99740:6,61898:8,15455:4,99913:18,276:19,63944:13,79618:17,51093:15,827
1:2,3715:14,74606:1,33432:3,58915:7,12302:12,56723:16,27519:11,64937:5,
85405:9,49756:10,17611:0}

 The buckets are:
   []
   [(99740, 6), (61898, 8)]
   [(15455, 4)]
   []
   [(99913, 18), (276, 19)]
   []
   []
   [(63944, 13), (79618, 17)]
   [(51093, 15)]
   [(8271, 2), (3715, 14)]
   [(74606, 1), (33432, 3), (58915, 7)]
   [(12302, 12), (56723, 16)]
   []
   [(27519, 11)]
   [(64937, 5), (85405, 9), (49756, 10)]
   []
   [(17611, 0)]
```

---

[65] Since the integers were chosen at random, you will probably get different results if you run it.

When we violate the abstraction barrier and peek at the representation of the intDict, we see that some of the hash buckets are empty. Others contain one, two, or three entries—depending upon the number of collisions that occurred.

What is the complexity of getValue? If there were no collisions it would be O(1), because each hash bucket would be of length 0 or 1. But, of course, there might be collisions. If everything hashed to the same bucket, it would be O(n) where n is the number of entries in the dictionary, because the code would perform a linear search on that hash bucket. By making the hash table large enough, we can reduce the number of collisions sufficiently to allow us to treat the complexity as O(1). That is, we can trade space for time. But what is the tradeoff? To answer this question, one needs to know a tiny bit of probability, so we defer the answer to Chapter 15.

11 PLOTTING AND MORE ABOUT CLASSES

Often text is the best way to communicate information, but sometimes there is a lot of truth to the Chinese proverb, 圖片的意義可以表達近萬字. Yet most programs rely on textual output to communicate with their users. Why? Because in many programming languages presenting visual data is too hard. Fortunately, it is simple to do in Python.

11.1 Plotting Using PyLab

PyLab is a Python standard library module that provides many of the facilities of MATLAB, "a high-level technical computing language and interactive environment for algorithm development, data visualization, data analysis, and numeric computation."[66] Later in the book we will look at some of the more advanced features of PyLab, but in this chapter we focus on some of its facilities for plotting data. Other plotting facilities are introduced in later chapters. A complete user's guide to the plotting capabilities of PyLab is at the Web site

> matplotlib.sourceforge.net/users/index.html

There are also a number of Web sites that provide excellent tutorials. We will not try to provide a user's guide or a complete tutorial here. Instead, in this chapter we will merely provide a few example plots and explain the code that generated them. Other examples appear in later chapters.

Let's start with a simple example that uses `pylab.plot` to produce two plots. Executing

```
import pylab

pylab.figure(1)                          #create figure 1
pylab.plot([1,2,3,4], [1,7,3,5])         #draw on figure 1
pylab.show()                             #show figure on screen
```

will cause a window to appear on your computer monitor. Its exact appearance may depend on your Python environment, but it will look similar to Figure 11.1 (which was produced using Anaconda). If you run this code with the default pa-

---

[66] www.mathworks.com/products/matlab/description1.html?s_cid=ML_b1008_desintro

rameter settings of most installations of PyLab, the line will probably not be as thick as the line in Figure 11.1. We have used nonstandard default values for line width and font sizes so that the figures will reproduce better in black and white. We discuss how this is done later in this section.

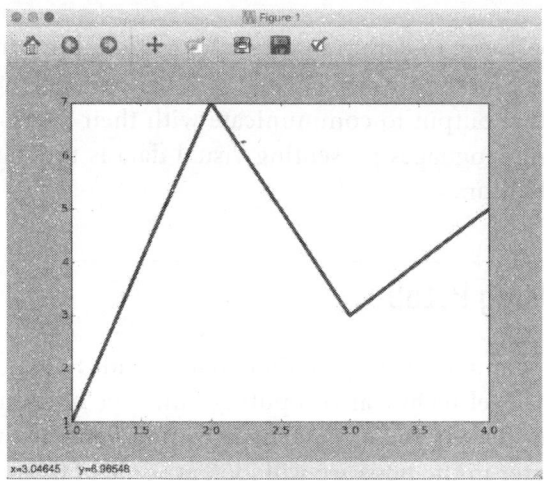

Figure 11.1 A simple plot

The bar at the top of the plot contains the name of the window, in this case "Figure 1."

The middle section of the window contains the plot generated by the invocation of pylab.plot. The two parameters of pylab.plot must be sequences of the same length. The first specifies the x-coordinates of the points to be plotted, and the second specifies the y-coordinates. Together, they provide a sequence of four <x, y> coordinate pairs, [(1,1), (2,7), (3,3), (4,5)]. These are plotted in order. As each point is plotted, a line is drawn connecting it to the previous point.

The final line of code, pylab.show(), causes the window to appear on the computer screen.[67] In some Python environments, if that line were not present, the figure would still have been produced, but it would not have been displayed. This is not as silly as it at first sounds, since one might well choose to write a figure directly to a file, as we will do later, rather than display it on the screen.

---

[67] In some Python environments, pylab.show() causes the process running Python to be suspended until the figure is closed (by clicking on the round red button at the upper left-hand corner of the window). This is unfortunate. The usual workaround is to ensure that pylab.show() is the last line of code to be executed.

CHAPTER 11. PLOTTING AND MORE ABOUT CLASSES

The bar at the top of the window contains a number of push buttons. The rightmost button pops up a window with options that can be used to adjust various aspects of the figure. The next button to the left is used to write the plot to a file.[68] The button to the left of that is used to adjust the appearance of the plot in the window. The next two buttons are used for zooming and panning. The two buttons that look like arrows are used to see previous views (like the forward and backward arrows of a Web browser). And the button on the extreme left is used to restore the figure to its original appearance after you are done playing with other buttons.

It is possible to produce multiple figures and to write them to files. These files can have any name you like, but they will all have the file extension .png. The file extension .png indicates that the file is in the Portable Networks Graphics format. This is a public domain standard for representing images.

The code

```
pylab.figure(1)                       #create figure 1
pylab.plot([1,2,3,4], [1,2,3,4])      #draw on figure 1
pylab.figure(2)                       #create figure 2
pylab.plot([1,4,2,3], [5,6,7,8])      #draw on figure 2
pylab.savefig('Figure-Addie')         #save figure 2
pylab.figure(1)                       #go back to working on figure 1
pylab.plot([5,6,10,3])                #draw again on figure 1
pylab.savefig('Figure-Jane')          #save figure 1
```

produces and saves to files named Figure-Jane.png and Figure-Addie.png the two plots in Figure 11.2.

Observe that the last call to pylab.plot is passed only one argument. This argument supplies the y values. The corresponding x values default to the sequence yielded by range(len([5, 6, 10, 3])), which is why they range from 0 to 3 in this case.

PyLab has a notion of "current figure." Executing pylab.figure(x) sets the current figure to the figure numbered x. Subsequently executed calls of plotting functions implicitly refer to that figure until another invocation of pylab.figure

---

[68] For those of you too young to know, the icon represents a "floppy disk." Floppy disks were first introduced by IBM in 1971. They were 8 inches in diameter and held all of 80,000 bytes. Unlike later floppy disks, they actually were floppy. The original IBM PC had a single 160Kbyte 5.5-inch floppy disk drive. For most of the 1970s and 1980s, floppy disks were the primary storage device for personal computers. The transition to rigid enclosures (as represented in the icon that launched this digression) started in the mid-1980s (with the Macintosh), which didn't stop people from continuing to call them floppy disks. By 1998 the world was consuming more than 2 billion floppy disks per year. Today, you'd be hard pressed of find a place to buy one. *Sic transit gloria.*

occurs. This explains why the figure written to the file Figure-Addie.png was the second figure created.

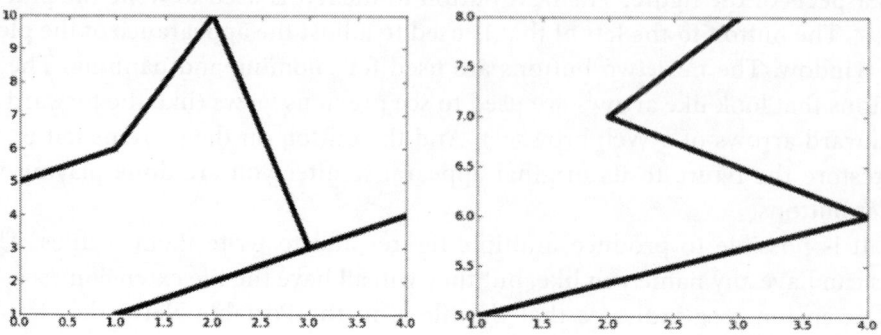

Figure 11.2 Contents of Figure-Jane.png (left) and Figure-Addie.png (right)

Let's look at another example. The code

```
principal = 10000 #initial investment
interestRate = 0.05
years = 20
values = []
for i in range(years + 1):
    values.append(principal)
    principal += principal*interestRate
pylab.plot(values)
```

produces the plot on the left in Figure 11.3.

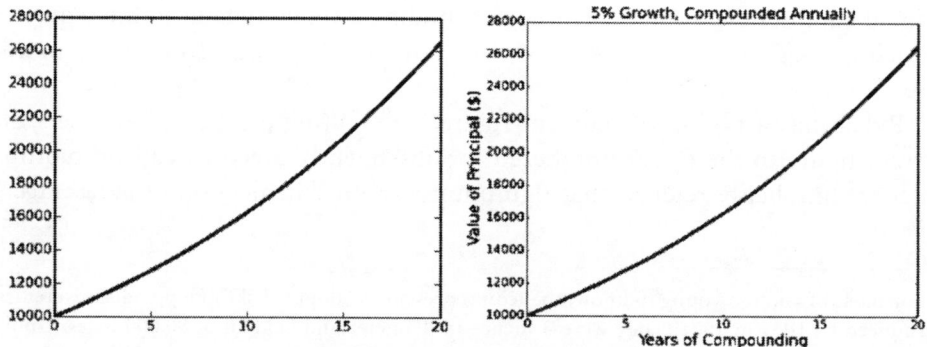

Figure 11.3 Plotting compound growth

If we look at the code, we can deduce that this is a plot showing the growth of an initial investment of $10,000 at an annually compounded interest rate of 5%. However, this cannot be easily inferred by looking only at the plot itself. That's a bad thing. All plots should have informative titles, and all axes should be labeled.

If we add to the end of our code the lines

```
pylab.title('5% Growth, Compounded Annually')
pylab.xlabel('Years of Compounding')
pylab.ylabel('Value of Principal ($)')
```

we get the plot on the right in Figure 11.3.

For every plotted curve, there is an optional argument that is a format string indicating the color and line type of the plot.[69] The letters and symbols of the format string are derived from those used in MATLAB, and are composed of a color indicator followed by an optional line-style indicator. The default format string is 'b-', which produces a solid blue line. To plot the the growth in principal with black circles, one would replace the call `pylab.plot(values)` by `pylab.plot(values, 'ko')`, which produces the plot in Figure 11.4. For a complete list of color and line-style indicators, see

`http://matplotlib.org/api/pyplot_api.html#matplotlib.pyplot.plot`

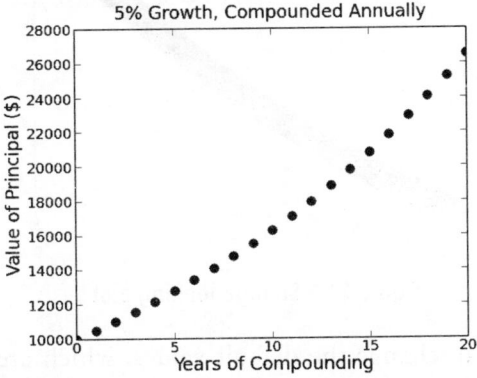

Figure 11.4 Another plot of compound growth

---

[69] In order to keep the price down, we chose to publish this book in black and white. That posed a dilemma: should we discuss how to use color in plots or not? We concluded that color is too important to ignore. However, we did use the color black far more often than we would have were we producing the book in color.

It is also possible to change the type size and line width used in plots. This can be done using keyword arguments in individual calls to functions. E.g., the code

```
principal = 10000 #initial investment
interestRate = 0.05
years = 20
values = []
for i in range(years + 1):
    values.append(principal)
    principal += principal*interestRate
pylab.plot(values, linewidth = 30)
pylab.title('5% Growth, Compounded Annually',
            fontsize = 'xx-large')
pylab.xlabel('Years of Compounding', fontsize = 'x-small')
pylab.ylabel('Value of Principal ($)')
```

produces the intentionally bizarre-looking plot in Figure 11.5.

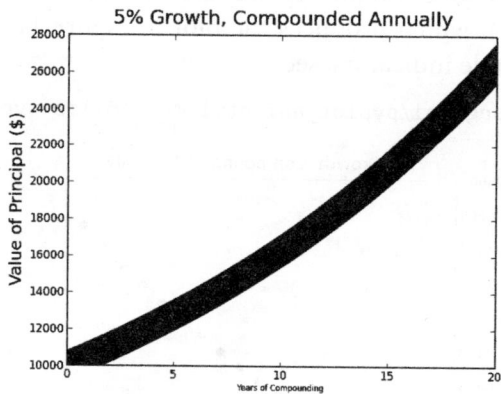

Figure 11.5 Strange-looking plot

It is also possible to change the default values, which are known as "rc settings." (The name "rc" is derived from the .rc file extension used for runtime configuration files in Unix.) These values are stored in a dictionary-like variable that can be accessed via the name pylab.rcParams. So, for example, you can set the default line width to 6 points[70] by executing the code

```
pylab.rcParams['lines.linewidth'] = 6.
```

---

[70] The point is a measure used in typography. It is equal to 1/72 of an inch, which is 0.3527mm.

CHAPTER 11. PLOTTING AND MORE ABOUT CLASSES

There are an enormous number `rcParams` settings. A complete list can be found at

`http://matplotlib.org/users/customizing.html`

If you don't want to worry about customizing individual parameters, there are pre-defined style sheets. A description of these can be found at

`http://matplotlib.org/users/style_sheets.html#style-sheets`

The values used in most of the remaining examples in this book were set with the code

```
#set line width
pylab.rcParams['lines.linewidth'] = 4
#set font size for titles
pylab.rcParams['axes.titlesize'] = 20
#set font size for labels on axes
pylab.rcParams['axes.labelsize'] = 20
#set size of numbers on x-axis
pylab.rcParams['xtick.labelsize'] = 16
#set size of numbers on y-axis
pylab.rcParams['ytick.labelsize'] = 16
#set size of ticks on x-axis
pylab.rcParams['xtick.major.size'] = 7
#set size of ticks on y-axis
pylab.rcParams['ytick.major.size'] = 7
#set size of markers, e.g., circles representing points
pylab.rcParams['lines.markersize'] = 10
#set number of times marker is shown when displaying legend
pylab.rcParams['legend.numpoints'] = 1
```

If you are viewing plots on a color display, you will have little reason to customize these settings. We customized the settings we used so that it would be easier to read the plots when we shrank them and converted them to black and white.

11.2 Plotting Mortgages, an Extended Example

In Chapter 8, we worked our way through a hierarchy of mortgages as way of illustrating the use of subclassing. We concluded that chapter by observing that "our program should be producing plots designed to show how the mortgage behaves over time." Figure 11.6 enhances class `Mortgage` by adding methods that make it convenient to produce such plots. (The function `findPayment`, which appears in Figure 8.9, is discussed in Section 8.4.)

```python
class Mortgage(object):
    """Abstract class for building different kinds of mortgages"""
    def __init__(self, loan, annRate, months):
        self.loan = loan
        self.rate = annRate/12.0
        self.months = months
        self.paid = [0.0]
        self.outstanding = [loan]
        self.payment = findPayment(loan, self.rate, months)
        self.legend = None #description of mortgage

    def makePayment(self):
        self.paid.append(self.payment)
        reduction = self.payment - self.outstanding[-1]*self.rate
        self.outstanding.append(self.outstanding[-1] - reduction)

    def getTotalPaid(self):
        return sum(self.paid)
    def __str__(self):
        return self.legend

    def plotPayments(self, style):
        pylab.plot(self.paid[1:], style, label = self.legend)

    def plotBalance(self, style):
        pylab.plot(self.outstanding, style, label = self.legend)

    def plotTotPd(self, style):
        totPd = [self.paid[0]]
        for i in range(1, len(self.paid)):
            totPd.append(totPd[-1] + self.paid[i])
        pylab.plot(totPd, style, label = self.legend)

    def plotNet(self, style):
        totPd = [self.paid[0]]
        for i in range(1, len(self.paid)):
            totPd.append(totPd[-1] + self.paid[i])
        equityAcquired = pylab.array([self.loan] * \
                         len(self.outstanding))
        equityAcquired = equityAcquired - \
                         pylab.array(self.outstanding)
        net = pylab.array(totPd) - equityAcquired
        pylab.plot(net, style, label = self.legend)
```

Figure 11.6 Class Mortgage with plotting methods

CHAPTER 11. PLOTTING AND MORE ABOUT CLASSES

The nontrivial methods in class Mortgage are plotTotPd and plotNet. The method plotTotPd simply plots the cumulative total of the payments made. The method plotNet plots an approximation to the total cost of the mortgage over time by plotting the cash expended minus the equity acquired by paying off part of the loan.[71]

The expression pylab.array(self.outstanding) in the function plotNet performs a type conversion. Thus far, we have been calling the plotting functions of PyLab with arguments of type list. Under the covers, PyLab has been converting these lists to a different type, array, which PyLab inherits from numpy.[72] The invocation pylab.array makes this explicit. There are a number of convenient ways to manipulate arrays that are not readily available for lists. In particular, expressions can be formed using arrays and arithmetic operators. There are a number of ways to create arrays in PyLab, but the most common way is to first create a list, and then convert it. Consider the code

```
a1 = pylab.array([1, 2, 4])
print('a1 =', a1)
a2 = a1*2
print('a2 =', a2)
print('a1 + 3 =', a1 + 3)
print('3 - a1 =', 3 - a1)
print('a1 - a2 =', a1 - a2)
print('a1*a2 =', a1*a2)
```

The expression a1*2 multiplies each element of a1 by the constant 2. The expression a1 + 3 adds the integer 3 to each element of a1. The expression a1 - a2 subtracts each element of a2 from the corresponding element of a1 (if the arrays had been of different length, an error would have occurred). The expression a1*a2 multiplies each element of a1 by the corresponding element of a2. When the above code is run it prints

```
a1 = [1 2 4]
a2 = [2 4 8]
a1 + 3 = [4 5 7]
3 - a1 = [ 2  1 -1]
a1 - a2 = [-1 -2 -4]
a1*a2 = [ 2  8 32]
```

---

[71] It is an approximation because it does not perform a net present value calculation to take into account the time value of cash.

[72] numpy is a Python module that provides tools for scientific computing. In addition to providing multi-dimensional arrays it provides a variety of linear algebra tools.

Figure 11.7 repeats the three subclasses of Mortgage from Figure 8.10. Each has a distinct __init__ method that overrides the __init__ method in Mortgage. The subclass TwoRate also overrides the makePayment method of Mortgage.

```
class Fixed(Mortgage):
    def __init__(self, loan, r, months):
        Mortgage.__init__(self, loan, r, months)
        self.legend = 'Fixed, ' + str(r*100) + '%'

class FixedWithPts(Mortgage):
    def __init__(self, loan, r, months, pts):
        Mortgage.__init__(self, loan, r, months)
        self.pts = pts
        self.paid = [loan*(pts/100.0)]
        self.legend = 'Fixed, ' + str(r*100) + '%, '\
                      + str(pts) + ' points'

class TwoRate(Mortgage):
    def __init__(self, loan, r, months, teaserRate, teaserMonths):
        Mortgage.__init__(self, loan, teaserRate, months)
        self.teaserMonths = teaserMonths
        self.teaserRate = teaserRate
        self.nextRate = r/12.0
        self.legend = str(teaserRate*100)\
                      + '% for ' + str(self.teaserMonths)\
                      + ' months, then ' + str(r*100) + '%'

    def makePayment(self):
        if len(self.paid) == self.teaserMonths + 1:
            self.rate = self.nextRate
            self.payment = findPayment(self.outstanding[-1],
                                       self.rate,
                                       self.months - self.teaserMonths)
        Mortgage.makePayment(self)
```

Figure 11.7 Subclasses of Mortgage

Figure 11.8 and Figure 11.9 contain functions that can be used to generate plots intended to provide insight about the different kinds of mortgages.

CHAPTER 11. PLOTTING AND MORE ABOUT CLASSES 179

The function compareMortgages, Figure 11.8, creates a list of different kinds of mortgages, and simulates making a series of payments on each, as it did in Figure 8.11. It then calls plotMortgages, Figure 11.9, to produce the plots.

```
def compareMortgages(amt, years, fixedRate, pts, ptsRate,
                    varRate1, varRate2, varMonths):
    totMonths = years*12
    fixed1 = Fixed(amt, fixedRate, totMonths)
    fixed2 = FixedWithPts(amt, ptsRate, totMonths, pts)
    twoRate = TwoRate(amt, varRate2, totMonths, varRate1, varMonths)
    morts = [fixed1, fixed2, twoRate]
    for m in range(totMonths):
        for mort in morts:
            mort.makePayment()
    plotMortgages(morts, amt)
```

Figure 11.8 Compare mortgages

The function plotMortgages in Figure 11.9 uses the plotting methods in Mortgage to produce plots containing information about each of three kinds of mortgages. The loop in plotMortgages uses the index i to select elements from the lists morts and styles in a way that ensures that different kinds of mortgages are represented in a consistent way across figures. For example, since the third element in morts is a variable-rate mortgage and the third element in styles is 'k:', the variable-rate mortgage is always plotted using a black dotted line. The local function labelPlot is used to generate appropriate titles and axis labels for each plot. The calls of pylab.figure ensure that titles and labels are associated with the appropriate plot.

The call

```
compareMortgages(amt=200000, years=30, fixedRate=0.07,
                pts = 3.25, ptsRate=0.05,
                varRate1=0.045, varRate2=0.095, varMonths=48)
```

produces plots (Figure 11.10 - Figure 11.12) that shed some light on the mortgages discussed in Section 8.4.

```
def plotMortgages(morts, amt):
    def labelPlot(figure, title, xLabel, yLabel):
        pylab.figure(figure)
        pylab.title(title)
        pylab.xlabel(xLabel)
        pylab.ylabel(yLabel)
        pylab.legend(loc = 'best')
    styles = ['k-', 'k-.', 'k:']
    #Give names to figure numbers
    payments, cost, balance, netCost = 0, 1, 2, 3
    for i in range(len(morts)):
        pylab.figure(payments)
        morts[i].plotPayments(styles[i])
        pylab.figure(cost)
        morts[i].plotTotPd(styles[i])
        pylab.figure(balance)
        morts[i].plotBalance(styles[i])
        pylab.figure(netCost)
        morts[i].plotNet(styles[i])
    labelPlot(payments, 'Monthly Payments of $' + str(amt) +
              ' Mortgages', 'Months', 'Monthly Payments')
    labelPlot(cost, 'Cash Outlay of $' + str(amt) +
              ' Mortgages', 'Months', 'Total Payments')
    labelPlot(balance, 'Balance Remaining of $' + str(amt) +
              ' Mortgages', 'Months', 'Remaining Loan Balance of $')
    labelPlot(netCost, 'Net Cost of $' + str(amt) + ' Mortgages',
              'Months', 'Payments - Equity $')
```

Figure 11.9 Generate mortgage plots

The plot in Figure 11.10, which was produced by invocations of plotPayments, simply plots each payment of each mortgage against time. The box containing the key appears where it does because of the value supplied to the keyword argument loc used in the call to pylab.legend. When loc is bound to 'best' the location is chosen automatically. This plot makes it clear how the monthly payments vary (or don't) over time, but doesn't shed much light on the relative costs of each kind of mortgage.

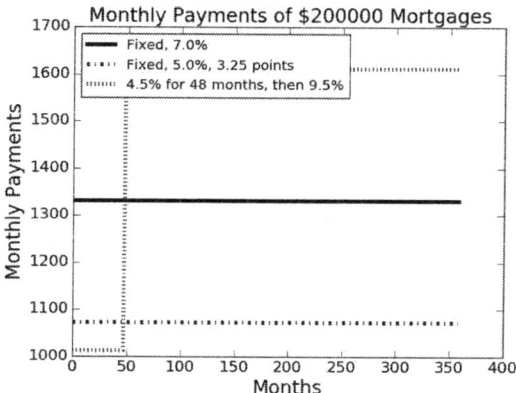

Figure 11.10 Monthly payments of different kinds of mortgages

The plots in Figure 11.11 were produced by invocations of plotTotPd. They shed some light on the cost of each kind of mortgage by plotting the cumulative costs that have been incurred at the start of each month. The entire plot is on the left, and an enlargement of the left part of the plot is on the right.

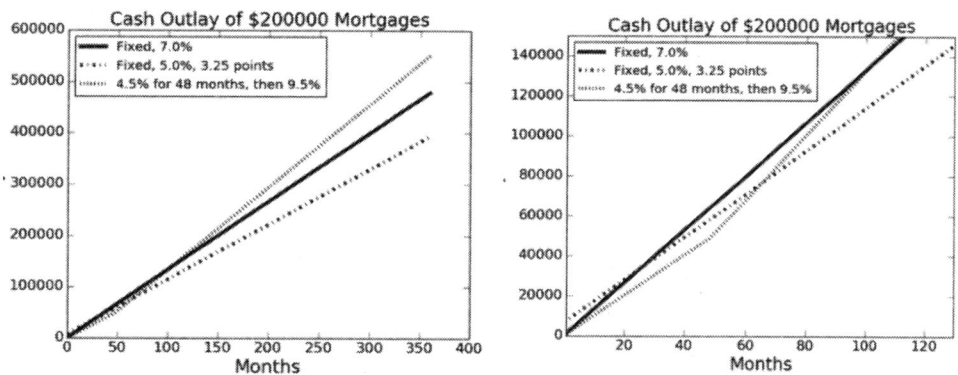

Figure 11.11 Cost over time of different kinds of mortgages

The plots in Figure 11.12 show the remaining debt (on the left) and the total net cost of having the mortgage (on the right).

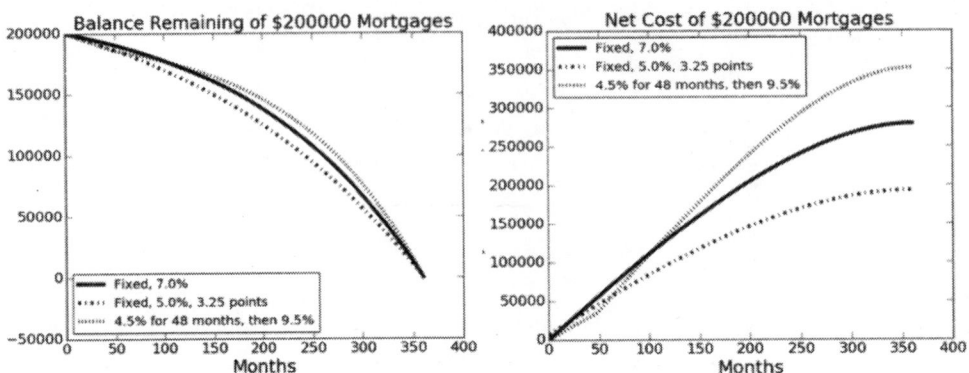

Figure 11.12 Balance remaining and net cost for different kinds of mortgages

12 KNAPSACK AND GRAPH OPTIMIZATION PROBLEMS

The notion of an optimization problem provides a structured way to think about solving lots of computational problems. Whenever you set about solving a problem that involves finding the biggest, the smallest, the most, the fewest, the fastest, the least expensive, etc., there is a good chance that you can map the problem onto a classic optimization problem for which there is a known computational solution.

In general, an **optimization problem** has two parts:

- An **objective function** that is to be maximized or minimized. For example, the airfare between Boston and Istanbul.
- A **set of constraints** (possibly empty) that must be honored. For example, an upper bound on the travel time.

In this chapter, we introduce the notion of an optimization problem and give a few examples. We also provide some simple algorithms that solve them. In Chapter 13, we discuss an efficient way of solving an important class of optimization problems.

The main things to take away from this chapter are:

- Many problems of real importance can be formulated in a simple way that leads naturally to a computational solution.
- Reducing a seemingly new problem to an instance of a well-known problem allows one to use preexisting solutions.
- Knapsack problems and graph problems are classes of problems to which other problems can often be reduced.
- Exhaustive enumeration algorithms provide a simple, but often computationally intractable, way to search for optimal solutions.
- A greedy algorithm is often a practical approach to finding a pretty good, but not always optimal, solution to an optimization problem.

As usual we will supplement the material on computational thinking with a few bits of Python and some tips about programming.

12.1 Knapsack Problems

It's not easy being a burglar. In addition to the obvious problems (making sure that a home is empty, picking locks, circumventing alarms, dealing with ethical quandaries, etc.), a burglar has to decide what to steal. The problem is that most homes contain more things of value than the average burglar can carry away. What's a poor burglar to do? He needs to find the set of things that provides the most value without exceeding his carrying capacity.

Suppose for example, a burglar who has a knapsack[73] that can hold at most 20 pounds of loot breaks into a house and finds the items in Figure 12.1. Clearly, he will not be able to fit it all in his knapsack, so he needs to decide what to take and what to leave behind.

	Value	Weight	Value/Weight
Clock	175	10	17.5
Painting	90	9	10
Radio	20	4	5
Vase	50	2	25
Book	10	1	10
Computer	200	20	10

Figure 12.1 Table of items

12.1.1 Greedy Algorithms

The simplest way to find an approximate solution to this problem is to use a **greedy algorithm**. The thief would choose the best item first, then the next best, and continue until he reached his limit. Of course, before doing this, the thief would have to decide what "best" should mean. Is the best item the most valuable, the least heavy, or maybe the item with the highest value-to-weight ratio? If he chose highest value, he would leave with just the computer, which he could fence for $200. If he chose lowest weight, he would take, in order, the book, the vase, the radio, and the painting—which would be worth a total of $170. Finally, if he decided that best meant highest value-to-weight ratio, he would start by taking the vase and the clock. That would leave three items with a value-to-weight ratio of 10, but of those only the book would still fit in the knapsack. After taking

---

[73] For those of you too young to remember, a "knapsack" is a simple bag that people used to carry on their back—long before "backpacks" became fashionable. If you happen to have been in scouting you might remember the words of the "Happy Wanderer," "I love to go a-wandering, Along the mountain track, And as I go, I love to sing, My knapsack on my back."

CHAPTER 12. KNAPSACK AND GRAPH OPTIMIZATION PROBLEMS

the book, he would take the remaining item that still fit, the radio. The total value of his loot would be $255.

Though greedy-by-density (value-to-weight ratio) happens to yield the best result for this data set, there is no guarantee that a greedy-by-density algorithm always finds a better solution than greedy by weight or value. More generally, there is no guarantee that any solution to this kind of knapsack problem that is found by a greedy algorithm will be optimal.[74] We will discuss this issue in more detail a bit later.

The code in the next three figures implements all three of these greedy algorithms. In Figure 12.2 we define class Item. Each Item has a name, value, and weight attribute. We also define three functions that can be bound to the argument keyFunction of our implementation of greedy, see Figure 12.3.

```
class Item(object):
    def __init__(self, n, v, w):
        self.name = n
        self.value = v
        self.weight = w
    def getName(self):
        return self.name
    def getValue(self):
        return self.value
    def getWeight(self):
        return self.weight
    def __str__(self):
        result = '<' + self.name + ', ' + str(self.value)\
                 + ', ' + str(self.weight) + '>'
        return result
def value(item):
    return item.getValue()

def weightInverse(item):
    return 1.0/item.getWeight()

def density(item):
    return item.getValue()/item.getWeight()
```

Figure 12.2 Class Item

---

[74] There is probably some deep moral lesson to be extracted from this fact, and it is probably not "greed is good."

```python
def greedy(items, maxWeight, keyFunction):
    """Assumes Items a list, maxWeight >= 0,
       keyFunction maps elements of Items to numbers"""
    itemsCopy = sorted(items, key=keyFunction, reverse = True)
    result = []
    totalValue, totalWeight = 0.0, 0.0
    for i in range(len(itemsCopy)):
        if (totalWeight + itemsCopy[i].getWeight()) <= maxWeight:
            result.append(itemsCopy[i])
            totalWeight += itemsCopy[i].getWeight()
            totalValue += itemsCopy[i].getValue()
    return (result, totalValue)
```

Figure 12.3 Implementation of a greedy algorithm

By introducing the parameter keyFunction, we make greedy independent of the order in which the elements of the list are to be considered. All that is required is that keyFunction defines an ordering on the elements in items. We then use this ordering to produce a sorted list containing the same elements as items. We use the built-in Python function sorted to do this. (We use sorted rather than sort because we want to generate a new list rather than mutate the list passed to the function.) We use the reverse parameter to indicate that we want the list sorted from largest (with respect to keyFunction) to smallest.

What is the algorithmic efficiency of greedy? There are two things to consider: the time complexity of the built-in function sorted, and the number of times through the for loop in the body of greedy. The number of iterations of the loop is bounded by the number of elements in items, i.e., it is O(n), where n is the length of items. However, the worst-case time for Python's built-in sorting function is roughly O(n log n), where n is the length of the list to be sorted.[75] Therefore the running time of greedy is O(n log n).

The code in Figure 12.4 builds a list of items and then tests the function greedy using different ways of ordering the list.

---

[75] As we discussed in Chapter 10, the time complexity of the sorting algorithm, timsort, used in most Python implementations is O(n log n).

```
def buildItems():
    names = ['clock','painting','radio','vase','book','computer']
    values = [175,90,20,50,10,200]
    weights = [10,9,4,2,1,20]
    Items = []
    for i in range(len(values)):
        Items.append(Item(names[i], values[i], weights[i]))
    return Items

def testGreedy(items, maxWeight, keyFunction):
    taken, val = greedy(items, maxWeight, keyFunction)
    print('Total value of items taken is', val)
    for item in taken:
        print('   ', item)

def testGreedys(maxWeight = 20):
    items = buildItems()
    print('Use greedy by value to fill knapsack of size', maxWeight)
    testGreedy(items, maxWeight, value)
    print('\nUse greedy by weight to fill knapsack of size',
          maxWeight)
    testGreedy(items, maxWeight, weightInverse)
    print('\nUse greedy by density to fill knapsack of size',
          maxWeight)
    testGreedy(items, maxWeight, density)
```

Figure 12.4 Using a greedy algorithm to choose items

When testGreedys() is executed it prints

```
Use greedy by value to fill knapsack of size 20
Total value of items taken is 200
    <computer, 200, 20>

Use greedy by weight to fill knapsack of size 20
Total value of items taken is 170
    <book, 10, 1>
    <vase, 50, 2>
    <radio, 20, 4>
    <painting, 90, 9>

Use greedy by density to fill knapsack of size 20
Total value of items taken is 255
    <vase, 50, 2>
    <clock, 175, 10>
    <book, 10, 1>
    <radio, 20, 4>
```

12.1.2 An Optimal Solution to the 0/1 Knapsack Problem

Suppose we decide that an approximation is not good enough, i.e., we want the best possible solution to this problem. Such a solution is called **optimal**, not surprising since we are solving an optimization problem. As it happens, the problem confronting our burglar is an instance of a classic optimization problem, called the **0/1 knapsack problem**. The 0/1 knapsack problem can be formalized as follows:

- Each item is represented by a pair, <*value, weight*>.
- The knapsack can accommodate items with a total weight of no more than w.
- A vector, I, of length n, represents the set of available items. Each element of the vector is an item.
- A vector, V, of length n, is used to indicate whether or not each item is taken by the burglar. If V[i] = 1, item I[i] is taken. If V[i] = 0, item I[i] is not taken.
- Find a V that maximizes

$$\sum_{i=0}^{n-1} V[i] * I[i].value$$

subject to the constraint that

$$\sum_{i=0}^{n-1} V[i] * I[i].weight \leq w$$

Let's see what happens if we try to implement this formulation of the problem in a straightforward way:

1. Enumerate all possible combinations of items. That is to say, generate all subsets of the set of items.[76] This is called the power set, and was discussed in Chapter 9.
2. Remove all of the combinations whose weight exceeds the allowed weight.
3. From the remaining combinations choose any one whose value is the largest.

This approach will certainly find an optimal answer. However, if the original set of items is large, it will take a very long time to run, because, as we saw in Section 9.3.6, the number of subsets grows exceedingly quickly with the number of items.

Figure 12.5 contains a straightforward implementation of this brute-force approach to solving the 0/1 knapsack problem. It uses the classes and functions defined in Figure 12.2 and Figure 12.4, and the function genPowerset defined in Figure 9.6.

---

[76] Recall that every set is a subset of itself and the empty set is a subset of every set.

```
def chooseBest(pset, maxWeight, getVal, getWeight):
    bestVal = 0.0
    bestSet = None
    for items in pset:
        itemsVal = 0.0
        itemsWeight = 0.0
        for item in items:
            itemsVal += getVal(item)
            itemsWeight += getWeight(item)
        if itemsWeight <= maxWeight and itemsVal > bestVal:
            bestVal = itemsVal
            bestSet = items
    return (bestSet, bestVal)

def testBest(maxWeight = 20):
    items = buildItems()
    pset = genPowerset(items)
    taken, val = chooseBest(pset, maxWeight, Item.getValue,
                            Item.getWeight)
    print('Total value of items taken is', val)
    for item in taken:
        print(item)
```

Figure 12.5 Brute-force optimal solution to the 0/1 knapsack problem

The complexity of this implementation is $O(n*2^n)$, where n is the length of items. The function genPowerset returns a list of lists of Items. This list is of length 2^n, and the longest list in it is of length n. Therefore the outer loop in chooseBest will be executed $O(2^n)$ times, and the number of times the inner loop will be executed is bounded by n.

Many small optimizations can be applied to speed this program up. For example, genPowerset could have had the header

```
def genPowerset(items, constraint, getVal, getWeight)
```

and returned only those combinations that meet the weight constraint. Alternatively, chooseBest could exit the inner loop as soon as the weight constraint is exceeded. While these kinds of optimizations are often worth doing, they don't address the fundamental issue. The complexity of chooseBest will still be $O(n*2^n)$, where n is the length of items, and chooseBest will therefore still take a very long time to run when items is large.

In a theoretical sense, the problem is hopeless. The 0/1 knapsack problem is inherently exponential in the number of items. In a practical sense, however, the problem is far from hopeless, as we will discuss in Section 13.2.

When testBest is run, it prints

```
Total value of items taken is 275.0
<clock, 175, 10>
<painting, 90, 9>
<book, 10, 1>
```

Notice that this solution is better than any of the solutions found by the greedy algorithms. The essence of a greedy algorithm is making the best (as defined by some metric) local choice at each step. It makes a choice that is **locally optimal**. However, as this example illustrates, a series of locally optimal decisions does not always lead to a solution that is **globally optimal**.

Despite the fact that they do not always find the best solution, greedy algorithms are often used in practice. They are usually easier to implement and more efficient to run than algorithms guaranteed to find optimal solutions. As Ivan Boesky once said, "I think greed is healthy. You can be greedy and still feel good about yourself." [77]

There is a variant of the knapsack problem, called the **fractional** (or **continuous**) **knapsack problem**, for which a greedy algorithm is guaranteed to find an optimal solution. Since the items are infinitely divisible, it always makes sense to take as much as possible of the item with the highest remaining value-to-weight ratio. Suppose, for example, that our burglar found only three things of value in the house: a sack of gold dust, a sack of silver dust, and a sack of raisins. In this case, a greedy-by-density algorithm will always find the optimal solution.

12.2 Graph Optimization Problems

Let's think about another kind of optimization problem. Suppose you had a list of the prices of all of the airline flights between each pair of cities in the United States. Suppose also that for all cities, A, B, and C, the cost of flying from A to C by way of B was the cost of flying from A to B plus the cost of flying from B to C. A few questions you might like to ask are:

---

[77] He said this, to enthusiastic applause, in a 1986 commencement address at the University of California at Berkeley Business School. A few months later he was indicted for insider trading, a charge that led to two years in prison and a $100,000,000 fine.

CHAPTER 12. KNAPSACK AND GRAPH OPTIMIZATION PROBLEMS

- What is the smallest number of stops between some pair of cities?
- What is the least expensive airfare between some pair of cities?
- What is the least expensive airfare between some pair of cities involving no more than two stops?
- What is the least expensive way to visit some collection of cities?

All of these problems (and many others) can be easily formalized as graph problems.

A **graph**[78] is a set of objects called **nodes** (or **vertices**) connected by a set of **edges** (or **arcs**). If the edges are unidirectional the graph is called a **directed graph** or **digraph**. In a directed graph, if there is an edge from $n1$ to $n2$, we refer to $n1$ as the **source** or **parent node** and $n2$ as the **destination** or **child node**.

Graphs are typically used to represent situations in which there are interesting relations among the parts. The first documented use of graphs in mathematics was in 1735 when the Swiss mathematician Leonhard Euler used what has come to be known as **graph theory** to formulate and solve the **Königsberg bridges problem**.

Königsberg, then the capital of East Prussia, was built at the intersection of two rivers that contained a number of islands. The islands were connected to each other and to the mainland by seven bridges, as shown on the map on the left side of Figure 12.6. For some reason, the residents of the city were obsessed with the question of whether it was possible to take a walk that crossed each bridge exactly once.

Euler's great insight was that the problem could be vastly simplified by viewing each separate landmass as a point (think "node") and each bridge as a line (think "edge") connecting two of these points. The map of the town could then be represented by the graph to the right of the map in Figure 12.6. Euler then reasoned that if a walk were to traverse each edge exactly once, it must be the case that each node in the middle of the walk (i.e., any island that is both entered and exited during the walk) must be connected by an even number of edges. Since none of the nodes in this graph has an even number of edges, Euler concluded that it is impossible to traverse each bridge exactly once.

---

[78] Computer scientists and mathematicians use the word "graph" in the sense used in this book. They typically use the word "plot" or "chart" to denote pictorial representations of information.

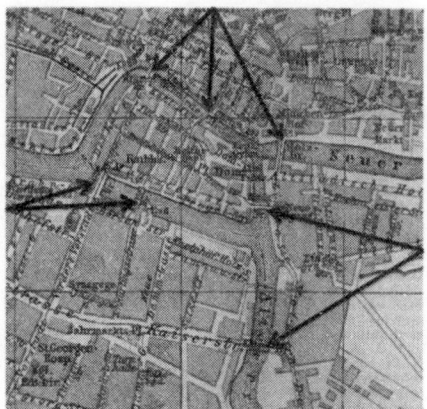 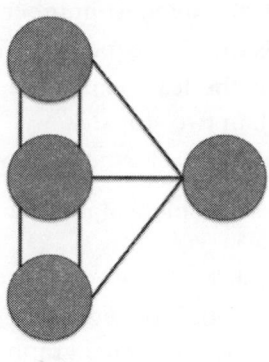

Figure 12.6 The bridges of Königsberg (left) and Euler's simplified map (right)

Of greater interest than the Königsberg bridges problem, or even Euler's theorem (which generalizes his solution to the Königsberg bridges problem), is the whole idea of using graph theory to help understand problems.

For example, only one small extension to the kind of graph used by Euler is needed to model a country's highway system. If a weight is associated with each edge in a graph (or digraph) it is called a **weighted graph**. Using weighted graphs, the highway system can be represented as a graph in which cities are represented by nodes and the highways connecting them as edges, where each edge is labeled with the distance between the two nodes. More generally, one can represent any road map (including those with one-way streets) by a weighted digraph.

Similarly, the structure of the World Wide Web can be represented as a digraph in which the nodes are Web pages and there is an edge from node A to node B if and only if there is a link to page B on page A. Traffic patterns could be modeled by adding a weight to each edge indicating how often is it used.

There are also many less obvious uses of graphs. Biologists use graphs to model things ranging from the way proteins interact with each other to gene expression networks. Physicists use graphs to describe phase transitions. Epidemiologists use graphs to model disease trajectories. And so on.

Figure 12.7 contains classes implementing abstract types corresponding to nodes, weighted edges, and edges.

CHAPTER 12. KNAPSACK AND GRAPH OPTIMIZATION PROBLEMS

```
class Node(object):
    def __init__(self, name):
        """Assumes name is a string"""
        self.name = name
    def getName(self):
        return self.name
    def __str__(self):
        return self.name

class Edge(object):
    def __init__(self, src, dest):
        """Assumes src and dest are nodes"""
        self.src = src
        self.dest = dest
    def getSource(self):
        return self.src
    def getDestination(self):
        return self.dest
    def __str__(self):
        return self.src.getName() + '->' + self.dest.getName()

class WeightedEdge(Edge):
    def __init__(self, src, dest, weight = 1.0):
        """Assumes src and dest are nodes, weight a number"""
        self.src = src
        self.dest = dest
        self.weight = weight
    def getWeight(self):
        return self.weight
    def __str__(self):
        return self.src.getName() + '->(' + str(self.weight) + ')'\
               + self.dest.getName()
```

Figure 12.7 Nodes and edges

Having a class for nodes may seem like overkill. After all, none of the methods in class Node perform any interesting computation. We introduced the class merely to give us the flexibility of deciding, perhaps at some later point, to introduce a subclass of Node with additional properties.

Figure 12.8 contains implementations of the classes Digraph and Graph.

```python
class Digraph(object):
    #nodes is a list of the nodes in the graph
    #edges is a dict mapping each node to a list of its children
    def __init__(self):
        self.nodes = []
        self.edges = {}
    def addNode(self, node):
        if node in self.nodes:
            raise ValueError('Duplicate node')
        else:
            self.nodes.append(node)
            self.edges[node] = []
    def addEdge(self, edge):
        src = edge.getSource()
        dest = edge.getDestination()
        if not (src in self.nodes and dest in self.nodes):
            raise ValueError('Node not in graph')
        self.edges[src].append(dest)
    def childrenOf(self, node):
        return self.edges[node]
    def hasNode(self, node):
        return node in self.nodes
    def __str__(self):
        result = ''
        for src in self.nodes:
            for dest in self.edges[src]:
                result = result + src.getName() + '->'\
                         + dest.getName() + '\n'
        return result[:-1] #omit final newline

class Graph(Digraph):
    def addEdge(self, edge):
        Digraph.addEdge(self, edge)
        rev = Edge(edge.getDestination(), edge.getSource())
        Digraph.addEdge(self, rev)
```

Figure 12.8 Classes Graph and Digraph

One important decision is the choice of data structure used to represent a Digraph. One common representation is an n × n **adjacency matrix**, where n is the number of nodes in the graph. Each cell of the matrix contains information (e.g., weights) about the edges connecting the pair of nodes <i, j>. If the edges are unweighted, each entry is True if and only if there is an edge from i to j.

Another common representation is an **adjacency list**, which we use here. Class Digraph has two instance variables. The variable nodes is a Python list containing the names of the nodes in the `Digraph`. The connectivity of the nodes is represented using an adjacency list implemented as a dictionary. The variable `edges` is a dictionary that maps each `Node` in the `Digraph` to a list of the children of that `Node`.

Class `Graph` is a subclass of `Digraph`. It inherits all of the methods of `Digraph` except `addEdge`, which it overrides. (This is not the most space-efficient way to implement `Graph`, since it stores each edge twice, once for each direction in the `Digraph`. But it has the virtue of simplicity.)

You might want to stop for a minute and think about why `Graph` is a subclass of `Digraph`, rather than the other way around. In many of the examples of subclassing we have looked at, the subclass adds attributes to the superclass. For example, class `WeightedEdge` added a `weight` attribute to class `Edge`.

Here, `Digraph` and `Graph` have the same attributes. The only difference is the implementation of the `addEdge` method. Either could have been easily implemented by inheriting methods from the other, but the choice of which to make the superclass was not arbitrary. In Chapter 8, we stressed the importance of obeying the substitution principle: If client code works correctly using an instance of the supertype, it should also work correctly when an instance of the subtype is substituted for the instance of the supertype.

And indeed if client code works correctly using an instance of `Digraph`, it will work correctly if an instance of `Graph` is substituted for the instance of `Digraph`. The converse is not true. There are many algorithms that work on graphs (by exploiting the symmetry of edges) that do not work on directed graphs.

12.2.1 Some Classic Graph-Theoretic Problems

One of the nice things about formulating a problem using graph theory is that there are well-known algorithms for solving many optimization problems on graphs. Some of the best-known graph optimization problems are:

- **Shortest path**. For some pair of nodes, $n1$ and $n2$, find the shortest sequence of edges $<s_n, d_n>$ (source node and destination node), such that
    - The source node in the first edge is $n1$
    - The destination node of the last edge is $n2$
    - For all edges $e1$ and $e2$ in the sequence, if $e2$ follows $e1$ in the sequence, the source node of $e2$ is the destination node of $e1$.
- **Shortest weighted path**. This is like the shortest path, except instead of choosing the shortest sequence of edges that connects two nodes, we define some function on the weights of the edges in the sequence (e.g., their sum) and min-

imize that value. This is the kind of problem solved by Google Maps when asked to compute driving directions between two points.
- **Maximum clique.** A **clique** is a set of nodes such that there is an edge between each pair of nodes in the set.[79] A maximum clique is a clique of the largest size in a graph.
- **Min cut.** Given two sets of nodes in a graph, a **cut** is a set of edges whose removal eliminates all paths from each node in one set to each node in the other. The minimum cut is the smallest set of edges whose removal accomplishes this.

12.2.2 Shortest Path: Depth-First Search and Breadth-First Search

Social networks are made up of individuals and relationships between individuals. These are typically modeled as graphs in which the individuals are nodes and the edges relationships. If the relationships are symmetric, the edges are undirected; if the relationships are asymmetric the edges are directed. Some social networks model multiple kinds of relationships, in which case labels on the edges indicate the kind of relationship.

In 1990 the playwright John Guare wrote *Six Degrees of Separation*. The dubious premise underlying the play is that "everybody on this planet is separated by only six other people." By this he meant that if one built a social network including every person on the earth using the relation "knows," the shortest path between any two individuals would pass through at most six other nodes.

A less hypothetical question is the distance using the "friend" relation between pairs of people on Facebook. For example, you might wonder if you have a friend who has a friend who has a friend who is a friend of Mick Jagger. Let's think about designing a program to answer such questions.

The friend relation (at least on Facebook) is symmetric, e.g., if Stephanie is a friend of Andrea, Andrea is a friend of Stephanie. We will, therefore, implement the social network using type Graph. We can then define the problem of finding the shortest connection between you and Mick Jagger as:
- Let *G* be the graph representing the friend relation.
- For *G*, find the shortest sequence of nodes, [You,...,Mick Jagger], such that
- If n_i and n_{i+1} are consecutive nodes in path, there is an edge in G connecting n_i and n_{i+1}.

---

[79] This notion is quite similar to the notion of a social clique, i.e., a group of people who feel closely connected to each other and are inclined to exclude those not in the clique. See, for example, the movie *Heathers*.

Figure 12.9 contains a recursive function that finds the shortest path between two nodes, start and end, in a `Digraph`. Since `Graph` is a subclass of `Digraph`, it will work for our Facebook problem.

```
def printPath(path):
    """Assumes path is a list of nodes"""
    result = ''
    for i in range(len(path)):
        result = result + str(path[i])
        if i != len(path) - 1:
            result = result + '->'
    return result

def DFS(graph, start, end, path, shortest, toPrint = False):
    """Assumes graph is a Digraph; start and end are nodes;
          path and shortest are lists of nodes
       Returns a shortest path from start to end in graph"""
    path = path + [start]
    if toPrint:
        print('Current DFS path:', printPath(path))
    if start == end:
        return path
    for node in graph.childrenOf(start):
        if node not in path: #avoid cycles
            if shortest == None or len(path) < len(shortest):
                newPath = DFS(graph, node, end, path, shortest,
                              toPrint)
                if newPath != None:
                    shortest = newPath
    return shortest

def shortestPath(graph, start, end, toPrint = False):
    """Assumes graph is a Digraph; start and end are nodes
       Returns a shortest path from start to end in graph"""
    return DFS(graph, start, end, [], None, toPrint)
```

Figure 12.9 Depth-first-search shortest-path algorithm

The algorithm implemented by DFS is an example of a recursive **depth-first-search (DFS)** algorithm. In general, a depth-first-search algorithm begins by choosing one child of the start node. It then chooses one child of that node and so on, going deeper and deeper until it either reaches the goal node or a node with no children. The search then **backtracks**, returning to the most recent node with children that it has not yet visited. When all paths have been explored, it chooses the shortest path (assuming that there is one) from the start to the goal.

The code is a bit more complicated than the algorithm we just described because it has to deal with the possibility of the graph containing cycles. It also avoids exploring paths longer than the shortest path that it has already found.

- The function shortestPath calls DFS with path == [] (to indicate that the current path being explored is empty) and shortest == None (to indicate that no path from start to end has yet been found).
- DFS begins by choosing one child of start. It then chooses one child of that node and so on, until either it reaches the node end or a node with no unvisited children.
    - The check if node not in path prevents the program from getting caught in a cycle.
    - The check if shortest == None or len(path) < len(shortest) is used to decide if it is possible that continuing to search this path might yield a shorter path than the best path found so far.
    - If so, DFS is called recursively. If it finds a path to end that is no longer than the best found so far, shortest is updated.
    - When the last node on path has no children left to visit, the program backtracks to the previously visited node and visits the next child of that node.
- The function returns when all possibly shortest paths from start to end have been explored.

Figure 12.10 contains some code that runs the code in Figure 12.9. The function testSP in Figure 12.10 first builds a directed graph like the one pictured in the figure, and then searches for a shortest path between node 0 and node 5.

When executed, testSP produces the output

```
Current DFS path: 0
Current DFS path: 0->1
Current DFS path: 0->1->2
Current DFS path: 0->1->2->3
Current DFS path: 0->1->2->3->4
Current DFS path: 0->1->2->3->5
Current DFS path: 0->1->2->4
Current DFS path: 0->2
Current DFS path: 0->2->3
Current DFS path: 0->2->3->4
Current DFS path: 0->2->3->5
Current DFS path: 0->2->3->1
Current DFS path: 0->2->4
Shortest path is 0->2->3->5
```

CHAPTER 12. KNAPSACK AND GRAPH OPTIMIZATION PROBLEMS

```
def testSP():
    nodes = []
    for name in range(6): #Create 6 nodes
        nodes.append(Node(str(name)))
    g = Digraph()
    for n in nodes:
        g.addNode(n)
    g.addEdge(Edge(nodes[0],nodes[1]))
    g.addEdge(Edge(nodes[1],nodes[2]))
    g.addEdge(Edge(nodes[2],nodes[3]))
    g.addEdge(Edge(nodes[2],nodes[4]))
    g.addEdge(Edge(nodes[3],nodes[4]))
    g.addEdge(Edge(nodes[3],nodes[5]))
    g.addEdge(Edge(nodes[0],nodes[2]))
    g.addEdge(Edge(nodes[1],nodes[0]))
    g.addEdge(Edge(nodes[3],nodes[1]))
    g.addEdge(Edge(nodes[4],nodes[0]))
    sp = shortestPath(g, nodes[0], nodes[5], toPrint = True)
    print('Shortest path is', printPath(sp))
```

Figure 12.10 Test depth-first-search code

Notice that after exploring the path 0->1->2->3->4, it backs up to node 3 and explores the path 0->1->2->3->5. After saving that as the shortest successful path so far, it backs up to node 2 and explores the path 0->1->2->4. When it reaches the end of that path (node 4), it backs up all the way to node 0 and investigates the path starting with the edge from 0 to 2. And so on.

The DFS algorithm implemented in Figure 12.9 finds the path with the minimum number of edges. If the edges have weights, it will not necessarily find the path that minimizes the sum of the weights of the edges. However, it is easily modified to do so.

Of course, there are other ways to traverse a graph than depth-first. Another common approach is **breadth-first search (BFS)**. In a breadth-first traversal one first visits all children of the start node. If none of those is the end node, one visits all children of each of those nodes. And so on. Unlike depth-first search, which is usually implemented recursively, breadth-first search is usually implemented iteratively. BFS explores many paths simultaneously, adding one node to each path on each iteration. Since it generates the paths in ascending order of length, the first path found with the goal as its last node is guaranteed to have a minimum number of edges.

Figure 12.11 contains code that uses a breadth-first search to find the shortest path in a directed graph. The variable pathQueue is used to store all of the paths currently being explored. Each iteration starts by removing a path from pathQueue and assigning that path to tmpPath. If the last node in tmpPath is end, tmpPath is a shortest path and is returned. Otherwise, a set of new paths is created, each of which extends tmpPath by adding one of its children. Each of these new paths is then added to pathQueue.

```
def BFS(graph, start, end, toPrint = False):
    """Assumes graph is a Digraph; start and end are nodes
       Returns a shortest path from start to end in graph"""
    initPath = [start]
    pathQueue = [initPath]
    if toPrint:
        print('Current BFS path:', printPath(path))
    while len(pathQueue) != 0:
        #Get and remove oldest element in pathQueue
        tmpPath = pathQueue.pop(0)
        print('Current BFS path:', printPath(tmpPath))
        lastNode = tmpPath[-1]
        if lastNode == end:
            return tmpPath
        for nextNode in graph.childrenOf(lastNode):
            if nextNode not in tmpPath:
                newPath = tmpPath + [nextNode]
                pathQueue.append(newPath)
    return None
```

Figure 12.11 Breadth-first-search shortest path algorithm

When the lines

```
sp = BFS(g, nodes[0], nodes[5])
print('Shortest path found by BFS:', printPath(sp))
```

are added at the end of testSP and the function is executed it prints

```
Current DFS path: 0
Current DFS path: 0->1
Current DFS path: 0->1->2
Current DFS path: 0->1->2->3
Current DFS path: 0->1->2->3->4
Current DFS path: 0->1->2->3->5
Current DFS path: 0->1->2->4
Current DFS path: 0->2
Current DFS path: 0->2->3
Current DFS path: 0->2->3->4
Current DFS path: 0->2->3->5
Current DFS path: 0->2->3->1
Current DFS path: 0->2->4
Shortest path found by DFS: 0->2->3->5
Current BFS path: 0
Current BFS path: 0->1
Current BFS path: 0->2
Current BFS path: 0->1->2
Current BFS path: 0->2->3
Current BFS path: 0->2->4
Current BFS path: 0->1->2->3
Current BFS path: 0->1->2->4
Current BFS path: 0->2->3->4
Current BFS path: 0->2->3->5
Shortest path found by BFS: 0->2->3->5
```

Comfortingly, each algorithm found a path of the same length. In this case, they found the same path. However, if a graph contains more than one shortest path between a pair of nodes, DFS and BFS will not necessarily find the same shortest path.

As mentioned above, BFS is a convenient way to search for a path with the fewest edges because the first time a path is found, it is guaranteed to be such a path.

Finger exercise: Consider a digraph with weighted edges. Is the first path found by BFS guaranteed to minimize the sum of the weights of the edges?

13 DYNAMIC PROGRAMMING

Dynamic programming was invented by Richard Bellman in the 1950s. Don't try to infer anything about the technique from its name. As Bellman described it, the name "dynamic programming" was chosen to hide from governmental sponsors "the fact that I was really doing mathematics... [the phrase dynamic programming] was something not even a Congressman could object to."[80]

Dynamic programming is a method for efficiently solving problems that exhibit the characteristics of overlapping subproblems and optimal substructure. Fortunately, many optimization problems exhibit these characteristics.

A problem has **optimal substructure** if a globally optimal solution can be found by combining optimal solutions to local subproblems. We've already looked at a number of such problems. Merge sort, for example, exploits the fact that a list can be sorted by first sorting sublists and then merging the solutions.

A problem has **overlapping subproblems** if an optimal solution involves solving the same problem multiple times. Merge sort does not exhibit this property. Even though we are performing a merge many times, we are merging different lists each time.

It's not immediately obvious, but the 0/1 knapsack problem exhibits both of these properties. First, however, we digress to look at a problem where the optimal substructure and overlapping subproblems are more obvious.

13.1 Fibonacci Sequences, Revisited

In Chapter 4, we looked at a straightforward recursive implementation of the Fibonacci function:

```
def fib(n):
    """Assumes n is an int >= 0
       Returns Fibonacci of n"""
    if n == 0 or n == 1:
        return 1
    else:
        return fib(n-1) + fib(n-2)
```

---

[80] As quoted in Stuart Dreyfus "Richard Bellman on the Birth of Dynamic Programming," *Operations Research*, vol. 50, no. 1 (2002).

While this implementation of the recurrence is obviously correct, it is terribly inefficient. Try, for example, running fib(120), but don't wait for it to complete. The complexity of the implementation is a bit hard to derive, but it is roughly O(fib(n)). That is, its growth is proportional to the growth in the value of the result, and the growth rate of the Fibonacci sequence is substantial. For example, fib(120) is 8,670,007,398,507,948,658,051,921. If each recursive call took a nanosecond, fib(120) would take about 250,000 years to finish.

Let's try and figure out why this implementation takes so long. Given the tiny amount of code in the body of fib, it's clear that the problem must be the number of times that fib calls itself. As an example, look at the tree of calls associated with the invocation fib(6).

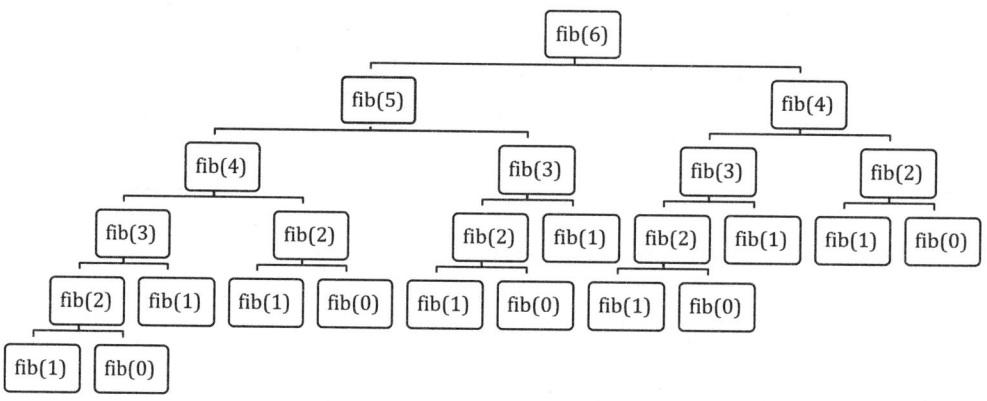

Figure 13.1 Tree of calls for recursive Fibonacci

Notice that we are computing the same values over and over again. For example, fib gets called with 3 three times, and each of these calls provokes four additional calls of fib. It doesn't require a genius to think that it might be a good idea to record the value returned by the first call, and then look it up rather than compute it each time it is needed. This is called **memoization**, and is the key idea behind dynamic programming.

Figure 13.2 contains an implementation of Fibonacci based on this idea. The function fastFib has a parameter, memo, that it uses to keep track of the numbers it has already evaluated. The parameter has a default value, the empty dictionary, so that clients of fastFib don't have to worry about supplying an initial value for memo. When fastFib is called with an n > 1, it attempts to look up n in memo. If it is not there (because this is the first time fastFib has been called with that value), an exception is raised. When this happens, fastFib uses the normal Fibonacci recurrence, and then stores the result in memo.

```
def fastFib(n, memo = {}):
    """Assumes n is an int >= 0, memo used only by recursive calls
        Returns Fibonacci of n"""
    if n == 0 or n == 1:
        return 1
    try:
        return memo[n]
    except KeyError:
        result = fastFib(n-1, memo) + fastFib(n-2, memo)
        memo[n] = result
        return result
```

Figure 13.2 Implementing Fibonacci using a memo

If you try running fastFib, you will see that it is indeed quite fast: fib(120) returns almost instantly. What is the complexity of fastFib? It calls fib exactly once for each value from 0 to n. Therefore, under the assumption that dictionary lookup can be done in constant time, the time complexity of fastFib(n) is O(n).[81]

13.2 Dynamic Programming and the 0/1 Knapsack Problem

One of the optimization problems we looked at in Chapter 12 was the 0/1 knapsack problem. Recall that we looked at a greedy algorithm that ran in n log n time, but was not guaranteed to find an optimal solution. We also looked at a brute-force algorithm that was guaranteed to find an optimal solution, but ran in exponential time. Finally, we discussed the fact that the problem is inherently exponential in the size of the input. In the worst case, one cannot find an optimal solution without looking at all possible answers.

Fortunately, the situation is not as bad as it seems. Dynamic programming provides a practical method for solving most 0/1 knapsack problems in a reasonable amount of time. As a first step in deriving such a solution, we begin with an exponential solution based on exhaustive enumeration. The key idea is to think about exploring the space of possible solutions by constructing a rooted binary tree that enumerates all states that satisfy the weight constraint.

---

[81] Though cute and pedagogically interesting, this is not the best way to implement Fibonacci. There is a simple linear-time iterative implementation.

A **rooted binary tree** is an acyclic directed graph in which
- There is exactly one node with no parents. This is called the **root**.
- Each non-root node has exactly one parent.
- Each node has at most two children. A childless node is called a **leaf**.

Each node in the search tree for the 0/1 knapsack problem is labeled with a quadruple that denotes a partial solution to the knapsack problem. The elements of the quadruple are:
- A set of items to be taken,
- The list of items for which a decision has not been made,
- The total value of the items in the set of items to be taken (this is merely an optimization, since the value could be computed from the set), and
- The remaining space in the knapsack. (Again, this is an optimization, since it is merely the difference between the weight allowed and the weight of all the items taken so far.)

The tree is built top-down starting with the root.[82] One element is selected from the still-to-be-considered items. If there is room for that item in the knapsack, a node is constructed that reflects the consequence of choosing to take that item. By convention, we draw that node as the left child. The right child shows the consequences of choosing not to take that item. The process is then applied recursively until either the knapsack is full or there are no more items to consider. Because each edge represents a decision (to take or not to take an item), such trees are called **decision trees**.[83]

Figure 13.3 is a table describing a set of items.

Name	Value	Weight
a	6	3
b	7	3
c	8	2
d	9	5

Figure 13.3 Table of items with values and weights

---

[82] It may seem odd to put the root of a tree at the top, but that is the way that mathematicians and computer scientists usually draw them. Perhaps it is evidence that those folks do not spend enough time contemplating nature.

[83] Decision trees, which need not be binary, provide a structured way to explore the consequences of making a series of sequential decisions. They are used extensively in many fields.

CHAPTER 13. DYNAMIC PROGRAMMING

Figure 13.4 is a decision tree for deciding which of those items to take under the assumption that the knapsack has a maximum weight of 5. The root of the tree (node 0) has a label <{}, [a,b,c,d], 0, 5>, indicating that no items have been taken, all items remain to be considered, the value of the items taken is 0, and a weight of 5 is still available. Node 1 indicates that item a has been taken, [b,c,d] remain to be considered, the value of the items taken is 6, and the knapsack can hold another 2 pounds. Node 1 has no left child since item b, which weighs 3 pounds, would not fit in the knapsack.

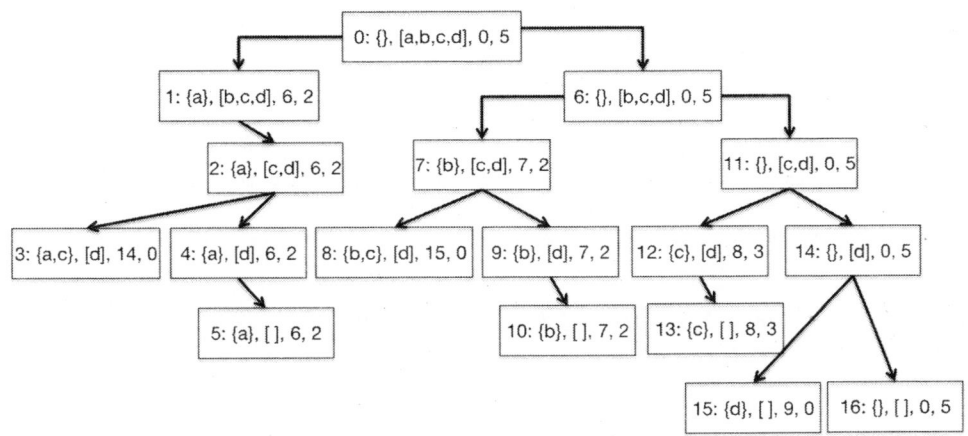

Figure 13.4 Decision tree for knapsack problem

In Figure 13.4, the numbers that precede the colon in each node indicate one order in which the nodes could be generated. This particular ordering is called left-first depth-first. At each node we attempt to generate a left node. If that is impossible, we attempt to generate a right node. If that too is impossible, we back up one node (to the parent) and repeat the process. Eventually, we find ourselves having generated all descendants of the root, and the process halts. When the process halts, each combination of items that could fit in the knapsack has been generated, and any leaf node with the greatest value represents an optimal solution. Notice that for each leaf node, either the second element is the empty list (indicating that there are no more items to consider taking) or the fourth element is 0 (indicating that there is no room left in the knapsack).

Unsurprisingly (especially if you read Chapter 12), the natural implementation of a depth-first tree search is recursive. Figure 13.5 contains such an implementation.

```python
def maxVal(toConsider, avail):
    """Assumes toConsider a list of items, avail a weight
       Returns a tuple of the total value of a solution to the
           0/1 knapsack problem and the items of that solution"""
    if toConsider == [] or avail == 0:
        result = (0, ())
    elif toConsider[0].getWeight() > avail:
        #Explore right branch only
        result = maxVal(toConsider[1:], avail)
    else:
        nextItem = toConsider[0]
        #Explore left branch
        withVal, withToTake = maxVal(toConsider[1:],
                                     avail - nextItem.getWeight())
        withVal += nextItem.getValue()
        #Explore right branch
        withoutVal, withoutToTake = maxVal(toConsider[1:], avail)
        #Choose better branch
        if withVal > withoutVal:
            result = (withVal, withToTake + (nextItem,))
        else:
            result = (withoutVal, withoutToTake)
    return result
```

Figure 13.5 Using a decision tree to solve a knapsack problem

The implementation uses class Item from Figure 12.2. The function maxVal returns two values, the set of items chosen and the total value of those items. It is called with two arguments, corresponding to the second and fourth elements of the labels of the nodes in the tree:

- toConsider. Those items that nodes higher up in the tree (corresponding to earlier calls in the recursive call stack) have not yet considered.
- avail. The amount of space still available.

Notice that the implementation of maxVal does not build the decision tree and then look for an optimal node. Instead, it uses the local variable result to record the best solution found so far. The code in Figure 13.6 can be used to test maxVal.

When smallTest (which uses the values in Figure 13.3) is run it prints a result indicating that node 8 in Figure 13.4 is an optimal solution:

```
<c, 8, 2>
<b, 7, 3>
Total value of items taken = 15
```

```
def smallTest():
    names = ['a', 'b', 'c', 'd']
    vals = [6, 7, 8, 9]
    weights = [3, 3, 2, 5]
    Items = []
    for i in range(len(vals)):
        Items.append(Item(names[i], vals[i], weights[i]))
    val, taken = maxVal(Items, 5)
    for item in taken:
        print(item)
    print('Total value of items taken =', val)

def buildManyItems(numItems, maxVal, maxWeight):
    items = []
    for i in range(numItems):
        items.append(Item(str(i),
                          random.randint(1, maxVal),
                          random.randint(1, maxWeight)))
    return items

def bigTest(numItems):
    items = buildManyItems(numItems, 10, 10)
    val, taken = maxVal(items, 40)
    print('Items Taken')
    for item in taken:
        print(item)
    print('Total value of items taken =', val)
```

Figure 13.6 Testing the decision tree-based implementation

The functions buildManyItems and bigTest can be used to test maxVal on randomly generated sets of items. Try bigTest(10). Now try bigTest(40). After you get tired of waiting for it to return, stop the computation and ask yourself what is going on.

Let's think about the size of the tree we are exploring. Since at each level of the tree we are deciding to keep or not keep one item, the maximum depth of the tree is len(items). At level 0 we have only one node, at level 1 up to two nodes, at level 2 up to four nodes, at level 3 up to eight nodes. At level 39 we have up to 2^{39} nodes. No wonder it takes a long time to run!

What should we do about this? Let's start by asking whether this program has anything in common with our first implementation of Fibonacci. In particular, is there optimal substructure and are there overlapping subproblems?

Optimal substructure is visible both in Figure 13.4 and in Figure 13.5. Each parent node combines the solutions reached by its children to derive an optimal solution for the subtree rooted at that parent. This is reflected in Figure 13.5 by the code following the comment #Choose better branch.

Are there also overlapping subproblems? At first glance, the answer seems to be "no." At each level of the tree we have a different set of available items to consider. This implies that if common subproblems do exist, they must be at the same level of the tree. And indeed, at each level of the tree each node has the same set of items to consider taking. However, we can see by looking at the labels in Figure 13.4 that each node at a level represents a different set of choices about the items considered higher in the tree.

Think about what problem is being solved at each node. The problem being solved is finding the optimal items to take from those left to consider, given the remaining available weight. The available weight depends upon the total weight of the items taken, but not on which items are taken or the total value of the items taken. So, for example, in Figure 13.4, nodes 2 and 7 are actually solving the same problem: deciding which elements of [c,d] should be taken, given that the available weight is 2.

The code in Figure 13.7 exploits the optimal substructure and overlapping subproblems to provide a dynamic programming solution to the 0/1 knapsack problem. An extra parameter, memo, has been added to keep track of solutions to subproblems that have already been solved. It is implemented using a dictionary with a key constructed from the length of toConsider and the available weight. The expression len(toConsider) is a compact way of representing the items still to be considered. This works because items are always removed from the same end (the front) of the list toConsider.

Figure 13.8 shows the number of calls made when we ran the code on problems of various sizes. The growth is hard to quantify, but it is clearly far less than exponential.[84] But how can this be, since we know that the 0/1 knapsack problem is inherently exponential in the number of items? Have we found a way to overturn fundamental laws of the universe? No, but we have discovered that computational complexity can be a subtle notion.[85]

The running time of fastMaxVal is governed by the number of distinct pairs, <toConsider, avail>, generated. This is because the decision about what to do next depends only upon the items still available and the total weight of the items already taken.

---

[84] Since $2^{128} = 340,282,366,920,938,463,463,374,607,431,768,211,456$

[85] OK, "discovered" may be too strong a word. People have known this for a long time. You probably figured it out around Chapter 9.

CHAPTER 13. DYNAMIC PROGRAMMING

```
def fastMaxVal(toConsider, avail, memo = {}):
    """Assumes toConsider a list of items, avail a weight
          memo supplied by recursive calls
       Returns a tuple of the total value of a solution to the
          0/1 knapsack problem and the items of that solution"""
    if (len(toConsider), avail) in memo:
        result = memo[(len(toConsider), avail)]
    elif toConsider == [] or avail == 0:
        result = (0, ())
    elif toConsider[0].getWeight() > avail:
        #Explore right branch only
        result = fastMaxVal(toConsider[1:], avail, memo)
    else:
        nextItem = toConsider[0]
        #Explore left branch
        withVal, withToTake =\
                fastMaxVal(toConsider[1:],
                            avail - nextItem.getWeight(), memo)
        withVal += nextItem.getValue()
        #Explore right branch
        withoutVal, withoutToTake = fastMaxVal(toConsider[1:],
                                                avail, memo)
        #Choose better branch
        if withVal > withoutVal:
            result = (withVal, withToTake + (nextItem,))
        else:
            result = (withoutVal, withoutToTake)
    memo[(len(toConsider), avail)] = result
    return result
```

Figure 13.7 Dynamic programming solution to knapsack problem

len(Items)	Number of items selected	Number of calls
4	4	31
8	6	337
16	9	1,493
32	12	3,650
64	19	8,707
128	27	18.306
256	40	36,675

Figure 13.8 Performance of dynamic programming solution

The number of possible values of toConsider is bounded by len(items). The number of possible values of avail is more difficult to characterize. It is bounded from above by the maximum number of distinct totals of weights of the items that the knapsack can hold. If the knapsack can hold at most n items (based on the capacity of the knapsack and the weights of the available items), avail can take on at most 2^n different values. In principle, this could be a rather large number. However, in practice, it is not usually so large. Even if the knapsack has a large capacity, if the weights of the items are chosen from a reasonably small set of possible weights, many sets of items will have the same total weight, greatly reducing the running time.

This algorithm falls into a complexity class called **pseudo-polynomial**. A careful explanation of this concept is beyond the scope of this book. Roughly speaking, fastMaxVal is exponential in the number of bits needed to represent the possible values of avail.

To see what happens when the values of avail are chosen from a considerably larger space, change the call to maxVal in the function bigTest in Figure 13.6 to

```
val, taken = fastMaxVal(items, 1000)
```

Finding a solution now takes 1,802,817 calls of fastMaxVal when the number of items is 256.

To see what happens when the weights are chosen from an enormous space, we can choose the possible weights from the positive reals rather than the positive integers. To do this, replace the line,

```
items.append(Item(str(i),
                random.randint(1, maxVal),
                random.randint(1, maxWeight)))
```

in buildManyItems by the line

```
items.append(Item(str(i),
                random.randint(1, maxVal),
                random.randint(1, maxWeight)*random.random()))
```

Each time it is called, random.random() returns a random floating point number between 0.0 and 1.0, so there are, for all intents and purposes, an infinite number of possible weights. Don't hold your breath waiting for this last test to finish. Dynamic programming may be a miraculous technique in the common sense of the word,[86] but it is not capable of performing miracles in the liturgical sense.

---

[86] Extraordinary and bringing welcome consequences.

13.3 Dynamic Programming and Divide-and-Conquer

Like divide-and-conquer algorithms, dynamic programming is based upon solving independent subproblems and then combining those solutions. There are, however, some important differences.

Divide-and-conquer algorithms are based upon finding subproblems that are substantially smaller than the original problem. For example, merge sort works by dividing the problem size in half at each step. In contrast, dynamic programming involves solving problems that are only slightly smaller than the original problem. For example, computing the 19th Fibonacci number is not a substantially smaller problem than computing the 20th Fibonacci number.

Another important distinction is that the efficiency of divide-and-conquer algorithms does not depend upon structuring the algorithm so that identical problems are solved repeatedly. In contrast, dynamic programming is efficient only when the number of distinct subproblems is significantly smaller than the total number of subproblems.

14 RANDOM WALKS AND MORE ABOUT DATA VISUALIZATION

This book is about using computation to solve problems. Thus far, we have focused our attention on problems that can be solved by a **deterministic program**. A program is deterministic if whenever it is run on the same input, it produces the same output. Such computations are highly useful, but clearly not sufficient to tackle some kinds of problems. Many aspects of the world in which we live can be accurately modeled only as **stochastic processes**.[87] A process is stochastic if its next state can depend upon some random element. The outcome of a stochastic process is usually uncertain. Therefore, we can rarely make definitive statements about what they will do. Instead, we make probabilistic statements about what they might do. The rest of this book deals with building programs that help to understand uncertain situations. Many of these programs will be simulation models.

A simulation mimics the activity of a real system. For example, the code in Figure 8.11 simulates a person making a series of mortgage payments. Think of that code as an experimental device, called a **simulation model**, that provides useful information about the possible behaviors of the system being modeled. Among other things, simulations are widely used to predict a future state of a physical system (e.g., the temperature of the planet 50 years from now), and in lieu of physical experiments that would be too expensive, time consuming, or dangerous to perform (e.g., the impact of a change in the tax code).

It is important to remember that simulation models, like all models, are only an approximation of reality. One can never be sure that the actual system will behave in the way predicted by the model. In fact, one can usually be pretty confident that the actual system will not behave exactly as predicted by the model. For example, not every borrower will make all mortgage payments on time. It is a commonly quoted truism that "all models are wrong, but some are useful."[88]

---

[87] The word stems from the Greek word *stokhastikos*, which means something like "capable of divining." A stochastic program, as we shall see, is aimed at getting a good result, but the exact results are not guaranteed.

[88] Usually attributed to the statistician George E.P. Box.

14.1 Random Walks

In 1827, the Scottish botanist Robert Brown observed that pollen particles suspended in water seemed to float around at random. He had no plausible explanation for what came to be known as Brownian motion, and made no attempt to model it mathematically.[89] A clear mathematical model of the phenomenon was first presented in 1900 in Louis Bachelier's doctoral thesis, *The Theory of Speculation*. However, since this thesis dealt with the then disreputable problem of understanding financial markets, it was largely ignored by respectable academics. Five years later, a young Albert Einstein brought this kind of stochastic thinking to the world of physics with a mathematical model almost the same as Bachelier's and a description of how it could be used to confirm the existence of atoms.[90] For some reason, people seemed to think that understanding physics was more important than making money, and the world started paying attention. Times were certainly different.

Brownian motion is an example of a **random walk**. Random walks are widely used to model physical processes (e.g., diffusion), biological processes (e.g., the kinetics of displacement of RNA from heteroduplexes by DNA), and social processes (e.g., movements of the stock market).

In this chapter we look at random walks for three reasons:

- Random walks are intrinsically interesting and widely used.
- It provides us with a good example of how to use abstract data types and inheritance to structure programs in general and simulation models in particular.
- It provides an opportunity to introduce a few more features of Python and to demonstrate some additional techniques for producing plots.

---

[89] Nor was he the first to observe it. As early as 60 BCE, the Roman Titus Lucretius, in his poem "On the Nature of Things," described a similar phenomenon, and even implied that it was caused by the random movement of atoms.

[90] "On the movement of small particles suspended in a stationary liquid demanded by the molecular-kinetic theory of heat," *Annalen der Physik*, May 1905. Einstein would come to describe 1905 as his "*annus mirabilis.*" That year, in addition to his paper on Brownian motion, he published papers on the production and transformation of light (pivotal to the development of quantum theory), on the electrodynamics of moving bodies (special relativity), and on the equivalence of matter and energy ($E = mc^2$). Not a bad year for a newly minted PhD.

14.2 The Drunkard's Walk

Let's look at a random walk that actually involves walking. A drunken farmer is standing in the middle of a field, and every second the farmer takes one step in a random direction. What is her (or his) expected distance from the origin in 1000 seconds? If she takes many steps, is she likely to move ever farther from the origin, or is she more likely to wander back to the origin over and over, and end up not far from where she started? Let's write a simulation to find out.

Before starting to design a program, it is always a good idea to try to develop some intuition about the situation the program is intended to model. Let's start by sketching a simple model of the situation using Cartesian coordinates. Assume that the farmer is standing in a field where the grass has, mysteriously, been cut to resemble a piece of graph paper. Assume further that each step the farmer takes is of length one and is parallel to either the x-axis or y-axis.

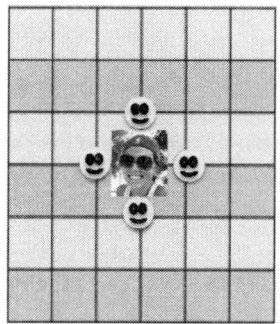 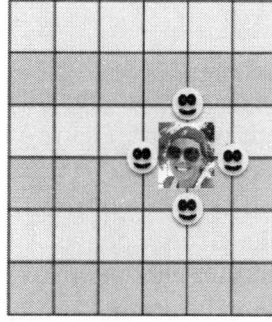

Figure 14.1 An unusual farmer

The picture on the left of Figure 14.1 depicts a farmer[91] standing in the middle of the field. The smiley faces indicate all the places the farmer might be after one step. Notice that after one step she is always exactly one unit away from where she started. Let's assume that she wanders eastward from her initial location on her first step. How far away might she be from her initial location after her second step?

Looking at the smiley faces in the picture on the right, we see that with a probability of 0.25 she will be 0 units away, with a probability of 0.25 she will be 2 units away, and with a probability of 0.5 she will be $\sqrt{2}$ units away.[92] So, on aver-

---

[91] To be honest, the person pictured here is an actor impersonating a farmer.
[92] Why $\sqrt{2}$? We are using the Pythagorean theorem.

age she will be farther away after two steps than after one step. What about the third step? If the second step is to the top or bottom smiley face, the third step will bring the farmer closer to the origin half the time and farther half the time. If the second step is to the left smiley face (the origin), the third step will be away from the origin. If the second step is to the right smiley face, the third step will be closer to the origin a quarter of the time, and farther away three quarters of the time.

It seems as if the more steps the drunk takes, the greater the expected distance from the origin. We could continue this exhaustive enumeration of possibilities and perhaps develop a pretty good intuition about how this distance grows with respect to the number of steps. However, it is getting pretty tedious, so it seems like a better idea to write a program to do it for us.

Let's begin the design process by thinking about some data abstractions that are likely to be useful in building this simulation and perhaps simulations of other kinds of random walks. As usual, we should try to invent types that correspond to the kinds of things that appear in the situation we are attempting to model. Three obvious types are `Location`, `Field`, and `Drunk`. As we look at the classes providing these types, it is worthwhile to think about what each might imply about the kinds of simulation models they will allow us to build.

Let's start with `Location`, Figure 14.2. This is a simple class, but it does embody two important decisions. It tells us that the simulation will involve at most two dimensions. E.g., the simulation will not model changes in altitude. This is consistent with the pictures above. Also, since the values supplied for `deltaX` and `deltaY` could be floats rather than integers, there is no built-in assumption in this class about the set of directions in which a drunk might move. This is a generalization of the informal model in which each step was of length one and was parallel to the x-axis or y-axis.

Class `Field`, Figure 14.2, is also quite simple, but it too embodies notable decisions. It simply maintains a mapping of drunks to locations. It places no constraints on locations, so presumably a `Field` is of unbounded size. It allows multiple drunks to be added into a `Field` at random locations. It says nothing about the patterns in which drunks move, nor does it prohibit multiple drunks from occupying the same location or moving through spaces occupied by other drunks.

```python
class Location(object):
    def __init__(self, x, y):
        """x and y are numbers"""
        self.x, self.y = x, y

    def move(self, deltaX, deltaY):
        """deltaX and deltaY are numbers"""
        return Location(self.x + deltaX, self.y + deltaY)

    def getX(self):
        return self.x

    def getY(self):
        return self.y

    def distFrom(self, other):
        ox, oy = other.x, other.y
        xDist, ydist = self.x - ox, self.y - oy
        return (xDist**2 + yDist**2)**0.5

    def __str__(self):
        return '<' + str(self.x) + ', ' + str(self.y) + '>'

class Field(object):
    def __init__(self):
        self.drunks = {}

    def addDrunk(self, drunk, loc):
        if drunk in self.drunks:
            raise ValueError('Duplicate drunk')
        else:
            self.drunks[drunk] = loc

    def moveDrunk(self, drunk):
        if drunk not in self.drunks:
            raise ValueError('Drunk not in field')
        xDist, yDist = drunk.takeStep()
        currentLocation = self.drunks[drunk]
        #use move method of Location to get new location
        self.drunks[drunk] = currentLocation.move(xDist, yDist)

    def getLoc(self, drunk):
        if drunk not in self.drunks:
            raise ValueError('Drunk not in field')
        return self.drunks[drunk]
```

Figure 14.2 Location and Field classes

The classes Drunk and UsualDrunk in Figure 14.3 define the ways in which a drunk might wander through the field. In particular the value of stepChoices in UsualDrunk introduces the restriction that each step is of length one and is parallel to either the x-axis or y-axis. Since the function random.choice returns a randomly chosen member of the sequence that it is passed, each kind of step is equally likely and not influenced by previous steps. A bit later we will look at subclasses of Drunk with different kinds of behaviors.

```
import random

class Drunk(object):
    def __init__(self, name = None):
        """Assumes name is a str"""
        self.name = name

    def __str__(self):
        if self != None:
            return self.name
        return 'Anonymous'

class UsualDrunk(Drunk):
    def takeStep(self):
        stepChoices = [(0,1), (0,-1), (1, 0), (-1, 0)]
        return random.choice(stepChoices)
        return random.choice(stepChoices)
```

Figure 14.3 Classes defining Drunks

The next step is to use these classes to build a simulation that answers the original question. Figure 14.4 contains three functions used in this simulation.

The function walk simulates one walk of numSteps steps. The function simWalks calls walk to simulate numTrials walks of numSteps steps each. The function drunkTest calls simWalks to simulate walks of varying lengths.

The parameter dClass of simWalks is of type class, and is used in the first line of code to create a Drunk of the appropriate subclass. Later, when drunk.takeStep is invoked from Field.moveDrunk, the method from the appropriate subclass is automatically selected.

The function drunkTest also has a parameter, dClass, of type class. It is used twice, once in the call to simWalks and once in the first print statement. In the print statement, the built-in class attribute __name__ is used to get a string with the name of the class.

```
def walk(f, d, numSteps):
    """Assumes: f a Field, d a Drunk in f, and numSteps an int >= 0.
       Moves d numSteps times; returns the distance between the
       final location and the location at the start of the  walk."""
    start = f.getLoc(d)
    for s in range(numSteps):
        f.moveDrunk(d)
    return start.distFrom(f.getLoc(d))

def simWalks(numSteps, numTrials, dClass):
    """Assumes numSteps an int >= 0, numTrials an int > 0,
         dClass a subclass of Drunk
       Simulates numTrials walks of numSteps steps each.
       Returns a list of the final distances for each trial"""
    Homer = dClass()
    origin = Location(0, 0)
    distances = []
    for t in range(numTrials):
        f = Field()
        f.addDrunk(Homer, origin)
        distances.append(round(walk(f, Homer, numTrials), 1))
    return distances

def drunkTest(walkLengths, numTrials, dClass):
    """Assumes walkLengths a sequence of ints >= 0
         numTrials an int > 0, dClass a subclass of Drunk
       For each number of steps in walkLengths, runs simWalks with
         numTrials walks and prints results"""
    for numSteps in walkLengths:
        distances = simWalks(numSteps, numTrials, dClass)
        print(dClass.__name__, 'random walk of', numSteps, 'steps')
        print(' Mean =', round(sum(distances)/len(distances), 4))
        print(' Max =', max(distances), 'Min =', min(distances))
```

Figure 14.4 The drunkard's walk (with a bug)

When we executed drunkTest((10, 100, 1000, 10000), 100, UsualDrunk), it printed

```
UsualDrunk random walk of 10 steps
 Mean = 8.634
 Max = 21.6 Min = 1.4
UsualDrunk random walk of 100 steps
 Mean = 8.57
 Max = 22.0 Min = 0.0
UsualDrunk random walk of 1000 steps
 Mean = 9.206
 Max = 21.6 Min = 1.4
UsualDrunk random walk of 10000 steps
 Mean = 8.727
 Max = 23.5 Min = 1.4
```

This is surprising, given the intuition we developed earlier that the mean distance should grow with the number of steps. It could mean that our intuition is wrong, or it could mean that our simulation is buggy, or both.

The first thing to do at this point is to run the simulation on values for which we already think we know the answer, and make sure that what the simulation produces matches the expected result. Let's try walks of zero steps (for which the mean, minimum and maximum distances from the origin should all be 0) and one step (for which the mean, minimum and maximum distances from the origin should all be 1).

When we ran drunkTest((0,1), 100, UsualDrunk), we got the highly suspect result

```
UsualDrunk random walk of 0 steps
 Mean = 8.634
 Max = 21.6 Min = 1.4
UsualDrunk random walk of 1 steps
 Mean = 8.57
 Max = 22.0 Min = 0.0
```

How on earth can the mean distance of a walk of zero steps be over 8? We must have at least one bug in our simulation. After some investigation, the problem is clear. In simWalks, the function call walk(f, Homer, numTrials) should have been walk(f, Homer, numSteps).

CHAPTER 14. RANDOM WALKS AND MORE ABOUT DATA VISUALIZATION

The moral here is an important one: Always bring some skepticism to bear when looking at the results of a simulation. Ask if the results are plausible, and "smoke test"[93] the simulation on parameters for which you have a strong intuition about what the results should be.

When the corrected version of the simulation is run on our two simple cases, it yields exactly the expected answers:

```
UsualDrunk random walk of 0 steps
  Mean = 0.0
  Max = 0.0 Min = 0.0
UsualDrunk random walk of 1 steps
  Mean = 1.0
  Max = 1.0 Min = 1.0
```

When run on longer walks it printed

```
UsualDrunk random walk of 10 steps
  Mean = 2.863
  Max = 7.2 Min = 0.0
UsualDrunk random walk of 100 steps
  Mean = 8.296
  Max = 21.6 Min = 1.4
UsualDrunk random walk of 1000 steps
  Mean = 27.297
  Max = 66.3 Min = 4.2
UsualDrunk random walk of 10000 steps
  Mean = 89.241
  Max = 226.5 Min = 10.0
```

As anticipated, the mean distance from the origin grows with the number of steps.

Now let's look at a plot of the mean distances from the origin, Figure 14.5. To give a sense of how fast the distance is growing, we have placed on the plot a line showing the square root of the number of steps (and increased the number of steps to 100,000). The plot showing the square root of the number of steps versus the distance from the origin is a straight line because we used a logarithmic scale on both axes.

---

[93] In the 19th century, it became standard practice for plumbers to test closed systems of pipes for leaks by filling the system with smoke. Later, electronic engineers adopted the term to cover the very first test of a piece of electronics—turning on the power and looking for smoke. Still later, software developers starting using the term for a quick test to see if a program did anything useful.

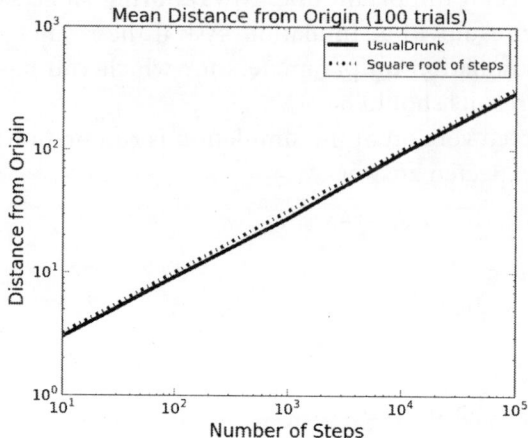

Figure 14.5 Distance from starting point versus steps taken

Does this plot provide any information about the expected final location of a drunk? It does tell us that on average the drunk will be somewhere on a circle with its center at the origin and with a radius equal to the expected distance from the origin. However, it tells us very little about where we might actually find the drunk at the end of any particular walk. We return to this topic in the next section.

14.3 Biased Random Walks

Now that we have a working simulation, we can start modifying it to investigate other kinds of random walks. Suppose, for example, that we want to consider the behavior of a drunken farmer in the northern hemisphere who hates the cold, and even in his drunken stupor is able to move twice as fast when his random movements take him in a southward direction. Or maybe a phototropic drunk who always moves towards the sun (east in the morning and west in the afternoon). These are examples of **biased random walks**. The walk is still stochastic, but there is a bias in the outcome.

Figure 14.6 defines two additional subclasses of Drunk. In each case the specialization involves choosing an appropriate value for stepChoices. The function simAll iterates over a sequence of subclasses of Drunk to generate information about how each kind behaves.

CHAPTER 14. RANDOM WALKS AND MORE ABOUT DATA VISUALIZATION

```
class ColdDrunk(Drunk):
    def takeStep(self):
        stepChoices = [(0.0,1.0), (0.0,-2.0), (1.0, 0.0),\
                       (-1.0, 0.0)]
        return random.choice(stepChoices)

class EWDrunk(Drunk):
    def takeStep(self):
        stepChoices = [(1.0, 0.0), (-1.0, 0.0)]
        return random.choice(stepChoices)

def simAll(drunkKinds, walkLengths, numTrials):
    for dClass in drunkKinds:
        drunkTest(walkLengths, numTrials, dClass)
```

Figure 14.6 Subclasses of Drunk base class

When we ran

`simAll((UsualDrunk, ColdDrunk, EWDrunk), (100, 1000), 10)`

it printed

```
UsualDrunk random walk of 100 steps
 Mean = 9.64
 Max = 17.2 Min = 4.2
UsualDrunk random walk of 1000 steps
 Mean = 22.37
 Max = 45.5 Min = 4.5
ColdDrunk random walk of 100 steps
 Mean = 27.96
 Max = 51.2 Min = 4.1
ColdDrunk random walk of 1000 steps
 Mean = 259.49
 Max = 320.7 Min = 215.1
EWDrunk random walk of 100 steps
 Mean = 7.8
 Max = 16.0 Min = 0.0
EWDrunk random walk of 1000 steps
 Mean = 20.2
 Max = 48.0 Min = 4.0
```

It appears that our heat-seeking drunk moves away from the origin faster than the other two kinds of drunk. However, it is not easy to digest all of the information in this output. It is once again time to move away from textual output and start using plots.

Since we are showing a number of different kinds of drunks on the same plot, we will associate a distinct style with each type of drunk so that it is easy to differentiate among them. The style will have three aspects:
- The color of the line and marker,
- The shape of the marker, and
- The kind of the line, e.g., solid or dotted.

The class styleIterator, Figure 14.7, rotates through a sequence of styles defined by the argument to styleIterator.__init__.

```
class styleIterator(object):
    def __init__(self, styles):
        self.index = 0
        self.styles = styles

    def nextStyle(self):
        result = self.styles[self.index]
        if self.index == len(self.styles) - 1:
            self.index = 0
        else:
            self.index += 1
        return result
```

Figure 14.7 **Iterating over styles**

The code in Figure 14.8 is similar in structure to that in Figure 14.4. The print statements in simDrunk and simAll1 contribute nothing to the result of the simulation. They are there because this simulation can take a rather long time to complete, and printing an occasional message indicating that progress is being made can be quite reassuring to a user who might be wondering if the program is actually making progress.

The code in Figure 14.8 produces the plot in Figure 14.9. Notice that both the x and y axes are on a **logarithmic scale**. This was done by calling the plotting functions pylab.semilogx and pylab.semilogy. These functions are always applied to the current figure.

```
def simDrunk(numTrials, dClass, walkLengths):
    meanDistances = []
    for numSteps in walkLengths:
        print('Starting simulation of', numSteps, 'steps')
        trials = simWalks(numSteps, numTrials, dClass)
        mean = sum(trials)/len(trials)
        meanDistances.append(mean)
    return meanDistances

def simAll1(drunkKinds, walkLengths, numTrials):
    styleChoice = styleIterator(('m-', 'r:', 'k-.'))
    for dClass in drunkKinds:
        curStyle = styleChoice.nextStyle()
        print('Starting simulation of', dClass.__name__)
        means = simDrunk(numTrials, dClass, walkLengths)
        pylab.plot(walkLengths, means, curStyle,
                   label = dClass.__name__)
    pylab.title('Mean Distance from Origin ('
                + str(numTrials) + ' trials)')
    pylab.xlabel('Number of Steps')
    pylab.ylabel('Distance from Origin')
    pylab.legend(loc = 'best')
    pylab.semilogx()
    pylab.semilogy()

simAll1((UsualDrunk, ColdDrunk, EWDrunk),
        (10,100,1000,10000,100000), 100)
```

Figure 14.8 Plotting the walks of different drunks

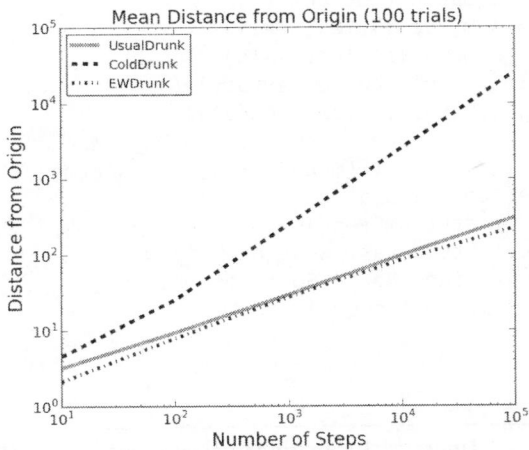

Figure 14.9 Mean distance for different kinds of drunks

The usual drunk and the phototropic drunk (EWDrunk) seem to be moving away from the origin at approximately the same pace, but the heat-seeking drunk (ColdDrunk) seems to be moving away orders of magnitude faster. This is interesting, since on average he is only moving 25% faster (he takes, on average, five steps for every four taken by the others).

Let's construct a different plot, that may help us get more insight into the behavior of these three classes. Instead of plotting the change in distance over time for an increasing number of steps, the code in Figure 14.10 plots the distribution of final locations for a single number of steps.

```python
def getFinalLocs(numSteps, numTrials, dClass):
    locs = []
    d = dClass()
    for t in range(numTrials):
        f = Field()
        f.addDrunk(d, Location(0, 0))
        for s in range(numSteps):
            f.moveDrunk(d)
        locs.append(f.getLoc(d))
    return locs

def plotLocs(drunkKinds, numSteps, numTrials):
    styleChoice = styleIterator(('k+', 'r^', 'mo'))
    for dClass in drunkKinds:
        locs = getFinalLocs(numSteps, numTrials, dClass)
        xVals, yVals = [], []
        for loc in locs:
            xVals.append(loc.getX())
            yVals.append(loc.getY())
        meanX = sum(xVals)/len(xVals)
        meanY = sum(yVals)/len(yVals)
        curStyle = styleChoice.nextStyle()
        pylab.plot(xVals, yVals, curStyle,
                   label = dClass.__name__ + ' mean loc. = <'
                   + str(meanX) + ', ' + str(meanY) + '>')
    pylab.title('Location at End of Walks ('
                + str(numSteps) + ' steps)')
    pylab.xlabel('Steps East/West of Origin')
    pylab.ylabel('Steps North/South of Origin')
    pylab.legend(loc = 'lower left')

plotLocs((UsualDrunk, ColdDrunk, EWDrunk), 100, 200)
```

Figure 14.10 Plotting final locations

The first thing `plotLocs` does is create an instance of `styleIterator` with three different styles of markers. It then uses `pylab.plot` to place a marker at a location corresponding to the end of each trial. The call to `pylab.plot` sets the color and shape of the marker to be plotted using the values returned by the iterator `styleIterator`.

The call `plotLocs((UsualDrunk, ColdDrunk, EWDrunk), 100, 200)` produces the plot in Figure 14.11.

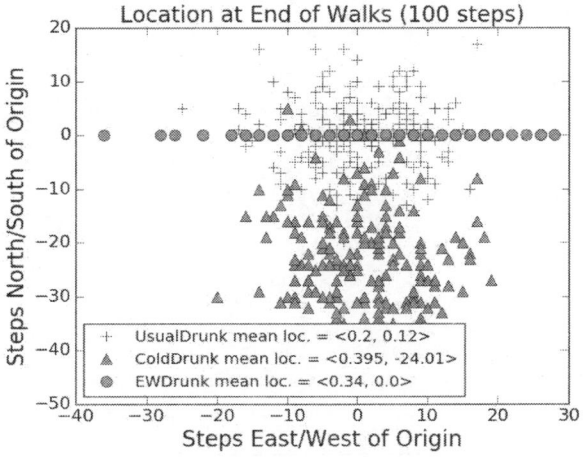

Figure 14.11 Where the drunk stops

The first thing to say is that our drunks seem to be behaving as advertised. The `EWDrunk` ends up on the x-axis, the `ColdDrunk` seem to have made progress southwards, and the `UsualDrunk` seem to have wandered aimlessly.

But why do there appear to be far fewer circle markers than triangle or + markers? Because many of the `EWDrunk`'s walks ended up at the same place. This is not surprising, given the small number of possible endpoints (200) for the EW-Drunk. Also the circle markers seem to be fairly uniformly spaced across the x-axis.

It is still not immediately obvious, at least to us, why the `ColdDrunk` manages, on average, to get so much farther from the origin than the other kinds of drunks. Perhaps it's time to look not at the endpoints of many walks, but at the path followed by a single walk. The code in Figure 14.12 produces the plot in Figure 14.13.

```
def traceWalk(drunkKinds, numSteps):
    styleChoice = styleIterator(('k+', 'r^', 'mo'))
    f = Field()
    for dClass in drunkKinds:
        d = dClass()
        f.addDrunk(d, Location(0, 0))
        locs = []
        for s in range(numSteps):
            f.moveDrunk(d)
            locs.append(f.getLoc(d))
        xVals, yVals = [], []
        for loc in locs:
            xVals.append(loc.getX())
            yVals.append(loc.getY())
        curStyle = styleChoice.nextStyle()
        pylab.plot(xVals, yVals, curStyle,
                   label = dClass.__name__)
    pylab.title('Spots Visited on Walk ('
                + str(numSteps) + ' steps)')
    pylab.xlabel('Steps East/West of Origin')
    pylab.ylabel('Steps North/South of Origin')
    pylab.legend(loc = 'best')

traceWalk((UsualDrunk, ColdDrunk, EWDrunk), 200)
```

Figure 14.12 Tracing walks

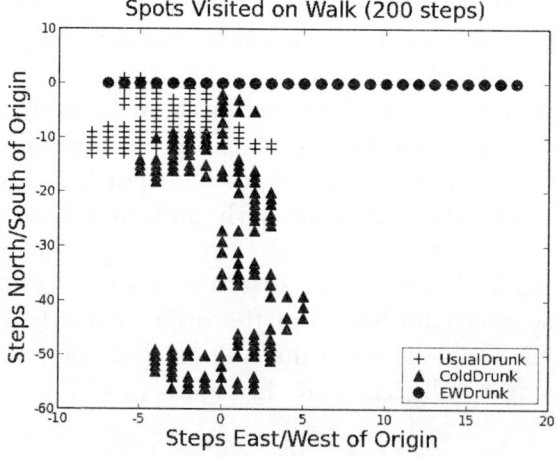

Figure 14.13 Trajectory of walks

Since the walk is 200 steps long and the `EWDrunk`'s walk visits fewer than 30 different locations, it's clear that he is spending a lot of time retracing his steps. The same kind of observation holds for the `UsualDrunk`. In contrast, while the `ColdDrunk` is not exactly making a beeline for Florida, he is managing to spend relatively less time visiting places he has already been.

None of these simulations is interesting in its own right. (In Chapter 16, we will look at more intrinsically interesting simulations.) But there are some points worth taking away:

- Initially we divided our simulation code into four separate chunks. Three of them were classes (`Location`, `Field`, and `Drunk`) corresponding to abstract data types that appeared in the informal description of the problem. The fourth chunk was a group of functions that used these classes to perform a simple simulation.
- We then elaborated `Drunk` into a hierarchy of classes so that we could observe different kinds of biased random walks. The code for `Location` and `Field` remained untouched, but the simulation code was changed to iterate through the different subclasses of `Drunk`. In doing this, we took advantage of the fact that a class is itself an object, and therefore can be passed as an argument.
- Finally, we made a series of incremental changes to the simulation that did not involve any changes to the classes representing the abstract types. These changes mostly involved introducing plots designed to provide insight into the different walks. This is very typical of the way in which simulations are developed. One gets the basic simulation working first, and then starts adding features.

14.4 Treacherous Fields

Did you ever play the board game known as *Chutes and Ladders* in the U.S. and *Snakes and Ladders* in the UK? This children's game originated in India (perhaps in the 2nd century BCE), where it was called *Moksha-patamu*. Landing on a square representing virtue (e.g., generosity) sent a player up a ladder to a higher tier of life. Landing on a square representing evil (e.g., lust), sent a player back to a lower tier of life.

We can easily add this kind of feature to our random walks by creating a Field with wormholes,[94] as shown in Figure 14.14, and replacing the second line of code in the function traceWalk by the line of code

```
f = oddField(1000, 100, 200)
```

In an oddField, a drunk who steps into a wormhole location is transported to the location at the other end of the wormhole.

```
class oddField(Field):
    def __init__(self, numHoles, xRange, yRange):
        Field.__init__(self)
        self.wormholes = {}
        for w in range(numHoles):
            x = random.randint(-xRange, xRange)
            y = random.randint(-yRange, yRange)
            newX = random.randint(-xRange, xRange)
            newY = random.randint(-yRange, yRange)
            newLoc = Location(newX, newY)
            self.wormholes[(x, y)] = newLoc

    def moveDrunk(self, drunk):
        Field.moveDrunk(self, drunk)
        x = self.drunks[drunk].getX()
        y = self.drunks[drunk].getY()
        if (x, y) in self.wormholes:
            self.drunks[drunk] = self.wormholes[(x, y)]
```

Figure 14.14 Fields with strange properties

When we ran traceWalk((UsualDrunk, ColdDrunk, EWDrunk), 500), we got the rather odd-looking plot in Figure 14.15.

---

[94] This kind of wormhole is a hypothetical concept invented by theoretical physicists (or maybe science fiction writers). It provides shortcuts through the time/space continuum.

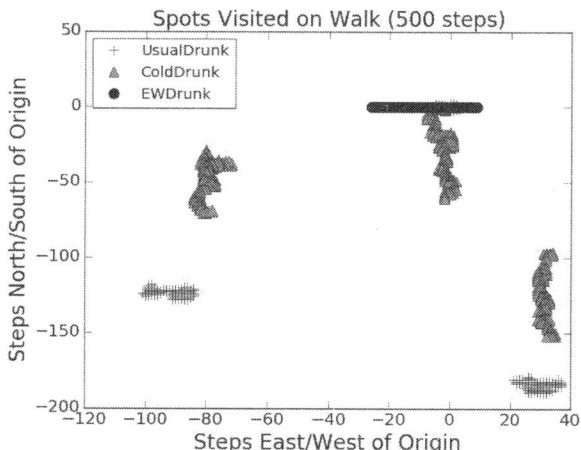

Figure 14.15 A strange walk

Clearly changing the properties of the field has had a dramatic effect. However, that is not the point of this example. The main points are:

- Because of the way we structured our code, it was easy to accommodate a significant change to the situation being modeled. Just as we could add different kinds of drunks without touching Field, we can add a new kind of Field without touching Drunk or any of its subclasses. (Had we been sufficiently prescient to make the field a parameter of traceWalk, we wouldn't have had to change traceWalk either.)
- While it would have been feasible to analytically derive different kinds of information about the expected behavior of the simple random walk and even the biased random walks, it would have been challenging to do so once the wormholes were introduced. Yet it was exceedingly simple to change the simulation to model the new situation. Simulation models often enjoy this advantage relative to analytic models.

15 STOCHASTIC PROGRAMS, PROBABILITY, AND DISTRIBUTIONS

There is something very comforting about Newtonian mechanics. You push down on one end of a lever, and the other end goes up. You throw a ball up in the air; it travels a parabolic path, and eventually comes down. $\vec{F} = m\vec{a}$. In short, everything happens for a reason. The physical world is a completely predictable place—all future states of a physical system can be derived from knowledge about its current state.

For centuries, this was the prevailing scientific wisdom; then along came quantum mechanics and the Copenhagen Doctrine. The doctrine's proponents, led by Bohr and Heisenberg, argued that at its most fundamental level the behavior of the physical world cannot be predicted. One can make probabilistic statements of the form "x is highly likely to occur," but not statements of the form "x is certain to occur." Other distinguished physicists, most notably Einstein and Schrödinger, vehemently disagreed.

This debate roiled the worlds of physics, philosophy, and even religion. The heart of the debate was the validity of **causal nondeterminism**, i.e., the belief that not every event is caused by previous events. Einstein and Schrödinger found this view philosophically unacceptable, as exemplified by Einstein's often-repeated comment, "God does not play dice." What they could accept was **predictive nondeterminism**, i.e., the concept that our inability to make accurate measurements about the physical world makes it impossible to make precise predictions about future states. This distinction was nicely summed up by Einstein, who said, "The essentially statistical character of contemporary theory is solely to be ascribed to the fact that this theory operates with an incomplete description of physical systems."

The question of causal nondeterminism is still unsettled. However, whether the reason we cannot predict events is because they are truly unpredictable or is because we simply don't have enough information to predict them is of no practical importance.

While the Bohr/Einstein debate was about how to understand the lowest levels of the physical world, the same issues arise at the macroscopic level. Perhaps the outcomes of horse races, spins of roulette wheels, and stock market investments are causally deterministic. However, there is ample evidence that it is perilous to treat them as predictably deterministic.[95]

15.1 Stochastic Programs

A program is **deterministic** if whenever it is run on the same input, it produces the same output. Notice that this is not the same as saying that the output is completely defined by the specification of the problem. Consider, for example, the specification of squareRoot:

```
def squareRoot(x, epsilon):
    """Assumes x and epsilon are of type float; x >= 0 and epsilon > 0
       Returns float y such that x-epsilon <= y*y <= x+epsilon"""
```

This specification admits many possible return values for the function call squareRoot(2, 0.001). However, the successive approximation algorithm that we looked at in Chapter 3 will always return the same value. The specification doesn't require that the implementation be deterministic, but it does allow deterministic implementations.

Not all interesting specifications can be met by deterministic implementations. Consider, for example, implementing a program to play a dice game, say backgammon or craps. Somewhere in the program there may be a function that simulates a fair roll of a single six-sided die.[96] Suppose it had a specification something like

```
def rollDie():
    """Returns an int between 1 and 6"""
```

This would be problematic, since it allows the implementation to return the same number each time it is called, which would make for a pretty boring game. It would be better to specify that rollDie "returns a randomly chosen int between 1 and 6," thus requiring a stochastic implementation.

Most programming languages, including Python, include simple ways to write stochastic programs, i.e., programs that exploit randomness. The tiny pro-

---

[95] Of course this doesn't stop people from believing that they are, and losing a lot of money based on that belief.

[96] A roll is fair if each of the six possible outcomes is equally likely. This is not always to be taken for granted. Excavations of Pompeii discovered "loaded" dice in which small lead weights had been inserted to bias the outcome of a roll. More recently, an online vendor's site said, "Are you unusually unlucky when it comes to rolling dice? Investing in a pair of dice that's more, uh, reliable might be just what you need."

gram in Figure 15.1 is a simulation model. Rather than asking some person to roll a die multiple times, we wrote a program to simulate that activity. The code uses one of several useful functions found in the imported Python standard library module random. As we saw earlier, the function random.choice takes a non-empty sequence as its argument and returns a randomly chosen member of that sequence. Almost all of the functions in random are built using the function random.random, which, as we saw earlier in the book, generates a random floating point number between 0.0 and 1.0.[97]

```
import random

def rollDie():
    """Returns a random int between 1 and 6"""
    return random.choice([1,2,3,4,5,6])

def rollN(n):
    result = ''
    for i in range(n):
        result = result + str(rollDie())
    print(result)
```

Figure 15.1 Roll die

Now, imagine running rollN(10). Would you be more surprised to see it print 1111111111 or 5442462412? Or, to put it another way, which of these two sequences is more random? It's a trick question. Each of these sequences is equally likely, because the value of each roll is independent of the values of earlier rolls. In a stochastic process, two events are **independent** if the outcome of one event has no influence on the outcome of the other.

This is a bit easier to see if we simplify the situation by thinking about a two-sided die (also known as a coin) with the values 0 and 1. This allows us to think of the output of a call of rollN as a binary number. When we use a binary die, there are 2^n possible sequences that testN might return. Each of these sequences is equally likely; therefore each has a probability of occurring of $(1/2)^n$.

Let's go back to our six-sided die. How many different sequences are there of length 10? 6^{10}. So, the probability of rolling ten consecutive 1's is $1/6^{10}$. Less than

---

[97] In point of fact, the values returned by random.random are not truly random. They are what mathematicians call **pseudorandom**. For almost all practical purposes, this distinction is not relevant and we shall ignore it.

one out of sixty million. Pretty low, but no lower than the probability of any other sequence, e.g., 5442462412.

15.2 Calculating Simple Probabilities

In general, when we talk about the **probability** of a result having some property (e.g., all 1's) we are asking what fraction of all possible results has that property. This is why probabilities range from 0 to 1. Suppose we want to know the probability of getting any sequence other than all 1's when rolling the die. It is simply $1 - (1/6^{10})$, because the probability of something happening and the probability of the same thing not happening must add up to 1.

Suppose we want to know the probability of rolling the die ten times without getting a single 1. One way to answer this question is to transform it into the question of how many of the 6^{10} possible sequences don't contain a 1. This can be computed as follows:

1. The probability of not rolling a 1 on any single roll is 5/6.
2. The probability of not rolling a 1 on either the first or the second roll is $(5/6)*(5/6)$, or $(5/6)^2$.
3. So, the probability of not rolling a 1 ten times in a row is $(5/6)^{10}$, slightly more than 0.16.

Step 2 is an application of the **multiplicative law** for independent probabilities. Consider, for example, two independent events A and B. If A occurs one 1/3 of the time and B occurs 1/4 of the time, the probability that both A and B occur is 1/4 of 1/3, i.e., (1/3)/4 or (1/3)*(1/4).

What about the probability of rolling at least one 1? It is simply 1 minus the probability of not rolling at least one 1, i.e., $1 - (5/6)^{10}$. Notice that this cannot be correctly computed by saying that the probability of rolling a 1 on any roll is 1/6, so the probability of rolling at least one 1 is 10*(1/6), i.e., 10/6. This is obviously incorrect, since a probability cannot be greater than 1.

How about the probability of rolling exactly two 1's in ten rolls? This is equivalent to asking what fraction of the first 6^{10} integers has exactly two 1's in its base 6 representation. We could easily write a program to generate all of these sequences and count the number that contained exactly one 1. Deriving the probability analytically is a bit tricky, and we defer it to Section 15.4.4.

15.3 Inferential Statistics

As we just saw, one can use a systematic process to derive the precise probability of some complex event based upon knowing the probability of one or more simpler events. For example, one can easily compute the probability of flipping a coin and getting ten consecutive heads based on the assumption that flips are independent and we know the probability of each flip coming up heads. Suppose, however, that we don't actually know the probability of the relevant simpler event. Suppose, for example, that we don't know whether the coin is fair (i.e., a coin where heads and tails are equally likely).

All is not lost. If we have some data about the behavior of the coin, we can combine that data with our knowledge of probability to derive an estimate of the true probability. We can use **inferential statistics** to estimate the probability of a single flip coming up heads, and then conventional probability to compute the probability of a coin with that behavior coming up heads ten times in a row.

In brief (since this is not a book about statistics), the guiding principle of inferential statistics is that a random sample tends to exhibit the same properties as the population from which it is drawn.

Suppose Harvey Dent (also known as Two-Face) flipped a coin, and it came up heads. You would not infer from this that the next flip would also come up heads. Suppose he flipped it twice, and it came up heads both time. You might reason that the probability of this happening for a fair coin was 0.25, so there was still no reason to assume the next flip would be heads. Suppose, however, 100 out of 100 flips came up heads. $(1/2)^{100}$ (the probability of this event, assuming a fair coin) is a pretty small number, so you might feel safe in inferring that the coin has a head on both sides.

Your belief in whether the coin is fair is based on the intuition that the behavior of a single sample of 100 flips is similar to the behavior of the population of all samples of 100 flips. This belief seems pretty sound when all 100 flips are heads. Suppose that 52 flips came up heads and 48 tails. Would you feel comfortable in predicting that the next 100 flips would have the same ratio of heads to tails? For that matter, how comfortable would you feel about even predicting that there would be more heads than tails in the next 100 flips? Take a few minutes to think about this, and then try the experiment. Or, if you don't happen to have a coin handy, simulate the flips using the code in Figure 15.2.

The function `flip` in Figure 15.2 simulates flipping a fair coin `numFlips` times, and returns the fraction of those flips that came up heads. For each flip, the call `random.choice(('H', 'T'))` randomly returns either `'H'` or `'T'`.

```
def flip(numFlips):
    """Assumes numFlips a positive int"""
    heads = 0
    for i in range(numFlips):
        if random.choice(('H', 'T')) == 'H':
            heads += 1
    return heads/numFlips

def flipSim(numFlipsPerTrial, numTrials):
    """Assumes numFlipsPerTrial and numTrials positive ints"""
    fracHeads = []
    for i in range(numTrials):
        fracHeads.append(flip(numFlipsPerTrial))
    mean = sum(fracHeads)/len(fracHeads)
    return mean
```

Figure 15.2 Flipping a coin

Try executing the function flipSim(10, 1) a couple of times. Here's what we saw the first two times we tried print('Mean =', flipSim(10, 1)):

Mean = 0.2
Mean = 0.6

It seems that it would be inappropriate to assume much (other than that the coin has both heads and tails) from any one trial of 10 flips. That's why we typically structure our simulations to include multiple trials and compare the results. Let's try flipSim(10, 100) a couple of times:

Mean = 0.5029999999999999
Mean = 0.496

Do you feel better about these results? When we tried flipSim(100, 100000), we got

Mean = 0.5005000000000038
Mean = 0.5003139999999954

This looks really good (especially since we know that the answer should be 0.5—but that's cheating). Now it seems we can safely conclude something about the next flip, i.e., that heads and tails are about equally likely. But why do we think that we can conclude that?

CHAPTER 15. STOCHASTIC PROGRAMS, PROBABILITY, AND DISTRIBUTIONS

What we are depending upon is the **law of large numbers** (also known as **Bernoulli's theorem**[98]). This law states that in repeated independent tests (flips in this case) with the same actual probability p of a particular outcome in each test (e.g., an actual probability of 0.5 of getting a head for each flip), the chance that the fraction of times that outcome occurs differs from p converges to zero as the number of trials goes to infinity.

It is worth noting that the law of large numbers does not imply, as too many seem to think, that if deviations from expected behavior occur, these deviations are likely to be "evened out" by opposite deviations in the future. This misapplication of the law of large numbers is known as the **gambler's fallacy**.[99]

People often confuse the gambler's fallacy with regression to the mean. **Regression to the mean**[100] states that following an extreme random event, the next random event is likely to be less extreme. If you were to flip a fair coin six times and get six heads, regression to the mean implies that the next sequence of six flips is likely to have closer to the expected value of three heads. It does not imply, as the gambler's fallacy suggests, that the next sequence of flips is likely to have fewer heads than tails.

Success in most endeavors requires a combination of skill and luck. The skill component determines the mean and the luck component accounts for the variability. The randomness of luck leads to regression to the mean.

The code in Figure 15.3 produces a plot, Figure 15.4, illustrating regression to the mean. The function `regressToMean` first generates `numTrials` trials of `numFlips` coin flips each. It then identifies all trials where the fraction of heads was either less than 1/3 or more than 2/3 and plots these extremal values as circles. Then, for each of these points, it plots the value of the subsequent trial as a triangle in the same column as the circle.

---

[98] Though the law of large numbers had been discussed in the 16th century by Cardano, the first proof was published by Jacob Bernoulli in the early 18th century. It is unrelated to the theorem about fluid dynamics called Bernoulli's theorem, which was proved by Jacob's nephew Daniel.

[99] "On August 18, 1913, at the casino in Monte Carlo, black came up a record twenty-six times in succession [in roulette]. ... [There] was a near-panicky rush to bet on red, beginning about the time black had come up a phenomenal fifteen times. In application of the maturity [of the chances] doctrine, players doubled and tripled their stakes, this doctrine leading them to believe after black came up the twentieth time that there was not a chance in a million of another repeat. In the end the unusual run enriched the Casino by some millions of francs." Huff and Geis, *How to Take a Chance*, pp. 28-29.

[100] The term "regression to the mean" was first used by Francis Galton in 1885 in a paper titled "Regression Toward Mediocrity in Hereditary Stature." In that study he observed that children of unusually tall parents were likely to be shorter than their parents.

The horizontal line at 0.5, the expected mean, is created using the `axhline` function. The function `pylab.xlim` controls the extent of the x-axis. The function call `pylab.xlim(xmin, xmax)` sets the minimum and maximum values of the x-axis of the current figure. The function call `pylab.xlim()` returns a tuple composed of the minimum and maximum values of the x-axis of the current figure. The function `pylab.ylim` works the same way.

```
def regressToMean(numFlips, numTrials):
    #Get fraction of heads for each trial of numFlips
    fracHeads = []
    for t in range(numTrials):
        fracHeads.append(flip(numFlips))
    #Find trials with extreme results and for each the next trial
    extremes, nextTrials = [], []
    for i in range(len(fracHeads) - 1):
        if fracHeads[i] < 0.33 or fracHeads[i] > 0.66:
            extremes.append(fracHeads[i])
            nextTrials.append(fracHeads[i+1])
    #Plot results
    pylab.plot(range(len(extremes)), extremes, 'ko',
               label = 'Extreme')
    pylab.plot(range(len(nextTrials)), nextTrials, 'k^',
               label = 'Next Trial')
    pylab.axhline(0.5)
    pylab.ylim(0, 1)
    pylab.xlim(-1, len(extremes) + 1)
    pylab.xlabel('Extreme Example and Next Trial')
    pylab.ylabel('Fraction Heads')
    pylab.title('Regression to the Mean')
    pylab.legend(loc = 'best')

regressToMean(15, 40)
```

Figure 15.3: Regression to the mean

Notice that while the trial following an extreme result is typically followed by a trial closer to the mean than the extreme result, that doesn't always occur—as shown by the boxed pair.

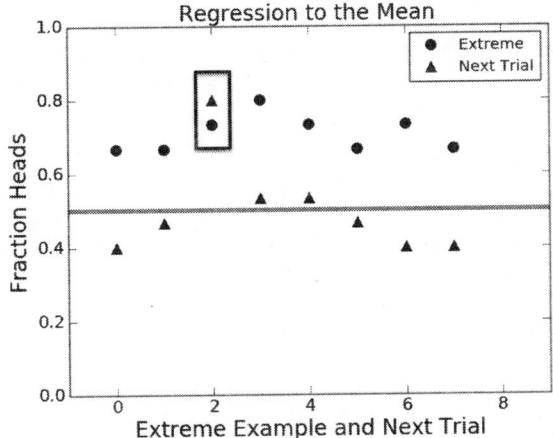

Figure 15.4: Illustration of regression to mean

Finger exercise: Sally averages 5 strokes a hole when she plays golf. One day, she took 40 strokes to complete the first nine holes. Her partner conjectured that she would probably regress to the mean and take 50 strokes to complete the next nine holes. Do you agree with her partner?

Figure 15.5 contains a function, flipPlot, that produces two plots, Figure 15.6, intended to show the law of large numbers at work. The first plot shows how the absolute value of the difference between the number of heads and number of tails changes with the number of flips. The second plot compares the ratio of heads to tails versus the number of flips. The line random.seed(0) near the bottom ensures that the pseudorandom number generator used by random.random will generate the same sequence of pseudorandom numbers each time this code is executed.[101] This is convenient for debugging. The function random.seed can be called with any number. If it is called with no argument, the seed is chosen at random.

---

[101] You should be aware of the fact that the random number generators in Python 2 and Python 3 are not identical. This means that even if you set the seed, you cannot assume that a program will behave the same way across versions of the language.

```
def flipPlot(minExp, maxExp):
    """Assumes minExp and maxExp positive integers; minExp < maxExp
       Plots results of 2**minExp to 2**maxExp coin flips"""
    ratios, diffs, xAxis = [], [], []
    for exp in range(minExp, maxExp + 1):
        xAxis.append(2**exp)
    for numFlips in xAxis:
        numHeads = 0
        for n in range(numFlips):
            if random.choice(('H', 'T')) == 'H':
                numHeads += 1
        numTails = numFlips - numHeads
        try:
            ratios.append(numHeads/numTails)
            diffs.append(abs(numHeads - numTails))
        except ZeroDivisionError:
            continue
    pylab.title('Difference Between Heads and Tails')
    pylab.xlabel('Number of Flips')
    pylab.ylabel('Abs(#Heads - #Tails)')
    pylab.plot(xAxis, diffs, 'k')
    pylab.figure()
    pylab.title('Heads/Tails Ratios')
    pylab.xlabel('Number of Flips')
    pylab.ylabel('#Heads/#Tails')
    pylab.plot(xAxis, ratios, 'k')

random.seed(0)
flipPlot(4, 20)
```

Figure 15.5 Plotting the results of coin flips

The plot on the left seems to suggest that the absolute difference between the number of heads and the number of tails fluctuates in the beginning, crashes downwards, and then moves rapidly upwards. However, we need to keep in mind that we have only two data points to the right of x = 300,000. The fact that pylab.plot connected these points with lines may mislead us into seeing trends when all we have are isolated points. This is not an uncommon phenomenon, so you should always ask how many points a plot actually contains before jumping to any conclusion about what it means.

It's hard to see much of anything in the plot on the right, which is mostly a flat line. This too is deceptive. Even though there are sixteen data points, most of them are crowded into a small amount of real estate on the left side of the plot, so that the detail is impossible to see. This occurs because the plotted points have x values of 2^4, 2^5, 2^6, ..., 2^{20}, so the values on the x-axis range from 16 to over a million, and unless instructed otherwise PyLab will place these points based on their relative distance from the origin. This is called **linear scaling**. Because most of the points have x values that are small relative to 2^{20}, they will appear relatively close to the origin.

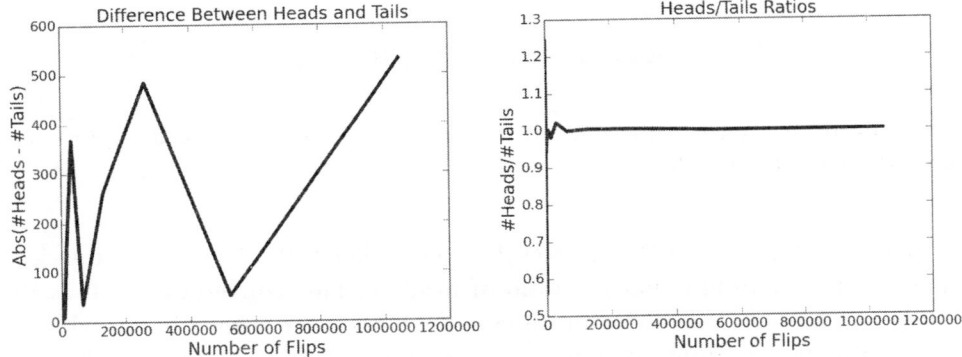

Figure 15.6 The law of large numbers at work

Fortunately, these visualization problems are easy to address in PyLab. As we saw in Chapter 11 and earlier in this chapter, we can easily instruct our program to plot unconnected points, e.g., by writing `pylab.plot(xAxis, diffs, 'ko')`.

Both plots in Figure 15.7 use a logarithmic scale on the x-axis. Since the x values generated by `flipPlot` are 2^{minExp}, $2^{minExp+1}$, .., 2^{maxExp}, using a logarithmic x-axis causes the points to be evenly spaced along the x-axis—providing maximum separation between points. The left-hand plot in Figure 15.7 uses a logarithmic scale on the y-axis as well as on the x-axis. The y values on this plot range from nearly 0 to around 550. If the y-axis were linearly scaled, it would be difficult to see the relatively small differences in y values on the left side of the plot. On the other hand, on the plot on the right the y values are fairly tightly grouped, so we use a linear y-axis.

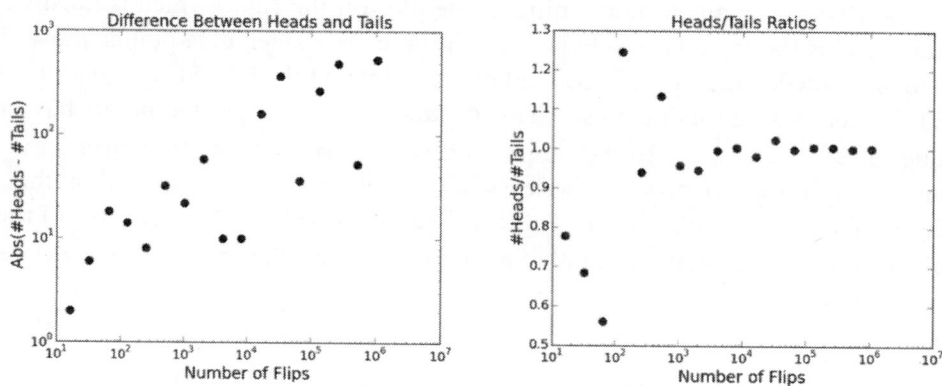

Figure 15.7 Impact of number of flips

Finger exercise: Modify the code in Figure 15.5 so that it produces plots like those shown in Figure 15.7.

These plots are easier to interpret than the earlier plots. The plot on the right suggests pretty strongly that the ratio of heads to tails converges to 1.0 as the number of flips gets large. The meaning of the plot on the left is a bit less clear. It appears that the absolute difference grows with the number of flips, but it is not completely convincing.

It is never possible to achieve perfect accuracy through sampling without sampling the entire population. No matter how many samples we examine, we can never be sure that the sample set is typical until we examine every element of the population (and since we are often dealing with infinite populations, e.g., all possible sequences of coin flips, this is often impossible). Of course, this is not to say that an estimate cannot be precisely correct. We might flip a coin twice, get one heads and one tails, and conclude that the true probability of each is 0.5. We would have reached the right conclusion, but our reasoning would have been faulty.

How many samples do we need to look at before we can have justified confidence in our answer? This depends on the **variance** in the underlying distribution. Roughly speaking, variance is a measure of how much spread there is in the possible different outcomes. More formally, the variance of a collection of values, X, is defined as

$$variance(X) = \frac{\sum_{x \in X}(x - \mu)^2}{|X|}$$

CHAPTER 15. STOCHASTIC PROGRAMS, PROBABILITY, AND DISTRIBUTIONS 247

where $|X|$ is the size of the collection and μ (mu) its mean. Informally, the variance describes what fraction of the values are close to the mean. If many values are relatively close to the mean, the variance is relatively small. If many values are relatively far from the mean, the variance is relatively large. If all values are the same, the variance is zero.

The **standard deviation** of a collection of values is the square root of the variance. While it contains exactly the same information as the variance, the standard deviation is easier to interpret because it is in the same units as the original data. For example, is easier to understand the statement "the mean height of a population is 70 inches with a standard deviation of 4 inches," than the sentence "the mean of height of a population is 70 inches with a variance of 16 inches^2."

Figure 15.8 contains implementations of variance and standard deviation.[102]

```
def variance(X):
    """Assumes that X is a list of numbers.
        Returns the standard deviation of X"""
    mean = sum(X)/len(X)
    tot = 0.0
    for x in X:
        tot += (x - mean)**2
    return tot/len(X)

def stdDev(X):
    """Assumes that X is a list of numbers.
        Returns the standard deviation of X"""
    return variance(X)**0.5
```

Figure 15.8 Variance and standard deviation

We can use the notion of standard deviation to think about the relationship between the number of samples we have looked at and how much confidence we should have in the answer we have computed. Figure 15.9 contains a modified version of flipPlot. It uses the helper functions defined at the top of the figure to run multiple trials of each number of coin flips, and then plots the means for abs(heads - tails) and the heads/tails ratio. It also plots the standard deviation of each. The helper function makePlot contains the code used to produce the plots. The function runTrial simulates one trial of numFlips coins.

---

[102] You'll probably never need to implement these yourself. Statistical libraries implement these and many other standard statistical functions. However, we present the code here on the off chance that some readers prefer looking at code to looking at equations.

```python
def makePlot(xVals, yVals, title, xLabel, yLabel, style,
             logX = False, logY = False):
    pylab.figure()
    pylab.title(title)
    pylab.xlabel(xLabel)
    pylab.ylabel(yLabel)
    pylab.plot(xVals, yVals, style)
    if logX:
        pylab.semilogx()
    if logY:
        pylab.semilogy()

def runTrial(numFlips):
    numHeads = 0
    for n in range(numFlips):
        if random.choice(('H', 'T')) == 'H':
            numHeads += 1
    numTails = numFlips - numHeads
    return (numHeads, numTails)

def flipPlot1(minExp, maxExp, numTrials):
    """Assumes minExp, maxExp, numTrials ints >0; minExp < maxExp
       Plots summaries of results of numTrials trials of
       2**minExp to 2**maxExp coin flips"""
    ratiosMeans, diffsMeans, ratiosSDs, diffsSDs = [], [], [], []
    xAxis = []
    for exp in range(minExp, maxExp + 1):
        xAxis.append(2**exp)
    for numFlips in xAxis:
        ratios, diffs = [], []
        for t in range(numTrials):
            numHeads, numTails = runTrial(numFlips)
            ratios.append(numHeads/numTails)
            diffs.append(abs(numHeads - numTails))
        ratiosMeans.append(sum(ratios)/numTrials)
        diffsMeans.append(sum(diffs)/numTrials)
        ratiosSDs.append(stdDev(ratios))
        diffsSDs.append(stdDev(diffs))
    numTrialsString = ' (' + str(numTrials) + ' Trials)'
    title = 'Mean Heads/Tails Ratios' + numTrialsString
    makePlot(xAxis, ratiosMeans, title, 'Number of flips',
             'Mean Heads/Tails', 'ko', logX = True)
    title = 'SD Heads/Tails Ratios' + numTrialsString
    makePlot(xAxis, ratiosSDs, title, 'Number of Flips',
             'Standard Deviation', 'ko', logX = True, logY = True)
```

Figure 15.9 Coin-flipping simulation

Let's try `flipPlot1(4, 20, 20)`. It generates the plots in Figure 15.10.

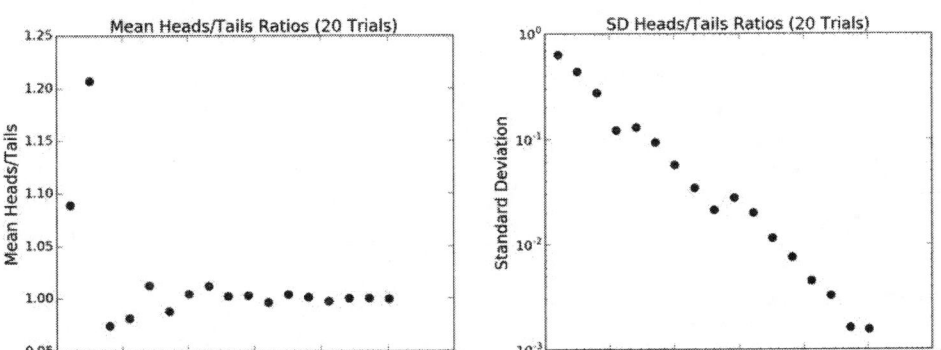

Figure 15.10 Convergence of heads/tails ratios

This is encouraging. The mean heads/tails ratio is converging towards 1 and the log of the standard deviation is falling linearly with the log of the number of flips per trial. By the time we get to about 10^6 coin flips per trial, the standard deviation (about 10^{-3}) is roughly three decimal orders of magnitude smaller than the mean (about 1), indicating that the variance across the trials was small. We can, therefore, have considerable confidence that the expected heads/tails ratio is quite close to 1.0. As we flip more coins, not only do we have a more precise answer, but more important, we also have reason to be more confident that it is close to the right answer.

What about the absolute difference between the number of heads and the number of tails? We can take a look at that by adding to the end of `flipPlot1` the code in Figure 15.11. This produces the plots in Figure 15.12.

```
title = 'Mean abs(#Heads - #Tails)' + numTrialsString
makePlot(xAxis, diffsMeans, title,
     'Number of Flips', 'Mean abs(#Heads - #Tails)', 'ko',
     logX = True, logY = True)
title = 'SD abs(#Heads - #Tails)' + numTrialsString
makePlot(xAxis, diffsSDs, title,
     'Number of Flips', 'Standard Deviation', 'ko',
     logX = True, logY = True)
```

Figure 15.11 Absolute differences

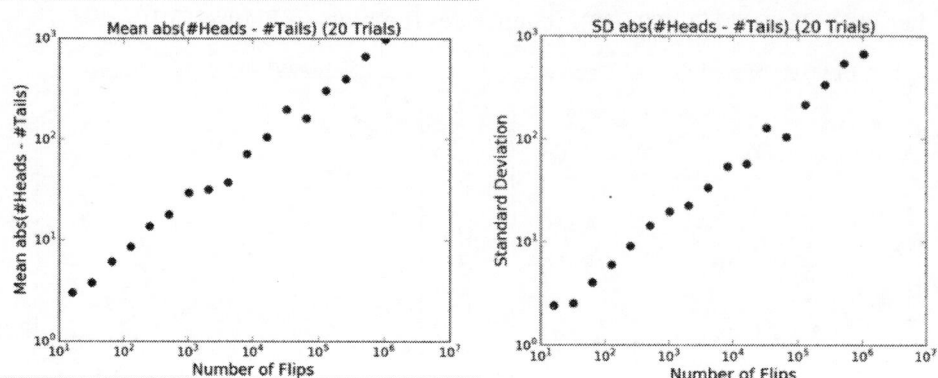

Figure 15.12 Mean and standard deviation of heads - tails

As expected, the absolute difference between the numbers of heads and tails grows with the number of flips. Furthermore, since we are averaging the results over twenty trials, the plot is considerably smoother than when we plotted the results of a single trial in Figure 15.7. But what's up with the plot on the right of Figure 15.12? The standard deviation is growing with the number of flips. Does this mean that as the number of flips increases we should have less rather than more confidence in the estimate of the expected value of the difference between heads and tails?

No, it does not. The standard deviation should always be viewed in the context of the mean. If the mean were a billion and the standard deviation 100, we would view the dispersion of the data as small. But if the mean were 100 and the standard deviation 100, we would view the dispersion as large.

The **coefficient of variation** is the standard deviation divided by the mean. When comparing data sets with different means (as here), the coefficient of variation is often more informative than the standard deviation. As you can see from its implementation in Figure 15.13, the coefficient of variation is not defined when the mean is 0.

```
def CV(X):
    mean = sum(X)/len(X)
    try:
        return stdDev(X)/mean
    except ZeroDivisionError:
        return float('nan')
```

Figure 15.13 Coefficient of variation

Figure 15.14 contains a function that plots coefficients of variation. In addition to the plots produced by flipPlot1, it produces the plots in Figure 15.15.

```
def flipPlot2(minExp, maxExp, numTrials):
    """Assumes minExp and maxExp positive ints; minExp < maxExp
         numTrials a positive integer
       Plots summaries of results of numTrials trials of
         2**minExp to 2**maxExp coin flips"""
    ratiosMeans, diffsMeans, ratiosSDs, diffsSDs = [], [], [], []
    ratiosCVs, diffsCVs, xAxis = [], [], []
    for exp in range(minExp, maxExp + 1):
        xAxis.append(2**exp)
    for numFlips in xAxis:
        ratios, diffs = [], []
        for t in range(numTrials):
            numHeads, numTails = runTrial(numFlips)
            ratios.append(numHeads/float(numTails))
            diffs.append(abs(numHeads - numTails))
        ratiosMeans.append(sum(ratios)/numTrials)
        diffsMeans.append(sum(diffs)/numTrials)
        ratiosSDs.append(stdDev(ratios))
        diffsSDs.append(stdDev(diffs))
        ratiosCVs.append(CV(ratios))
        diffsCVs.append(CV(diffs))
    numTrialsString = ' (' + str(numTrials) + ' Trials)'
    title = 'Mean Heads/Tails Ratios' + numTrialsString
    makePlot(xAxis, ratiosMeans, title, 'Number of flips',
             'Mean Heads/Tails', 'ko', logX = True)
    title = 'SD Heads/Tails Ratios' + numTrialsString
    makePlot(xAxis, ratiosSDs, title, 'Number of flips',
             'Standard Deviation', 'ko', logX = True, logY = True)
    title = 'Mean abs(#Heads - #Tails)' + numTrialsString
    makePlot(xAxis, diffsMeans, title,'Number of Flips',
             'Mean abs(#Heads - #Tails)', 'ko',
             logX = True, logY = True)
    title = 'SD abs(#Heads - #Tails)' + numTrialsString
    makePlot(xAxis, diffsSDs, title, 'Number of Flips',
             'Standard Deviation', 'ko', logX = True, logY = True)
    title = 'Coeff. of Var. abs(#Heads - #Tails)' + numTrialsString
    makePlot(xAxis, diffsCVs, title, 'Number of Flips',
             'Coeff. of Var.', 'ko', logX = True)
    title = 'Coeff. of Var. Heads/Tails Ratio' + numTrialsString
    makePlot(xAxis, ratiosCVs, title, 'Number of Flips',
             'Coeff. of Var.', 'ko', logX = True, logY = True)
```

Figure 15.14 Final version of flipPlot1

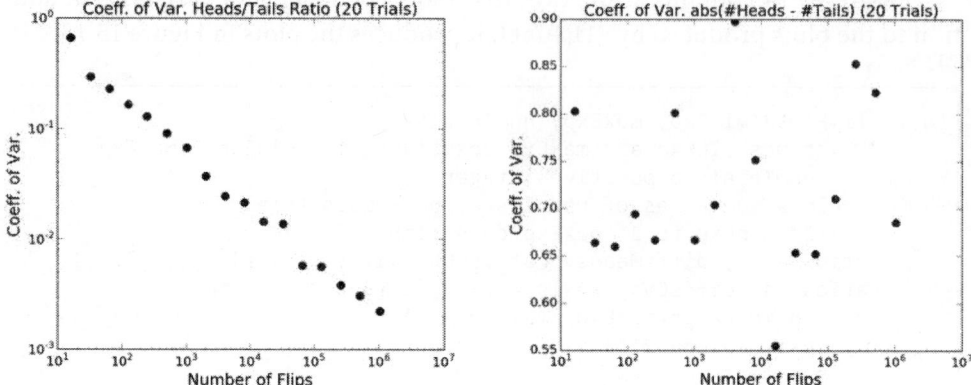

Figure 15.15 Coefficient of variation of heads/tails and abs(heads − tails)

In this case we see that the plot of coefficient of variation for the heads/tails ratio is not much different from the plot of the standard deviation in Figure 15.10. This is not surprising, since the only difference between the two is the division by the mean, and since the mean is close to 1 that makes little difference.

On the other hand, the plot of the coefficient of variation for the absolute difference between heads and tails is a different story. While the standard deviation exhibited a clear trend in Figure 15.12, it would take a brave person to argue that the coefficient of variation is trending in any direction. It seems to be fluctuating wildly. This suggests that dispersion in the values of abs(heads - tails) is independent of the number of flips. It's not growing, as the standard deviation might have misled us to believe, but it's not shrinking either. Perhaps a trend would appear if we tried 1000 trials instead of 20. Let's see.

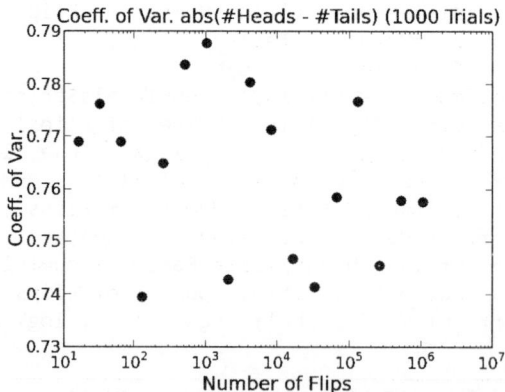

Figure 15.16 A large number of trials

In Figure 15.16, it looks as if the coefficient of variation settles in somewhere in the neighborhood of 0.74-0.78. In general, distributions with a coefficient of variation of less than 1 are considered low-variance.

The main advantage of the coefficient of variation over the standard deviation is that it allows us to compare the dispersion of sets with different means. Consider, for example, the distribution of weekly income in different regions of Australia, as depicted in Figure 15.17.

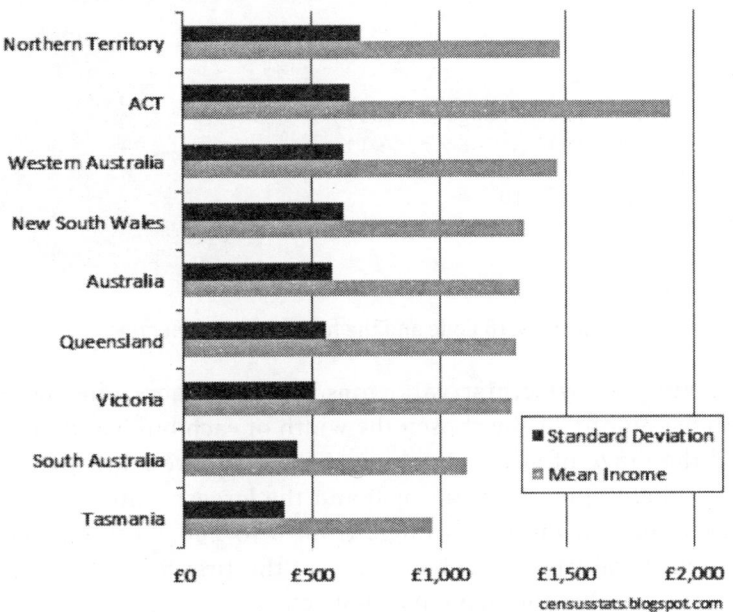

Figure 15.17 Income distribution in Australia

If we use standard deviation as a measure of income inequality, it appears that there is considerably less income inequality in Tasmania than in the ACT (Australian Capital Territory). However, if we look at the coefficients of variation (about 0.32 for ACT and 0.42 for Tasmania), we reach a rather different conclusion.

That isn't to say that the coefficient of variation is always more useful than the standard deviation. If the mean is near 0, small changes in the mean lead to large (but not necessarily meaningful) changes in the coefficient of variation, and when the mean is 0, the coefficient of variation is undefined. Also, as we shall see in Section 15.4.2, the standard deviation can be used to construct a confidence interval, but the coefficient of variation cannot.

15.4 Distributions

A **histogram** is a plot designed to show the distribution of values in a set of data. The values are first sorted, and then divided into a fixed number of equal-width bins. A plot is then drawn that shows the number of elements in each bin. The code on the left of Figure 15.18 produces the plot on the right of that figure.

```
vals = []
for i in range(1000):
    num1 = random.choice(range(0, 101))
    num2 = random.choice(range(0, 101))
    vals.append(num1+num2)
pylab.hist(vals, bins = 10)
pylab.xlabel('Number of Occurrences')
```

Figure 15.18 Code and the histogram it generates

The function call `pylab.hist(vals, bins = 10)` produces a histogram with ten bins. PyLab has automatically chosen the width of each bin based on the number of bins and the range of values. Looking at the code, we know that the smallest number that might appears in vals is 0 and the largest number 200. Therefore, the possible values on the x-axis range from 0 to 200. Each bin represents an equal fraction of the values on the x-axis, so the first bin will contain the elements 0-19, the next bin the elements 20-39, etc.

Finger exercise: In Figure 15.18, why are the bins near the middle of the histogram taller than the the bins near the sides? Hint: think about why 7 is the most common outcome of rolling a pair of dice.

By now you must be getting awfully bored with flipping coins. Nevertheless, we are going to ask you to look at yet one more coin-flipping simulation. The simulation in Figure 15.19 illustrates more of PyLab's plotting capabilities, and gives us an opportunity to get a visual notion of what standard deviation means. It produces two histograms. The first shows the result of a simulation of 100,000 trials of 100 flips of a fair coin. The second shows the result of a simulation of 100,000 trials of 1,000 flips of a fair coin.

The method `pylab.annotate` is used to place some statistics on the figure showing the histogram. The first argument is the string to be displayed on the

CHAPTER 15. STOCHASTIC PROGRAMS, PROBABILITY, AND DISTRIBUTIONS

figure. The next two arguments control where the string is placed. The argument xycoords = 'axes fraction' indicates the placement of the text will be expressed as a fraction of the width and height of the figure. The argument xy = (0.67, 0.5) indicates that the text should begin two thirds of the way from the left edge of the figure and half way from the bottom edge of the figure.

```
def flip(numFlips):
    """Assumes numFlips a positive int"""
    heads = 0
    for i in range(numFlips):
        if random.choice(('H', 'T')) == 'H':
            heads += 1
    return heads/float(numFlips)

def flipSim(numFlipsPerTrial, numTrials):
    fracHeads = []
    for i in range(numTrials):
        fracHeads.append(flip(numFlipsPerTrial))
    mean = sum(fracHeads)/len(fracHeads)
    sd = stdDev(fracHeads)
    return (fracHeads, mean, sd)

def labelPlot(numFlips, numTrials, mean, sd):
    pylab.title(str(numTrials) + ' trials of '
                + str(numFlips) + ' flips each')
    pylab.xlabel('Fraction of Heads')
    pylab.ylabel('Number of Trials')
    pylab.annotate('Mean = ' + str(round(mean, 4))\
                   + '\nSD = ' + str(round(sd, 4)), size='x-large',
                   xycoords = 'axes fraction', xy = (0.67, 0.5))

def makePlots(numFlips1, numFlips2, numTrials):
    val1, mean1, sd1 = flipSim(numFlips1, numTrials)
    pylab.hist(val1, bins = 20)
    xmin,xmax = pylab.xlim()
    labelPlot(numFlips1, numTrials, mean1, sd1)
    pylab.figure()
    val2, mean2, sd2 = flipSim(numFlips2, numTrials)
    pylab.hist(val2, bins = 20)
    pylab.xlim(xmin, xmax)
    labelPlot(numFlips2, numTrials, mean2, sd2)

makePlots(100, 1000, 100000)
```

Figure 15.19 Plot histograms of coin flips

To facilitate comparing the two figures, we have used pylab.xlim to force the bounds of the x-axis in the second plot to match those in the first plot, rather than letting PyLab choose the bounds.

When the code in Figure 15.19 is run, it produces the plots in Figure 15.20. Notice that while the means in both plots are about the same, the standard deviations are quite different. The spread of outcomes is much tighter when we flip the coin 1000 times per trial than when we flip the coin 100 times per trial.

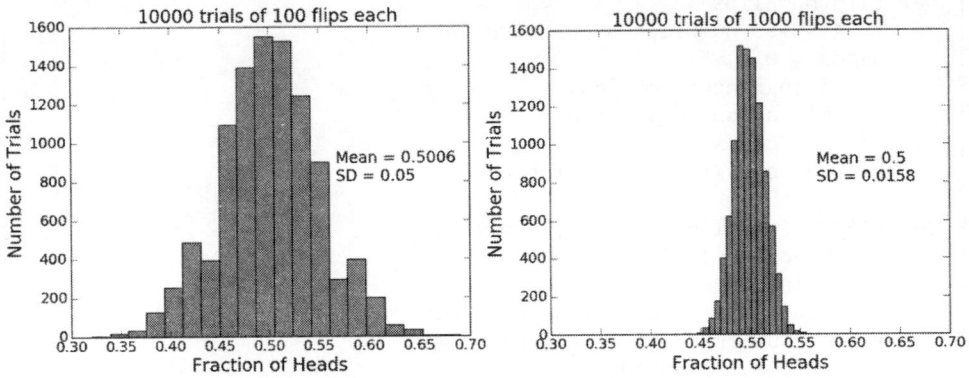

Figure 15.20 Histograms of coin flips

15.4.1 Probability Distributions

A histogram is a depiction of a **frequency distribution**. It tells us how often a random variable has taken on a value in some range, e.g., how often the fraction of times a coin came up heads was between 0.4 and 0.5. It also provides information about the relative frequency of various ranges. For example, we can easily see that the fraction of heads falls between 0.4 and 0.5 far more frequently than it falls between 0.3 and 0.4. A **probability distribution** captures the notion of relative frequency by giving the probability of a random value taking on a value within a range.

Probability distributions fall into two groups: discrete probability distributions and continuous probability distributions, depending upon whether they define the probability distribution for a discrete or a continuous random variable. A **discrete random variable** can take on one of a finite set of values, e.g., the values associated with a roll of a die. A **continuous random variable** can take on any of the infinite real values between two real numbers, e.g., the speed of a car traveling between 0 miles per hour and the car's maximum speed.

Discrete probability distributions are easier to describe. Since there are a finite number of values that the variable can take on, the distribution can be described by simply listing the probability of each value.

Continuous probability distributions are trickier. Since there are an infinite number of possible values, the probability that a continuous random variable will take on a specific value is usually 0. For example, the probability that a car is travelling at exactly 81.3457283 miles per hour is probably 0. Mathematicians like to describe continuous probability distributions using a **probability density function**, often abbreviated as **PDF**. A PDF describes the probability of a random variable lying between two values. Think of the PDF as defining a curve where the values on the x-axis lie between the minimum and maximum value of the random variable. (In some cases the x-axis is infinitely long.) Under the assumption that x1 and x2 lie in the domain of the random variable, the probability of the variable having a value between x1 and x2 is the area under the curve between x1 and x2. Figure 15.21 shows the probability density functions for the expressions random.random() and random.random() + random.random().

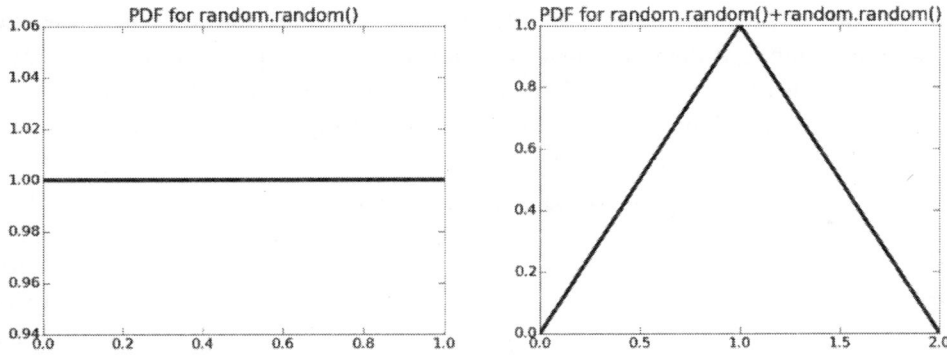

Figure 15.21: PDF for random.random

For random.random() the area under the curve from 0 to 1 is 1. This makes sense because we know that the probability of random.random() returning a value between 0 and 1 is 1. On the other hand, if we consider the area under the part of the curve for random.random() between 0.2 and 0.4, it is 0.2—indicating that the probability of random.random() returning a value between 0.2 and 0.4 is 0.2. Similarly, the area under the curve for random.random() + random.random() from 0 to 2 is 1, and the area under the curve from 0 to 1 is 0.5. Notice, by the way that the PDF for random.random() indicates that every possible interval of the same length has the same probability, whereas the PDF for random.random() + random.random() indicates that some intervals are more probable than others.

15.4.2 Normal Distributions

A **normal** (or **Gaussian**) **distribution** is defined by the probability density function

$$P(x) = \frac{1}{\sigma\sqrt{2\pi}} * e^{-\frac{(x-\mu)^2}{2\sigma^2}}$$

where μ is the mean, σ the standard deviation, and e is Euler's number (roughly 2.718).[103]

If you don't feel like studying this equation, that's fine. Just remember that normal distributions peak at the mean, fall off symmetrically above and below the mean, and asymptotically approach 0. They have the nice mathematical property of being completely specified by two parameters: the mean and the standard deviation (the only two parameters in the equation). Knowing these is equivalent to knowing the entire distribution. The shape of the normal distribution resembles (in the eyes of some) that of a bell, so it sometimes is referred to as a **bell curve**.

Figure 15.22 shows part of the PDF for a normal distribution with a mean of 0 and and standard deviation of 1. We can only show a portion of the PDF, because the tails of a normal distribution converge towards 0, but don't reach it. In principle, no value has a zero probability of occurring.

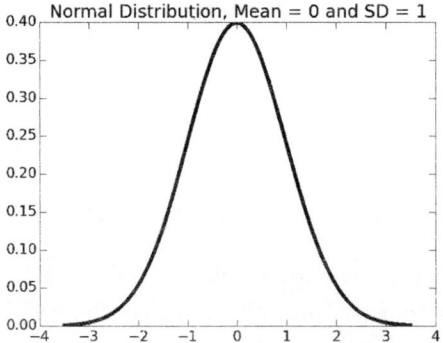

Figure 15.22: A normal distribution

---

[103] e is one of those magic irrational constants, like π, that show up all over the place in mathematics. The most common use is as the base of what are called "natural logarithms." There are many equivalent ways of defining e, including as the value of $(1 + \frac{1}{x})^x$ as x approaches infinity.

CHAPTER 15. STOCHASTIC PROGRAMS, PROBABILITY, AND DISTRIBUTIONS

Normal distributions can be easily generated in Python programs by calling random.gauss(mu, sigma), which returns a randomly chosen floating point number from a normal distribution with mean and standard deviation sigma.

Normal distributions are frequently used in constructing probabilistic models because they have nice mathematical properties. Of course, finding a mathematically nice model is of no use if it provides a bad model of the actual data. Fortunately, many random variables have an approximately normal distribution. For example, physical properties of plants and animals (e.g., height, weight, body temperature) typically have approximately normal distributions. Importantly, many experiments have normally distributed measurement errors. This assumption was used in the early 1800s by the German mathematician and physicist Karl Gauss, who assumed a normal distribution of measurement errors in his analysis of astronomical data (which led to the normal distribution becoming known as the **Gaussian distribution** in much of the scientific community).

One of the nice properties of normal distributions is that independent of the mean and standard deviation, the number of standard deviations from the mean needed to encompass a fixed fraction of the data is a constant. For example, ~68.27% of the data will always lie with one standard deviation of the mean, ~95.45% within two standard deviations of the mean, and ~99.73% within three standard deviations of the mean. This is sometimes called the **68-95-99.7** rule, but is more often called the **empirical rule**.

The rule can be derived by integrating the formula defining a normal distribution to get the area under the curve. Looking at Figure 15.22, it is easy to believe that roughly two thirds of the total area under the curve lies between −1 and 1, roughly 95% between -2 and 2, and almost all of it between -3 and 3. But that's only one example, and it is always dangerous to generalize from a single example. We could accept the empirical rule on the unimpeachable authority of Wikipedia. However, just to be sure, and as an excuse to introduce a Python library worth knowing about, let's check it ourselves.

The SciPy library contains many mathematical functions commonly used by scientists and engineers. SciPy is organized into modules covering different scientific computing domains, such as signal processing and image processing. We will use a number of functions from SciPy later in this book. Here we use the function scipy.integrate.quad, which finds an approximation to the value of integrating a function between two points.

The function scipy.integrate.quad has three required parameters and one optional parameter:

- a function or method to be integrated (if the function takes more than one argument, it is integrated along the axis corresponding to the first argument).
- a number representing the lower limit of the integration,
- a number representing the upper limit of the integration, and
- an optional tuple supplying values for all arguments, except the first, of the function to be integrated.

The quad function returns a tuple of two floating point numbers. The first is an approximation to the value of the integral, and the second an estimate of the absolute error in the result.

Consider, for example, evaluating the integral of the unary function abs in the interval 0 to 5. We don't need any fancy math to compute the area under this curve: it's simply the area of a right triangle with base and altitude of length 5, i.e., 12.5. So, it shouldn't be a surprise that

```
print scipy.integrate.quad(abs, 0, 5)[0]
```

prints 12.5. (The second value in the tuple returned by quad is roughly 10^{-13}, indicating that the approximation is quite good.)

The code in Figure 15.23 computes the area under portions of normal distributions for some randomly chosen means and standard deviations. Notice that gaussian is a ternary function, and therefore the code

```
print scipy.integrate.quad(gaussian, -2, 2, (0, 1))[0]
```

prints the integral from -2 to 2 of a normal distribution with mean 0 and standard deviation 1.

When we ran the code in Figure 15.23, it printed what the empirical rule predicts:

```
For mu = -1 and sigma = 6
   Fraction within 1 std = 0.6827
   Fraction within 2 std = 0.9545
   Fraction within 3 std = 0.9973
For mu = 9 and sigma = 9
   Fraction within 1 std = 0.6827
   Fraction within 2 std = 0.9545
   Fraction within 3 std = 0.9973
For mu = 1 and sigma = 5
   Fraction within 1 std = 0.6827
   Fraction within 2 std = 0.9545
   Fraction within 3 std = 0.9973
```

```
import scipy.integrate

def gaussian(x, mu, sigma):
    factor1 = (1.0/(sigma*((2*pylab.pi)**0.5)))
    factor2 = pylab.e**-(((x-mu)**2)/(2*sigma**2))
    return factor1*factor2

def checkEmpirical(numTrials):
    for t in range(numTrials):
        mu = random.randint(-10, 10)
        sigma = random.randint(1, 10)
        print('For mu =', mu, 'and sigma =', sigma)
        for numStd in (1, 2, 3):
            area = scipy.integrate.quad(gaussian, mu-numStd*sigma,
                                        mu+numStd*sigma,
                                        (mu, sigma))[0]
            print('  Fraction within', numStd, 'std =',
                  round(area, 4))

checkEmpirical(3)
```

Figure 15.23: Checking the empirical rule

People frequently use the empirical rule to derive confidence intervals. Instead of estimating an unknown value (e.g., the expected number of heads) by a single value, a **confidence interval** provides a range that is likely to contain the unknown value and a degree of confidence that the unknown value lies within that range. For example, a political poll might indicate that a candidate is likely to get 52% of the vote ±4% (i.e., the confidence interval is of size 8) with a **confidence level** of 95%. What this means is that the pollster believes that 95% of the time the candidate will receive between 48% and 56% of the vote.[104] Together the confidence interval and the confidence level are intended to indicate the reliability of the estimate. Almost always, increasing the confidence level will require widening the confidence interval.

Suppose that we run 100 trials of 100 coin flips each. Suppose further that the mean fraction of heads is 0.4999 and the standard deviation 0.0497. For reasons we will discuss in Section 17.2, we can assume that the distribution of the means of the trials was normal. Therefore, we can conclude that if we conducted more trials of 100 flips each,

---

[104] For polls, confidence intervals are not typically estimated by looking at the standard deviation of multiple polls. Instead, they use something called standard error, see Section 17.3.

- ~95% of the time the fraction of heads will be 0.4999 ±0.0994 and
- >99% of the time the fraction of heads will be 0.4999 ±0.1491.

It is often useful to visualize confidence intervals using **error bars**. The function showErrorBars in Figure 15.24 calls the version of flipSim in Figure 15.19 and then uses

```
pylab.errorbar(xVals, means, yerr = 1.96*pylab.array(sds))
```

to produce a plot. The first two arguments give the x and y values to be plotted. The third argument says that the values in sds should be multiplied by 1.96 and used to create vertical error bars. We multiply by 1.96 because 95% of the data in a normal distribution falls within 1.96 standard deviations of the mean.

```
def showErrorBars(minExp, maxExp, numTrials):
    """Assumes minExp and maxExp positive ints; minExp < maxExp
          numTrials a positive integer
       Plots mean fraction of heads with error bars"""
    means, sds, xVals = [], [], []
    for exp in range(minExp, maxExp + 1):
        xVals.append(2**exp)
        fracHeads, mean, sd = flipSim(2**exp, numTrials)
        means.append(mean)
        sds.append(sd)
    pylab.errorbar(xVals, means, yerr=1.96*pylab.array(sds))
    pylab.semilogx()
    pylab.title('Mean Fraction of Heads ('
                + str(numTrials) + ' trials)')
    pylab.xlabel('Number of flips per trial')
    pylab.ylabel('Fraction of heads & 95% confidence')
```

Figure 15.24 Produce plot with error bars

The call showErrorBars(3, 10, 100) produces the plot in Figure 15.25. Unsurprisingly, the error bars shrink (the standard deviation gets smaller) as the number of flips per trial grows.

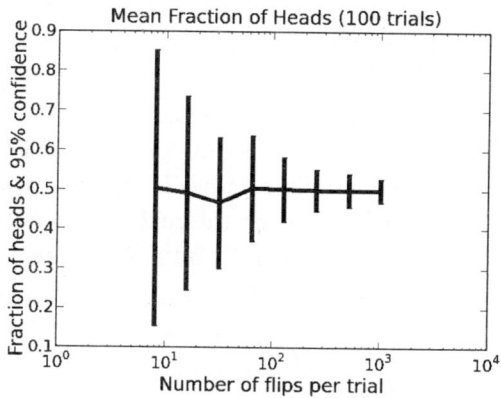

Figure 15.25 Estimates with error bars

15.4.3 Continuous and Discrete Uniform Distributions

Imagine that you take a bus that arrives at your stop every 15 minutes. If you make no effort to time your arrival at the stop to correspond to the bus schedule, your expected waiting time is uniformly distributed between 0 and 15 minutes.

A uniform distribution can be either discrete or continuous. A **continuous uniform distribution** also called a **rectangular distribution**, has the property that all intervals of the same length have the same probability. Consider the function random.random. As we saw in Section 15.4.1, the area under the PDF for any interval of a given length is the same. For example, the area under the curve between 0.23 and 0.33 is the same as the area under the curve between 0.53 and 0.63.

One can fully characterize a continuous uniform distribution with a single parameter, its range (i.e., minimum and maximum values). If the range of possible values is from min to max, the probability of a value falling in the range x to y is given by

$$P(x, y) = \begin{cases} \dfrac{y - x}{max - min} & \text{if } x \geq min \text{ and } y \leq max \\ 0 & otherwise \end{cases}$$

Elements drawn from a continuous uniform distributions can be generated by calling random.uniform(min, max), which returns a randomly chosen floating point number between min and max.

Discrete uniform distributions occur when each possible value occurs equally often, but the space of possible values is not continuous. For example, when a fair die is rolled, each of the six possible values is equally probable, but the outcomes are not uniformly distributed over the real numbers between 1 and 6—most values, e.g., 2.5, have a probability of 0 and a few values, e.g. 3, have a probability of $\frac{1}{6}$. One can fully characterize a discrete uniform distribution by

$$P(x) = \begin{cases} \frac{1}{|S|} & \text{if } x \in S \\ 0 & \text{otherwise} \end{cases}$$

where S is the set of possible values and $|S|$ the number of elements in S.

15.4.4 Binomial and Multinomial Distributions

Random variables that can take on only a discrete set of values are called **categorical** (also **nominal** or **discrete**) **variables**.

When a categorical variable has only two possible values (e.g., success or failure), the probability distribution is called a **binomial distribution**. One way to think about a binomial distribution is as the probability of a test succeeding exactly k times times in n independent trials. If the probability of a success in a single trial is p, the probability of exactly k successes in n independent trials is given by the formula

$$\binom{n}{k} * p^k * (1-p)^{n-k}$$

where

$$\binom{n}{k} = \frac{n!}{k! * (n-k)!}$$

The formula $\binom{n}{k}$ is known as the **binomial coefficient**. One way to read it is as "n choose k," since it is equivalent to the number of subsets of size k that can be constructed from a set of size n. For example, there are

$$\binom{4}{2} = \frac{4!}{2! * 2!} = \frac{24}{4} = 6$$

subsets of size two that can be constructed from the set {1,2,3,4}.

CHAPTER 15. STOCHASTIC PROGRAMS, PROBABILITY, AND DISTRIBUTIONS

In Section 15.2, we asked about the probability of rolling exactly two 1's in ten rolls of a die. We now have the tools in hand to calculate this probability. Think of the ten rolls as ten independent trials, where the trial is a success if a 1 is rolled and a failure otherwise. The binomial distribution tells us that the probability of having exactly two successful trials out of ten is

$$\binom{10}{2} * \left(\frac{1}{6}\right)^2 * \left(\frac{5}{6}\right)^8 = 45 * \frac{1}{36} * \frac{390625}{1679616} \approx 0.291$$

Finger exercise: Implement a function that calculates the probability of rolling exactly two 3's in k rolls of a fair die. Use this function to plot the probability as k varies from 2 to 100.

The **multinomial distribution** is a generalization of the binomial distribution to categorical data with more than two possible values. It applies when there are n independent trials each of which has m mutually exclusive outcomes, with each outcome having a fixed probability of occurring. The multinomial distribution gives the probability of any given combination of numbers of occurrences of the various categories.

15.4.5 Exponential and Geometric Distributions

Exponential distributions occur quite commonly. They are often used to model inter-arrival times, e.g., of cars entering a highway or requests for a Web page.

Consider, for example, the concentration of a drug in the human body. Assume that at each time step each molecule has a constant probability p of being cleared (i.e., of no longer being in the body). The system is memoryless in the sense that at each time step the probability of a molecule being cleared is independent of what happened at previous times. At time $t = 0$, the probability of an individual molecule still being in the body is 1. At time $t = 1$, the probability of that molecule still being in the body is $1 - p$. At time $t = 2$, the probability of that molecule still being in the body is $(1 - p)^2$. More generally, at time t the probability of an individual molecule having survived is $(1 - p)^t$, i.e., it is exponential in t.

Suppose that at time t_0 there are M_0 molecules of the drug. In general, at time t, the number of molecules will be M_0 multiplied by the probability that an individual module has survived to time t. The function clear implemented in Figure 15.26 plots the expected number of remaining molecules versus time.

```
def clear(n, p, steps):
    """Assumes n & steps positive ints, p a float
       n: the initial number of molecules
       p: the probability of a molecule being cleared
       steps: the length of the simulation"""
    numRemaining = [n]
    for t in range(steps):
        numRemaining.append(n*((1-p)**t))
    pylab.plot(numRemaining)
    pylab.xlabel('Time')
    pylab.ylabel('Molecules Remaining')
    pylab.title('Clearance of Drug')
```

Figure 15.26 Exponential clearance of molecules

The call `clear(1000, 0.01, 1000)` produces the plot in Figure 15.27.

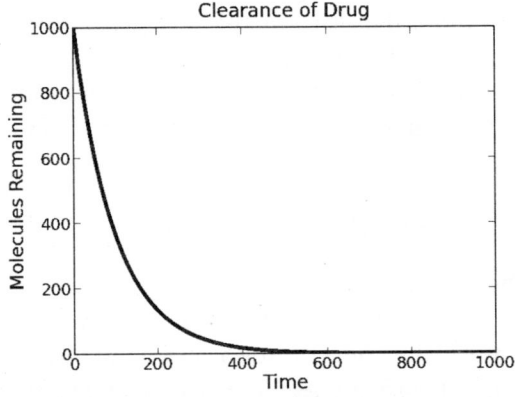

Figure 15.27: Exponential decay

This is an example of **exponential decay**. In practice, exponential decay is often talked about in terms of **half-life**, i.e., the expected time required for the initial value to decay by 50%. One can also talk about the half-life of a single item. For example, the half-life of a single molecule is the time at which the probability of that molecule having been cleared is 0.5. Notice that as time increases, the number of remaining molecules approaches 0. But it will never quite get there. This should not be interpreted as suggesting that a fraction of a molecule remains. Rather it should be interpreted as saying that since the system is probabilistic, one can never guarantee that all of the molecules have been cleared.

What happens if we make the y-axis logarithmic (by using `pylab.semilogy`)? We get the plot in Figure 15.28. In the plot in Figure 15.27, the values on the y-axis are changing exponentially quickly relative to the values on the x-axis. If we make the y-axis itself change exponentially quickly, we get a straight line. The slope of that line is the **rate of decay**.

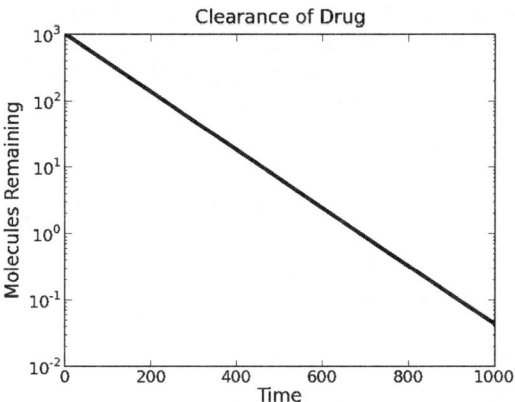

Figure 15.28: Plotting exponential decay with a logarithmic axis

Exponential growth is the inverse of exponential decay. It too is quite commonly seen in nature. Compound interest, the growth of algae in a swimming pool, and the chain reaction in an atomic bomb are all examples of exponential growth.

Exponential distributions can easily be generated in Python by calling the function `random.expovariate(lambd)`,[105] where `lambd` is 1.0 divided by the desired mean. The function returns a value between 0 and positive infinity if `lambd` is positive, and between negative infinity and 0 if `lambd` is negative.

The **geometric distribution** is the discrete analog of the exponential distribution.[106] It is usually thought of as describing the number of independent attempts required to achieve a first success (or a first failure). Imagine, for example, that you have a balky car that starts only half of the time you turn the key (or push the starter button). A geometric distribution could be used to characterize the ex-

---

[105] The parameter would have been called `lambda`, but as we saw in Section 5.4, `lambda` is a reserved word in Python.

[106] The name "geometric distribution" arises from its similarity to a "geometric progression." A geometric progression is any sequence of numbers in which each number other than the first is derived by multiplying the previous number by a constant nonzero number. Euclid's *Elements* proves a number of interesting theorems about geometric progressions.

pected number of times you would have to attempt to start the car before being successful. This is illustrated by the histogram in Figure 15.30, which was produced by the code in Figure 15.29.

```
def successfulStarts(successProb, numTrials):
    """Assumes successProb is a float representing probability of a
          single attempt being successful. numTrials a positive int
       Returns a list of the number of attempts needed before a
          success for each trial."""
    triesBeforeSuccess = []
    for t in range(numTrials):
        consecFailures = 0
        while random.random() > successProb:
            consecFailures += 1
        triesBeforeSuccess.append(consecFailures)
    return triesBeforeSuccess

probOfSuccess = 0.5
numTrials = 5000
distribution = successfulStarts(probOfSuccess, numTrials)
pylab.hist(distribution, bins = 14)
pylab.xlabel('Tries Before Success')
pylab.ylabel('Number of Occurrences Out of ' + str(numTrials))
pylab.title('Probability of Starting Each Try = '\
            + str(probOfSuccess))
```

Figure 15.29 Producing a Geometric Distribution

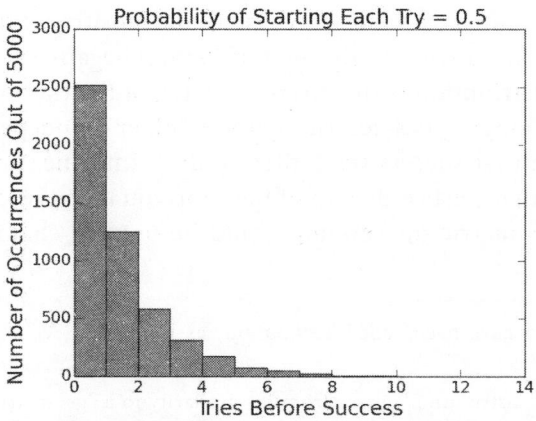

Figure 15.30 A geometric distribution

The histogram implies that most of the time you'll get the car going within a few attempts. On the other hand, the long tail suggests that on occasion you may run the risk of draining your battery before the car gets going.

15.4.6 Benford's Distribution

Benford's law defines a really strange distribution. Let S be a large set of decimal integers. How frequently would you expect each nonzero digit to appear as the first digit? Most of us would probably guess one ninth of the time. And when people are making up sets of numbers (e.g., faking experimental data or perpetrating financial fraud) this is typically true. It is not, however, typically true of many naturally occurring data sets. Instead, they follow a distribution predicted by Benford's law.

A set of decimal numbers is said to satisfy **Benford's law**[107] if the probability of the first digit being d is consistent with $P(d) = \log_{10}(1 + 1/d)$.

For example, this law predicts that the probability of the first digit being 1 is about 30%! Shockingly, many actual data sets seem to observe this law. It is possible to show that the Fibonacci sequence, for example, satisfies it perfectly. That's kind of plausible, since the sequence is generated by a formula. It's less easy to understand why such diverse data sets as iPhone pass codes, the number of Twitter followers per user, the population of countries, or the distances of stars from the earth closely approximate Benford's law.[108]

15.5 Hashing and Collisions

In Section 10.3 we pointed out that by using a larger hash table one could reduce the incidence of collisions, and thus reduce the expected time to retrieve a value. We now have the intellectual tools we need to examine that tradeoff more precisely.

First, let's get a precise formulation of the problem.

- Assume:
    - The range of the hash function is 1 to n,
    - The number of insertions is K, and

---

[107] The law is named after the physicist Frank Benford, who published a paper in 1938 showing that the law held on over 20,000 observations drawn from twenty different domains. However, it was first postulated in 1881 by the astronomer Simon Newcomb.

[108] http://testingbenfordslaw.com/

- ○ The hash function produces a perfectly uniform distribution of the keys used in insertions, i.e., for all keys, key, and for all integers, i, in the range 1 to n, the probability that hash(key) = i is 1/n.
- What is the probability that at least one collision occurs?

The question is exactly equivalent to asking "given K randomly generated integers in the range 1 to n, what is the probability that at least two of them are equal." If K ≥ n, the probability is clearly 1. But what about when K < n?

As is often the case, it is easiest to start by answering the inverse question, "given K randomly generated integers in the range 1 to n, what is the probability that none of them are equal?"

When we insert the first element, the probability of not having a collision is clearly 1. How about the second insertion? Since there are n-1 hash results left that are not equal to the result of the first hash, n-1 out of n choices will not yield a collision. So, the probability of not getting a collision on the second insertion is $\frac{n-1}{n}$, and the probability of not getting a collision on either of the first two insertions is $1 * \frac{n-1}{n}$. We can multiply these probabilities because for each insertion the value produced by the hash function is independent of anything that has preceded it.

The probability of not having a collision after three insertions is $1 * \frac{n-1}{n} * \frac{n-2}{n}$. And after K insertions it is $1 * \frac{n-1}{n} * \frac{n-2}{n} * \ldots * \frac{n-(K-1)}{n}$.

To get the probability of having at least one collision, we subtract this value from 1, i.e., the probability is

$$1 - \left(\frac{n-1}{n} * \frac{n-2}{n} * \ldots * \frac{n-(K-1)}{n}\right)$$

Given the size of the hash table and the number of expected insertions, we can use this formula to calculate the probability of at least one collision. If K were reasonably large, say 10,000, it would be a bit tedious to compute the probability with pencil and paper. That leaves two choices, mathematics and programming. Mathematicians have used some fairly advanced techniques to find a way to approximate the value of this series. But unless K is very large, it is easier to run some code to compute the exact value of the series:

```
def collisionProb(n, k):
    prob = 1.0
    for i in range(1, k):
        prob = prob * ((n - i)/n)
    return 1 - prob
```

If we try collisionProb(1000, 50) we get a probability of about 0.71 of there being at least one collision. If we consider 200 insertions, the probability of a collision is nearly 1. Does that seem a bit high to you? Let's write a simulation, Figure 15.31, to estimate the probability of at least one collision, and see if we get similar results.

```
def simInsertions(numIndices, numInsertions):
    """Assumes numIndices and numInsertions are positive ints.
       Returns 1 if there is a collision; 0 otherwise"""
    choices = range(numIndices) #list of possible indices
    used = []
    for i in range(numInsertions):
        hashVal = random.choice(choices)
        if hashVal in used: #there is a collision
            return 1
        else:
            used.append(hashVal)
    return 0

def findProb(numIndices, numInsertions, numTrials):
    collisions = 0
    for t in range(numTrials):
        collisions += simInsertions(numIndices, numInsertions)
    return collisions/numTrials
```

Figure 15.31 Simulating a hash table

If we run the code

```
print('Actual probability of a collision =', collisionProb(1000, 50))
print('Est. probability of a collision =', findProb(1000, 50, 10000))
print('Actual probability of a collision =', collisionProb(1000, 200))
print('Est. probability of a collision =', findProb(1000, 200, 10000))
```

it prints

```
Actual probability of a collision = 0.7122686568799875
Est. probability of a collision = 0.7097
Actual probability of a collision = 0.9999999994781328
Est. probability of a collision = 1.0
```

The simulation results are comfortingly similar to what we derived analytically.

Should the high probability of a collision make us think that hash tables have to be enormous to be useful? No. The probability of there being at least one collision tells us little about the expected lookup time. The expected time to look up a value depends upon the average length of the lists implementing the buckets that hold the values that collided. Assuming a uniform distribution of hash values, this is simply the number of insertions divided by the number of buckets.

15.6 How Often Does the Better Team Win?

Almost every October two teams from American Major League Baseball meet in something called the World Series. They play each other repeatedly until one of the teams has won four games, and that team is called (not entirely appropriately) the "world champion."

Setting aside the question of whether there is reason to believe that one of the participants in the World Series is indeed the best team in the world, how likely is it that a contest that can be at most seven games long will determine which of the two participants is better?

Clearly, each year one team will emerge victorious. So the question is whether we should attribute that victory to skill or to luck.

Figure 15.32 contains code that can provide us with some insight into that question. The function simSeries has one argument, numSeries, a positive integer describing the number of seven-game series to be simulated. It plots the probability of the better team winning the series against the probability of that team winning a single game. It varies the probability of the better team winning a single game from 0.5 to 1.0, and produces the plot in Figure 15.33.

Notice that for the better team to win 95% of the time (0.95 on the y-axis), it needs to be so much better that it would win more than three out of every four games between the two teams. For comparison, in 2015, the two teams in the World Series had regular season winning percentages of 58.6% (Kansas City Royals) and 55.5% (New York Mets).

```
def playSeries(numGames, teamProb):
    numWon = 0
    for game in range(numGames):
        if random.random() <= teamProb:
            numWon += 1
    return (numWon > numGames//2)

def fractionWon(teamProb, numSeries, seriesLen):
    won = 0
    for series in range(numSeries):
        if playSeries(seriesLen, teamProb):
            won += 1
    return won/float(numSeries)

def simSeries(numSeries):
    prob = 0.5
    fracsWon, probs = [], []
    while prob <= 1.0:
        fracsWon.append(fractionWon(prob, numSeries, 7))
        probs.append(prob)
        prob += 0.01
    pylab.axhline(0.95) #Draw line at 95%
    pylab.plot(probs, fracsWon, 'k', linewidth = 5)
    pylab.xlabel('Probability of Winning a Game')
    pylab.ylabel('Probability of Winning a Series')
    pylab.title(str(numSeries) + ' Seven-Game Series')

simSeries(400)
```

Figure 15.32 World Series simulation

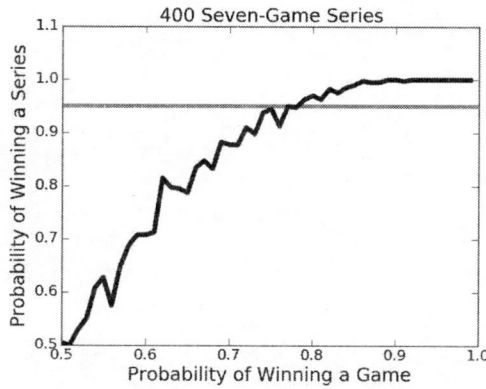

Figure 15.33 Probability of winning a 7-game series

16 MONTE CARLO SIMULATION

In Chapters 14 and 15, we looked at different ways of using randomness in computations. Many of the examples we presented fall into the class of computation known as **Monte Carlo simulation**. Monte Carlo simulation is a technique used to approximate the probability of an event by running the same simulation multiple times and averaging the results.

Stanislaw Ulam and Nicholas Metropolis coined the term Monte Carlo simulation in 1949 in homage to the games of chance played in the casino in the Principality of Monaco. Ulam, who is best known for designing the hydrogen bomb with Edward Teller, described the invention of the model as follows:

> *The first thoughts and attempts I made to practice [the Monte Carlo Method] were suggested by a question which occurred to me in 1946 as I was convalescing from an illness and playing solitaires. The question was what are the chances that a Canfield solitaire laid out with 52 cards will come out successfully? After spending a lot of time trying to estimate them by pure combinatorial calculations, I wondered whether a more practical method than "abstract thinking" might not be to lay it out say one hundred times and simply observe and count the number of successful plays. This was already possible to envisage with the beginning of the new era of fast computers,[109] and I immediately thought of problems of neutron diffusion and other questions of mathematical physics, and more generally how to change processes described by certain differential equations into an equivalent form interpretable as a succession of random operations. Later ... [in 1946, I] described the idea to John von Neumann, and we began to plan actual calculations.[110]*

The technique was used during the Manhattan Project to predict what would happen during a nuclear fission reaction, but did not really take off until the 1950s, when computers became both more common and more powerful.

---

[109] Ulam was probably referring to the ENIAC, which performed about 10^3 additions a second (and weighed 25 tons). Today's computers perform about 10^9 additions a second.

[110] Eckhardt, Roger (1987). "Stan Ulam, John von Neumann, and the Monte Carlo method," *Los Alamos Science*, Special Issue (15), 131-137.

Ulam was not the first mathematician to think about using the tools of probability to understand a game of chance. The history of probability is intimately connected to the history of gambling. It is the existence of uncertainty that makes gambling possible. And the existence of gambling provoked the development of much of the mathematics needed to reason about uncertainty. Contributions to the foundations of probability theory by Cardano, Pascal, Fermat, Bernoulli, de Moivre, and Laplace were all motivated by a desire to better understand (and perhaps profit from) games of chance.

16.1 Pascal's Problem

Most of the early work on probability theory revolved around games using dice.[111] Reputedly, Pascal's interest in the field that came to be known as probability theory began when a friend asked him whether or not it would be profitable to bet that within twenty-four rolls of a pair of dice he would roll a double 6. This was considered a hard problem in the mid-17th century. Pascal and Fermat, two pretty smart guys, exchanged a number of letters about how to resolve the issue, but it now seems like an easy question to answer:

- On the first roll the probability of rolling a 6 on each die is 1/6, so the probability of rolling a 6 with both dice is 1/36.
- Therefore, the probability of not rolling a double 6 on the first roll is 1 - 1/36 = 35/36.
- Therefore the probability of not rolling a double 6 twenty-four consecutive times is $(35/36)^{24}$, nearly 0.51, and therefore the probability of rolling a double 6 is 1 - $(35/36)^{24}$, about 0.49. In the long run it would not be profitable to bet on rolling a double 6 within twenty-four rolls.

Just to be safe, let's write a little program, Figure 16.1, to simulate Pascal's friend's game and confirm that we get the same answer as Pascal. When run the first time, the call checkPascal(1000000) printed

```
Probability of winning = 0.490761
```

This is indeed quite close to 1 - $(35/36)^{24}$; typing 1-(35.0/36.0)**24 into the Python shell produces 0.49140387613090342.

---

[111] Archeological excavations suggest that dice are the human race's oldest gambling implement. The oldest known "modern" six-sided die dates to about 600 BCE, but Egyptian tombs dating to about 2000 BCE contain artifacts resembling dice. Typically, these early dice were made from animal bones; in gambling circles people still use the phrase "rolling the bones."

```
def rollDie():
    return random.choice([1,2,3,4,5,6])

def checkPascal(numTrials):
    """Assumes numTrials an int > 0
       Prints an estimate of the probability of winning"""
    numWins = 0
    for i in range(numTrials):
        for j in range(24):
            d1 = rollDie()
            d2 = rollDie()
            if d1 == 6 and d2 == 6:
                numWins += 1
                break
    print('Probability of winning =', numWins/numTrials)
```

Figure 16.1 Checking Pascal's analysis

16.2 Pass or Don't Pass?

Not all questions about games of chance are so easily answered. In the game craps, the shooter (the person who rolls the dice) chooses between making a "pass line" or a "don't pass line" bet.

- Pass Line: Shooter wins if the first roll is a "natural" (7 or 11) and loses if it is "craps" (2, 3, or 12). If some other number is rolled, that number becomes the "point" and the shooter keeps rolling. If the shooter rolls the point before rolling a 7, the shooter wins. Otherwise the shooter loses.
- Don't Pass Line: Shooter loses if the first roll is 7 or 11, wins if it is 2 or 3, and ties (a "push" in gambling jargon) if it is 12. If some other number is rolled, that number becomes the point and shooter keeps rolling. If the shooter rolls a 7 before rolling the point, the shooter wins. Otherwise the shooter loses.

Is one of these a better bet than the other? Is either a good bet? It is possible to analytically derive the answer to these questions, but it seems easier (at least to us) to write a program that simulates a craps game, and see what happens. Figure 16.2 contains the heart of such a simulation.

```python
class CrapsGame(object):
    def __init__(self):
        self.passWins, self.passLosses = 0, 0
        self.dpWins, self.dpLosses, self.dpPushes = 0, 0, 0

    def playHand(self):
        throw = rollDie() + rollDie()
        if throw == 7 or throw == 11:
            self.passWins += 1
            self.dpLosses += 1
        elif throw == 2 or throw == 3 or throw == 12:
            self.passLosses += 1
            if throw == 12:
                self.dpPushes += 1
            else:
                self.dpWins += 1
        else:
            point = throw
            while True:
                throw = rollDie() + rollDie()
                if throw == point:
                    self.passWins += 1
                    self.dpLosses += 1
                    break
                elif throw == 7:
                    self.passLosses += 1
                    self.dpWins += 1
                    break

    def passResults(self):
        return (self.passWins, self.passLosses)

    def dpResults(self):
        return (self.dpWins, self.dpLosses, self.dpPushes)
```

Figure 16.2 CrapsGame class

The values of the instance variables of an instance of class CrapsGame record the performance of the pass and don't pass lines since the start of the game. The observer methods passResults and dpResults return these values. The method playHand simulates one hand of a game. A "hand" starts when the shooter is "coming out," the term used in craps for a roll before a point is established. A hand ends when the shooter has won or lost his or her initial bet. The bulk of the code in playHand is merely an algorithmic description of the rules stated above. Notice that there is a loop in the else clause corresponding to what happens after a point is established. It is exited using a break statement when either a seven or the point is rolled.

Figure 16.3 contains a function that uses class CrapsGame to simulate a series of craps games.

```python
def crapsSim(handsPerGame, numGames):
    """Assumes handsPerGame and numGames are ints > 0
       Play numGames games of handsPerGame hands; print results"""
    games = []

    #Play numGames games
    for t in range(numGames):
        c = CrapsGame()
        for i in range(handsPerGame):
            c.playHand()
        games.append(c)

    #Produce statistics for each game
    pROIPerGame, dpROIPerGame = [], []
    for g in games:
        wins, losses = g.passResults()
        pROIPerGame.append((wins - losses)/float(handsPerGame))
        wins, losses, pushes = g.dpResults()
        dpROIPerGame.append((wins - losses)/float(handsPerGame))

    #Produce and print summary statistics
    meanROI = str(round((100*sum(pROIPerGame)/numGames), 4)) + '%'
    sigma = str(round(100*stdDev(pROIPerGame), 4)) + '%'
    print('Pass:', 'Mean ROI =', meanROI, 'Std. Dev. =', sigma)
    meanROI = str(round((100*sum(dpROIPerGame)/numGames), 4)) +'%'
    sigma = str(round(100*stdDev(dpROIPerGame), 4)) + '%'
    print('Don\'t pass:','Mean ROI =', meanROI, 'Std Dev =', sigma)
```

Figure 16.3 Simulating a craps game

The structure of crapsSim is typical of many simulation programs:

1. It runs multiple games (think of each game as analogous to a trial in our earlier simulations) and accumulates the results. Each game includes multiple hands, so there is a nested loop.
2. It then produces and stores statistics for each game.
3. Finally, it produces and outputs summary statistics. In this case, it prints the expected return on investment (ROI) or each kind of betting line and the standard deviation of that ROI.

Return on investment is defined by the equation[112]

$$ROI = \frac{gain\ from\ investment - cost\ of\ investment}{cost\ of\ investment}$$

Since the pass and don't pass lines pay even money (if you bet $1 and win, you gain is $1), the ROI is

$$ROI = \frac{number\ of\ wins - number\ of\ losses}{number\ of\ bets}$$

For example, if you made 100 pass line bets and won half, your ROI would be

$$\frac{50-50}{100} = 0$$

If you bet the don't pass line 100 times and had 25 wins and 5 pushes the ROI would be

$$\frac{25-70}{100} = \frac{-45}{100} = -4.5$$

Let's run our craps game simulation and see what happens when we try `crapsSim(20, 10)`:[113]

```
Pass: Mean ROI = -7.0% Std. Dev. = 23.6854%
Don't pass: Mean ROI = 4.0% Std Dev = 23.5372%
```

It looks as if it would be a good idea to avoid the pass line—where the expected return on investment is a 7% loss. But the don't pass line looks like a pretty good bet. Or does it?

Looking at the standard deviations, it seems that perhaps the don't pass line is not such a good bet after all. Recall that under the assumption that the distribution is normal, the 95% confidence interval is encompassed by 1.96 standard deviations on either side of the mean. For the don't pass line, the 95% confidence

---

[112] More precisely, this equation defines what is often called "simple ROI." It does not account for the possiblity that there might be a gap in time between when the investment is made and when the gain attributable to that investment occurs. This gap should be accounted for when the time between making an investment and seeing the financial return is large (e.g., investing in a college education). This is probably not an issue at the craps table.

[113] Since these programs incorporate randomness, you should not expect to get identical results if you run the code yourself. More important, do not place any bets until you have read the entire section!

CHAPTER 16. MONTE CARLO SIMULATION

interval is [4.0−1.96∗23.5372, 4.0+1.96∗23.5372]—roughly [-43%, +51%]. That certainly doesn't suggest that betting the don't pass line is a sure thing.

Time to put the law of large numbers to work; crapsSim(1000000, 10) prints

```
Pass: Mean ROI = -1.4204% Std. Dev. = 0.0614%
Don't pass: Mean ROI = -1.3571% Std Dev = 0.0593%
```

We can now be pretty safe in assuming that neither of these is a good bet.[114] It looks as if the don't pass line might be slightly less bad, but we probably shouldn't count on that. If the 95% confidence intervals for the pass and don't pass lines did not overlap, it would be safe to assume that the difference in the two means was statistically significant.[115] However, they do overlap, so no conclusion can be safely drawn.

Suppose that instead of increasing the number of hands per game, we increased the number of games, e.g., by making the call crapsSim(20, 1000000):

```
Pass: Mean ROI = -1.4133% Std. Dev. = 22.3571%
Don't pass: Mean ROI = -1.3649% Std Dev = 22.0446%
```

The standard deviations are high—indicating that the outcome of a single game of 20 hands is highly uncertain.

One of the nice things about simulations is that they make it easy to perform "what if" experiments. For example, what if a player could sneak in a pair of cheater's dice that favored 5 over 2 (5 and 2 are on the opposite sides of a die)? To test this out, all we have to do is replace the implementation of rollDie by something like

```
def rollDie():
    return random.choice([1,1,2,3,3,4,4,5,5,5,6,6])
```

This relatively small change in the die makes a dramatic difference in the odds. Running crapsSim(1000000, 10) yields

```
Pass: Mean ROI = 6.7385% Std. Dev. = 0.13%
Don't pass: Mean ROI = -9.5186% Std Dev = 0.1226%
```

No wonder casinos go to a lot of trouble to make sure that players don't introduce their own dice into the game!

---

[114] In fact, the means of the estimated ROIs are close to the actual ROIs. Grinding through the probabilities yields an ROI of -1.414% for the pass line and -1.364% for the don't pass line.

[115] We discuss statistical significance in more detail in Chapter 19.

16.3 Using Table Lookup to Improve Performance

You might not want to try running crapsSim(100000000, 10) at home. It takes a long time to complete on most computers. That raises the question of whether there is a simple way to speed up the simulation.

The complexity of crapsSim is O(playHand)*handsPerGame*numGames. The running time of playHand depends upon the number of times the loop in it is executed. In principle, the loop could be executed an unbounded number of times since there is no bound on how long it could take to roll either a 7 or the point. In practice, of course, we have every reason to believe it will always terminate.

Notice, however, that the result of a call to playHand does not depend on how many times the loop is executed, but only on which exit condition is reached. For each possible point, one can easily calculate the probability of rolling that point before rolling a 7. For example, using a pair of dice one can roll a 4 in three different ways: <1, 3>, <3, 1>, and <2, 2>; and one can roll a 7 in six different ways: <1, 6>, <6, 1>, <2, 5>, <5, 2>, <3, 4>, and <4, 3>. Therefore, exiting the loop by rolling a 7 is twice as likely as exiting the loop by rolling a 4.

Figure 16.4 contains an implementation of playHand that exploits this thinking. We first compute the probability of making the point before rolling a 7 for each possible value of the point, and store those values in a dictionary. Suppose, for example, that the point is 8. The shooter continues to roll until he either rolls the point or rolls craps. There are five ways of rolling an 8 (<6,2>, <2,6>, <5,3>, <3,5>, and <4,4>) and six ways of rolling a 7. So, the value for the dictionary key 8 is the value of the expression 5/11. Having this table allows us to replace the inner loop, which contained an unbounded number of rolls, with a test against one call to random.random. The asymptotic complexity of this version of playHand is O(1).

The idea of replacing computation by **table lookup** has broad applicability and is frequently used when speed is an issue. Table lookup is an example of the general idea of **trading time for space**. As we saw in Chapter 13, it is is the key idea behind dynamic programming. We saw another example of this technique in our analysis of hashing: the larger the table, the fewer the collisions, and the faster the average lookup. In this case, the table is small, so the space cost is negligible.

CHAPTER 16. MONTE CARLO SIMULATION

```python
def playHand(self):
    #An alternative, faster, implementation of playHand
    pointsDict = {4:1/3, 5:2/5, 6:5/11, 8:5/11, 9:2/5, 10:1/3}
    throw = rollDie() + rollDie()
    if throw == 7 or throw == 11:
        self.passWins += 1
        self.dpLosses += 1
    elif throw == 2 or throw == 3 or throw == 12:
        self.passLosses += 1
        if throw == 12:
            self.dpPushes += 1
        else:
            self.dpWins += 1
    else:
        if random.random() <= pointsDict[throw]: # point before 7
            self.passWins += 1
            self.dpLosses += 1
        else:                                    # 7 before point
            self.passLosses += 1
            self.dpWins += 1
```

Figure 16.4 Using table lookup to improve performance

16.4 Finding π

It is easy to see how Monte Carlo simulation is useful for tackling problems in which nondeterminism plays a role. Interestingly, however, Monte Carlo simulation (and randomized algorithms in general) can be used to solve problems that are not inherently stochastic, i.e., for which there is no uncertainty about outcomes.

Consider π. For thousands of years, people have known that there is a constant (called π since the 18th century) such that the circumference of a circle is equal to π*diameter and the area of the circle equal to $\pi * radius^2$. What they did not know was the value of this constant.

One of the earliest estimates, $4*(8/9)^2 = 3.16$, can found in the Egyptian *Rhind Papyrus*, circa 1650 BC. More than a thousand years later, the *Old Testament* implied a different value for π when giving the specifications of one of King Solomon's construction projects,

And he made a molten sea, ten cubits from the one brim to the other: it was round all about, and his height was five cubits: and a line of thirty cubits did compass it round about.[116]

Solving for π, $10\pi = 30$, so $\pi = 3$. Perhaps the *Bible* is simply wrong, or perhaps the molten sea wasn't perfectly circular, or perhaps the circumference was measured from the outside of the wall and the diameter from the inside, or perhaps it's just poetic license. We leave it to the reader to decide.

Archimedes of Syracuse (287-212 BCE) derived upper and lower bounds on the value of π by using a high-degree polygon to approximate a circular shape. Using a polygon with 96 sides, he concluded that $223/71 < \pi < 22/7$. Giving upper and lower bounds was a rather sophisticated approach for the time. Also, if we take his best estimate as the average of his two bounds we obtain 3.1418, an error of about 0.0002. Not bad!

Long before computers were invented, the French mathematicians Buffon (1707-1788) and Laplace (1749-1827) proposed using a stochastic simulation to estimate the value of π.[117] Think about inscribing a circle in a square with sides of length 2, so that the radius, r, of the circle is of length 1.

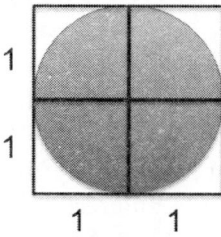

Figure 16.5 Unit circle inscribed in a square

By the definition of π, $area = \pi r^2$. Since r is 1, π = area. But what's the area of the circle? Buffon suggested that he could estimate the area of a circle by a dropping a large number of needles (which he argued would follow a random path as they fell) in the vicinity of the square. The ratio of the number of needles with tips lying within the square to the number of needles with tips lying within the circle could then be used to estimate the area of the circle.

---

[116]King James Bible, 1 Kings 7.23.

[117] Buffon proposed the idea first, but there was an error in his formulation that was later corrected by Laplace.

CHAPTER 16. MONTE CARLO SIMULATION

If the locations of the needles are truly random, we know that

$$\frac{\text{needles in circle}}{\text{needles in square}} = \frac{\text{area of circle}}{\text{area of square}}$$

and solving for the area of the circle,

$$\text{area of circle} = \frac{\text{area of square} * \text{needles in circle}}{\text{needles in square}}$$

Recall that the area of a 2 by 2 square is 4, so,

$$\text{area of circle} = \frac{4 * \text{needles in circle}}{\text{needles in square}}$$

In general, to estimate the area of some region R
1. Pick an enclosing region, E, such that the area of E is easy to calculate and R lies completely within E.
2. Pick a set of random points that lie within E.
3. Let F be the fraction of the points that fall within R.
4. Multiply the area of E by F.

If you try Buffon's experiment, you'll soon realize that the places where the needles land are not truly random. Moreover, even if you could drop them randomly, it would take a very large number of needles to get an approximation of π as good as even the *Bible*'s. Fortunately, computers can randomly drop simulated needles at a ferocious rate.

Figure 16.6 contains a program that estimates π using the Buffon-Laplace method. For simplicity, it considers only those needles that fall in the upper right-hand quadrant of the square.

The function throwNeedles simulates dropping a needle by first using random.random to get a pair of positive Cartesian coordinates (x and y values) representing the position of the needle with respect to the center of the square. It then uses the Pythagorean theorem to compute the hypotenuse of the right triangle with base x and height y. This is the distance of the tip of the needle from the origin (the center of the square). Since the radius of the circle is 1, we know that the needle lies within the circle if and only if the distance from the origin is no greater than 1. We use this fact to count the number of needles in the circle.

The function getEst uses throwNeedles to find an estimate of π by first dropping numNeedles needles, and then averaging the result over numTrials trials. It then returns the mean and standard deviation of the trials.

The function estPi calls getEst with an ever-growing number of needles until the standard deviation returned by getEst is no larger than precision/1.96. Under the assumption that the errors are normally distributed, this implies that 95% of the values lie within precision of the mean.

```python
def throwNeedles(numNeedles):
    inCircle = 0
    for Needles in range(1, numNeedles + 1):
        x = random.random()
        y = random.random()
        if (x*x + y*y)**0.5 <= 1:
            inCircle += 1
    #Counting needles in one quadrant only, so multiply by 4
    return 3*(inCircle/numNeedles)

def getEst(numNeedles, numTrials):
    estimates = []
    for t in range(numTrials):
        piGuess = throwNeedles(numNeedles)
        estimates.append(piGuess)
    sDev = stdDev(estimates)
    curEst = sum(estimates)/len(estimates)
    print('Est. =', str(round(curEst, 5)) + ',',
          'Std. dev. =', str(round(sDev, 5)) + ',',
          'Needles =', numNeedles)
    return (curEst, sDev)

def estPi(precision, numTrials):
    numNeedles = 1000
    sDev = precision
    while sDev > precision/1.96:
        curEst, sDev = getEst(numNeedles, numTrials)
        numNeedles *= 2
    return curEst
```

Figure 16.6 Estimating π

When we ran estPi(0.01, 100) it printed
```
Est. = 3.14844, Std. dev. = 0.04789, Needles = 1000
Est. = 3.13918, Std. dev. = 0.0355, Needles = 2000
Est. = 3.14108, Std. dev. = 0.02713, Needles = 4000
Est. = 3.14143, Std. dev. = 0.0168, Needles = 8000
Est. = 3.14135, Std. dev. = 0.0137, Needles = 16000
Est. = 3.14131, Std. dev. = 0.00848, Needles = 32000
Est. = 3.14117, Std. dev. = 0.00703, Needles = 64000
Est. = 3.14159, Std. dev. = 0.00403, Needles = 128000
```

As one would expect, the standard deviations decreased monotonically as we increased the number of samples. In the beginning the estimates of the value of π also improved steadily. Some were above the true value and some below, but each increase in numNeedles led to an improved estimate. With 1000 samples per trial, the simulation's estimate was already better than those of the *Bible* and the *Rhind Papyrus*.

Curiously, the estimate got worse when the number of needles went from 8,000 to 16,000, since 3.14135 is farther from the true value of π than is 3.14143. However, if we look at the ranges defined by one standard deviation around each of the means, both ranges contain the true value of π, and the range associated with the larger sample size is smaller. Even though the estimate generated with 16,000 samples happens to be farther from the actual value of π, we should have more confidence in its accuracy. This is an extremely important notion. It is not sufficient to produce a good answer. We have to have a valid reason to be confident that it is in fact a good answer. And when we drop a large enough number of needles, the small standard deviation gives us reason to be confident that we have a correct answer. Right?

Not exactly. Having a small standard deviation is a necessary condition for having confidence in the validity of the result. It is not a sufficient condition. The notion of a statistically valid conclusion should never be confused with the notion of a correct conclusion.

Each statistical analysis starts with a set of assumptions. The key assumption here is that our simulation is an accurate model of reality. Recall that the design of our Buffon-Laplace simulation started with a little algebra demonstrating how we could use the ratio of two areas to find the value of π. We then translated this idea into code that depended upon a little geometry and on the randomness of random.random.

Let's see what happens if we get any of this wrong. Suppose, for example, we replace the 4 in the last line of the function throwNeedles by a 2, and again run estPi(0.01, 100). This time it prints

```
Est. = 1.57422, Std. dev. = 0.02394, Needles = 1000
Est. = 1.56959, Std. dev. = 0.01775, Needles = 2000
Est. = 1.57054, Std. dev. = 0.01356, Needles = 4000
Est. = 1.57072, Std. dev. = 0.0084, Needles = 8000
Est. = 1.57068, Std. dev. = 0.00685, Needles = 16000
Est. = 1.57066, Std. dev. = 0.00424, Needles = 32000
```

The standard deviation for a mere 32,000 needles suggests that we should have a fair amount of confidence in the estimate. But what does that really mean? It means that we can be reasonably confident that if we were to draw more samples from the same distribution, we would get a similar value. It says nothing about whether or not this value is close to the actual value of π. If you are going to remember only one thing about statistics, remember this: a statistically valid conclusion should not be confused with a correct conclusion!

Before believing the results of a simulation, we need to have confidence both that our conceptual model is correct and that we have correctly implemented that model. Whenever possible, one should attempt to validate results against reality. In this case, one could use some other means to compute an approximation to the area of a circle (e.g., physical measurement) and check that the computed value of π is at least in the right neighborhood.

16.5 Some Closing Remarks About Simulation Models

For most of the history of science, theorists used mathematical techniques to construct purely analytical models that could be used to predict the behavior of a system from a set of parameters and initial conditions. This led to the development of important mathematical tools ranging from calculus to probability theory. These tools helped scientists develop a reasonably accurate understanding of the macroscopic physical world.

As the 20th century progressed, the limitations of this approach became increasingly clear. Reasons for this include:

- An increased interest in the social sciences, e.g., economics, led to a desire to construct good models of systems that were not mathematically tractable.

CHAPTER 16. MONTE CARLO SIMULATION

- As the systems to be modeled grew increasingly complex, it seemed easier to successively refine a series of simulation models than to construct accurate analytic models.
- It is often easier to extract useful intermediate results from a simulation than from an analytical model, e.g., to play "what if" games.
- The availability of computers made it feasible to run large-scale simulations. Until the advent of the modern computer in the middle of the 20th century the utility of simulation was limited by the time required to perform calculations by hand.

Simulation models are **descriptive**, not **prescriptive**. They tell how a system works under given conditions; not how to arrange the conditions to make the system work best. A simulation does not optimize, it merely describes. That is not to say that simulation cannot be used as part of an optimization process. For example, simulation is often used as part of a search process in finding an optimal set of parameter settings.

Simulation models can be classified along three dimensions:

- Deterministic versus stochastic,
- Static versus dynamic, and
- Discrete versus continuous.

The behavior of a **deterministic simulation** is completely defined by the model. Rerunning a simulation will not change the outcome. Deterministic simulations are typically used when the system being modeled is too complex to analyze analytically, e.g., the performance of a processor chip. **Stochastic simulations** incorporate randomness in the model. Multiple runs of the same model may generate different values. This random element forces us to generate many outcomes to see the range of possibilities. The question of whether to generate 10 or 1000 or 100,000 outcomes is a statistical question, as discussed earlier.

In a **static model**, time plays no essential role. The needle-dropping simulation used to estimate π in this chapter is an example of a static simulation. In a **dynamic model**, time, or some analog, plays an essential role. In the series of random walks simulated in Chapter 14, the number of steps taken was used as a surrogate for time.

In a **discrete model**, the values of pertinent variables are enumerable, e.g., they are integers. In a **continuous model**, the values of pertinent variables range over non-enumerable sets, e.g., the real numbers. Imagine analyzing the flow of traffic along a highway. We might choose to model each individual car, in which case we have a discrete model. Alternatively, we might choose to treat traffic as a flow, where changes in the flow can be described by differential equations. This leads to a continuous model. In this example, the discrete model more closely resembles the physical situation (nobody drives half a car, though some cars are half the size of others), but is more computationally complex than a continuous one. In practice, models often have both discrete and continuous components. For example, one might choose to model the flow of blood through the human body using a discrete model for blood (i.e., modeling individual corpuscles) and a continuous model for blood pressure.

17 SAMPLING AND CONFIDENCE INTERVALS

Recall that inferential statistics involves making inferences about a **population** of examples by analyzing a randomly chosen subset of that population. This subset is called a **sample**.

Sampling is important because it is often not possible to observe the entire population of interest. A physician cannot count the number of a species of bacterium in a patient's blood stream, but it is possible to measure the population in a small sample of the patient's blood, and from that to infer characteristics of the total population. If you wanted to know the average weight of eighteen-year-old Americans, you could try and round them all up, put them on a very large scale, and then divide by the number of people. Alternatively, you could round up fifty randomly chose eighteen-year-olds, compute their mean weight, and assume that their mean weight was a reasonable estimate of the mean weight of the entire population of eighteen-year-olds.

The correspondence between the sample and the population of interest is of overriding importance. If the sample is not representative of the population, no amount of fancy mathematics will lead to valid inferences. A sample of fifty women or fifty Asian-Americans or fifty football players cannot be used to make valid inferences about the average weight of the population of all eighteen-year-olds in America.

In this book, we focus on **probability sampling**. With probability sampling, each member of the population of interest has some nonzero probability of being included in the sample. In a **simple random sample**, each member of the population has an equal chance of being chosen for the sample. In **stratified sampling**, the population is first partitioned into subgroups, and then the sample is built by randomly sampling from each subgroup. Stratified sampling can be used to increase the probability that a sample is representative of the population as a whole. For example, ensuring that the fraction of men and women in a sample matches the fraction of men and women in the population increases the probability that that the mean weight of the sample, the **sample mean**, will be a good estimate of the mean weight of the whole population, the **population mean**.

17.1 Sampling the Boston Marathon

Each year since 1897, athletes (mostly runners, but since 1975 there has been a wheelchair division) have gathered in Massachusetts to participate in the Boston Marathon. In recent years, around twenty thousand hardy souls per year have successfully taken on the 42.195 km (26 mile, 385 yard) course.

A file containing data from the 2012 race is available on the Web site associated with this book. The file (bm_results2012.txt) is in a comma-separated format, and contain the name, gender, age, division, country, and time for each participant. Figure 17.1 contains the first few lines of the contents of the file.

```
"Gebremariam Gebregziabher",M,27,14,ETH,142.93
"Matebo Levy",M,22,2,KEN,133.10
"Cherop Sharon",F,28,1,KEN,151.83
"Chebet Wilson",M,26,5,KEN,134.93
"Dado Firehiwot",F,28,4,ETH,154.93
"Korir Laban",M,26,6,KEN,135.48
"Jeptoo Rita",F,31,6,KEN,155.88
"Korir Wesley",M,29,1,KEN,132.67
"Kipyego Bernard",M,25,3,KEN,133.22
```

Figure 17.1 The first few lines in bm_results2012.txt

Since complete data about the results of each race is easily available, there is no pragmatic need to using sampling to derive statistics about a race. However, it is pedagogically useful to compare statistical estimates derived from samples to the actual value being estimated.

The code in Figure 17.2 produces the plot shown in Figure 17.3. The function getBMData reads data from a file containing information about each of the competitors in the race. It returns the data in a dictionary with six elements. Each key describes the type of data (e.g., 'name' or 'gender') contained in the elements of a list associated with that key. For example, data['time'] is a list of floats containing the finishing time of each competitor, data['name'][i] is the name of the ith competitor, and data['time'][i] is the finishing time of the ith competitor. The function makeHist produces a visual representation of the finishing times.

CHAPTER 17. SAMPLING AND CONFIDENCE INTERVALS

```
def getBMData(filename):
    """Read the contents of the given file. Assumes the file
    in a comma-separated format, with 6 elements in each entry:
    0. Name (string), 1. Gender (string), 2. Age (int)
    3. Division (int), 4. Country (string), 5. Overall time (float)
    Returns: dict containing a list for each of the 6 variables."""

    data = {}
    f = open(filename)
    line = f.readline()
    data['name'], data['gender'], data['age'] = [], [], []
    data['division'], data['country'], data['time'] = [], [], []
    while line != '':
        split = line.split(',')
        data['name'].append(split[0])
        data['gender'].append(split[1])
        data['age'].append(int(split[2]))
        data['division'].append(int(split[3]))
        data['country'].append(split[4])
        data['time'].append(float(split[5][:-1])) #remove \n
        line = f.readline()
    f.close()
    return data

def makeHist(data, bins, title, xLabel, yLabel):
    pylab.hist(data, bins)
    pylab.title(title)
    pylab.xlabel(xLabel)
    pylab.ylabel(yLabel)
    mean = sum(data)/len(data)
    std = stdDev(data)
    pylab.annotate('Mean = ' + str(round(mean, 2)) +\
              '\nSD = ' + str(round(std, 2)), fontsize = 20,
              xy = (0.65, 0.75), xycoords = 'axes fraction')

times = getBMData('bm_results2012.txt')['time']
makeHist(times, 20, '2012 Boston Marathon',
         'Minutes to Complete Race', 'Number of Runners')
```

Figure 17.2: Read data and produce plot of Boston Marathon

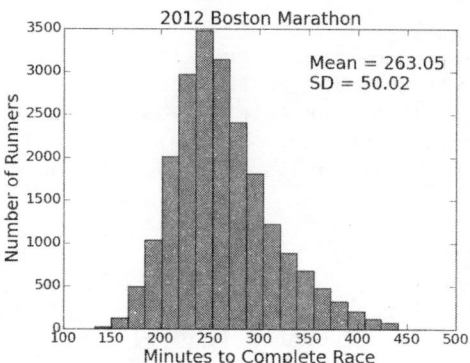

Figure 17.3: Boston Marathon finishing times

The distribution of finishing times resembles a normal distribution, but is clearly not normal because of the fat tail on the right.

Now, let's pretend that we don't have access to the data about all competitors, and instead want to estimate some statistics about the finishing times of the entire field by sampling a small number of randomly chosen competitors.

The code in Figure 17.4 creates a simple random sample of the elements of times, and then uses that sample to estimate the mean and standard deviation of times. The function sampleTimes uses random.sample(times, numExamples) to extract the sample. The invocation of random.sample returns a list of size numExamples of randomly chosen distinct elements from the list times. After extracting the sample, sampleTimes produces a histogram showing the distribution of values in the sample.

```
def sampleTimes(times, numExamples):
    """Assumes times a list of floats representing finishing
       times of all runners. numExamples an int
       Generates a random sample of size numExamples, and produces
       a histogram showing the distribution along with its mean and
       standard deviation"""
    sample = random.sample(times, numExamples)
    makeHist(sample, 10, 'Sample of Size ' + str(numExamples),
             'Minutes to Complete Race', 'Number of Runners')

sampleSize = 40
sampleTimes(times, sampleSize)
```

Figure 17.4: Sampling finishing times

As Figure 17.5 shows, the distribution of the sample is much farther from normal than the distribution from which it was drawn. This is not surprising, given the small sample size. What's more surprising is that despite the small sample size (40 out of about 21,000) the estimated mean differs from the population mean by less than 2%. Did we get lucky, or is there reason to expect that the estimate of the mean will be pretty good? To put it another way, can we express in a quantitative way how much confidence we should have in our estimate?

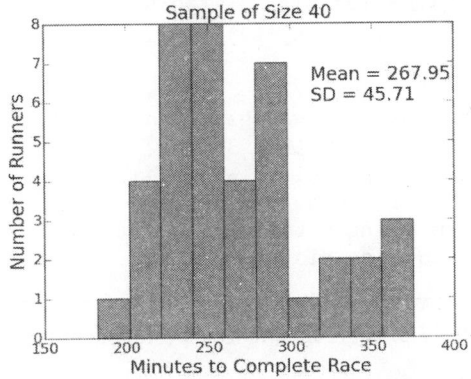

Figure 17.5: Analyzing a small sample

As we discussed in Chapters 15 and 16, it is often useful to provide a confidence interval and confidence level to indicate the reliability of the estimate. Given a single sample (of any size) drawn from a larger population, the best estimate of the mean of the population is the mean of the sample. Estimating the width of the confidence interval required to achieve a desired confidence level is trickier. It depends, in part, upon the size of the sample.

It's easy to understand why the size of the sample is important. The law of large numbers tells us that as the sample size grows, the distribution of the values of the sample is more likely to resemble the distribution of the population from which the sample is drawn. Consequently, as the sample size grows, the sample mean and the sample standard deviation are likely to be closer to the population mean and population standard deviation.

So, bigger is better, but how big is big enough? That depends upon the variance of the population. The higher the variance, the more samples are needed. Consider two normal distributions, one with a mean of 0 and standard deviation of 1, and the other with a mean of 0 and a standard deviation of 100. If we were to select one randomly chosen element from one of these distributions and use it to estimate the mean of the distribution, the probability of that estimate being within any desired accuracy, ϵ, of the true mean (0), would be equal to the area under the probability density function between $-\epsilon$ and ϵ (see Section 15.4.1). The code in Figure 17.6 computes and prints these probabilities for $\epsilon = 3$ minutes.

```
import scipy.integrate

def gaussian(x, mu, sigma):
    factor1 = (1/(sigma*((2*pylab.pi)**0.5)))
    factor2 = pylab.e**-(((x-mu)**2)/(2*sigma**2))
    return factor1*factor2

area = round(scipy.integrate.quad(gaussian, -3, 3, (0, 1))[0], 4)
print('Probability of being within 3',
      'of true mean of tight dist. =', area)
area = round(scipy.integrate.quad(gaussian, -3, 3, (0, 100))[0], 4)
print('Probability of being within 3',
      'of true mean of wide dist. =', area)
```

Figure 17.6: Effect of variance on estimate of mean

When the code in Figure 17.6 is run it prints

```
Probability of being within 3 of true mean of tight dist. = 0.9973
Probability of being within 3 of true mean of wide dist. = 0.0239
```

The code in Figure 17.7 plots the mean of each of 1000 samples of size 40 from two normal distributions. Again, each distribution has a mean of 0, but one has a standard deviation of 1 and the other a standard deviation of 100.

The left side of Figure 17.8 shows the mean of each sample. As expected, when the population standard deviation is 1, the sample means are all near the population mean of 0, which is why no distinct circles are visible—they are so dense that they merge into what appears to be a bar. In contrast, when the standard deviation of the population is 100, the sample means are scattered in a hard-to-discern pattern.

However, when we look at a histogram of the means when the standard deviation is 100, the right side of Figure 17.8, something important emerges: the means form a distribution that is close to a normal distribution centered around 0. That the right side of Figure 17.8 looks the way it does is not an accident. It is a consequence of the Central Limit Theorem, the most famous theorem in all of probability and statistics.

CHAPTER 17. SAMPLING AND CONFIDENCE INTERVALS

```
def testSamples(numTrials, sampleSize):
    tightMeans, wideMeans = [], []
    for t in range(numTrials):
        sampleTight, sampleWide = [], []
        for i in range(sampleSize):
            sampleTight.append(random.gauss(0, 1))
            sampleWide.append(random.gauss(0, 100))
        tightMeans.append(sum(sampleTight)/len(sampleTight))
        wideMeans.append(sum(sampleWide)/len(sampleWide))
    return tightMeans, wideMeans

tightMeans, wideMeans = testSamples(1000, 40)
pylab.plot(wideMeans, 'y*', label = ' SD = 100')
pylab.plot(tightMeans, 'bo', label = 'SD = 1')
pylab.xlabel('Sample Number')
pylab.ylabel('Sample Mean')
pylab.title('Means of Samples of Size ' + str(40))
pylab.legend()

pylab.figure()
pylab.hist(wideMeans, bins = 20, label = 'SD = 100')
pylab.title('Distribution of Sample Means')
pylab.xlabel('Sample Mean')
pylab.ylabel('Frequency of Occurrence')
pylab.legend()
```

Figure 17.7: Compute and plot sample means

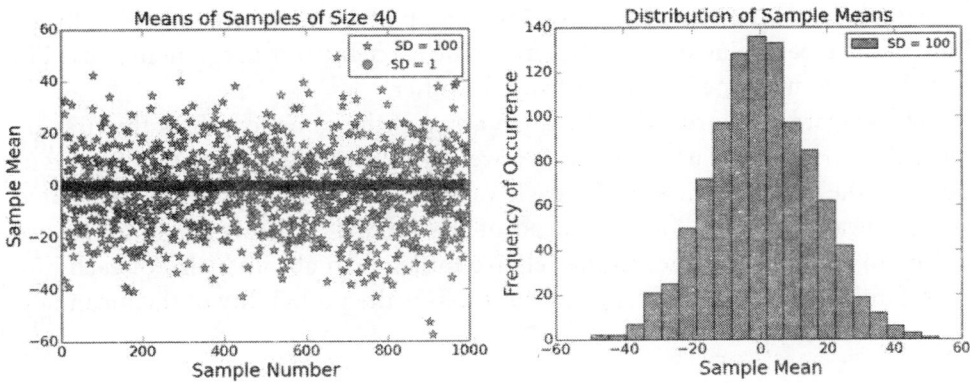

Figure 17.8: Sample means

17.2 The Central Limit Theorem

The central limit theorem explains why it is possible to use a single sample drawn from a population to estimate the variability of the means of a set of hypothetical samples drawn from the same population.

A version of the **Central Limit Theorem** (**CLT** to its friends) was first published by Laplace in 1810, and then refined by Poisson in the 1820s. But the CLT as we know it today is a product of work done by a sequence of prominent mathematicians in the first half of the 20th century.

Despite (or maybe because of) the impressive list of mathematicians who have worked on it, the CLT is really quite simple. It says that

- Given a set of sufficiently large samples drawn from the same population, the means of the samples (the sample means) will be approximately normally distributed,
- This normal distribution will have a mean close to the mean of the population, and
- The variance (as defined in Section 15.3) of the sample means will be close to the variance of the population divided by the sample size.

Let's look at an example of the CLT in action. Imagine that you had a die with the property that that each roll would yield a random real number between 0 and 5. The code in Figure 17.9 simulates rolling such a die many times, prints the mean and variance (the function variance is defined in Figure 15.8), and then plots a histogram showing the probability of ranges of numbers getting rolled. It also simulates rolling 100 dice many times and plots (on the same figure) a histogram of the mean value of those 100 dice. The hatch keyword argument is used to visually distinguish one histogram from the other.

The weights keyword is bound to an array of the same length as the first argument to hist, and is used to assign a weight to each element in the first argument. In the resulting histogram, each value in a bin contributes its associated weight towards the bin count (instead of the usual 1). In this example, we use weights to scale the y values to the relative rather than absolute size of each bin. Therefore, for each bin, the value on the y-axis is the probability of the mean falling within that bin.

```
def plotMeans(numDicePerTrial, numDiceThrown, numBins, legend,
              color, style):
    means = []
    numTrials = numDiceThrown//numDicePerTrial
    for i in range(numTrials):
        vals = 0
        for j in range(numDicePerTrial):
            vals += 5*random.random()
        means.append(vals/numDicePerTrial)
    pylab.hist(means, numBins, color = color, label = legend,
               weights = pylab.array(len(means)*[1])/len(means),
               hatch = style)
    return sum(means)/len(means), variance(means)

mean, var = plotMeans(1, 100000, 11, '1 die', 'w', '*')
print('Mean of rolling 1 die =', round(mean,4),
      'Variance =', round(var,4))
mean, var = plotMeans(100, 100000, 11,
                      'Mean of 100 dice', 'w', '//')
print('Mean of rolling 100 dice =', round(mean, 4),
      'Variance =', round(var, 4))
pylab.title('Rolling Continuous Dice')
pylab.xlabel('Value')
pylab.ylabel('Probability')
pylab.legend()
```

Figure 17.9: Estimating the mean of a continuous die

When run, the code produced the plot in Figure 17.10, and printed,

```
Mean of rolling 1 die = 2.4974 Variance = 2.0904
Mean of rolling 100 dice = 2.4981 Variance = 0.02
```

In each case the mean was quite close to the expected mean of 2.5. Since our die is fair, the probability distribution for one die is almost perfectly uniform,[118] i.e., very far from normal. However, when we look at the average value of 100 dice, the distribution is almost perfectly normal, with the peak including the expected mean. Furthermore, the variance of the mean of the 100 rolls is close to the variance of the value of a single roll divided by 100. All is as predicted by the CLT.

---

[118] "Almost" because we rolled the die a finite number of times.

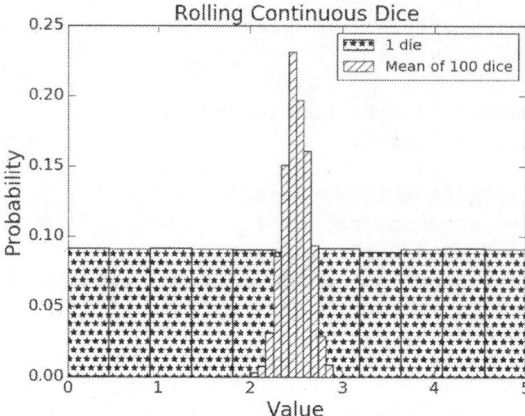

Figure 17.10: An illustration of the CLT

It's nice that the CLT seems to work, but what good is it? Perhaps it could prove useful in winning bar bets for those who drink in particularly nerdy bars. However, the primary value of the CLT is that it allows us to compute confidence levels and intervals even when the underlying population distribution is not normal. When we looked at confidence intervals in Section 15.4.2, we pointed out that the empirical rule is based on assumptions about the nature of the space being sampled. We assumed that

- The mean estimation error is 0, and
- The distribution of the errors in the estimates is normal.

When these assumptions hold, the empirical rule for normal distributions provides a handy way to estimate confidence intervals and levels given the mean and standard deviation.

Let's return to the Boston Marathon example. The code in Figure 17.11, which produced the plot in Figure 17.12, draws twenty simple random samples for each of a variety of sample sizes. For each sample size, it computes the mean of each of the twenty samples; it then computes the mean and standard deviation of those means. Since the CLT tells us that the sample means will be normally distributed, we can use the standard deviation and the empirical rule to compute a 95% confidence interval for each sample size.

As the plot in Figure 17.12 shows, all of the estimates are reasonably close to the actual population mean. Notice, however, that the error in the estimated mean does not decrease monotonically with the size of the samples—the estimate using 250 examples happens to be worse than the estimate using 50 examples. What does change monotonically with the sample size is our confidence in our estimate of the mean. As the sample size grows from 50 to 1,850, the confidence interval decreases from about ±15 to about ±2. This is important. It's not good enough to get lucky and happen to get a good estimate. We need to know how much confidence to have in our estimate.

```
times = getBMData('bm_results2012.txt')['time']
meanOfMeans, stdOfMeans = [], []
sampleSizes = range(50, 2000, 200)
for sampleSize in sampleSizes:
    sampleMeans = []
    for t in range(20):
        sample = random.sample(times, sampleSize)
        sampleMeans.append(sum(sample)/sampleSize)
    meanOfMeans.append(sum(sampleMeans)/len(sampleMeans))
    stdOfMeans.append(stdDev(sampleMeans))
pylab.errorbar(sampleSizes, meanOfMeans,
               yerr = 1.96*pylab.array(stdOfMeans),
               label = 'Estimated mean and 95% confidence interval')
pylab.xlim(0, max(sampleSizes) + 50)
pylab.axhline(sum(times)/len(times), linestyle = '--',
              label = 'Population mean')
pylab.title('Estimates of Mean Finishing Time')
pylab.xlabel('Sample Size')
pylab.ylabel('Finshing Time (minutes)')
pylab.legend(loc = 'best')
```

Figure 17.11 Produce plot with error bars

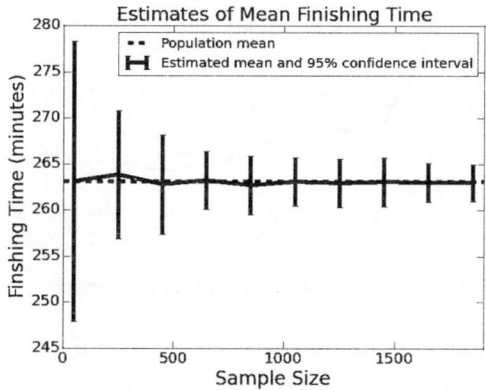

Figure 17.12: Estimates of finishing times with error bars

17.3 Standard Error of the Mean

We just saw that if we chose twenty random samples of 1,850 competitors, we could, with 95% confidence, estimate the mean finishing time within a range of about four minutes. We did this using the standard deviation of the sample means. Unfortunately, since this involves using more total examples (20*1,850 = 37,000) than there were competitors, it doesn't seem like a very useful result. We would have been better off computing the actual mean directly using the entire population. What we need is a way to estimate a confidence interval using a single example. Enter the concept of the **standard error** of the mean (**SE** or **SEM**).

The SE for a sample of size n is the standard deviation of the means of an infinite number of samples of size n drawn from the same population. Unsurprisingly, it depends upon both n and σ, the standard deviation of the population:

$$SE = \frac{\sigma}{\sqrt{n}}$$

Figure 17.13 compares the SE for the sample sizes used in Figure 17.12 to the standard deviation of the means of the twenty samples we generated for each sample size.

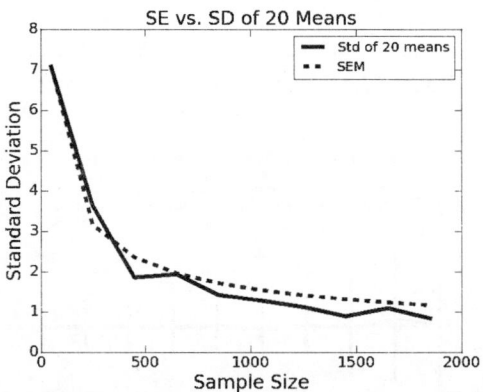

Figure 17.13: Standard error of the mean

The actual standard deviations of the means of our twenty samples closely tracks the SE. In both cases, the standard deviation drops rapidly at the start and then more slowly as the sample size gets large. The is because the reduction in standard deviation depends upon the square root of the sample size. E.g., to cut the standard deviation in half, one needs to quadruple the sample size.

CHAPTER 17. SAMPLING AND CONFIDENCE INTERVALS

Alas, if all we have is a single sample, we don't know the standard deviation of the population. Typically, we assume that the standard deviation of the sample, the sample standard deviation, is a reasonable proxy for the standard deviation of the population. This will be the case when the population distribution is not terribly skewed.

The code in Figure 17.14 creates 100 samples of various sizes from the Boston Marathon data, and compares the mean standard deviation of the samples of each size to the standard deviation of the population. It produces the plot in Figure 17.15.

```
times = getBMData('bm_results2012.txt')['time']
popStd = stdDev(times)
sampleSizes = range(2, 200, 2)
diffsMeans = []
for sampleSize in sampleSizes:
    diffs = []
    for t in range(100):
        diffs.append(abs(popStd - stdDev(random.sample(times,
                                                        sampleSize))))
    diffsMeans.append(sum(diffs)/len(diffs))
pylab.plot(sampleSizes, diffsMeans)
pylab.xlabel('Sample Size')
pylab.ylabel('Abs(Pop. Std - Sample Std)')
pylab.title('Sample SD vs Population SD')
```

Figure 17.14: Sample standard deviation vs. population standard deviation

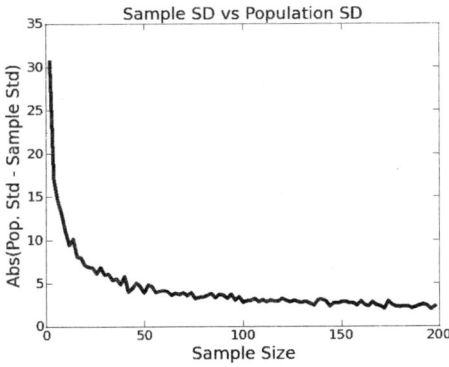

Figure 17.15: Sample standard deviations

By the time the sample size reaches 100, the difference between the sample standard deviation and the population standard deviation is relatively small.

In practice, people usually use the sample standard deviation in place of the (usually unknown) population standard deviation to estimate the SE. If the sample size is large enough,[119] and the population distribution is not too far from normal, it is safe to use this estimate to compute confidence intervals using the empirical rule.

What does this imply? If we take a single sample of say 200 runners, we can

- Compute the mean and standard deviation of that sample,
- Use the standard deviation of that sample to estimate the SE, and
- Use the estimated SE to generate confidence intervals around the sample mean.

The code in Figure 17.16 does this 10,000 times and then prints the fraction of times the sample mean is more than 1.96 estimated SE's from the population mean. (Recall that for a normal distribution 95% of the data falls within 1.96 standard deviations of the mean.)

```
times = getBMData('bm_results2012.txt')['time']
popMean = sum(times)/len(times)
sampleSize = 200
numBad = 0
for t in range(10000):
    sample = random.sample(times, sampleSize)
    sampleMean = sum(sample)/sampleSize
    se = stdDev(sample)/sampleSize**0.5
    if abs(popMean - sampleMean) > 1.96*se:
        numBad += 1
print('Fraction outside 95% confidence interval =', numBad/10000)
```

Figure 17.16 Estimating the population mean 10,000 times

When the code is run it prints,

```
Fraction outside 95% confidence interval = 0.0533
```

I.e., pretty much what the theory predicts. Score one for the CLT!

---

[119] Don't you just love following instructions with phrases like, "choose a large enough sample." Unfortunately, there is no simple recipe for choosing a sufficient sample size when you know little about the underlying population. Many statisticians say that a sample size of 30-40 is large enough when the population distribution is roughly normal. For smaller sample sizes, it is better to use something called the t-distribution to compute the size of the interval. The t-distribution is similar to a normal distribution, but it has fatter tails, so the confidence intervals will be a bit wider.

18 UNDERSTANDING EXPERIMENTAL DATA

This chapter is about understanding experimental data. We will make extensive use of plotting to visualize the data, and show how to use linear regression to build a model of experimental data. We will also talk about the interplay between physical and computational experiments. We defer our discussion of how to draw a valid statistical conclusion to Chapter 19.

18.1 The Behavior of Springs

Springs are wonderful things. When they are compressed or stretched by some force, they store energy. When that force is no longer applied they release the stored energy. This property allows them to smooth the ride in cars, help mattresses conform to our bodies, retract seat belts, and launch projectiles.

In 1676 the British physicist Robert Hooke formulated **Hooke's law** of elasticity: *Ut tensio, sic vis*, in English, $F = -kx$. In other words, the force F stored in a spring is linearly related to the distance the spring has been compressed (or stretched). (The minus sign indicates that the force exerted by the spring is in the opposite direction of the displacement.) Hooke's law holds for a wide variety of materials and systems, including many biological systems. Of course, it does not hold for an arbitrarily large force. All springs have an **elastic limit**, beyond which the law fails. Those of you who have stretched a Slinky too far know this all too well.

The constant of proportionality, k, is called the **spring constant**. If the spring is stiff (like the ones in the suspension of a car or the limbs of an archer's bow), k is large. If the spring is weak, like the spring in a ballpoint pen, k is small.

Knowing the spring constant of a particular spring can be a matter of some import. The calibrations of both simple scales and atomic force microscopes depend upon knowing the spring constants of components. The mechanical behavior of a strand of DNA is related to the force required to compress it. The force with which a bow launches an arrow is related to the spring constant of its limbs. And so on.

Generations of physics students have learned to estimate spring constants using an experimental apparatus similar to that pictured here.

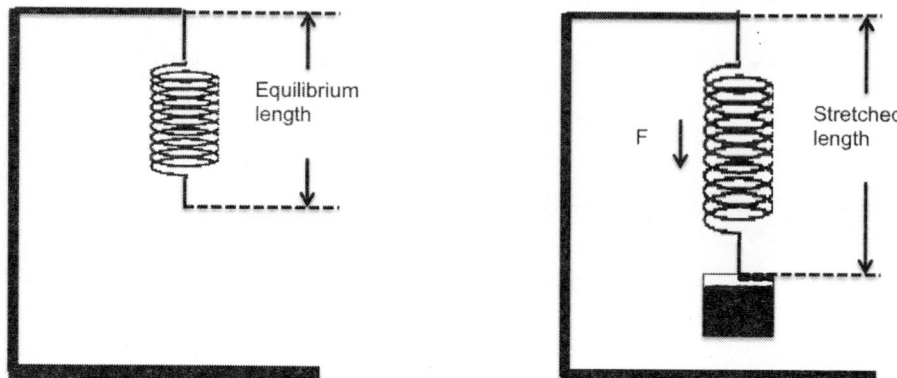

Figure 18.1 A classic experiment

We start with a spring with no weight on it, and measure the distance to the bottom of the spring from the top of the stand. We then hang a known mass on the spring, and wait for it to stop moving. At this point, the force stored in the spring is the force exerted on the spring by the weight hanging from it. This is the value of F in Hooke's law. We again measure the distance from the bottom of the spring to the top of the stand. The difference between this distance and the distance before we hung the weight then becomes the value of x in Hooke's law.

We know that the force, F, being exerted on the spring is equal to the mass, m, multiplied by the acceleration due to gravity, g (9.81 m/s² is a pretty good approximation of g on this planet), so we substitute m*g for F. By simple algebra we know that k = -(m*g)/x.

Suppose, for example, that m = 1kg and x = 0.1m, then

$$k = -\frac{1kg * 9.81 m/s^2}{0.1m} = -\frac{9.81N}{0.1m} = -98.1 N/m$$

According to this calculation, it will take *98.1* Newtons[120] of force to stretch the spring one meter.

This would all be well and good if

---

[120] The Newton, written *N*, is the standard international unit for measuring force. It is the amount of force needed to accelerate a mass of one kilogram at a rate of one meter per second per second. A Slinky, by the way, has a spring constant of approximately *1N/m*.

CHAPTER 18. UNDERSTANDING EXPERIMENTAL DATA

- We had complete confidence that we would conduct this experiment perfectly. In that case, we could take one measurement, perform the calculation, and know that we had found k. Unfortunately, experimental science hardly ever works this way.
- We could be sure that we were operating below the elastic limit of the spring.

A more robust experiment would be to hang a series of increasingly heavier weights on the spring, measure the stretch of the spring each time, and plot the results. We ran such an experiment, and typed the results into a file named springData.txt:

```
Distance (m) Mass (kg)
0.0865 0.1
0.1015 0.15
...
0.4416 0.9
0.4304 0.95
0.437 1.0
```

The function in Figure 18.2 reads data from a file such as the one we saved, and returns lists containing the distances and masses.

```
def getData(fileName):
    dataFile = open(fileName, 'r')
    distances = []
    masses = []
    dataFile.readline() #ignore header
    for line in dataFile:
        d, m = line.split(' ')
        distances.append(float(d))
        masses.append(float(m))
    dataFile.close()
    return (masses, distances)
```

Figure 18.2 Extracting the data from a file

The function in Figure 18.3 uses getData to extract the experimental data from the file and then produces the plot in Figure 18.4.

```
def plotData(inputFile):
    masses, distances = getData(inputFile)
    distances = pylab.array(distances)
    masses = pylab.array(masses)
    forces = masses*9.81
    pylab.plot(forces, distances, 'bo',
               label = 'Measured displacements')
    pylab.title('Measured Displacement of Spring')
    pylab.xlabel('|Force| (Newtons)')
    pylab.ylabel('Distance (meters)')

plotData('springData.txt')
```

Figure 18.3 Plotting the data

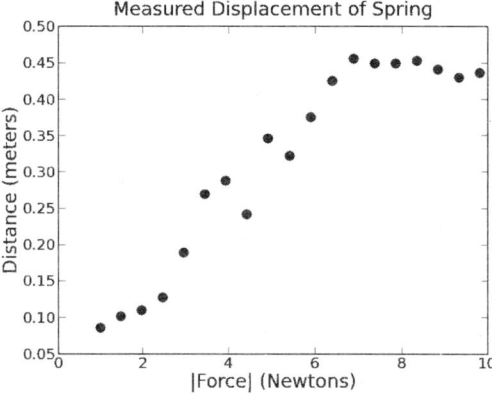

Figure 18.4 Displacement of spring

This is not what Hooke's law predicts. Hooke's law tells us that the distance should increase linearly with the mass, i.e., the points should lie on a straight line the slope of which is determined by the spring constant. Of course, we know that when we take real measurements the experimental data are rarely a perfect match for the theory. Measurement error is to be expected, so we should expect the points to lie around a line rather than on it.

Still, it would be nice to see a line that represents our best guess of where the points would have been if we had no measurement error. The usual way to do this is to fit a line to the data.

18.1.1 Using Linear Regression to Find a Fit

Whenever we fit any curve (including a line) to data we need some way to decide which curve is the best **fit** for the data. This means that we need to define an **objective function** that provides a quantitative assessment of how well the curve fits the data. Once we have such a function, finding the best fit can be formulated as finding a curve that minimizes (or maximizes) the value of that function, i.e., as an optimization problem (see Chapters 12 and 13).

The most commonly used objective function is called **least squares**. Let *observed* and *predicted* be vectors of equal length, where *observed* contains the measured points and *predicted* the corresponding data points on the proposed fit. The objective function is then defined as:

$$\sum_{i=0}^{len(observed)-1} (observed[i] - predicted[i])^2$$

Squaring the difference between observed and predicted points makes large differences between observed and predicted points relatively more important than small differences. Squaring the difference also discards information about whether the difference is positive or negative.

How might we go about finding the best least-squares fit? One way to do this would be to use a successive approximation algorithm similar to the Newton-Raphson algorithm in Chapter 3. Alternatively, there is are analytic solutions that is often applicable. But we don't have to implement either, because PyLab provides a built-in function, polyfit, that finds an approximation to the best least-squares fit. The call

```
pylab.polyfit (observedXVals, observedYVals, n)
```

finds the coefficients of a polynomial of degree n that provides a best least-squares fit for the set of points defined by the two arrays observedXVals and observedYVals. For example, the call

```
pylab.polyfit(observedXVals, observedYVals, 1)
```

will find a line described by the polynomial $y = ax + b$, where a is the slope of the line and b the y-intercept. In this case, the call returns an array with two floating point values. Similarly, a parabola is described by the quadratic equation $y = ax^2 + bx + c$. Therefore, the call

```
pylab.polyfit(observedXVals, observedYVals, 2)
```

returns an array with three floating point values.

The algorithm used by polyfit is called **linear regression**. This may seem a bit confusing, since we can use it to fit curves other than lines. Some authors do make a distinction between linear regression (when the model is a line) and **polynomial regression** (when the model is a polynomial with degree greater than 1), but most do not.[121]

The function fitData in Figure 18.5 extends the plotData function in Figure 18.3 by adding a line that represents the best fit for the data. It uses polyfit to find the coefficients a and b, and then uses those coefficients to generate the predicted spring displacement for each force. Notice that there is an asymmetry in the way forces and distance are treated. The values in forces (which are derived from the mass suspended from the spring) are treated as independent, and used to produce the values in the dependent variable predictedDistances (a prediction of the displacements produced by suspending the mass).

The function also computes the spring constant, k. The slope of the line, a, is $\Delta distance/\Delta force$. The spring constant, on the other hand, is $\Delta force/\Delta distance$. Consequently, k is the inverse of a.

The call fitData('springData.txt') produces the plot in Figure 18.6.

```
def fitData(inputFile):
    masses, distances = getData(inputFile)
    distances = pylab.array(distances)
    forces = pylab.array(masses)*9.81
    pylab.plot(forces, distances, 'ko',
               label = 'Measured displacements')
    pylab.title('Measured Displacement of Spring')
    pylab.xlabel('|Force| (Newtons)')
    pylab.ylabel('Distance (meters)')
    #find linear fit
    a,b = pylab.polyfit(forces, distances, 1)
    predictedDistances = a*pylab.array(forces) + b
    k = 1.0/a #see explanation in text
    pylab.plot(forces, predictedDistances,
               label = 'Displacements predicted by\nlinear fit, k = '
               + str(round(k, 5)))
    pylab.legend(loc = 'best')
```

Figure 18.5 Fitting a curve to data

---

[121] The reason they do not is that although polynomial regression fits a nonlinear model to the data, the model is linear in the unknown parameters that it estimates.

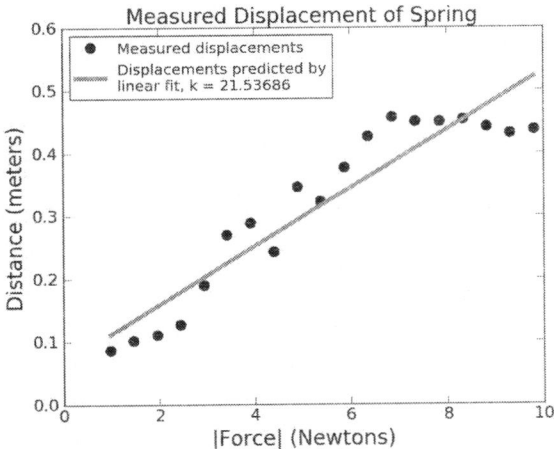

Figure 18.6 Measured points and linear model

It is interesting to observe that very few points actually lie on the least-squares fit. This is plausible because we are trying to minimize the sum of the squared errors, rather than maximize the number of points that lie on the line. Still, it doesn't look like a great fit. Let's try a cubic fit by adding to fitData the code

```
#find cubic fit
fit = pylab.polyfit(forces, distances, 3)
predictedDistances = pylab.polyval(fit, forces)
pylab.plot(forces, predictedDistances, 'k:', label = 'cubic fit')
```

In this code, we have used the function polyval to generate the points associated with the cubic fit. This function takes two arguments: a sequence of polynomial coefficients and a sequence of values at which the polynomial is to be evaluated. The code fragments

```
fit = pylab.polyfit(forces, distances, 3)
predictedDistances = pylab.polyval(fit, forces)
```

and

```
a,b,c,d = pylab.polyfit(forces, distances, 3)
predictedDistances = a*(forces**3) + b*forces**2 + c*forces + d
```

are equivalent.

This produces the plot in Figure 18.7. The cubic fit looks like a much better model of the data than the linear fit, but is it? Probably not.

As Figure 18.9 shows, eliminating those points certainly makes a difference: k has dropped dramatically and the linear and cubic fits are almost indistinguishable. But how do we know which of the two linear fits is a better representation of how our spring performs up to its elastic limit? We could use some statistical test to determine which line is a better fit for the data, but that would be beside the point. This is not a question that can be answered by statistics. After all we could throw out all the data except any two points and know that `polyfit` would find a line that would be a perfect fit for those two points. One should never throw out experimental results merely to get a better fit.[122] Here we justified throwing out the rightmost points by appealing to the theory underlying Hooke's law, i.e., that springs have an elastic limit. That justification could not have been appropriately used to eliminate points elsewhere in the data.

18.2 The Behavior of Projectiles

Growing bored with merely stretching springs, we decided to use one of our springs to build a device capable of launching a projectile.[123] We used the device four times to fire a projectile at a target 30 yards (1080 inches) from the launching point. Each time, we measured the height of the projectile at various distances from the launching point. The launching point and the target were at the same height, which we treated as 0.0 in our measurements.

The data was stored in a file with the contents shown in Figure 18.10. The first column contains distances of the projectile from the target. The other columns contain the height of the projectile at that distance for each of the four trials. All of the measurements are in inches.

---

[122] Which isn't to say that people never do.

[123] A projectile is an object that is propelled through space by the exertion of a force that stops after the projectile is launched. In the interest of public safety, we will not describe the launching device used in this experiment. Suffice it to say that it was awesome.

CHAPTER 18. UNDERSTANDING EXPERIMENTAL DATA

Distance	trial1	trial2	trial3	trial4
1080	0.0	0.0	0.0	0.0
1044	2.25	3.25	4.5	6.5
1008	5.25	6.5	6.5	8.75
972	7.5	7.75	8.25	9.25
936	8.75	9.25	9.5	10.5
900	12.0	12.25	12.5	14.75
864	13.75	16.0	16.0	16.5
828	14.75	15.25	15.5	17.5
792	15.5	16.0	16.6	16.75
756	17.0	17.0	17.5	19.25
720	17.5	18.5	18.5	19.0
540	19.5	20.0	20.25	20.5
360	18.5	18.5	19.0	19.0
180	13.0	13.0	13.0	13.0
0	0.0	0.0	0.0	0.0

Figure 18.10 Data from projectile experiment

The code in Figure 18.11 was used to plot the mean altitude of the projectile in the four trials against the distance from the point of launch. It also plots the best linear and quadratic fits to those points. (In case you have forgotten the meaning of multiplying a list by an integer, the expression [0]*len(distances) produces a list of len(distances) 0's.)

By comparing the estimation errors (the numerator) with the variability of the original values (the denominator), R^2 is intended to capture the proportion of variability (relative to the mean) in a data set that is accounted for by the statistical model provided by the fit. When the model being evaluated is produced by a linear regression, the value of R^2 always lies between 0 and 1. If $R^2 = 1$, the model is a perfect fit to the data. If $R^2 = 0$, there is no relationship between the values predicted by the model and the way the data is distributed around the mean.

The code in Figure 18.13 provides a straightforward implementation of this statistical measure. Its compactness stems from the expressiveness of the operations on arrays. The expression (predicted - measured)**2 subtracts the elements of one array from the elements of another, and then squares each element in the result. The expression (measured - meanOfMeasured)**2 subtracts the scalar value meanOfMeasured from each element of the array measured, and then squares each element of the results.

```
def rSquared(measured, predicted):
    """Assumes measured a one-dimensional array of measured values
                predicted a one-dimensional array of predicted values
       Returns coefficient of determination"""
    estimateError = ((predicted - measured)**2).sum()
    meanOfMeasured = measured.sum()/len(measured)
    variability = ((measured - meanOfMeasured)**2).sum()
    return 1 - estimateError/variability
```

Figure 18.13 Computing R^2

When the lines of code

`print('RSquare of linear fit =', rSquared(meanHeights, altitudes))`

and

`print('RSquare of quadratic fit =', rSquared(meanHeights, altitudes))`

are inserted after the appropriate calls to pylab.plot in processTrajectories (see Figure 18.11), they print

```
RSquared of linear fit = 0.0177433205441
RSquared of quadratic fit = 0.985765369287
```

CHAPTER 18. UNDERSTANDING EXPERIMENTAL DATA

Roughly speaking, this tells us that less than 2% of the variation in the measured data can be explained by the linear model, but more than 98% of the variation can be explained by the quadratic model.

18.2.2 Using a Computational Model

Now that we have what seems to be a good model of our data, we can use this model to help answer questions about our original data. One interesting question is the horizontal speed at which the projectile is traveling when it hits the target. We might use the following train of thought to design a computation that answers this question:

1. We know that the trajectory of the projectile is given by a formula of the form y = ax² + bx + c, i.e., it is a parabola. Since every parabola is symmetrical around its vertex, we know that its peak occurs halfway between the launch point and the target; call this distance xMid. The peak height, yPeak, is therefore given by yPeak = a * xMid² + b * xMid + c.

2. If we ignore air resistance (remember that no model is perfect), we can compute the amount of time it takes for the projectile to fall from yPeak to the height of the target, because that is purely a function of gravity. It is given by the equation t = $\sqrt{(2 * yPeak)/g}$.[126] This is also the amount of time it takes for the projectile to travel the horizontal distance from xMid to the target, because once it reaches the target it stops moving.

3. Given the time to go from xMid to the target, we can easily compute the average horizontal speed of the projectile over that interval. If we assume that the projectile was neither accelerating nor decelerating in the horizontal direction during that interval, we can use the average horizontal speed as an estimate of the horizontal speed when the projectile hits the target.

Figure 18.14 implements this technique for estimating the horizontal velocity of the projectile.[127]

---

[126] This equation can be derived from first principles, but it is easier to just look it up. We found it at http://en.wikipedia.org/wiki/Equations_for_a_falling_body.

[127] The vertical component of the velocity is also easily estimated, since it is merely the product of the g and t in Figure 18.14.

it does not, because we can use polyfit to find a curve that fits the original independent values and the log of the dependent values.

Consider the sequence [1, 2, 4, 8, 16, 32, 64, 128, 256, 512]. If we take the log base 2 of each value. we get the sequence [0, 1, 2, 3, 4, 5, 6, 7, 8, 9], i.e., a sequence that grows linearly. In fact, if a function y = f(x), exhibits exponential growth, the log (to any base) of f(x) grows linearly. This can be visualized by plotting an exponential function with a logarithmic y-axis. The code

```
xVals, yVals = [], []
for i in range(10):
    xVals.append(i)
    yVals.append(3**i)
pylab.plot(xVals, yVals, 'k')
pylab.semilogy()
```

produces the plot in Figure 18.17.

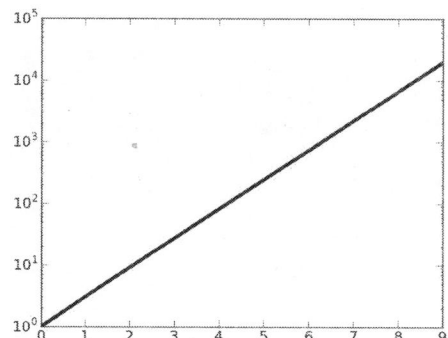

Figure 18.17 An exponential on a semilog plot

That taking the log of an exponential function produces a linear function can be used to construct a model for an exponentially distributed set of data points, as illustrated by the code in Figure 18.18. We use polyfit to find a curve that fits the x values and log of the y values. Notice that we use yet another Python standard library module, math, which supplies a log function. We also use a lambda expression, see Section 5.4.

When run, this code produces the plot in Figure 18.19, in which the actual values and the predicted values coincide. Moreover, when the model is tested on a value (20) that was not used to produce the fit, it prints

```
f(20) = 3486784401
Predicted value = 3486784401
```

```
import math

def createData(f, xVals):
    """Asssumes f is afunction of one argument
                 xVals is an array of suitable arguments for f
       Returns array containing results of applying f to the
                 elements of xVals"""
    yVals = []
    for i in xVals:
        yVals.append(f(xVals[i]))
    return pylab.array(yVals)

def fitExpData(xVals, yVals):
    """Assumes xVals and yVals arrays of numbers such that
          yVals[i] == f(xVals[i]), where f is an exponential function
       Returns a, b, base such that log(f(x), base) == ax + b"""
    logVals = []
    for y in yVals:
        logVals.append(math.log(y, 2.0)) #get log base 2
    fit = pylab.polyfit(xVals, logVals, 1)
    return fit, 2.0

xVals = range(10)
f = lambda x: 3**x
yVals = createData(f, xVals)
pylab.plot(xVals, yVals, 'ko', label = 'Actual values')
fit, base = fitExpData(xVals, yVals)
predictedYVals = []
for x in xVals:
    predictedYVals.append(base**pylab.polyval(fit, x))
pylab.plot(xVals, predictedYVals, label = 'Predicted values')
pylab.title('Fitting an Exponential Function')
pylab.legend(loc = 'upper left')
#Look at a value for x not in original data
print('f(20) =', f(20))
print('Predicted value =', int(base**(pylab.polyval(fit, [20]))))
```

Figure 18.18 Using polyfit to fit an exponential

This method of using polyfit to find a model for data works when the relationship can be described by an equation of the form $y = base^{ax+b}$. If used on data that cannot be described this way, it will yield erroneous results.

19 RANDOMIZED TRIALS AND HYPOTHESIS CHECKING

Dr. X invented a drug, PED-X, designed to help professional bicycle racers ride faster. When he tried to market it, the racers insisted that Dr. X demonstrate that his drug was superior to PED-Y, the banned drug that they had been using for years. Dr. X raised money from some investors, and launched a **randomized trial**.

He persuaded 200 professional cyclists to participate in his trial. He then divided them randomly into two groups: treatment and control. Each member of the **treatment group** received a dose of PED-X. Members of the **control group** were told that they were being given a dose of PED-X, but were instead given a dose of PED-Y.

Each cyclist was asked to bike 50 miles as fast as possible. The finishing times for each group were normally distributed. The mean finishing time of the treatment group was 118.79 minutes, and that of the control group was 120.17 minutes. Figure 19.1 shows the time for each cyclist.

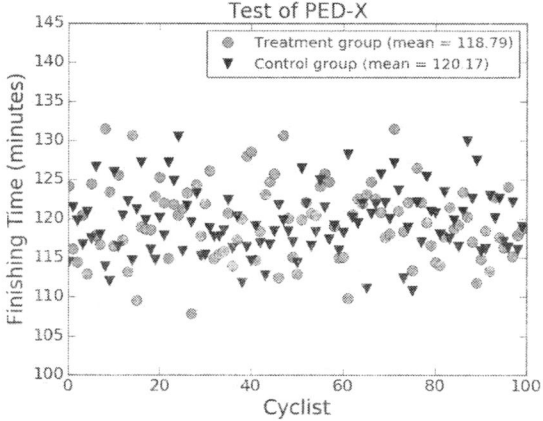

Figure 19.1: Finishing times for cyclists

Dr. X was elated until he ran into a statistician who pointed out that it was almost inevitable that one of the two groups would have a lower mean than the other, and perhaps the difference in means was merely a random occurrence. When she saw the crestfallen look on the scientist's face, the statistician offered to show him how to check the statistical significance of his study.

19.1 Checking Significance

In any experiment that involves drawing samples at random from a population, there is always the possibility that an observed effect occurred purely by chance. Figure 19.2 is a visualization of how temperatures in January of 2014 varied from the average temperatures in January from 1951 to 1980. Now, imagine that you constructed a sample by choosing twenty random spots on the planet, and then discovered that the mean change in temperature for the sample was +1 degree Celsius. What is the probability that the observed change in mean temperature was an artifact of the sites you happened to sample rather than an indication that the planet as a whole is warming? Answering this kind of question is what **statistical significance** is all about.

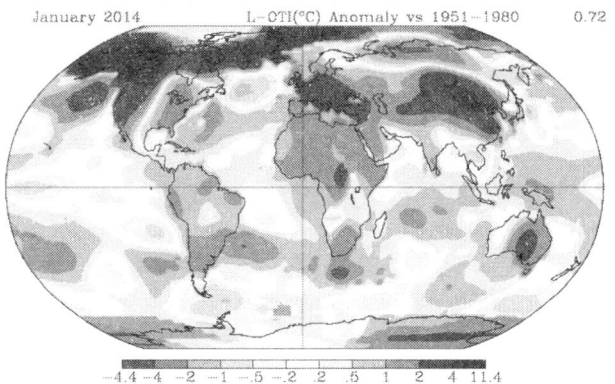

Figure 19.2 January temperature difference in degrees Celsius from the 1951-1980 average[128]

In the early part of the 20th century, Ronald Fisher developed an approach to statistical **hypothesis testing** that has become the most commonly used approach for evaluating the probability of an observed effect having occurred purely by chance. Fisher claims to have invented the method in response to a claim by Dr. Muriel Bristol-Roach that when she drank tea with milk in it she could detect whether the tea or the milk was poured into the teacup first. Fisher challenged her to a "tea test" in which she was given eight cups of tea (four for each order of adding tea and milk), and asked to identify those cups into which the tea had been poured before the milk. She did this perfectly. Fisher then calculated the probability of her having done this purely by chance. As we saw in Section 15.4.4,

---

[128] This is a gray-scale version of a color image provided by the U.S. National Aeronautics and Space Administration.

$\binom{8}{4}$ = 70, i.e., there are 70 different ways to choose 4 cups out of 8. Since only one of these 70 combinations includes all 4 cups in which the tea was poured first, Fisher calculated that the probability of Dr. Bristol-Roach having chosen correctly by pure luck was $\frac{1}{70} \approx 0.014$. From this he concluded that it was highly unlikely that her success could be attributed to luck.

Fisher's approach to significance testing can be summarized as

1. State a **null hypothesis** and an **alternative hypothesis**. The null hypothesis is that the "treatment" has no interesting effect. For the "tea test," the null hypothesis was that Dr. Bristol-Roach had no ability to taste the difference. The alternative hypothesis is a hypothesis that can be true only if the null hypothesis is false, e.g., that Dr. Bristol-Roach could taste the difference.[129]
2. Understand statistical assumptions about the sample being evaluated. For the "tea test" Fisher assumed that Dr. Bristol-Roach was making independent decisions for each cup.
3. Compute a relevant **test statistic**. In this case, the test statistic was the fraction of correct answers given by Dr. Bristol-Roach.
4. Derive the probability of that test statistic under the null hypothesis. In this case, the probability of getting all of the cups right by accident, i.e., 0.014.
5. Decide whether that probability is sufficiently small that you are willing to assume that the null hypothesis is false, i.e., to **reject** the null hypothesis. Common values for the rejection level, which should be chosen in advance, are 0.05 and 0.01.

Returning to our cyclists, imagine that the times for the treatment and control groups were samples drawn from infinite populations of finishing times for PED-X users and PED-Y users. The null hypothesis for this experiment is that the means of those two larger populations are the same, i.e., the difference between the population mean of the treatment group and the population mean of the control group is 0. The alternative hypothesis is that they are not the same, i.e., the difference in means is not equal to 0.

Next, we go about trying to reject the null hypothesis. We choose a threshold, α, for statistical significance, and try to show that the probability of the data having been drawn from distributions consistent with the null hypothesis is less than α. We then say that we can reject the null hypothesis with confidence α, and accept the negation of the null hypothesis with probability $1 - \alpha$.

---

[129] In his formulation, Fisher had only a null hypothesis. The idea of an alternative hypothesis was introduced later by Jerzy Neyman and Egon Pearson.

The choice of α affects the kind of errors we make. The larger α, the more often we will reject a null hypothesis that is actually true. These are known as **type I errors**. When α is smaller, we will more often accept a null hypothesis that is actually false. These are known as **type II errors**.

Most commonly, people choose α = 0.05. However, depending upon the consequences of being wrong, it might be preferable to choose a smaller or larger α. Imagine, for example, that the null hypothesis is that there is no difference in the rate of premature death between those taking PED-X and those taking PED-Y. One might well want to choose a small α, say 0.01, as the basis for rejecting that hypothesis before deciding whether or not one drug was safer than the other. On the other hand, if the null hypothesis were that there is no difference in the taste of PED-X and PED-Y, one might comfortably choose a pretty large α.[130]

The next step is to compute the test statistic. The most common test statistic is the **t-statistic**. The t-statistic tells us how different, measured in units of standard error, the estimate derived from the data is from the null hypothesis. The larger the t-statistic, the more likely the null hypothesis can be rejected. For our example, the t-statistic tells us how many standard errors the difference in the two means (118.79 − 120.17 = -1.38) is from 0. The t-statistic for our PED-X example is -2.13165598142. What does this mean? How do we use it?

We use the t-statistic in much the same way we use the number of standard deviations from the mean to compute confidence intervals (see Section 15.4.2). Recall that for all normal distributions the probability of an example lying within a fixed number of standard deviations of the mean is fixed. Here we do something slightly more complex that takes into account the number of samples used to compute the standard error. Instead of assuming a normal distribution, we assume a **t-distribution**.

T-distributions were first described, in 1908, by William Gosset, a statistician working for the Arthur Guinness and Son brewery.[131] The t-distribution is actually a family of distributions, since the shape of the distribution depends upon the degrees of freedom in the sample.

---

[130] Many researchers, including the author of this book, believe strongly that the "rejectionist" approach to reporting statistics is unfortunate. It is almost always preferable to report the actual significance level rather than merely stating that "the null hypothesis has been rejected at the 5% level."

[131] Guiness forbade Gosset from publishing under his own name. He used the pseudonym "Student" when he published his seminal 1908 paper, "Probable Error of a Mean," about t-distributions. As a result, the distribution is frequently called "Student's t-distribution."

CHAPTER 19. RANDOMIZED TRIALS AND HYPOTHESIS CHECKING

The **degrees of freedom** describes the amount of independent information used to derive the t-statistic. In general, we can think of degrees of freedom as the number of independent observations in a sample that are available to estimate some statistic about the population from which that sample is drawn.

A t-distribution looks a lot like a normal distribution, and the larger the degrees of freedom the closer it is to a normal distribution. For small degrees of freedom, the t-distributions have notably fatter tails than normal distributions. For degrees of freedom of 30 or more, t-distributions are very close to normal.

Now, let's use the sample variance to to estimate the population variance. Recall that

$$variance(X) = \frac{\sum_{x \in X}(x - \mu)^2}{|X|}$$

so the variance of our sample is

$$\frac{(100 - 200)^2 + (200 - 200)^2 + (300 - 200)^2}{3}$$

It might appear that we are using three independent pieces of information, but we are not. The three terms in the numerator are not independent of each other, because all three observations were used to compute the mean of the sample of 200 riders. The degrees of freedom is 2, since once we know the mean and any two of the three observations, the value of the third observation is fixed.

The larger the degrees of freedom, the higher the probability that the sample statistic is representative of the population. The degrees of freedom in a t-statistic computed from a single sample is one less than the sample size, because the mean of the sample is used in calculating the t-statistic. If two samples are used, the degrees of freedom is two less than the sum of the sample sizes, because the mean of each sample is used in calculating the t-statistic. For example, for the PED-X/PED-Y experiment, the degrees of freedom is 198.

Given the degrees of freedom, we can draw a plot showing the appropriate t-distribution, and then see where the t-statistic we have computed for our PED-X example lies on the distribution. The code in Figure 19.3 does that, and produces the plot in Figure 19.4. The code first uses the function scipy.random.standard_t to generate a large number of examples drawn from a t-distribution with 198 degrees of freedom. It then draws white lines at the t-statistic and the negative of the t-statistic for the PED-X sample.

```
tStat = -2.13165598142 #t-statistic for PED-X example
tDist = []
numBins = 1000
for i in range(10000000):
    tDist.append(scipy.random.standard_t(198))

pylab.hist(tDist, bins = numBins,
           weights = pylab.array(len(tDist)*[1.0])/len(tDist))
pylab.axvline(tStat, color = 'w')
pylab.axvline(-tStat, color = 'w')
pylab.title('T-distribution with 198 Degrees of Freedom')
pylab.xlabel('T-statistic')
pylab.ylabel('Probability')
```

Figure 19.3: Plotting a t-distribution

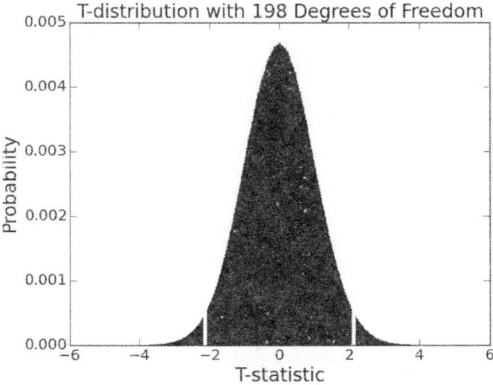

Figure 19.4: Visualizing the t-statistic

The sum of the fractions of the area of the histogram to the left and right of the white lines equals the probability of getting a value at least as extreme as the observed value if

- the sample is representative of the population, and
- the null hypothesis is true.

We need to look at both tails because our null hypothesis is that the population means are equal. So, the test should fail if the mean of the treatment group is either significantly larger or significantly smaller than the mean of the control group.

CHAPTER 19. RANDOMIZED TRIALS AND HYPOTHESIS CHECKING

Under the assumption that the null hypothesis holds, the probability of getting a value at least as extreme as the observed value is called a **p-value**. For our PED-X example, the p-value is the probability of seeing a difference in the means at least as large as the observed difference, under the assumption that the actual population means of the treatment and controls are identical.

It may seem a bit odd that p-values tell us something about the probability of an event occurring if the null hypothesis holds, when what we are usually hoping is that the null hypothesis doesn't hold. However, it is not so different in character from the classic "scientific method," which is based upon designing experiments that have the potential to refute a hypothesis. The code in Figure 19.5 computes and prints the t-statistic and p-value for our two samples. The library function stats.ttest_ind performs a two-tailed two-sample **t-test** and returns both the t-statistic and the p-value. Setting the parameter equal_var to False indicates that we don't know whether the two populations have the same variance.

```
controlMean = sum(controlTimes)/len(controlTimes)
treatmentMean = sum(treatmentTimes)/len(treatmentTimes)
print('Treatment mean - control mean =',
      treatmentMean - controlMean, 'minutes')
twoSampleTest = stats.ttest_ind(treatmentTimes, controlTimes,
                                equal_var = False)
print('The t-statistic from two-sample test is', twoSampleTest[0])
print('The p-value from two-sample test is', twoSampleTest[1])
```

Figure 19.5 Compute and print t-statistic and p-value

When we run the code, it reports

```
Treatment mean - control mean = -1.3766016405102306 minutes
The t-statistic from two-sample test is -2.13165598142
The p-value from two-sample test is 0.0343720799815
```

"Yes," Dr. X crowed, "it seems that the probability of PED-X being no better than PED-Y is less than 3.5%, and therefore the probability that PED-X has an effect is more than 96.5%. Let the cash registers start ringing." Alas, his elation lasted only until he read the next section of this chapter.

19.2 Beware of P-values

It is way too easy to read something into a p-value that it doesn't really imply. It is tempting to think of a p-value as the probability of the null hypothesis being true. But this is not what it actually means.

The null hypothesis is analogous to a defendant in the Anglo-American criminal justice system. That system is based on a principle called "presumption of innocence," i.e., innocent until proven guilty. Analogously, we assume that the null hypothesis is true unless we see enough evidence to the contrary. In a trial, a jury can rule that a defendant is "guilty" or "not guilty." A "not guilty" verdict implies that the evidence was insufficient to convince the jury that the defendant was guilty "beyond a reasonable doubt."[132] Think of it as equivalent to "guilt was not proven." A verdict of "not guilty" does not imply that the evidence was sufficient to convince the jury that the defendant was innocent. And it says nothing about what the jury would have concluded had it seen different evidence. Think of a p-value as a jury verdict where the standard "beyond a reasonable doubt" corresponds to choosing a very small α, and the evidence is the data from which the t-statistic was constructed.

A small p-value indicates that a particular sample is unlikely if the null hypothesis is true. It is analogous to a jury concluding that it was unlikely that it would have been presented with this set of evidence if the defendant were innocent, and therefore reaching a guilty verdict. Of course, that doesn't mean that the defendant is actually guilty. Perhaps the jury was presented with misleading evidence. Analogously, a low p-value might be attributable to the null hypothesis actually being false, or it could simply be that the sample is unrepresentative of the population from which it is drawn, i.e., the evidence is misleading.

As you might expect, Dr. X staunchly claimed that his experiment showed that the null hypothesis was probably false. Dr. Y insisted that the low p-value was probably attributable to an unrepresentative sample, and funded another experiment of the same size as Dr. X's. When the statistics were computed using the samples from her experiment, the code printed

---

[132] The "beyond a reasonable doubt" standard implies that society believes that in the case of a criminal trial, type I errors (convicting an innocent person) are much less desirable than type II errors (acquitting a guilty person). In civil cases, the standard is "the preponderance of the evidence," suggesting that society believes that the two kinds of errors are equally undesirable.

CHAPTER 19. RANDOMIZED TRIALS AND HYPOTHESIS CHECKING

```
Treatment mean - control mean = 0.1760912816 minutes
The t-statistic from two-sample test is -0.274609731618
The p-value from two-sample test is 0.783908632676
```

This p-value is almost 24 times larger than that obtained from Dr. X's experiment, and since it is considerably larger than 0.5, provides no reason to doubt the null hypothesis. Confusion reigned. But we can clear it up!

You may not be surprised to discover that this is not a true story—after all, the idea of a cyclist taking a performance-enhancing drug strains credulity. In fact, the samples for the experiments were generated by the code in Figure 19.6.

```
treatmentDist = (119.5, 5.0)
controlDist = (120, 4.0)
sampleSize = 100
treatmentTimes, controlTimes = [], []
for s in range(sampleSize):
    treatmentTimes.append(random.gauss(treatmentDist[0],
                                      treatmentDist[1]))
    controlTimes.append(random.gauss(controlDist[0],
                                     controlDist[1]))
```

Figure 19.6 Code for generating racing examples

Since the experiment is purely computational, we can run it many times to get many different samples. When we generated 10,000 pairs of samples (one from each distribution) and plotted the probability of the p-values, we got the plot in Figure 19.7.

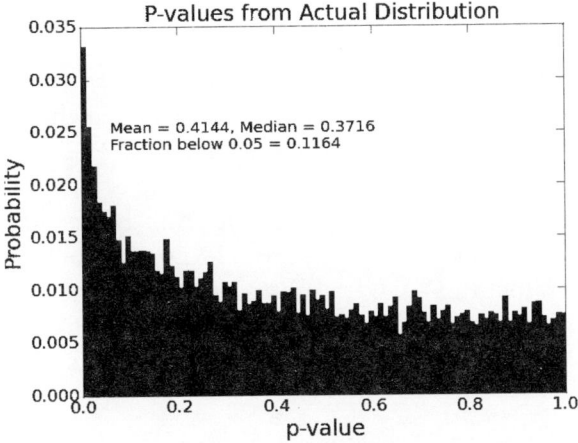

Figure 19.7: Probability of p-values

Since more than 11.6% of the p-values lie below 0.05, it is not terribly surprising that the first experiment we ran happened to show significance at the 5% level. On the other hand, that the second experiment yielded a completely different result is also not surprising. What does seem surprising is that given that we know that the means of the two distributions are actually different, we get a result that is significant at the 5% level only about 11.6% of the time. More than 88% of the time we would fail to reject a fallacious null hypothesis at the 5% level. (If we increase the sample size in our example to 2000, we fail to reject the fallacious null hypothesis only about 6% of the time.)

That p-values can be unreliable indicators of whether it is truly appropriate to reject a null hypothesis is one of the reasons that so many of the results appearing in the scientific literature cannot be reproduced by other scientists. One problem is that there is a strong relationship between the **study power** (the size of the samples) and the credibility of the statistical finding.[133]

Why are so many studies under-powered? If we were truly running an experiment with people (rather than a simulation) it would be twenty times more expensive to draw samples of size 2000 than samples of size 100.

The problem of sample size is an intrinsic attribute of what is called the frequentist approach to statistics. In Chapter 20, we discuss an alternative approach that attempts to mitigate this problem.

19.3 One-tail and One-sample Tests

Thus far in this chapter, we have looked only at two-tailed two-sample tests. There are times when it is more appropriate to use a **one-tailed** and/or a **one-sample** t-test.

Let's first consider a one-tailed two-sample test. In our two-tailed test of the relative effectiveness of PED-X and PED-Y, we considered three cases: 1) they were equally effective, 2) PED-X was more effective than PED-Y, and 3) PED-Y was more effective than PED-X. The goal was to reject the null hypothesis (case 1) by arguing that if it were true, it would be unlikely to see as large a difference as observed in the means of the PED-X and PED-Y samples.

Suppose, however, that PED-X were substantially less expensive than PED-Y. To find a market for his compound, Dr. X would only need to show that PED-X is at least as effective as PED-Y. One way to think about this is that we want to

---

[133] Katherine S. Button, John P. A. Ioannidis, Claire Mokrysz, Brian A. Nosek, Jonathan Flint, Emma S. J. Robinson, and Marcus R. Munafò (2013) "Power failure: why small sample size undermines the reliability of neuroscience," *Nature Reviews Neuroscience*, 14: 365-376.

CHAPTER 19. RANDOMIZED TRIALS AND HYPOTHESIS CHECKING 337

reject the hypothesis that the means are equal or that the PED-X mean is larger. Note that this is strictly weaker than the hypothesis that the means are equal. (Hypothesis A is strictly weaker than hypothesis B, if whenever B is true A is true, but not vice versa.)

To do this, we start with the a two-sample test with the original null hypothesis computed by the code in Figure 19.5. It printed

```
Treatment mean - control mean = -1.37660164051 minutes
The t-statistic from two-sample test is -2.13165598142
The p-value from two-sample test is 0.0343720799815
```

allowing us to reject the null hypothesis at about the 3.5% level.

How about our weaker hypothesis? Recall Figure 19.4. We observed that under the assumption that the null hypothesis holds, the sum of the fractions of the areas of the histogram to the left and right of the white lines equals the probability of getting a value at least as extreme as the observed value. However, to reject our weaker hypothesis we don't need to take into account the area under the left tail, because that corresponds to PED-X being more effective than PED-Y (a negative time difference), and we're interested only in rejecting the hypothesis that PED-X is less effective. I.e., we can do a one-tailed test.

Since the t-distribution is symmetric, to get the value for a one-tailed test we divide the p-value from the two-tailed test in half. So the p-value for the one-tailed test is 0.01718603999075. This allows us to reject our weaker hypothesis at about the 1.7% level, something that we could not do using the two-tailed test.

Because a one-tailed test provides more power to detect an effect, it is tempting to use a one-tailed test whenever one has a hypothesis about the direction of an effect. This is usually not a good idea. A one-tailed test is appropriate only if the consequences of missing an effect in the untested direction are negligible.

Now let's look at a one-sample test. Suppose that, after years of experience of people using PED-Y, it was well established that the mean time for a racer on PED-Y to complete a fifty-mile course is 120 minutes. To discover whether or not PED-X had a different effect than PED-Y, we would test the null hypothesis that the mean time for a single PED-X sample is equal to 120. We can do this using the function `scipy.stats.ttest_1samp`, which takes as arguments a single sample and the population mean against which it is to be compared. It returns a tuple containing the t-statistic and p-value. For example, if we append to the end of the code in Figure 19.5 the code

```
oneSampleTest = stats.ttest_1samp(treatmentTimes, 120)
print('The t-statistic from one-sample test is', oneSampleTest[0])
print('The p-value from one-sample test is', oneSampleTest[1])
```

it prints

```
The t-statistic from one-sample test is -2.32665745939
The p-value from one-sample test is 0.0220215196873
```

It is not surprising that the p-value is smaller than the one we got using the two-sample two-tail test. By assuming that we know one of the two means, we have removed a source of uncertainty.

So, after all this, what have we learned from our statistical analysis of PED-X and PED-Y? Even though there is a difference in the expected performance of PED-X and and PED-Y users, no finite sample of PED-X and PED-Y users is guaranteed to reveal that difference. Moreover, because the difference in the expected means is small (less than half a percent), it is unlikely that an experiment of the size Dr. X ran (100 riders in each group) will yield evidence that would allow us to conclude at the 95% confidence level that there is a difference in means. We could increase the likelihood of getting a result that is statistically significant at the 95% level by using a one-tailed test, but that would be misleading, because we have no reason to assume that PED-X is not less effective than PED-Y.

19.4 Significant or Not?

Lyndsay and John have wasted an inordinate amount of time over the last several years playing a game called Words with Friends. They have played each other 1,273 times, and Lyndsay has won 666 of those games, prompting her to boast, "I'm way better at this game than you are." John asserted that Lyndsay's claim was nonsense, and that the difference in wins could be (and probably should be) attributed entirely to luck.

John, who had recently read a book about statistics, proposed the following way to find out whether it was reasonable to attribute Lyndsay's relative success to skill:

- Treat each of the 1,273 games as an experiment returning 1 if Lyndsay was the victor and 0 if she was not.
- Choose the null hypothesis that the mean value of those experiments is 0.5.
- Perform a two-tailed one-sample test for that null hypothesis.

When he ran the code

CHAPTER 19. RANDOMIZED TRIALS AND HYPOTHESIS CHECKING

```
numGames = 1273
lyndsayWins = 666
outcomes = [1.0]*lyndsayWins + [0.0]*(numGames-lyndsayWins)
print('The p-value from a one-sample test is',
      stats.ttest_1samp(outcomes, 0.5)[1])
```

it printed

```
The p-value from a one-sample test is 0.0982205871244
```

prompting John to claim that the difference wasn't even close to being significant at the 5% level.

Lyndsay, who had not studied statistics, but had read Chapter 16 of this book, was not satisfied. "Let's run a Monte Carlo simulation," she suggested, and supplied the code in Figure 19.8.

```
numGames = 1273
lyndsayWins = 666
numTrials = 10000
atLeast = 0
for t in range(numTrials):
    LWins = 0
    for g in range(numGames):
        if random.random() < 0.5:
            LWins += 1
    if LWins >= lyndsayWins:
        atLeast += 1
print('Probability of result at least this',
      'extreme by accident =', atLeast/numTrials)
```

Figure 19.8: Lyndsay's simulation of games

When Lyndsay's code was run it printed,

```
Probability of result at least this extreme by accident = 0.0491
```

prompting her to claim that John's statistical test was completely bogus and that the difference in wins was statistically significant at the 5% level.

"No," John explained patiently, "It's your simulation that's bogus. It assumed that you were the better player, and performed the equivalent of a one-tailed test. The inner loop of your simulation is wrong. You should have performed the equivalent of a two-tailed test by testing whether, in the simulation, either player won more than the 666 games that you won in actual competition." John then ran the simulation in Figure 19.9.

```
numGames = 1273
lyndsayWins = 666
numTrials = 10000
atLeast = 0
for t in range(numTrials):
    LWins, JWins = 0, 0
    for g in range(numGames):
        if random.random() < 0.5:
            LWins += 1
        else:
            JWins += 1
    if LWins >= lyndsayWins or JWins >= lyndsayWins:
        atLeast += 1
print('Probability of result at least this',
      'extreme by accident =', atLeast/numTrials)
```

Figure 19.9 Correct simulation of games

John's simulation printed

```
Probability of result at least this extreme by accident = 0.0986
```

"That's pretty darned close to what my two-tailed test predicted," crowed John. Lyndsay's unladylike response was not appropriate for inclusion in a family-oriented book.

19.5 Which N?

A professor wondered whether attending lectures was correlated with grades in his department. He recruited 40 freshmen and gave them all ankle bracelets so that he could track their whereabouts. Half of the students were not allowed to attend any of the lectures in any of their classes,[134] and half were required to attend all of the lectures.[135] Over the next four years, each student took 40 different classes, yielding 800 grades for each group of students.

When the professor performed a two-tailed t-test on the means of these two samples of size 800, the p-value was about 0.01. This disappointed the professor, who was hoping that there would be no statistically significant effect—so that he would feel less guilty about canceling lectures and going to the beach. In desperation, he took a look at the mean GPAs of the two groups, and discovered that

---

[134] They should have been given a tuition rebate, but weren't.

[135] They should have been given combat pay, but weren't.

CHAPTER 19. RANDOMIZED TRIALS AND HYPOTHESIS CHECKING

there was very little difference. How, he wondered, could such a small difference in means be significant at that level?

When the sample size is large enough, even a small effect can be highly statistically significant. I.e., N matters, a lot. Figure 19.10 plots the mean p-value of 1000 trials against the size of the samples used in those trials. For each sample size and each trial we generated two samples. Each was was drawn from a Gaussian with a standard deviation of 5. One had a mean of 100 and the other a mean of 100.5. The mean p-value drops linearly with the sample size. The 0.5% difference in means becomes consistently statistically significant at the 5% level when the sample size reaches about 1500, and at the 1% level when the sample size exceeds about 2600.

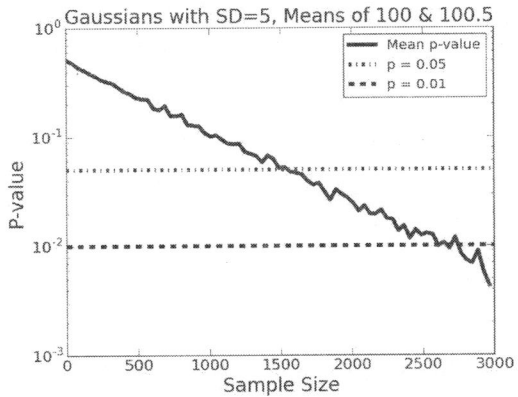

Figure 19.10 Impact of sample size on p-value

Returning to our example, was the professor justified in using an N of 800 for each **arm** of his study? To put it another way, were there really 800 independent examples for each cohort of 20 students? Probably not. There were 800 grades per sample, but only 20 students, and the 40 grades associated with each student should probably not be viewed as independent examples. After all, some students consistently get good grades, and some students consistently get grades that disappoint.

The professor decided to look at the data a different way. He computed the GPA for each student. When he performed a two-tailed t-test on these two samples, each of size 20, the p-value was about 0.3. He felt much better.

19.6 Multiple Hypotheses

In Chapter 17, we looked at sampling using data from the Boston Marathon. The code in Figure 19.11 reads in data from the 2012 race and looks for statistically significant differences in the mean finishing times of the women from a small set of countries. It uses the getBMData function defined in Figure 17.2.

```
data = getBMData('bm_results2012.txt')
countriesToCompare = ['BEL', 'BRA', 'FRA', 'JPN', 'ITA']
#Build mapping from country to list of female finishing times
countryTimes = {}
for i in range(len(data['name'])): #for each racer
    if data['country'][i] in countriesToCompare and\
       data['gender'][i] == 'F':
        try:
            countryTimes[data['country'][i]].append(data['time'][i])
        except KeyError:
            countryTimes[data['country'][i]] = [data['time'][i]]

#Compare finishing times of countries
for c1 in countriesToCompare:
    for c2 in countriesToCompare:
        if c1 < c2: # < rather than != so each pair examined once
            pVal = stats.ttest_ind(countryTimes[c1],
                                   countryTimes[c2],
                                   equal_var = False)[1]
            if pVal < 0.05:
                print(c1, 'and', c2,
                      'have significantly different means,',
                      'p-value =', round(pVal, 4))
```

Figure 19.11: Comparing mean finishing times for selected countries

When the code is run, it prints

`ITA and JPN have significantly different means, p-value = 0.025`

It looks as if either Italy or Japan can claim to have faster women runners than the other.[136] However, such a conclusion would be pretty tenuous. While one set of runners did have a faster mean time than the other, the sample sizes

---

[136] We could easily find out which by looking at the sign of the t-statistic, but in the interest of not offending potential purchasers of this book, we won't.

CHAPTER 19. RANDOMIZED TRIALS AND HYPOTHESIS CHECKING

(20 and 32) were small and perhaps not representative of the capabilities of women marathoners in each country.

More important, there is a flaw in the way we constructed our experiment. We checked 10 null hypotheses (one for each distinct pair of countries), and discovered that one of them could be rejected at the 5% level. One way to think about it is that we were actually checking the null hypothesis: "for all pairs of countries, the mean finishing times of their female marathon runners are the same." It might be fine to reject that null hypothesis, but that is not the same as rejecting the null hypothesis that women marathon runners from Italy and Japan are equally fast.

The point is made starkly by the example in Figure 19.12. In that example, we draw twenty pairs of samples of size 200 from the same population, and for each we test whether the means of the samples are statistically different.

```
numHyps = 20
sampleSize = 30
population = []
for i in range(5000): #Create large population
    population.append(random.gauss(0, 1))
sample1s, sample2s = [], []
for i in range(numHyps): #Generate many pairs of small sanples
    sample1s.append(random.sample(population, sampleSize))
    sample2s.append(random.sample(population, sampleSize))
#Check pairs for statistically significant difference
numSig = 0
for i in range(numHyps):
    if scipy.stats.ttest_ind(sample1s[i], sample2s[i])[1] < 0.05:
        numSig += 1
print('Number of statistically significant (p < 0.05) results  =',
      numSig)
```

Figure 19.12: Checking multiple hypotheses

Since the samples are all drawn from the same population, we know that the null hypothesis is true. Yet, when we run the code it prints

```
Number of statistically significant (p < 0.05) results  = 1
```

indicating that the null hypothesis can be rejected for one pair.

This is not particularly surprising. Recall that a p-value of 0.05 indicates that if the null hypothesis holds, the probability of seeing a difference in means at least as large as the difference for the two samples is 0.05. Therefore, it is not terribly surprising that if we examine twenty pairs of samples, at least one of them has means that are statistically significantly different from each other. Running large sets of related experiments, and then cherry-picking the result you like, can be kindly described as sloppy. An unkind person might call it something else.

Returning to our Boston Marathon experiment, we checked whether or not we could reject the null hypothesis (no difference in means) for 10 pairs of samples. When running an experiment involving multiple hypotheses, the simplest and most conservative approach is to use something called the **Bonferroni correction**. The intuition behind it is simple: when checking a family of m hypotheses, one way of maintaining an appropriate **family-wise error rate** is to test each individual hypothesis at a level of $\frac{1}{m} * \alpha$. Using the Bonferroni correction to see if the difference between Italy and Japan is significant at the $\alpha = 0.05$ level, we should check if the p-value is less that 0.05/10 i.e., 0.005—which it is not.

The Bonferroni correction is conservative (i.e., it fails to reject the null hypothesis more often than necessary) if there are a large number of tests or the test statistics for the tests are positively correlated. An additional issue is the absence of a generally accepted definition of "family of hypotheses." It is obvious that the hypotheses generated by the code in Figure 19.12 are related, and therefore a correction needs to be applied. But the situation is not always so clear cut.

20 CONDITIONAL PROBABILITY AND BAYESIAN STATISTICS

Up to this point we have taken what is called a **frequentist** approach to statistics. We have drawn conclusions from samples based entirely on the frequency or proportion of the data. This is the most commonly used inference framework, and leads to the well-established methodologies of statistical hypothesis testing and confidence intervals covered earlier in this book. In principle, it has the advantage of being unbiased. Conclusions are reached solely on the basis of the observed data.

In some situations, however, an alternative approach to statistics, **Bayesian statistics**, is more appropriate. Consider the cartoon in Figure 20.1.[137]

Figure 20.1 Has the sun exploded?

---

[137] http://imgs.xkcd.com/comics/frequentists_vs_bayesians.png

What's going on here? The frequentist knows that there are only two possibilities: the machine rolls a pair of sixes and is lying, or it doesn't roll a pair of sixes and is telling the truth. Since the probability of not rolling a pair of sixes is 35/36 (97.22%) the frequentist concludes that the machine is probably telling the truth, and therefore the sun has probably exploded.[138]

The Bayesian utilizes additional information in building his probability model. He agrees that it is unlikely that the machine rolls a pair of sixes, however he argues that the probability of that happening needs to be compared to the *a priori* probability that the sun has not exploded. He concludes that the likelihood of the sun having not exploded is even higher than 97.22%, and decides to bet that "the sun will come out tomorrow."

20.1 Conditional Probabilities

The key idea underlying Bayesian reasoning is **conditional probability**.

In our earlier discussion of probability, we relied on the assumption that events were independent. For example, we assumed that whether a coin flip came up heads or tails was unrelated to whether the previous flip came up heads or tails. This is convenient mathematically, but life doesn't always work that way. In many practical situations, independence is a bad assumption.

Consider the probability that a randomly chosen adult American is male and weighs over 180 pounds. The probability of being male is about 0.5 and the probability of weighing more than 180 pounds (the average weight in the U.S.[139]) is also about 0.5.[140] So, if these were independent events the probability of the selected person being both male and weighing more than 180 pounds would be 0.25. However, these events are not independent, since the average American male weighs about 30 pounds more than the average female. So, a better question to ask is 1) what is the probability of the selected person being a male, and 2) given that the selected person is a male, what is the probability of that person weigh-

---

[138] If you are of the frequentist persuasion, keep in mind that this cartoon is a parody—not a serious critique of your religious beliefs.

[139] This number may strike you as high. It is. The average American adult weighs about 40 pounds more than the average adult in Japan. The only three countries on earth with higher average adult weights than the U.S. are Nauru, Tonga, and Micronesia.

[140] The probability of weighing more than the *median* weight is 0.5, but that doesn't imply that the probability of weighing more than the *mean* is 0.5. However, for the purposes of this discussion, let's pretend that it does.

CHAPTER 20. CONDITIONAL PROBABILITY AND BAYESIAN STATISTICS

ing more than 180 pounds. The notation of conditional probability makes it easy to say just that.

The notation P(A|B) stands for the probability of A being true under the assumption that B is true. It is often read as "the probability of A, given B." Therefore, the formula

$$P(male) * P(weight > 180 \mid male)$$

expresses exactly the probability we are looking for. If P(A) and P(B) are independent, P(A|B) = P(A). For the above example, B is male and A is weight > 180.

In general, if $P(B) \neq 0$,

$$P(A|B) = \frac{P(A \text{ and } B)}{P(B)}$$

Like conventional probabilities, conditional probabilities always lie between 0 and 1. Furthermore, if $\bar{A}$ stands for *not A*, $P(A|B) + P(\bar{A}|B) = 1$. People often incorrectly assume that $P(A|B)$ is equal to $P(B|A)$. There is no reason to expect this to be true. For example, the value of $P(male|Maltese)$ is roughly 0.5, but $P(Maltese|male)$ is about 0.000064.[141]

Finger exercise: Estimate the probability that a randomly chosen American is both male and weighs more than 180 pounds. Assume that 50% of the population is male, and that the weights of the male population are normally distributed with a mean of 210 pounds and a standard deviation of 30 pounds. (Hint: think about using the empirical rule.)

The formula $P(A|B, C)$ stands for the probability of A, given that both B and C hold. Assuming that B and C are independent of each other, the definition of a conditional probability and the multiplication rule for independent probabilities imply that

$$P(A \mid B, C) = \frac{P(A, B, C)}{P(B, C)}$$

where the formula $P(A, B, C)$ stands for the probability of all of A, B, and C being true.

---

[141] By "Maltese" we mean somebody from the country of Malta. We have no idea what fraction of the world's males are cute little dogs.

Similarly, $P(A, B|C)$ stands for the probability of A and B, given C. Assuming that A and B are independent of each other

$$P(A, B|C) = P(A|C) * P(B|C)$$

20.2 Bayes' Theorem

Suppose that an asymptomatic woman in her forties goes for a mammogram and receives bad news: the mammogram is "positive."[142]

The probability that a woman who has breast cancer will get a **true positive** result on a mammogram is 0.9. The probability that a woman who does not have breast cancer will get a **false positive** on a mammogram is 0.07.

We can use conditional probabilities to express these facts. Let

```
Canc = has breast cancer
TP = true positive
FP = false positive
```

Using these variables, we write the conditional probabilities

```
P(TP | Canc) = 0.9
P(FP | not Canc) = 0.07
```

Given these conditional probabilities, how worried should a woman in her forties with a positive mammogram be? What is the probability that she actually has breast cancer? Is it 0.93, since the false positive rate is 7%? More? less?

It's a trick question: We haven't supplied enough information to allow you to answer the question in a sensible way. To do that, you need to know the **prior probabilities** for breast cancer for a woman in her forties. The fraction of women in their forties who have breast cancer is 0.008 (8 out of 1000). The fraction who do not have breast cancer is therefore 1 − 0.008 = 0.992. I.e.,

```
P(Canc | woman in her 40s) = 0.008
P(not Canc | woman in her 40s) = 0.992
```

We now have all the information we need to address the question of how worried that woman in her forties should be. To compute the probability that she

---

[142] In medical jargon, a "positive" test is usually bad news. It implies that a marker of disease has been found.

CHAPTER 20. CONDITIONAL PROBABILITY AND BAYESIAN STATISTICS

has breast cancer we use something called **Bayes' Theorem**[143] (often called Bayes' Law or Bayes' Rule) :

$$P(A|B) = \frac{P(A) * P(B|A)}{P(B)}$$

In the Bayesian world, probability measures a **degree of belief**. Bayes' theorem links the degree of belief in a proposition before and after accounting for evidence. The formula to the left of the equal sign, P(A|B), is the **posterior** probability, the degree of belief in A, having accounted for B. The posterior is defined in terms of the **prior**, P(A), and the **support** that the evidence, B, provides for A. The support is the ratio of the probability of B holding if A holds and the probability of B holding independently of A, i.e., $\frac{P(B|A)}{P(B)}$.

If we use Bayes' Theorem to estimate the probability of the woman actually having breast cancer we get (where Canc plays the role of A, and Pos the role of B in our statement of Bayes' Theorem)

$$P(Canc|Pos) = \frac{P(Canc) * P(Pos|Canc)}{P(Pos)}$$

The probability of having a positive test is

$$P(Pos) = P(Pos|Canc) * P(Canc) + P(Pos|\text{ not } Canc) * (1 - P(Canc))$$

so

$$P(Canc|Pos) = \frac{0.008 * 0.9}{0.9 * 0.008 + 0.07 * 0.992} = \frac{0.0072}{0.07664} \approx 0.094$$

I.e., approximately 90% of the positive mammograms are false positives![144] Bayes' Theorem helped us here because we had an accurate estimate of the prior probability of a woman in her forties having breast cancer.

It is important to keep in mind that if we had started with an incorrect prior, incorporating that prior into our probability estimate would make the estimate worse rather than better. For example, if we had started with the prior

```
P(Canc | women in her 40's) = 0.6
```

---

[143] Bayes' theorem is named after Rev. Thomas Bayes (1701–1761), and was first published two years after his death. It was popularized by Laplace, who published the modern formulation of the theorem in 1812 in his *Théorie analytique des probabilités*.

[144] This is one of the reasons that there is considerable controversy in the medical community about the value of mammography as a routine screening tool for some cohorts.

we would have concluded that the false positive rate was about 5%, i.e., that the probability of a woman in her forties with a positive mammogram having breast cancer is roughly 0.95.

Finger exercise: You are wandering through a forest and see a field of delicious-looking mushrooms. You fill your basket with them, and head home prepared to cook them up and serve them to your husband. Before you cook them, however, he demands that you consult a book about local mushroom species to check whether they are poisonous. The book says that 80% of the mushrooms in the local forest are poisonous. However, you compare your mushrooms to the ones pictured in the book, and decide that you are 95% certain that your mushrooms are safe. How comfortable you should you be about serving them to your husband (assuming that you would rather not become a widow)?

20.3 Bayesian Updating

Bayesian inference provides a principled way of combining new evidence with prior beliefs, through the application of Bayes' theorem. Bayes' theorem can be applied iteratively: After observing some evidence, the resulting posterior probability can then be treated as a prior probability, and a new posterior probability computed from new evidence. This allows for Bayesian principles to be applied to various kinds of evidence, whether viewed all at once or over time. This procedure is termed **Bayesian updating**.

Let's look at an example. Assume that you have a bag containing equal numbers of three different kinds of dice—each with a different probability of coming up 6 when rolled. Type A dice come up 6 with a probability of one fifth, type B dice with a probability of one sixth, and type C dice with a probability of one seventh. Reach into the bag, grab one die, and estimate the probability of it being of type A. You don't need to know much probability to know that the best estimate is 1/3. Now roll the die twice and revise the estimate based on the outcome of the rolls. If it comes up 6 both times, it seems clear that it is somewhat more likely that the die is of type A. How much more likely? We can use Bayesian updating to answer that question.

By Bayes' theorem, after rolling the first 6, the probability that the die is of type A is

$$P(A|6) = \frac{P(A) * P(6|A)}{P(6)}$$

CHAPTER 20. CONDITIONAL PROBABILITY AND BAYESIAN STATISTICS

where

$$P(A) = \frac{1}{3}, \quad P(6|A) = \frac{1}{5}, \quad P(6) = \frac{\frac{1}{5}+\frac{1}{6}+\frac{1}{7}}{3}$$

The code in Figure 20.2 implements Bayes' theorem and uses it to calculate the probability that the die is of type A. Notice that the second call of calcBayes uses the result of the first call as the prior value for A.

```
def calcBayes(priorA, probBifA, probB):
    """priorA: initial estimate of probability of A independent of B
       priorBifA: est. of probability of B assuming A is true
       priorBifNotA: est. of probability of B
       returns probability of A given B"""
    return priorA*probBifA/probB

priorA = 1/3
prob6ifA = 1/5
prob6 = (1/5 + 1/6 + 1/7)/3

postA = calcBayes(priorA, prob6ifA, prob6)
print('Probability of type A =', round(postA, 4))
postA = calcBayes(postA, prob6ifA, prob6)
print('Probability of type A =', round(postA, 4))
```

Figure 20.2: Bayesian updating

When the code is run, it prints,

```
Probability of type A = 0.3925
Probability of type A = 0.4622
```

indicating that we should revise our estimate of the probability upwards.

What if we had thrown something other than 6 on both rolls of the die? Replacing the last four lines of the code in Figure 20.2 with

```
postA = calcBayes(priorA, 1 - prob6ifA, 1 - prob6)
print('Probability of type A =', round(postA, 4))
postA = calcBayes(postA, 1 - prob6ifA, 1 - prob6)
print('Probability of type A =', round(postA, 4))
```

causes the program to print

```
Probability of type A = 0.3212
Probability of type A = 0.3096
```

indicating that we should revise our estimate of the probability downwards.

Let's suppose that we have reason to believe that 90% of the dice in the bag are of type A. All we need to do is change our original prior, priorA in the code, to 0.9. Now, if we simulate getting something other than 6 on both rolls, it prints

```
Probability of type A = 0.8673
Probability of type A = 0.8358
```

The prior makes a big difference!

Let's try one more experiment. We'll stick with priorA = 0.9, and see what happens if the die is actually of type C. The code in Figure 20.3 simulates 200 rolls of a die of type C (which has a probability of 1/7 of coming up 6), and prints a revised estimate of the probability of the die being of type A after every 20 rolls.

```
numRolls = 200
postA = priorA
for i in range(numRolls+1):
    if i%(numRolls//10) == 0:
        print('After', i, 'rolls. Probability of type A =',
              round(postA, 4))
    isSix = random.random() <= 1/7 #because die of type C
    if isSix:
        postA = calcBayes(postA, prob6ifA, prob6)
    else:
        postA = calcBayes(postA, 1 - prob6ifA, 1 - prob6)
```

Figure 20.3: Bayesian updating with a bad prior

When we ran the code it printed

```
After 0 rolls. Probability of type A = 0.9
After 20 rolls. Probability of type A = 0.4294
After 40 rolls. Probability of type A = 0.3059
After 60 rolls. Probability of type A = 0.2662
After 80 rolls. Probability of type A = 0.1552
After 100 rolls. Probability of type A = 0.0905
After 120 rolls. Probability of type A = 0.0962
After 140 rolls. Probability of type A = 0.1251
After 160 rolls. Probability of type A = 0.1089
After 180 rolls. Probability of type A = 0.0776
After 200 rolls. Probability of type A = 0.0553
```

CHAPTER 20. CONDITIONAL PROBABILITY AND BAYESIAN STATISTICS

The good news is that even given a misleading prior, the probability converges towards the truth as the number of examples grows. Notice, by the way, that it didn't converge monotonically. The probability after 120 rolls was higher than after 100—indicating that those 20 rolls were more consistent with a die of type A than with a die of type B or C.

Had we started with a better prior, it would have converged faster. If we go back to 1/3 as the initial prior, the probability is 0.0335 after 100 rolls, and 0.0205 after 200 rolls.

21 LIES, DAMNED LIES, AND STATISTICS

"If you can't prove what you want to prove, demonstrate something else and pretend they are the same thing. In the daze that follows the collision of statistics with the human mind, hardly anyone will notice the difference."[145]

Statistical thinking is a relatively new invention. For most of recorded history things were assessed qualitatively rather than quantitatively. People must have had an intuitive sense of some statistical facts (e.g., that women are usually shorter than men), but they had no mathematical tools that would allow them to proceed from anecdotal evidence to statistical conclusions. This started to change in the middle of the 17th century, most notably with the publication of John Graunt's *Natural and Political Observations Made Upon the Bills of Mortality*. This pioneering work used statistical analysis to estimate the population of London from death rolls, and attempted to provide a model that could be used to predict the spread of plague.

Alas, since that time people have used statistics as much to mislead as to inform. Some have willfully used statistics to mislead; others have merely been incompetent. In this chapter we discuss a few ways in which people can be fooled into drawing inappropriate inferences from statistical data. We trust that you will use this information only for good—to become a better consumer and a more honest purveyor of statistical information.

21.1 Garbage In Garbage Out (GIGO)

"On two occasions I have been asked [by members of Parliament], 'Pray, Mr. Babbage, if you put into the machine wrong figures, will the right answers come out?' I am not able rightly to apprehend the kind of confusion of ideas that could provoke such a question." — Charles Babbage[146]

---

[145] Darrell Huff, *How to Lie with Statistics*, 1954.

[146] Charles Babbage, 1791-1871, was an English mathematician and mechanical engineer who is credited with having designed the first programmable computer. He never succeeded in building a working machine, but in 1991 a working mechanical device for evaluating polynomials was built from his original plans.

The message here is a simple one. If the input data is seriously flawed, no amount of statistical massaging will produce a meaningful result.

The 1840 United States census showed that insanity among free blacks and mulattoes was roughly ten times more common than among enslaved blacks and mulattoes. The conclusion was obvious. As U.S. Senator (and former Vice President and future Secretary of State) John C. Calhoun put it, "The data on insanity revealed in this census is unimpeachable. From it our nation must conclude that the abolition of slavery would be to the African a curse." Never mind that it was soon clear that the census was riddled with errors. As Calhoun reportedly explained to John Quincy Adams, "there were so many errors they balanced one another, and led to the same conclusion as if they were all correct."

Calhoun's (perhaps willfully) spurious response to Adams was based on a classical error, the **assumption of independence**. Were he more sophisticated mathematically, he might have said something like, "I believe that the measurement errors are unbiased and independent of each other, and therefore evenly distributed on either side of the mean." In fact, later analysis showed that the errors were so heavily biased that no statistically valid conclusions could be drawn.[147]

21.2 Tests Are Imperfect

Every experiment should be viewed as a potentially flawed test. We can perform a test for a chemical, a phenomenon, a disease, etc. However, the event for which we are testing is not necessarily the same as the result of the test. Professors design exams with the goal of understanding how well a student has mastered some subject matter, but the result of the exam should not be confused with how much a student actually understands. Every test has some inherent error rate. Imagine that a student learning a second language has been asked to learn the meaning of 100 words, but has learned the meaning of only 80 of them. His rate of understanding is 80%, but the probability that he will score 80% on a test with 20 words is certainly not 1.

Tests can have both false negatives and false positives. As we saw in Chapter 20, a negative mammogram does not guarantee absence of breast cancer, and a positive mammogram doesn't guarantee its presence. Furthermore, the test probability and the event probability are not the same thing. This is especially relevant when testing for a rare event, e.g., the presence of a rare disease. If the cost of a

---

[147] We should note that Calhoun was in office over 150 years ago. It goes without saying that no contemporary politician would find ways to abuse statistics to support a wrong-headed position.

false negative is high (e.g., missing the presence of a serious but curable disease), the test should be designed to be highly sensitive, even at the cost of there being a large number of false positives.

21.3 Pictures Can Be Deceiving

There can be no doubt about the utility of graphics for quickly conveying information. However, when used carelessly (or maliciously) a plot can be highly misleading. Consider, for example, the charts in Figure 21.1 depicting housing prices in the U.S. Midwestern states.

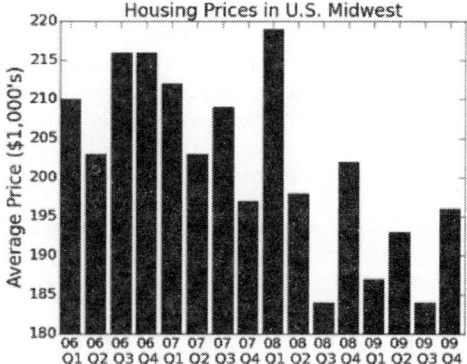

Figure 21.1 Housing prices in the U.S. Midwest

Looking at the chart on the left of Figure 21.1, it seems as if housing prices were pretty stable during the period 2006-2009. But wait a minute! Wasn't there a collapse of U.S. residential real estate followed by a global financial crisis in late 2008? There was indeed, as shown in the chart on the right.

These two charts show exactly the same data, but convey very different impressions. The chart on the left was designed to give the impression that housing prices had been stable. On the y-axis, the designer used a scale ranging from the absurdly low average price for a house of $1,000 to the improbably high average price of $500,000. This minimized the amount of space devoted to the area where prices are changing, giving the impression that the changes were relatively small. The chart on the right was designed to give the impression that housing prices moved erratically, and then crashed. The designer used a narrow range of prices, so the sizes of the changes were exaggerated.

The code in Figure 21.2 produces the two plots we looked at above and a plot intended to give an accurate impression of the movement of housing prices. It uses two plotting facilities that we have not yet seen. The call `pylab.bar(quarters, prices, width)` produces a **bar chart** with bars of the given width. The left edges of the bars are the values of the elements of the list quarters and the heights of the bars are the values of the corresponding elements of the list prices. The function call `pylab.xticks(quarters+width/2, labels)` describes the labels to be associated with the bars. The first argument specifies where each label is to be placed and the second argument the text of the labels. The function yticks behaves analogously. The call `plotHousing('fair')` produces the plot in Figure 21.3.

```
def plotHousing(impression):
    """Assumes impression a str. Must be one of 'flat',
         'volatile,' and 'fair'
       Produce bar chart of housing prices over time"""
    f = open('midWestHousingPrices.txt', 'r')
    #Each line of file contains year quarter price
    #for Midwest region of U.S.
    labels, prices = ([], [])
    for line in f:
        year, quarter, price = line.split()
        label = year[2:4] + '\n Q' + quarter[1]
        labels.append(label)
        prices.append(int(price)/1000)
    quarters = pylab.arange(len(labels)) #x coords of bars
    width = 0.8 #Width of bars
    pylab.bar(quarters, prices, width)
    pylab.xticks(quarters+width/2, labels)
    pylab.title('Housing Prices in U.S. Midwest')
    pylab.xlabel('Quarter')
    pylab.ylabel('Average Price ($1,000\'s)')
    if impression == 'flat':
        pylab.ylim(1, 500)
    elif impression == 'volatile':
        pylab.ylim(180, 220)
    elif impression == 'fair':
        pylab.ylim(150, 250)
    else:
        raise ValueError

plotHousing('flat')
pylab.figure()
plotHousing('volatile')
```

Figure 21.2 Plotting housing prices

CHAPTER 21. LIES, DAMNED LIES, AND STATISTICS

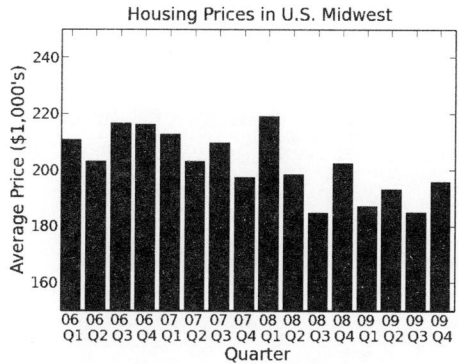

Figure 21.3 A different view of housing prices

21.4 Cum Hoc Ergo Propter Hoc[148]

It has been shown that college students who regularly attend class have higher average grades than students who attend class only sporadically. Those of us who teach these classes would like to believe that this is because the students learn something from the classes we teach. Of course, it is at least equally likely that those students get better grades because students who are more likely to attend classes are also more likely to study hard.

Correlation is a measure of the degree to which two variables move in the same direction. If x moves in the same direction as y, the variables are positively correlated. If they move in opposite directions they are negatively correlated. If there is no relationship, the correlation is 0. People's heights are positively correlated with the heights of their parents. The correlation between hours spent playing video games and grade point average is negative.

When two things are correlated, there is a temptation to assume that one has caused the other. Consider the incidence of flu in North America. The number of cases rises and falls in a predictable pattern. There are almost no cases in the summer; the number of cases starts to rise in the early fall and then starts dropping as summer approaches. Now consider the number of children attending school. There are very few children in school in the summer, enrollment starts to rise in the early fall, and then drops as summer approaches.

---

[148]Statisticians, like attorneys and physicians, sometimes use Latin for no obvious reason other than to seem erudite. This phrase means, "with this, therefore because of this."

The correlation between the opening of schools and the rise in the incidence of flu is inarguable. This has led many to conclude that that going to school is an important causative factor in the spread of flu. That might be true, but one cannot conclude it based simply on the correlation. Correlation does not imply causation! After all, the correlation could be used just as easily to justify the belief that flu outbreaks cause schools to be in session. Or perhaps there is no causal relationship in either direction, and there is some **lurking variable** that we have not considered that causes each. In fact, as it happens, the flu virus survives considerably longer in cool dry air than it does in warm wet air, and in North America both the flu season and school sessions are correlated with cooler and dryer weather.

Given enough retrospective data, it is always possible to find two variables that are correlated, as illustrated by the chart in Figure 21.4.[149]

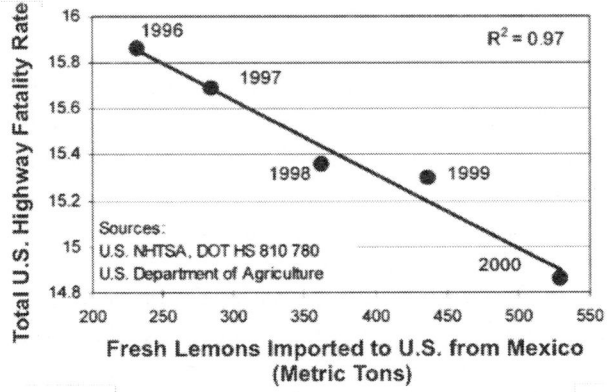

Figure 21.4 Do Mexican lemons save lives?

When such correlations are found, the first thing to do is to ask whether there is a plausible theory explaining the correlation.

Falling prey to the *cum hoc ergo propter hoc* fallacy can be quite dangerous. At the start of 2002, roughly six million American women were being prescribed hormone replacement therapy (HRT) in the belief that it would substantially lower their risk of cardiovascular disease. That belief was supported by several highly reputable published studies that demonstrated a reduced incidence of cardiovascular death among women using HRT.

---

[149] Stephen R. Johnson, "The Trouble with QSAR (or How I Learned to Stop Worrying and Embrace Fallacy)," *J. Chem. Inf. Model.*, 2008.

CHAPTER 21. LIES, DAMNED LIES, AND STATISTICS

Many women, and their physicians, were taken by surprise when the *Journal of the American Medical Society* published an article asserting that HRT in fact increased the risk of cardiovascular disease.[150] How could this have happened?

Reanalysis of some of the earlier studies showed that women undertaking HRT were likely to be from groups with better than average diet and exercise regimes. Perhaps the women undertaking HRT were on average more health conscious than the other women in the study, so that taking HRT and improved cardiac health were coincident effects of a common cause.

21.5 Statistical Measures Don't Tell the Whole Story

There are an enormous number of different statistics that can be extracted from a data set. By carefully choosing among these, it is possible to convey a variety of different impressions about the same data. A good antidote is to look at the data set itself.

In 1973, the statistician F.J. Anscombe published a paper with the table in Figure 21.5. It contains the <x, y> coordinates of points from each of four data sets. Each of the four data sets has the same mean value for x (9.0), the same mean value for y (7.5), the same variance for x (10.0), the same variance for y (3.75), and the same correlation between x and y (0.816). And if we use linear regression to fit a line to each, we get the same result for each, y = 0.5x + 3.

x	y	x	y	x	y	x	y
10.0	8.04	10.0	9.14	10.0	7.46	8.0	6.58
8.0	6.95	8.0	8.14	8.0	6.77	8.0	5.76
13.0	7.58	13.0	8.74	13.0	12.74	8.0	7.71
9.0	8.81	9.0	8.77	9.0	7.11	8.0	8.84
11.0	8.33	11.0	9.26	11.0	7.81	8.0	8.47
14.0	9.96	14.0	8.10	14.0	8.84	8.0	7.04
6.0	7.24	6.0	6.13	6.0	6.08	8.0	5.25
4.0	4.26	4.0	3.10	4.0	5.39	19.0	12.50
12.0	10.84	12.0	9.13	12.0	8.15	8.0	5.56
7.0	4.82	7.0	7.26	7.0	6.42	8.0	7.91
5.0	5.68	5.0	4.74	5.0	5.73	8.0	6.89

Figure 21.5 Statistics for Anscombe's Quartet

---

[150] Nelson HD, Humphrey LL, Nygren P, Teutsch SM, Allan JD. Postmenopausal hormone replacement therapy: scientific review. *JAMA*. 2002;288:872-881.

Does this mean that there is no obvious way to distinguish these data sets from each other? No. One simply needs to plot the data to see that the data sets are not at all alike (Figure 21.6).

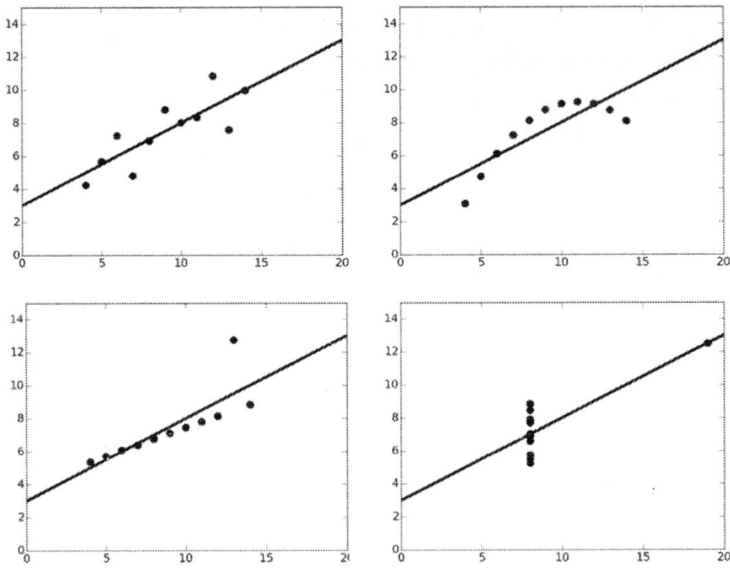

Figure 21.6 Data for Ancsombe's Quartet

The moral is simple: if possible, always take a look at some representation of the raw data.

21.6 Sampling Bias

During World War II, whenever an Allied plane would return from a mission over Europe the plane would be inspected to see where the flak from antiaircraft artillery had impacted. Based upon this data, mechanics reinforced those areas of the planes that seemed most likely to be hit by flak.

What's wrong with this? They did not inspect the planes that failed to return from missions because they had been downed by flak. Perhaps these unexamined planes failed to return precisely because they were hit in the places where the flak would do the most damage. This particular error is called **non-response bias**. It is quite common in surveys. At many universities, for example, students are asked during one of the lectures late in the term to fill out a form rating the quality of the professor's lectures. Though the results of such surveys are often unflattering, they could be worse. Those students who think that the lectures are so bad that they aren't worth attending are not included in the survey.[151]

As discussed in Chapter 17, all statistical techniques are based upon the assumption that by sampling a subset of a population we can infer things about the population as a whole. If random sampling is used, we can make precise mathematical statements about the expected relationship of the sample to the entire population. Unfortunately, many studies, particularly in the social sciences, are based on what is called **convenience** (or **accidental**) **sampling**. This involves choosing samples based on how easy they are to procure. Why do so many psychological studies use populations of undergraduates? Because they are easy to find on college campuses. A convenience sample *might* be representative, but there is no way of knowing whether it actually *is* representative.

21.7 Context Matters

It is easy to read more into the data than it actually implies, especially when viewing the data out of context. On April 29, 2009, CNN reported that, "Mexican health officials suspect that the swine flu outbreak has caused more than 159 deaths and roughly 2,500 illnesses." Pretty scary stuff—until one compares it to the 36,000 deaths attributable annually to the seasonal flu in the U.S.

An often quoted, and accurate, statistic is that most auto accidents happen within 10 miles of home. So what? Most driving is done within 10 miles of home! And besides, what does "home" mean in this context? The statistic is computed using the address at which the automobile is registered as "home." Might one reduce the probability of getting into an accident by merely registering one's car in some distant place?

Opponents of government initiatives to reduce the prevalence of guns in the United States are fond of quoting the statistic that roughly 99.8% of the firearms in the U.S. will not be used to commit a violent crime in any given year. But without some context, it's hard to know what that implies. Does it imply that there is not much gun violence in the U.S.? The National Rifle Association reports that there are roughly 300 million privately owned firearms in the U.S.— 0.2% of 300 million is 600,000!

---

[151] The move to online surveys, which allows students who do not attend class to participate in the survey, does not augur well for the egos of professors.

21.8 Beware of Extrapolation

It is all too easy to extrapolate from data. We did that in Section 18.1.1 when we extended fits derived from linear regression beyond the data used in the regression. Extrapolation should be done only when one has a sound theoretical justification for doing so. Be especially wary of straight-line extrapolations.

Consider the plot on the left in Figure 21.7. It shows the growth of Internet usage in the United States from 1994 to 2000. As you can see, a straight line provides a pretty good fit.

The plot on the right of Figure 21.7 uses this fit to project the percentage of the U.S. population using the Internet in following years. The projection is a bit hard to believe. It seems unlikely that by 2009 everybody in the U.S. was using the Internet, and even less likely that by 2015 more than 140% of the U.S. population was using the Internet.

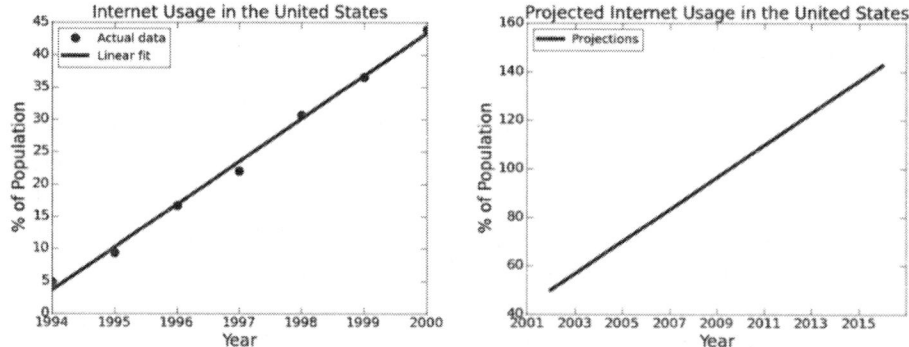

Figure 21.7 Growth of Internet usage in U.S.

21.9 The Texas Sharpshooter Fallacy

Imagine that you are driving down a country road in Texas. You see a barn that has six targets painted on it, and a bullet hole at the very center of each target. "Yes sir," says the owner of the barn, "I never miss." "That's right," says his spouse, "there ain't a man in the state of Texas who's more accurate with a paint brush." Got it? He fired the six shots, and then painted the targets around them.

CHAPTER 21. LIES, DAMNED LIES, AND STATISTICS

Figure 21.8 Professor puzzles over students' chalk-throwing accuracy

A classic of the genre appeared in 2001.[152] It reported that a research team at the Royal Cornhill Hospital in Aberdeen had discovered that "anorexic women are most likely to have been born in the spring or early summer... Between March and June there were 13% more anorexics born than average, and 30% more in June itself."

Let's look at that worrisome statistic for those women born in June. The team studied 446 women who had been diagnosed as anorexic, so the mean number of births per month was slightly more than 37. This suggests that the number born in June was 48 (37*1.3). Let's write a short program (Figure 21.9) to estimate the probability that this occurred purely by chance.

```
def juneProb(numTrials):
    june48 = 0
    for trial in range(numTrials):
        june = 0
        for i in range(446):
            if random.randint(1,12) == 6:
                june += 1
        if june >= 48:
            june48 += 1
    jProb = round(june48/numTrials, 4)
    print('Probability of at least 48 births in June =', jProb)
```

Figure 21.9 Probability of 48 anorexics being born in June

---

[152] Eagles, John, et al., "Season of birth in females with anorexia nervosa in Northeast Scotland," *International Journal of Eating Disorders*, 30, 2, September 2001.

When we ran juneProb(10000) it printed

`Probability of at least 48 births in June = 0.0427`

It looks as if the probability of at least 48 babies being born in June purely by chance is around 4.5%. So perhaps those researchers in Aberdeen are on to something. Well, they might have been on to something had they started with the hypothesis that more babies who will become anorexic are born in June, and then run a study designed to check that hypothesis.

But that is not what they did. Instead, they looked at the data and then, imitating the Texas sharpshooter, drew a circle around June. The right statistical question to have asked is what is the probability that there was at least one month (out of 12) in which at least 48 babies were born. The program in Figure 21.10 answers that question.

```
def anyProb(numTrials):
    anyMonth48 = 0
    for trial in range(numTrials):
        months = [0]*12
        for i in range(446):
            months[random.randint(0,11)] += 1
        if max(months) >= 48:
            anyMonth48 += 1
    aProb = round(anyMonth48/numTrials, 4)
    print('Probability of at least 48 births in some month =',aProb)
```

Figure 21.10 Probability of 48 anorexics being born in some month

The call anyProb(10000) printed

`Probability of at least 48 births in some month = 0.4357`

It appears that it is not so unlikely after all that the results reported in the study reflect a chance occurrence rather a real association between birth month and anorexia. One doesn't have to come from Texas to fall victim to the Texas Sharpshooter Fallacy.

What we see here is that the statistical significance of a result depends upon the way the experiment was conducted. If the Aberdeen group had started out with the hypothesis that more anorexics are born in June, their result would be worth considering. But if they started off with the hypothesis that there exists a month in which an unusually large proportion of anorexics are born, their result is not very compelling. In effect, they were testing multiple hypothesis and probably should have applied a Bonferroni correction (see Section 19.6).

CHAPTER 21. LIES, DAMNED LIES, AND STATISTICS

What next steps might the Aberdeen group have taken to test their newfound hypothesis? One possibility is to conduct a **prospective study**. In a prospective study, one starts with a set of hypotheses, recruits subjects before they have developed the outcome of interest (anorexia in this case), and then follows the subjects for a period of time. If the group had conducted a prospective study with a specific hypothesis and gotten similar results, one might be convinced.

Prospective studies can be expensive and time-consuming to perform. In a **retrospective study**, one has to examine existing data in ways that reduce the likelihood of getting misleading results. One common technique, as discussed in Section 18.4, is to split the data into a training set and a held out test set. For example, they could have chosen 446/2 women at random from their data (the training set), and tallied the number of births for each month. They could have then compared that to the number of births each month for the remaining women (the holdout set).

21.10 Percentages Can Confuse

An investment advisor called a client to report that the value of his stock portfolio had risen 16% over the last month. He admitted that there had been some ups and downs over the year, but was pleased to report that the average monthly change was +0.5%. Image the client's surprise when he got his statement for the year, and observed that the value of his portfolio had declined over the year.

He called his advisor, and accused him of being a liar. "It looks to me," he said, "like my portfolio declined by about 8%, and you told me that it went up by 0.5% a month." "I did not," the financial advisor replied, "I told you that the average monthly change was +0.5%." When he examined his monthly statements, the investor realized that he had not been lied to, just misled. His portfolio went down by 15% in each month during the first half of the year, and then went up by 16% in each month during the second half of the year.

When thinking about percentages, we always need to pay attention to the basis on which the percentage is computed. In this case, the 15% declines were on a higher average basis than the 16% increases.

Percentages can be particularly misleading when applied to a small basis. You might read about a drug that has a side effect of increasing the incidence of some illness by 200%. But if the base incidence of the disease is very low, say one in 1,000,000, you might well decide that the risk of taking the drug was more than counterbalanced by the drug's positive effects.

21.11 Statistically Significant Differences Can Be Insignificant

An admissions officer at the Maui Institute of Technology (MIT), wishing to convince the world that MIT's admissions process is "gender-blind," trumpeted, "At MIT, there is no significant difference between the grade point averages of men and women." The same day, an ardent female chauvinist proclaimed that "At MIT, the women have a significantly higher grade point average than the men." A puzzled reporter at the student newspaper decided to examine the data and expose the liar. But when she finally managed to pry the data out of the university, she concluded that both were telling the truth.

What does the sentence, "At MIT, the women have a significantly higher grade point average than the men," actually mean? People who have not studied statistics (most of the population) would probably conclude that there is a "meaningful" difference between the GPAs of women and men attending MIT. In contrast, those who have recently studied statistics might conclude only that 1) the average GPA of women is higher than that of men, and 2) the null hypothesis that the difference in GPA can be attributed to randomness can be rejected at the 5% level.

Suppose, for example, that there were 2500 women and 2500 men studying at MIT. Suppose further that the mean GPA of men was 3.5, the mean GPA of women was 3.51, and the standard deviation of the GPA for both men and women was 0.25. Most sensible people would consider the difference in GPAs "insignificant." However, from a statistical point of view the difference is "significant" at close to the 2% level. What is the root of this strange dichotomy? As we showed in Section 19.5, when a study has enough power—i.e, enough examples—even insignificant differences can be statistically significant.

A related problem arises when a study is very small. Suppose you flipped a coin twice and it came up heads both times. Now, let's use the two-tailed one-sample t-test we saw in Section 19.3 to test the null hypothesis that the coin is fair. If we assume that the value of heads is 1 and the value of tails is 0, we can get the p-value using the code

```
stats.ttest_1samp([1, 1], 0.5)[1]
```

It returns a p-value of 0, indicating that if the coin is fair the probability of getting two consecutive heads is nil.

21.12 The Regressive Fallacy

The **regressive fallacy** occurs when people fail to take into account the natural fluctuations of events.

All athletes have good days and bad days. When they have good days, they try not to change anything. When they have a series of unusually bad days, however, they often try to make changes. Whether or not the changes are actually constructive, regression to the mean (Section 15.3) makes it likely that over the next few days the athlete's performance will be better than the unusually poor performances preceding the changes. But that may not stop the athlete from assuming that there is a **treatment effect**, i.e., attributing the improved performance to the changes he or she made.

The Nobel prize-winning psychologist Daniel Kahneman tells a story about an Israeli Air Force flight instructor who rejected Kahneman's assertion that "rewards for improved performance work better than punishment for mistakes." The instructor's argument was "On many occasions I have praised flights cadets for clean execution of some aerobatic maneuver. The next time they try the same maneuver they usually do worse. On the other hand, I have often screamed into a cadet's earphone for bad execution, and in general he does better on the next try."[153] It is natural for humans to imagine a treatment effect, because we like to think causally. But sometimes it is simply a matter of luck.

Imagining a treatment effect when there is none can be dangerous. It can lead to the belief that vaccinations are harmful, that snake oil cures all aches and pains, or that investing exclusively in mutual funds that "beat the market" last year is a good strategy.

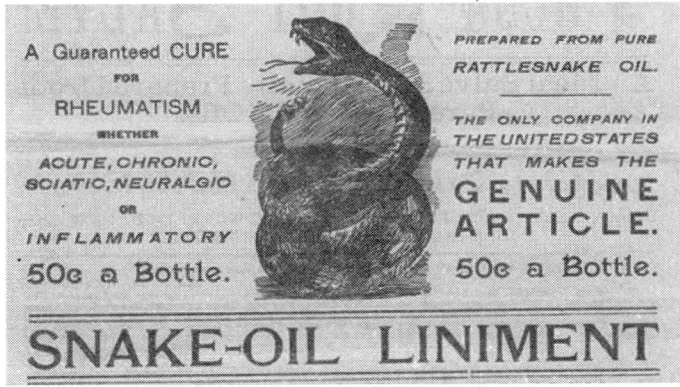

---

[153] *Thinking, Fast and Slow*, Daniel Kahneman, Farrar, Straus and Giroux, 2011, p.175.

21.13 Just Beware

It would be easy, and fun, to fill a few hundred pages with a history of statistical abuses. But by now you probably got the message: It's just as easy to lie with numbers as it is to lie with words. Make sure that you understand what is actually being measured and how those "statistically significant" results were computed before you jump to conclusions. As Darrell Huff said, "If you torture the data long enough, it will confess to anything."[154]

---

[154] Darrell Huff, *How to Lie with Statistics*, 1954. A similar remark is attributed to the Nobel prize winning economist Ronald Coase.

22 A QUICK LOOK AT MACHINE LEARNING

The amount of digital data in the world has been growing at a rate that defies human comprehension. The world's data storage capacity has doubled about every three years since the 1980s. During the time it will take you to read this chapter, approximately 10^{18} bits of data will be added to the world's store. It's not easy to relate to a number that large. One way to think about it is that 10^{18} Canadian pennies would have a surface area roughly twice that of the earth.

Of course, more data does not always lead to more useful information. Evolution is a slow process, and the ability of the human mind to assimilate data does not, alas, double every three years. One approach that the world is using to attempt to wring more useful information from "big data" is **statistical machine learning**.

Machine learning is hard to define. In some sense, every useful program learns something. For example, an implementation of Newton's method learns the roots of a polynomial. One of the earliest definitions was proposed by the American electrical engineer and computer scientist Arthur Samuel,[155] who defined it as a "field of study that gives computers the ability to learn without being explicitly programmed."

Humans learn things in two ways—memorization and generalization. We use memorization to accumulate individual facts. In England, for example, primary school students might learn a list of English monarchs. Humans use **generalization** to deduce new facts from old facts. A student of political science, for example, might observe the behavior of a large number of politicians, and generalize from those observations to conclude that all politicians lie on the campaign trail.

When computer scientists speak about machine learning, they most often mean the discipline of writing programs that automatically learn to make useful inferences from implicit patterns in data. For example, linear regression (see

---

[155] Samuel is probably best known as the author of a program that played checkers. The program, which he started working on in the 1950s and continued to work on into the 1970s, was impressive for its time, though not particularly good by modern standards. However, while working on it Samuel invented several techniques that are still used today. Among other things, Samuel's checker-playing program was quite possibly the first program ever written that improved based upon "experience."

Chapter 18) learns a curve that is a model of a collection of examples. That model can then be used to make predictions about previously unseen examples. The basic paradigm is

1. Observe a set of examples, frequently called the **training data**, that represent incomplete information about some statistical phenomenon
2. Use inference techniques to create a model of a process that could have generated the observed examples, and
3. Use that model to make predictions about previously unseen examples.

Suppose, for example, you were given the two sets of names in Figure 22.1 and the **feature vectors** in Figure 22.2.

```
A: {Abraham Lincoln, George Washington, Charles de Gaulle}
B: {Benjamin Harrison, James Madison, Louis Napoleon}
```

Figure 22.1: Two sets of names

```
Abraham Lincoln: [American, President, 193 cm tall]
George Washington: [American, President, 189 cm tall]
Charles de Gaulle: [French, President, 196 cm tall]
Benjamin Harrison: [American, President, 168 cm tall]
James Madison: [American, President, 163 cm tall]
Louis Napoleon: [French, President, 169 cm tall]
```

Figure 22.2: Associating a feature vector with each name

Each element of a vector corresponds to some aspect (i.e., feature) of the person. Based on this limited information about these historical figures, you might infer that the process that assigned either the label A or the label B to each of these examples was intended to separate tall presidents from shorter ones.

There are a large number of different approaches to machine learning, but all try to learn a model that is a generalization of the provided examples. All have three components:

- A representation of the model,
- An objective function for assessing the goodness of the model, and
- An optimization method for learning a model that minimizes or maximizes the value of the objective function.

Broadly speaking, machine learning algorithms can be thought of as either supervised or unsupervised.

CHAPTER 22. A QUICK LOOK AT MACHINE LEARNING

In **supervised learning**, we start with a set of feature vector/value pairs. The goal is to derive from these pairs a rule that predicts the value associated with a previously unseen feature vector. **Regression models** associate a real number with each feature vector. **Classification models** associate one of a finite number of **labels** with each feature vector.[156]

In Chapter 18, we looked at one kind of regression model, linear regression. Each feature vector was an x-coordinate, and the value associate with it was the corresponding y-coordinate. From the set of feature vector/value pairs we learned a model that could be used to predict the y-coordinate associated with any x-coordinate.

Now, let's look at a simple classification model. Given the sets of presidents we labeled A and B in Figure 22.1 and the feature vectors in Figure 22.2, we can generate the feature vector/label pairs in Figure 22.3.

```
[American, President, 193 cm tall], A
[American, President, 189 cm tall], A
[French, President, 196 cm tall], A
[American, President, 168 cm tall], B
[American, President, 163 cm tall], B
[French, President, 169 cm tall], B
```

Figure 22.3 Feature vector/label pairs for presidents

From these labeled examples, a learning algorithm might infer that all tall presidents should be labeled A and all short presidents labeled B. When asked to assign a label to

`[American, President, 189 cm.]`[157]

it would use the rule it had learned to choose label A.

Supervised machine learning is broadly used in practice for such tasks as detecting fraudulent use of credit cards and recommending movies to people.

In **unsupervised learning**, we are given a set of feature vectors but no labels. The goal of unsupervised learning is to uncover latent structure in the set of feature vectors. For example, given the set of presidential feature vectors, an unsupervised learning algorithm might separate the presidents into tall and short, or

---

[156] Much of the machine learning literature uses the word "class" rather than "label." Since we have used the word "class" for something else in this book, we will stick to using "label" for this concept.

[157] In case you are curious, Thomas Jefferson was 189 cm. tall.

perhaps into American and French. Broadly speaking, approaches to unsupervised machine learning can be categorized as either methods for clustering or methods for learning latent variable models.

A **latent variable** is a variable whose value is not directly observed, but can be inferred from the values of variables that are observed. Admissions officers at universities, for example, try to infer the probability of an applicant being a successful student (the latent variable), based on a set of observable values such as secondary school grades and performance on standardized tests. There is a rich set of methods for learning latent variable models, but we do not cover them in this book.

Clustering partitions a set of examples into groups (called clusters) such that examples in the same group are more similar to each other than they are to examples in other groups. Geneticists, for example, use clustering to find groups of related genes. Many popular clustering methods are surprisingly simple.

We present a widely used clustering algorithm in Chapter 23, and several approaches to supervised learning in Chapter 24. In the remainder of this chapter, we discuss the process of building feature vectors and different ways of calculating the similarity between two feature vectors.

22.1 Feature Vectors

The concept of **signal-to-noise ratio** (**SNR**) is used in many branches of engineering and science. The precise definition varies across applications, but the basic idea is simple. Think of it as the ratio of useful input to irrelevant input. In a restaurant, the signal might be the voice of your dinner date, and the noise the voices of the other diners.[158] If we were trying to predict which students would do well in a programming course, previous programming experience and mathematical aptitude would be part of the signal, but hair color merely noise. Separating the signal from the noise is not always easy. And when it is done poorly, the noise can be a distraction that obscures the truth in the signal.

---

[158] Unless your dinner date is exceedingly boring. In that case, your dinner date's conversation becomes the noise, and the conversation at the next table the signal.

The purpose of **feature engineering** is to separate those features in the available data that contribute to the signal from those that are merely noise. Failure to do an adequate job of this can lead to a bad model. The danger is particularly high when the **dimensionality** of the data (i.e., the number of different features) is large relative to the number of samples.

Successful feature engineering is an abstraction process that reduces the vast amount of information that might be available to information from which it will be productive to generalize. Imagine, for example, that your goal is to learn a model that will predict whether a person is likely to suffer a heart attack. Some features, such as their age, are likely to highly relevant. Other features, such as whether they are left-handed, are less likely to be relevant.

There are **feature elimination** techniques that can be used to automatically identify which features in a given set of features are most likely to be helpful. For example, in the context of supervised learning, one can select those features that are most strongly correlated with the labels of the examples.[159] However, these feature elimination techniques are of little help if relevant features are not there to start with. Suppose that our original feature set for the heart attack example includes height and weight. It might be the case that while neither height or weight is highly predictive of a heart attack, body mass index (BMI) is. While BMI can be computed from height and weight, the relationship (weight in kilograms divided by the square of height in meters) is too complicated to be automatically found by current machine learning techniques. Successful machine learning often involves the design of features by those with domain expertise.

In unsupervised learning, the problem is even harder. Typically, we choose features based upon our intuition about which features might be relevant to the kinds of structure we would like to find. However, relying on intuition about the potential relevance of features is problematical. How good is your intuition about whether one's dental history is a good predictor of a future heart attack?

Consider Figure 22.4, which contains a table of feature vectors and the label (reptile or not) with which each vector is associated.

---

[159] Since features are often strongly correlated with each other, this can lead to a large number of redundant features. There are more sophisticated feature elimination techniques, but we do not cover them in this book.

Name	Egg-laying	Scales	Poisonous	Cold-blooded	# Legs	Reptile
Cobra	True	True	True	True	0	Yes
Rattlesnake	True	True	True	True	0	Yes
Boa constrictor	False	True	False	True	0	Yes
Alligator	True	True	False	True	4	Yes
Dart frog	True	False	True	False	4	No
Salmon	True	True	False	True	0	No
Python	True	True	False	True	0	Yes

Figure 22.4 Name, features and labels for assorted animals

A supervised machine learning algorithm (or a human) given only the information about cobras—i.e., only the first row of the table—cannot do much more than to remember the fact that a cobra is a reptile. Now, let's add the information about rattlesnakes. We can begin to generalize, and might infer the rule that an animal is a reptile if it lays eggs, has scales, is poisonous, is cold-blooded, and has no legs.

Now, suppose we are asked to decide if a boa constrictor is a reptile. We might answer "no," because a boa constrictor is neither poisonous nor egg-laying. But this would be the wrong answer. Of course, it is hardly surprising that attempting to generalize from two examples might lead us astray. Once we include the boa constrictor in our training data, we might formulate the new rule that an animal is a reptile if it has scales, is cold-blooded, and is legless. In doing so, we are discarding the features egg-laying and poisonous as irrelevant to the classification problem.

If we use the new rule to classify the alligator, we conclude incorrectly that since it has legs it is not a reptile. Once we include the alligator in the training data we reformulate the rule to allow reptiles to have either none or four legs. When we look at the dart frog, we correctly conclude that it is not a reptile, since it is not cold-blooded. However, when we use our current rule to classify the salmon, we incorrectly conclude that a salmon is a reptile. We can add yet more complexity to our rule, to separate salmon from alligators, but it's a losing battle. There is no way to modify our rule so that it will correctly classify both salmon and pythons, since the feature vectors of these two species are identical.

This kind of problem is more common than not in machine learning. It is quite rare to have feature vectors that contain enough information to classify things perfectly. In this case, the problem is that we don't have enough features.

CHAPTER 22. A QUICK LOOK AT MACHINE LEARNING

If we had included the fact that reptile eggs have amnios,[160] we could devise a rule that separates reptiles from fish. Unfortunately, in most practical applications of machine learning it is not possible to construct feature vectors that allow for perfect discrimination.

Does this mean that we should give up because all of the available features are mere noise? No. In this case, the features scales and cold-blooded are necessary conditions for being a reptile, but not sufficient conditions. The rule that an animal is a reptile if it has scales and is cold-blooded will not yield any false negatives, i.e., any animal classified as a non-reptile will indeed not be a reptile. However, it will yield some false positives, i.e., some of the animals classified as reptiles will not be reptiles.

22.2 Distance Metrics

In Figure 22.4 we described animals using four binary features and one integer feature. Suppose we want to use these features to evaluate the similarity of two animals, for example, to ask whether a rattlesnake is more similar to a boa constrictor or to a dart frog.[161]

The first step in doing this kind of comparison is converting the features for each animal into a sequence of numbers. If we say True = 1 and False = 0, we get the following feature vectors:

```
Rattlesnake: [1,1,1,1,0]
Boa constrictor: [0,1,0,1,0]
Dart frog: [1,0,1,0,4]
```

There are many different ways to compare the similarity of vectors of numbers. The most commonly used metrics for comparing equal-length vectors are based on the **Minkowski distance**:[162]

$$distance(V, W, p) = \left(\sum_{i=1}^{len} abs(V_i - W_i)^p\right)^{1/p}$$

where *len* is the length of the vectors.

---

[160] Amnios are protective outer layers that allow eggs to be laid on land rather than in the water.

[161] This question is not quite as silly as it sounds. A naturalist and a toxicologist (or someone looking to enhance the effectiveness of a blow dart) might give different answers to this question.

[162] Another popular distance metric is cosine similarity. This captures the difference in the angle of the two vectors rather than the difference in magnitude. It is is often useful for high-dimensional vectors.

The parameter p, which must be at least 1, defines the kinds of paths that can be followed in traversing the distance between the vectors V and W.[163] This can be mostly easily visualized if the vectors are of length two, and can therefore be represented using Cartesian coordinates. Consider the picture in Figure 22.5.

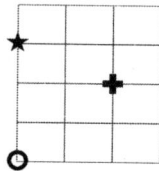

Figure 22.5 Visualizing distance metrics

Is the circle in the bottom left corner closer to the cross or closer to the star? It depends. If we can travel in a straight line, the cross is closer. The Pythagorean Theorem tells us that the cross is the square root of 8 units from the circle, about 2.8 units, whereas we can easily see that the star is 3 units from the circle. These distances are called Euclidean distances, and correspond to using the Minkowski distance with p = 2. But imagine that the lines in the picture correspond to streets, and that we have to stay on the streets to get from one place to another. The star remains 3 units from the circle, but the cross is now 4 units away. These distances are called **Manhattan distances**,[164] and they correspond to using the Minkowski distance with p = 1. Figure 22.6 contains a function implementing the Minkowski distance.

Figure 22.7 contains class Animal. It defines the distance between two animals as the Euclidean distance between the feature vectors associated with the animals.

---

[163] When p < 1, peculiar things happen. Consider, for example p = 0.5 and the points A = (0,0), B = (1,1), and C = (0,1). If you compute the pairwise distances beween these points, you will discover that the distance from A to B is 4, the distance from A to C is 1, and the distance from C to B is 1. Common sense dictates that the distance from A to B via C cannot be less than the distance from A to B. (Mathematicians refer to this as the triangle inequality, which states that for any triangle the sum of the lengths of any two sides must not be less than the length of the third side.)

[164] Manhattan Island is the most densely populated borough of New York City. On most of the island, the streets are laid out in a rectangular grid, so using the Minkowski distance with p = 1 provides a good approximation of the distance one has to travel to walk from one place to another. Driving in Manhattan is a totally different story.

```
def minkowskiDist(v1, v2, p):
    """Assumes v1 and v2 are equal-length arrays of numbers
       Returns Minkowski distance of order p between v1 and v2"""
    dist = 0.0
    for i in range(len(v1)):
        dist += abs(v1[i] - v2[i])**p
    return dist**(1/p)
```

Figure 22.6 Minkowski distance

```
class Animal(object):
    def __init__(self, name, features):
        """Assumes name a string; features a list of numbers"""
        self.name = name
        self.features = pylab.array(features)

    def getName(self):
        return self.name

    def getFeatures(self):
        return self.features

    def distance(self, other):
        """Assumes other an Animal
           Returns the Euclidean distance between feature vectors
              of self and other"""
        return minkowskiDist(self.getFeatures(),
                             other.getFeatures(), 2)
```

Figure 22.7 Class Animal

Figure 22.8 contains a function that compares a list of animals to each other and produces a table showing the pairwise distances. The code uses a PyLab plotting facility that we have not previously used: table.

The table function produces a plot that (surprise!) looks like a table. The keyword arguments rowLabels and colLabels are used to supply the labels (in this example the names of the animals) for the rows and columns. The keyword argument cellText is used to supply the values appearing in the cells of the table. In the example, cellText is bound to tableVals, which is a list of lists of strings. Each element in tableVals is a list of the values for the cells in one row of the table. The keyword argument cellLoc is used to specify where in each cell the text should appear, and the keyword argument loc is used to specify where in the figure the table itself should appear. The last keyword parameter used in the example is colWidths. It is bound to a list of floats giving the width (in inches) of each column in the table. The code table.scale(1, 2.5) instructs PyLab to leave the horizontal width of the cells unchanged, but to increase the height of the cells by a factor of 2.5 (so the tables look prettier).

```
def compareAnimals(animals, precision):
    """Assumes animals is a list of animals, precision an int >= 0
       Builds a table of Euclidean distance between each animal"""
    #Get labels for columns and rows
    columnLabels = []
    for a in animals:
        columnLabels.append(a.getName())
    rowLabels = columnLabels[:]
    tableVals = []
    #Get distances between pairs of animals
    #For each row
    for a1 in animals:
        row = []
        #For each column
        for a2 in animals:
            if a1 == a2:
                row.append('--')
            else:
                distance = a1.distance(a2)
                row.append(str(round(distance, precision)))
        tableVals.append(row)
    #Produce table
    table = pylab.table(rowLabels = rowLabels,
                        colLabels = columnLabels,
                        cellText = tableVals,
                        cellLoc = 'center',
                        loc = 'center',
                        colWidths = [0.2]*len(animals))
    table.scale(1, 2.5)
    pylab.savefig('distances')
```

Figure 22.8 Build table of distances between pairs of animals

CHAPTER 22. A QUICK LOOK AT MACHINE LEARNING

If we run the code

```
rattlesnake = Animal('rattlesnake', [1,1,1,1,0])
boa = Animal('boa\nconstrictor', [0,1,0,1,0])
dartFrog = Animal('dart frog', [1,0,1,0,4])
animals = [rattlesnake, boa, dartFrog]
compareAnimals(animals, 3)
```

it produces the table in Figure 22.9 and saves it in a file named distances.

As you probably expected, the distance between the rattlesnake and the boa constrictor is less than that between either of the snakes and the dart frog. Notice, by the way, that the dart frog is a bit closer to the rattlesnake than to the boa constrictor.

	rattlesnake	boa constrictor	dart frog
rattlesnake	--	1.414	4.243
boa constrictor	1.414	--	4.472
dart frog	4.243	4.472	--

Figure 22.9 Distances between three animals

Now, let's insert before the last line of the above code the lines

```
alligator = Animal('alligator', [1,1,0,1,4])
animals.append(alligator)
```

It produces the table in Figure 22.10.

	rattlesnake	boa constrictor	dart frog	alligator
rattlesnake	--	1.414	4.243	4.123
boa constrictor	1.414	--	4.472	4.123
dart frog	4.243	4.472	--	1.732
alligator	4.123	4.123	1.732	--

Figure 22.10 Distances between four animals

Perhaps you're surprised that the alligator is considerably closer to the dart frog than to either the rattlesnake or the boa constrictor. Take a minute to think about why.

The feature vector for the alligator differs from that of the rattlesnake in two places: whether it is poisonous and the number of legs. The feature vector for the alligator differs from that of the dart frog in three places: whether it is poisonous, whether it has scales, and whether it is cold-blooded. Yet according to our distance metric the alligator is more like the dart frog than like the rattlesnake. What's going on?

The root of the problem is that the different features have different ranges of values. All but one of the features range between 0 and 1, but the number of legs ranges from 0 to 4. This means that when we calculate the Euclidean distance the number of legs gets disproportionate weight. Let's see what happens if we turn the feature into a binary feature, with a value of 0 if the animal is legless and 1 otherwise.

	rattlesnake	boa constrictor	dart frog	alligator
rattlesnake	--	1.414	1.732	1.414
boa constrictor	1.414	--	2.236	1.414
dart frog	1.732	2.236	--	1.732
alligator	1.414	1.414	1.732	--

Figure 22.11 **Distances using a different feature representation**

This looks a lot more plausible.

Of course, it is not always convenient to use only binary features. In Section 23.4, we will present a more general approach to dealing with differences in scale among features.

23 CLUSTERING

Unsupervised learning involves finding hidden structure in unlabeled data. The most commonly used unsupervised machine learning technique is clustering.

Clustering can be defined as the process of organizing objects into groups whose members are similar in some way. A key issue is defining the meaning of "similar." Consider the plot in Figure 23.1, which shows the height, weight, and shirt color for 13 people.

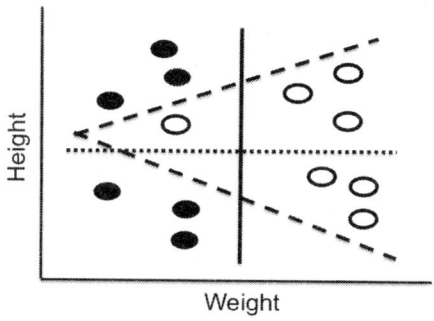

Figure 23.1 Height, weight, and kind of shirt

If we cluster people by height, there are two obvious clusters—delimited by the dotted horizontal line. If we cluster people by weight, there are two different obvious clusters—delimited by the solid vertical line. If we cluster people based on their shirts, there is yet a third clustering—delimited by the angled dashed lines. Notice, by the way, that this last division is not linear, i.e., we cannot separate the people by shirt color using a single straight line.

Clustering is an optimization problem. The goal is to find a set of clusters that optimizes an objective function, subject to some set of constraints. Given a distance metric that can be used to decide how close two examples are to each other, we need to define an objective function that minimizes the distance between examples in the same cluster, i.e., minimizes the dissimilarity of the examples within a cluster.

One measure, which we call variability, of how different the examples within a single cluster, *c*, are from each other is

$$variability(c) = \sum_{e \in c} distance(mean(c), e)^2$$

where *mean(c)* is the mean of the feature vectors of all the examples in the cluster. The mean of a set of vectors is computed component-wise. The corresponding elements are added, and the result divided by the number of vectors. If v1 and v2 are arrays of numbers, the value of the expression (v1+v2)/2 is their **Euclidean mean.**

What we are calling variability is quite similar to the notion of variance presented in Chapter 15. The difference is that variability is not normalized by the size of the cluster, so clusters with more points are likely to look less cohesive according to this measure. If one wants to compare the coherence of two clusters of different sizes, one needs to divide the variability of each cluster by the size of the cluster.

The definition of variability within a single cluster, *c*, can be extended to define a dissimilarity metric for a set of clusters, *C*:

$$dissimilarity(C) = \sum_{c \in C} variability(c)$$

Notice that since we don't divide the variability by the size of the cluster, a large incoherent cluster increases the value of *dissimilarity(C)* more than a small incoherent cluster does. This is by design.

So, is the optimization problem to find a set of clusters, *C*, such that *dissimilarity(C)* is minimized? Not exactly. It can easily be minimized by putting each example in its own cluster. We need to add some constraint. For example, we could put a constraint on the minimum distance between clusters or require that the maximum number of clusters is some *k*.

In general, solving this optimization problem is computationally prohibitive for most interesting problems. Consequently, people rely on greedy algorithms that provide approximate solutions. In Section 23.2, we present one such algorithm, k-means clustering. But first we will introduce some abstractions that are useful for implementing that algorithm (and other clustering algorithms as well).

23.1 Class Cluster

Class `Example` will be used to build the samples to be clustered. Associated with each example is a name, a feature vector, and an optional label. The `distance` method returns the Euclidean distance between two examples.

```python
class Example(object):

    def __init__(self, name, features, label = None):
        #Assumes features is an array of floats
        self.name = name
        self.features = features
        self.label = label

    def dimensionality(self):
        return len(self.features)

    def getFeatures(self):
        return self.features[:]

    def getLabel(self):
        return self.label

    def getName(self):
        return self.name

    def distance(self, other):
        return minkowskiDist(self.features, other.getFeatures(), 2)

    def __str__(self):
        return self.name +':'+ str(self.features) + ':'\
            + str(self.label)
```

Figure 23.2 Class `Example`

Class `Cluster`, Figure 23.3, is slightly more complex. A cluster is a set of examples. The two interesting methods in `Cluster` are `computeCentroid` and `variability`. Think of the **centroid** of a cluster as its center of mass. The method `computeCentroid` returns an example with a feature vector equal to the Euclidean mean of the feature vectors of the examples in the cluster. The method `variability` provides a measure of the coherence of the cluster.

```python
class Cluster(object):

    def __init__(self, examples):
        """Assumes examples a non-empty list of Examples"""
        self.examples = examples
        self.centroid = self.computeCentroid()

    def update(self, examples):
        """Assume examples is a non-empty list of Examples
           Replace examples; return amount centroid has changed"""
        oldCentroid = self.centroid
        self.examples = examples
        self.centroid = self.computeCentroid()
        return oldCentroid.distance(self.centroid)

    def computeCentroid(self):
        vals = pylab.array([0.0]*self.examples[0].dimensionality())
        for e in self.examples: #compute mean
            vals += e.getFeatures()
        centroid = Example('centroid', vals/len(self.examples))
        return centroid

    def getCentroid(self):
        return self.centroid

    def variability(self):
        totDist = 0.0
        for e in self.examples:
            totDist += (e.distance(self.centroid))**2
        return totDist

    def members(self):
        for e in self.examples:
            yield e

    def __str__(self):
        names = []
        for e in self.examples:
            names.append(e.getName())
        names.sort()
        result = 'Cluster with centroid '\
               + str(self.centroid.getFeatures()) + ' contains:\n  '
        for e in names:
            result = result + e + ', '
        return result[:-2] #remove trailing comma and space
```

Figure 23.3 Class Cluster

23.2 K-means Clustering

K-means clustering is probably the most widely used clustering method.[165] Its goal is to partition a set of examples into k clusters such that

- Each example is in the cluster whose centroid is the closest centroid to that example, and
- The dissimilarity of the set of clusters is minimized.

Unfortunately, finding an optimal solution to this problem on a large data set is computationally intractable. Fortunately, there is an efficient greedy algorithm[166] that can be used to find a useful approximation. It is described by the pseudocode

```
randomly choose k examples as initial centroids of clusters
while true:
    1. Create k clusters by assigning each example to closest centroid
    2. Compute k new centroids by averaging the examples in each
       cluster
    3. If none of the centroids differ from the previous iteration:
          return the current set of clusters
```

The complexity of step 1 is O(k*n*d), where k is the number of clusters, n is the number of examples, and d the time required to compute the distance between a pair of examples. The complexity of step 2 is O(n), and the complexity of step 3 is O(k). Hence, the complexity of a single iteration is O(k*n*d). If the examples are compared using the Minkowski distance, d is linear in the length of the feature vector.[167] Of course, the complexity of the entire algorithm depends upon the number of iterations. That is not easy to characterize, but suffice it to say that it is usually small.

One problem with the k-means algorithm is that the value returned depends upon the initial set of randomly chosen centroids. If a particularly unfortunate set of initial centroids is chosen, the algorithm might settle into a local optimum that is far from the global optimum. In practice, this problem is typically ad-

---

[165] Though k-means clustering is probably the most commonly used clustering method, it is not the most appropriate method in all situations. Two other widely used methods, not covered in this book, are hierarchical clustering and EM-clustering.

[166] The most widely used k-means algorithm is attributed to James McQueen, and was first published in 1967. However, other approaches to k-means clustering were used as early as the 1950s.

[167] Unfortunately, in many applications we need to use a distance metric, e.g., earth-movers distance or dynamic-time-warping distance, that has a higher computational complexity.

dressed by running k-means multiple times with randomly chosen initial centroids. We then choose the solution with the minimum dissimilarity of clusters.

Figure 23.4 contains a function, trykmeans, that calls kmeans (see Figure 23.5) multiple times and selects the result with the lowest dissimilarity. If a trial fails because kmeans generated an empty cluster and therefore raised an exception, trykmeans merely tries again—assuming that eventually kmeans will choose an initial set of centroids that successfully converges.

```python
def dissimilarity(clusters):
    totDist = 0.0
    for c in clusters:
        totDist += c.variability()
    return totDist

def trykmeans(examples, numClusters, numTrials, verbose = False):
    """Calls kmeans numTrials times and returns the result with the
          lowest dissimilarity"""
    best = kmeans(examples, numClusters, verbose)
    minDissimilarity = dissimilarity(best)
    trial = 1
    while trial < numTrials:
        try:
            clusters = kmeans(examples, numClusters, verbose)
        except ValueError:
            continue #If failed, try again
        currDissimilarity = dissimilarity(clusters)
        if currDissimilarity < minDissimilarity:
            best = clusters
            minDissimilarity = currDissimilarity
        trial += 1
    return best
```

Figure 23.4 Finding the best k-means clustering

Figure 23.5 contains a translation into Python of the pseudocode describing k-means. The only wrinkle is that it raises an exception if any iteration creates a cluster with no members. Generating an empty cluster is rare. It can't occur on the first iteration, but it can occur on subsequent iterations. It usually results from choosing too large a k or an unlucky choice of initial centroids. Treating an empty cluster as an error is one of the options used by Matlab. Another is creating a new cluster containing a single point—the point furthest from the centroid in the other clusters. We chose to treat it an error to keep the implementation relatively simple.

```
def kmeans(examples, k, verbose = False):
    #Get k randomly chosen initial centroids, create cluster for each
    initialCentroids = random.sample(examples, k)
    clusters = []
    for e in initialCentroids:
        clusters.append(Cluster([e]))

    #Iterate until centroids do not change
    converged = False
    numIterations = 0
    while not converged:
        numIterations += 1
        #Create a list containing k distinct empty lists
        newClusters = []
        for i in range(k):
            newClusters.append([])

        #Associate each example with closest centroid
        for e in examples:
            #Find the centroid closest to e
            smallestDistance = e.distance(clusters[0].getCentroid())
            index = 0
            for i in range(1, k):
                distance = e.distance(clusters[i].getCentroid())
                if distance < smallestDistance:
                    smallestDistance = distance
                    index = i
            #Add e to the list of examples for appropriate cluster
            newClusters[index].append(e)

        for c in newClusters: #Avoid having empty clusters
            if len(c) == 0:
                raise ValueError('Empty Cluster')

        #Update each cluster; check if a centroid has changed
        converged = True
        for i in range(k):
            if clusters[i].update(newClusters[i]) > 0.0:
                converged = False
        if verbose:
            print('Iteration #' + str(numIterations))
            for c in clusters:
                print(c)
            print('') #add blank line
    return clusters
```

Figure 23.5 K-means clustering

23.3 A Contrived Example

Figure 23.7 contains code that generates, plots, and clusters examples drawn from two distributions.

The function genDistributions generates a list of n examples with two-dimensional feature vectors. The values of the elements of these feature vectors are drawn from normal distributions.

The function plotSamples plots the feature vectors of a set of examples. It uses pylab.annotate to place text next to points on the plot. The first argument is the text, the second argument the point with which the text is associated, and the third argument the location of the text relative to the point with which it is associated.

The function contrivedTest uses genDistributions to create two distributions of ten examples (each with the same standard deviation but different means), plots the examples using plotSamples, and then clusters them using trykmeans.

The call contrivedTest(1, 2, True) produced the plot in Figure 23.6 and printed the lines in Figure 23.8.

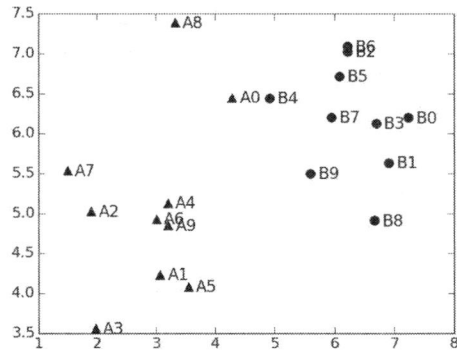

Figure 23.6 Examples from two distributions

```python
def genDistribution(xMean, xSD, yMean, ySD, n, namePrefix):
    samples = []
    for s in range(n):
        x = random.gauss(xMean, xSD)
        y = random.gauss(yMean, ySD)
        samples.append(Example(namePrefix+str(s), [x, y]))
    return samples

def plotSamples(samples, marker):
    xVals, yVals = [], []
    for s in samples:
        x = s.getFeatures()[0]
        y = s.getFeatures()[1]
        pylab.annotate(s.getName(), xy = (x, y),
                       xytext = (x+0.13, y-0.07),
                       fontsize = 'x-large')
        xVals.append(x)
        yVals.append(y)
    pylab.plot(xVals, yVals, marker)

def contrivedTest(numTrials, k, verbose = False):
    xMean = 3
    xSD = 1
    yMean = 5
    ySD = 1
    n = 10
    d1Samples = genDistribution(xMean, xSD, yMean, ySD, n, 'A')
    plotSamples(d1Samples, 'k^')
    d2Samples = genDistribution(xMean+3, xSD, yMean+1, ySD, n, 'B')
    plotSamples(d2Samples, 'ko')
    clusters = trykmeans(d1Samples+d2Samples, k, numTrials, verbose)
    print('Final result')
    for c in clusters:
        print('', c)
```

Figure 23.7 A test of k-means

```
Iteration #1
Cluster with centroid [ 4.71113345  5.76359152] contains:
  A0, A1, A2, A4, A5, A6, A7, A8, A9, B0, B1, B2, B3, B4, B5, B6,
  B7, B8, B9
Cluster with centroid [ 1.97789683  3.56317055] contains:
  A3

Iteration #2
Cluster with centroid [ 5.46369488  6.12015454] contains:
  A0, A4, A8, A9, B0, B1, B2, B3, B4, B5, B6, B7, B8, B9
Cluster with centroid [ 2.49961733  4.56487432] contains:
  A1, A2, A3, A5, A6, A7

Iteration #3
Cluster with centroid [ 5.84078727  6.30779094] contains:
  A0, A8, B0, B1, B2, B3, B4, B5, B6, B7, B8, B9
Cluster with centroid [ 2.67499815  4.67223977] contains:
  A1, A2, A3, A4, A5, A6, A7, A9

Iteration #4
Cluster with centroid [ 5.84078727  6.30779094] contains:
  A0, A8, B0, B1, B2, B3, B4, B5, B6, B7, B8, B9
Cluster with centroid [ 2.67499815  4.67223977] contains:
  A1, A2, A3, A4, A5, A6, A7, A9

Final result
 Cluster with centroid [ 5.84078727  6.30779094] contains:
  A0, A8, B0, B1, B2, B3, B4, B5, B6, B7, B8, B9
 Cluster with centroid [ 2.67499815  4.67223977] contains:
  A1, A2, A3, A4, A5, A6, A7, A9
```

Figure 23.8 Lines printed by call contrivedTest(1, 2, True)

Notice that the initial (randomly chosen) centroids led to a highly skewed clustering in which a single cluster contained all but one of the points. By the fourth iteration, however, the centroids had moved to places such that the points from the two distributions were reasonably well separated into two clusters. The only "mistakes" were made on A0 and A8.

When we tried 50 trials rather than 1, by calling contrivedTest(50, 2, False), it printed

CHAPTER 23. CLUSTERING

```
Final result
 Cluster with centroid [ 2.74674403  4.97411447] contains:
   A1, A2, A3, A4, A5, A6, A7, A8, A9
 Cluster with centroid [ 6.0698851   6.20948902] contains:
   A0, B0, B1, B2, B3, B4, B5, B6, B7, B8, B9
```

A0 is still mixed in with the B's, but A8 is not. If we try 1000 trials, we get the same result. That might surprise you, since a glance at Figure 23.6 reveals that if A0 and B0 are chosen as the initial centroids (which would probably happen with 1000 trials), the first iteration will yield clusters that perfectly separate the A's and B's. However, in the second iteration new centroids will be computed, and A0 will be assigned to a cluster with the B's. Is this bad? Recall that clustering is a form of unsupervised learning that looks for structure in unlabeled data. Grouping A0 with the B's is not unreasonable.

One of the key issues in using k-means clustering is choosing k. The function contrivedTest2 in Figure 23.9 generates, plots, and clusters points from three overlapping Gaussian distributions. We will use it to look at the results of clustering this data for various values of k. The data points are shows in Figure 23.10.

```
def contrivedTest2(numTrials, k, verbose = False):
    xMean = 3
    xSD = 1
    yMean = 5
    ySD = 1
    n = 8
    d1Samples = genDistribution(xMean,xSD, yMean, ySD, n, 'A')
    plotSamples(d1Samples, 'k^')
    d2Samples = genDistribution(xMean+3,xSD,yMean, ySD, n, 'B')
    plotSamples(d2Samples, 'ko')
    d3Samples = genDistribution(xMean, xSD, yMean+3, ySD, n, 'C')
    plotSamples(d3Samples, 'kx')
    clusters = trykmeans(d1Samples + d2Samples + d3Samples,
                        k, numTrials, verbose)
    pylab.ylim(0,11)
    print('Final result has dissimilarity',
          round(dissimilarity(clusters), 3))
    for c in clusters:
        print('', c)
```

Figure 23.9 Generating points from three distributions

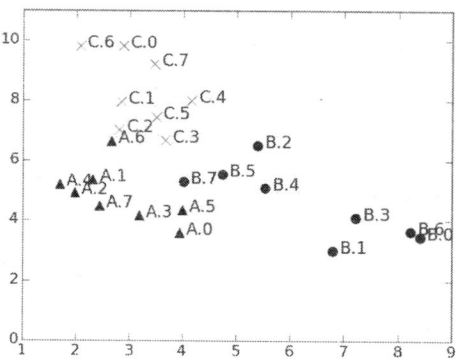

Figure 23.10 Points from three overlapping Gaussians

The invocation contrivedTest2(40, 2) prints

```
Final result has dissimilarity 90.128
  Cluster with centroid [ 5.5884966    4.43260236] contains:
   A.0, A.3, A.5, B.0, B.1, B.2, B.3, B.4, B.5, B.6, B.7
  Cluster with centroid [ 2.80949911   7.11735738] contains:
   A.1, A.2, A.4, A.6, A.7, C.0, C.1, C.2, C.3, C.4, C.5, C.6, C.7
```

The invocation contrivedTest2(40, 3) prints

```
Final result has dissimilarity 42.757
  Cluster with centroid [ 7.66239972   3.55222681] contains:
   B.0, B.1, B.3, B.6
  Cluster with centroid [ 3.56907939   4.95707576] contains:
   A.0, A.1, A.2, A.3, A.4, A.5, A.7, B.2, B.4, B.5, B.7
  Cluster with centroid [ 3.12083099   8.06083681] contains:
   A.6, C.0, C.1, C.2, C.3, C.4, C.5, C.6, C.7
```

And the invocation contrivedTest2(40, 6) prints

```
Final result has dissimilarity 11.441
  Cluster with centroid [ 2.10900238   4.99452866] contains:
   A.1, A.2, A.4, A.7
  Cluster with centroid [ 4.92742554   5.60609442] contains:
   B.2, B.4, B.5, B.7
  Cluster with centroid [ 2.80974427   9.60386549] contains:
   C.0, C.6, C.7
  Cluster with centroid [ 3.27637435   7.28932247] contains:
   A.6, C.1, C.2, C.3, C.4, C.5
  Cluster with centroid [ 3.70472053   4.04178035] contains:
   A.0, A.3, A.5
  Cluster with centroid [ 7.66239972   3.55222681] contains:
   B.0, B.1, B.3, B.6
```

CHAPTER 23. CLUSTERING

The last clustering is the tightest fit, i.e., the clustering has the lowest dissimilarity (11.441). Does this mean that it is the "best" clustering? Not necessarily. Recall that when we looked at linear regression in Section 18.1.1, we observed that by increasing the degree of the polynomial we got a more complex model that provided a tighter fit to the data. We also observed that when we increased the degree of the polynomial we ran the risk of finding a model with poor predictive value—because it overfit the data.

Choosing the right value for k is exactly analogous to choosing the right degree polynomial for a linear regression. By increasing k, we can decrease dissimilarity, at the risk of overfitting. (When k is equal to the number of examples to be clustered, the dissimilarity is 0!) If we have information about how the examples to be clustered were generated, e.g., chosen from m distributions, we can use that information to choose k. Absent such information, there are a variety of heuristic procedures for choosing k. Going into them is beyond the scope of this book.

23.4 A Less Contrived Example

Different species of mammals have different eating habits. Some species (e.g., elephants and beavers) eat only plants, others (e.g., lions and tigers) eat only meat, and some (e.g., pigs and humans) eat anything they can get into their mouths. The vegetarian species are called herbivores, the meat eaters are called carnivores, and those species that eat both plants and animals are called omnivores.

Over the millennia, evolution (or some other mysterious process) has equipped species with teeth suitable for consumption of their preferred foods.[168] That raises the question of whether clustering mammals based on their dentition produces clusters that have some relation to their diets.

Figure 23.11 shows the contents of a file listing some species of mammals, their dental formulas (the first 8 numbers), their average adult weight in pounds,[169] and a code indicating their preferred diet. The comments at the top describe the items associated with each mammal, e.g., the first item following the name is the number of top incisors.

---

[168] Or, perhaps, species have chosen food based on their dentition. As we pointed out in Section 21.4, correlation does not imply causation.

[169] We included the information about weight because the author has been told, on more than one occasion, that there is a relationship between weight and eating habits.

```
#Name
#top incisors
#top canines
#top premolars
#top molars
#bottom incisors
#bottom canines
#bottom premolars
#bottom molars
#weight
#Label: 0=herbivore, 1=carnivore, 2=omnivore
Badger,3,1,3,1,3,1,3,2,10,1
Bear,3,1,4,2,3,1,4,3,278,2
Beaver,1,0,2,3,1,0,1,3,20,0
Brown bat,2,1,1,3,3,1,2,3,0.5,1
Cat,3,1,3,1,3,1,2,1,4,1
Cougar,3,1,3,1,3,1,2,1,63,1
Cow,0,0,3,3,3,1,2,1,400,0
Deer,0,0,3,3,4,0,3,3,200,0
Dog,3,1,4,2,3,1,4,3,20,1
Elk,0,1,3,3,3,1,3,3,500,0
Fox,3,1,4,2,3,1,4,3,5,1
Fur seal,3,1,4,1,2,1,4,1,200,1
Grey seal,3,1,3,2,2,1,3,2,268,1
Guinea pig,1,0,1,3,1,0,1,3,1,0
Human,2,1,2,3,2,1,2,3,150,2
Jaguar,3,1,3,1,3,1,2,1,81,1
Kangaroo,3,1,2,4,1,0,2,4,55,0
Lion,3,1,3,1,3,1,2,1,175,1
Mink,3,1,3,1,3,1,3,2,1,1
Mole,3,1,4,3,3,1,4,3,0.75,1
Moose,0,0,3,3,4,0,3,3,900,0
Mouse,1,0,0,3,1,0,0,3,0.3,2
Pig,3,1,4,3,3,1,4,3,50,2
Porcupine,1,0,1,3,1,0,1,3,3,0
Rabbit,2,0,3,3,1,0,2,3,1,0
Raccoon,3,1,4,2,3,1,4,2,40,2
Rat,1,0,0,3,1,0,0,3,.75,2
Red bat,1,1,2,3,3,1,2,3,1,1
Sea lion,3,1,4,1,2,1,4,1,415,1
Skunk,3,1,3,1,3,1,3,2,2,2
Squirrel,1,0,2,3,1,0,1,3,2,2
Wolf,3,1,4,2,3,1,4,3,27,1
Woodchuck,1,0,2,3,1,0,1,3,4,2
```

Figure 23.11 Mammal dentition

CHAPTER 23. CLUSTERING

Figure 23.12 contains a function, readMammalData, for reading a file formatted in this way and processing the contents of the file to produce a set of examples representing the information in the file. It first processes the header information at the start of the file to get a count of the number of features to be associated with each example. It then uses the lines corresponding to each species to build three lists:

- speciesNames is a list of the names of the mammals.
- labelList is a list of the labels associated with the mammals.
- featureVals is a list of lists. Each element of featureVals contains the list of values, one for each mammal, for a single feature—for example, a list of weights. The value of the expression featureVals[i][j] is the ith feature of the jth mammal.

The last part of readMammalData uses the values in featureVals to create a list of feature vectors, one for each mammal. (The code could be simplified by not constructing featureVals and instead directly constructing the feature vectors for each mammal. However, we chose not to do that in anticipation of an enhancement to readMammalData that we make later in this section.)

The function buildMammalExamples in Figure 23.12 builds a list of examples from the data in the lists created by readMammalData.

The function testTeeth, Figure 23.13, uses trykmeans to cluster the examples built by buildMammalExamples. It then reports the number of herbivores, carnivores, and omnivores in each cluster.

```python
def readMammalData(fName):
    dataFile = open(fName, 'r')
    numFeatures = 0
    #Process lines at top of file
    for line in dataFile: #Find number of features
        if line[0:6] == '#Label': #indicates end of features
            break
        if line[0:5] != '#Name':
            numFeatures += 1
    featureVals = []

    #Produce featureVals, speciesNames, and labelList
    featureVals, speciesNames, labelList = [], [], []
    for i in range(numFeatures):
        featureVals.append([])

    #Continue processing lines in file, starting after comments
    for line in dataFile:
        #remove newline, then split
        dataLine = line[:-1].split(',')
        speciesNames.append(dataLine[0])
        classLabel = dataLine[-1]
        labelList.append(classLabel)
        for i in range(numFeatures):
            featureVals[i].append(float(dataLine[i+1]))

    #Use featureVals to build list containing the feature vectors
    #for each mammal
    featureVectorList = []
    for mammal in range(len(speciesNames)):
        featureVector = []
        for feature in range(numFeatures):
            featureVector.append(featureVals[feature][mammal])
        featureVectorList.append(featureVector)
    return featureVectorList, labelList, speciesNames

def buildMammalExamples(featureList, labelList, speciesNames):
    examples = []
    for i in range(len(speciesNames)):
        features = pylab.array(featureList[i])
        example = Example(speciesNames[i], features, labelList[i])
        examples.append(example)
    return examples
```

Figure 23.12 Read and process file

CHAPTER 23. CLUSTERING

```
def testTeeth(numClusters, numTrials):
    features, labels, species = readMammalData('dentalFormulas.txt')
    examples = buildMammalExamples(features, labels, species)
    bestClustering = trykmeans(examples, numClusters, numTrials)
    for c in bestClustering:
        names = ''
        for p in c.members():
            names += p.getName() + ', '
        print('\n' + names[:-2]) #remove trailing comma and space
        herbivores, carnivores, omnivores = 0, 0, 0
        for p in c.members():
            if p.getLabel() == '0':
                herbivores += 1
            elif p.getLabel() == '1':
                carnivores += 1
            else:
                omnivores += 1
        print(herbivores, 'herbivores,', carnivores, 'carnivores,',
              omnivores, 'omnivores')
```

Figure 23.13 Clustering animals

When we executed the code testTeeth(3, 40) it printed

```
Bear, Cow, Deer, Elk, Fur seal, Grey seal, Lion, Sea lion
3 herbivores, 4 carnivores, 1 omnivores

Badger, Cougar, Dog, Fox, Guinea pig, Human, Jaguar, Kangaroo, Mink,
Mole, Mouse, Pig, Porcupine, Rabbit, Raccoon, Rat, Red bat, Skunk,
Squirrel, Wolf, Woodchuck
4 herbivores, 9 carnivores, 8 omnivores

Moose
1 herbivores, 0 carnivores, 0 omnivores
```

So much for our conjecture that the clustering would be related to the eating habits of the various species. A cursory inspection suggests that we have a clustering totally dominated by the weights of the animals. The problem is that the range of weights is much larger than the range of any of the other features. Therefore, when the Euclidean distance between examples is computed, the only feature that truly matters is weight.

We encountered a similar problem in Section 22.2 when we found that the distance between animals was dominated by the number of legs. We solved the problem there by turning the number of legs into a binary feature (legged or legless). That was fine for that data set, because all of the animals happened to have either zero or four legs. Here, however, there is no obvious way to turn weight into a single binary feature without losing a great deal of information.

This is a common problem, which is often addressed by scaling the features so that each feature has a mean of 0 and a standard deviation of 1,[170] as done by the function zScaleFeatures in Figure 23.14. It's easy to see why the statement result = result - mean ensures that the mean of the returned array will always be close to 0.[171] That the standard deviation will always be 1 is not obvious. It can be shown by a long and tedious chain of algebraic manipulations, which we will not bore you with. This kind of scaling is often called **z-scaling** because the normal distribution is sometimes referred to as the Z-distribution.

Another common approach to scaling is to map the minimum feature value to 0, map the maximum feature value to 1, and use linear interpolation in between, as done by the function iScaleFeatures in Figure 23.14.

```
def zScaleFeatures(vals):
    """Assumes vals is a sequence of floats"""
    result = pylab.array(vals)
    mean = sum(result)/len(result)
    result = result - mean
    return result/stdDev(result)

def iScaleFeatures(vals):
    """Assumes vals is a sequence of floats"""
    minVal, maxVal = min(vals), max(vals)
    fit = pylab.polyfit([minVal, maxVal], [0, 1], 1)
    return pylab.polyval(fit, vals)
```

Figure 23.14 Scaling attributes

Figure 23.15 contains a version of readMammalData that allows scaling of features using the function bound to the parameter scale. Notice that it depends upon that fact that we collect all of the values for a single feature into a single vector. The version of the function testTeeth in Figure 23.15 supplies the scaling function used by readMammalData. When testTeeth is called with only two arguments, it calls readMammalData with the identity function, which is equivalent to doing no scaling.

---

[170] A normal distribution with a mean of 0 and a standard deviation of 1 is called a **standard normal distribution**.

[171] We say "close," because floating point numbers are only an approximation to the reals.

```
def readMammalData(fName, scale):
    Same code as in Figure 23.11

        #Produce featureVals, speciesNames, and labelList
        Same code as in Figure 23.11

        #Continue processing lines in file, starting after comments
        Same code as in Figure 23.11

        #Use featureVals to build list containing the feature vectors
        #for each mammal, scaling features as indicated
        for i in range(numFeatures):
            featureVals[i] = scale(featureVals[i])
        featureVectorList = []
        for mammal in range(len(speciesNames)):
            featureVector = []
            for feature in range(numFeatures):
                featureVector.append(featureVals[feature][mammal])
            featureVectorList.append(featureVector)
        return featureVectorList, labelList, speciesNames

def testTeeth(numClusters, numTrials, scale = lambda x: x):
    features, labels, species =\
             readMammalData('dentalFormulas.txt', scale)
    examples = buildMammalExamples(features, labels, species)

    ###Remainder of testTeeth is the same as in Figure 23.13###
```

Figure 23.15 Code that allows scaling of features

When we executed the code

```
random.seed(0) #so two clusterings starts with same seed
print('Clustering without scaling')
testTeeth(3, 40)
random.seed(0) #so two clusterings starts with same seed
print('\nClustering with z-scaling')
testTeeth(3, 40, zScaleFeatures)
print('\nClustering with i-scaling')
testTeeth(3, 40, iScaleFeatures)
```

it printed

```
Clustering without scaling

Bear, Cow, Deer, Elk, Fur seal, Grey seal, Lion, Sea lion
3 herbivores, 4 carnivores, 1 omnivores

Badger, Cougar, Dog, Fox, Guinea pig, Human, Jaguar, Kangaroo, Mink,
Mole, Mouse, Pig, Porcupine, Rabbit, Raccoon, Rat, Red bat, Skunk,
Squirrel, Wolf, Woodchuck
4 herbivores, 9 carnivores, 8 omnivores

Moose
1 herbivores, 0 carnivores, 0 omnivores

Clustering with z-scaling

Badger, Bear, Cougar, Dog, Fox, Fur seal, Grey seal, Human, Jaguar,
Lion, Mink, Mole, Pig, Raccoon, Red bat, Sea lion, Skunk, Wolf
0 herbivores, 13 carnivores, 5 omnivores

Guinea pig, Kangaroo, Mouse, Porcupine, Rabbit, Rat, Squirrel,
Woodchuck
4 herbivores, 0 carnivores, 4 omnivores

Cow, Deer, Elk, Moose
4 herbivores, 0 carnivores, 0 omnivores

Clustering with i-scaling

Cow, Deer, Elk, Moose
4 herbivores, 0 carnivores, 0 omnivores

Badger, Bear, Cougar, Dog, Fox, Fur seal, Grey seal, Human, Jaguar,
Lion, Mink, Mole, Pig, Raccoon, Red bat, Sea lion, Skunk, Wolf
0 herbivores, 13 carnivores, 5 omnivores

Guinea pig, Kangaroo, Mouse, Porcupine, Rabbit, Rat, Squirrel,
Woodchuck
4 herbivores, 0 carnivores, 4 omnivores
```

The clustering with scaling (the two methods of scaling yield the same clusters) does not perfectly partition the animals based upon their eating habits, but it is certainly correlated with what they eat. It does a good job of separating the carnivores from the herbivores, but there is no obvious pattern in where the omnivores appear. This suggests that perhaps features other than dentition and weight might be needed to separate omnivores from herbivores and carnivores.

24 CLASSIFICATION METHODS

The most common application of supervised machine learning is building classification models. A **classification model**, or classifier, is used to label an example as belonging to one of a finite set of categories. Deciding whether an email message is spam, for example, is a classification problem. In the literature, these categories are typically called **classes** (hence the name classification). Equivalently, one can describe an example as belonging to a class or a having **label**.

In **one-class learning**, the training set contains examples drawn from only one class. The goal is to learn a model that predicts whether an example belongs to that class. One-class learning is useful when it is difficult to find training examples that lie outside the class. One-class learning is frequently used for building anomaly detectors, e.g., detecting previously unseen kinds of attacks on a computer network.

In **two-class learning** (often called **binary classification**), the training set contains examples drawn from exactly two classes (typically called positive and negative), and the objective is to find a boundary that separates the two classes. **Multiclass learning** involves finding boundaries that separate more than two classes from each other.

In this chapter, we look at two widely used supervised learning methods for solving classification problems: k-nearest neighbors and regression. Before we do, we address the question of how to evaluate the classifiers produced by these methods.

24.1 Evaluating Classifiers

Those of you who read Chapter 18 might recall that part of that chapter addressed the question of choosing a degree for a linear regression that would 1) provide a reasonably good fit for the available data, and 2) have a reasonable chance of making good predictions about as yet unseen data. The same issues arise when using supervised machine learning to train a classifier.

We start by dividing our data into two sets, a training set and a **test set**. The training set is used to learn a model, and the test set is used to evaluate that model. When we train the classifier, we attempt to minimize **training error**, i.e., errors in classifying the examples in the training set, subject to certain constraints. The constraints are designed to increase the probability that the model will perform reasonably well on as yet unseen data. Let's look at this pictorially.

The chart on the left of Figure 24.1 shows a representation of voting patterns for sixty (simulated) American citizens. The x-axis is the distance of the voter's home from Boston, Massachusetts. The y-axis is the age of the voter. The stars indicate voters who usually vote Democratic, and the triangles voters who usually vote Republican. The chart on the right in Figure 24.1 shows a training set containing a randomly chosen sample of thirty of those voters. The solid and dashed lines show two possible boundaries between the two populations. For the model based on the solid line, points below the line are classified as Democratic voters. For the model based on the dotted line, points to the left of the line are classified as Democratic voters.

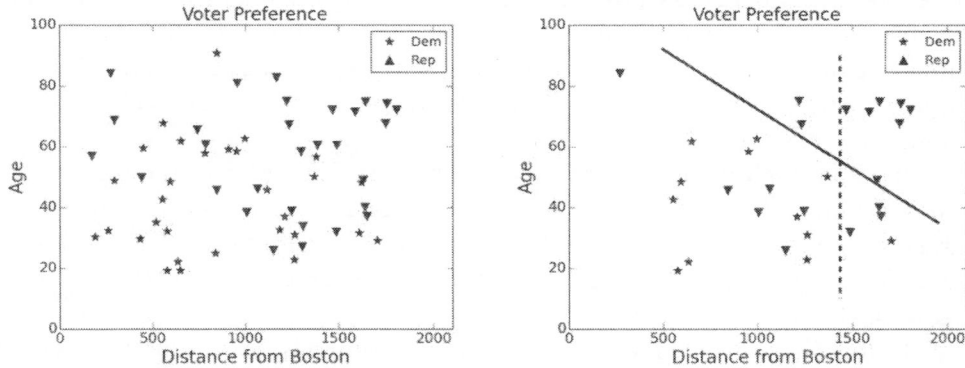

Figure 24.1 Plots of voter preferences

Neither boundary separates the training data perfectly. The training errors for the two models are shown in the **confusion matrices** in Figure 24.2. The top left corner of each shows the number of examples classified as Democratic that are actually Democratic, i.e., the true positives. The bottom left corner shows the number of examples classified as Democratic that are actually Republican, i.e., the false positives. The right-hand column shows the number of false negatives on the top and the number of true negatives on the bottom.

CHAPTER 24. CLASSIFICATION METHODS

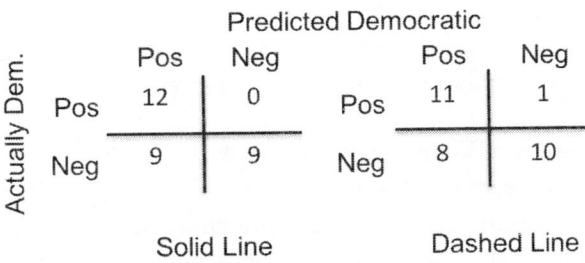

Figure 24.2 Confusion matrices

The **accuracy** of each classifier on the training data can be calculated as

$$accuracy = \frac{true\ positive + true\ negative}{true\ positive + true\ negative + false\ positive + false\ negative}$$

In this case, each classifier has an accuracy of 0.7. Which does a better job of fitting the training data? It depends upon whether one is more concerned about misclassifying Republicans as Democrats, or vice versa.

If we are willing to draw a more complex boundary, we can get a classifier that does a more accurate job of classifying the training data. The classifier pictured in Figure 24.3, for example, has an accuracy of about 0.83 on the training data, as depicted in the left plot of the figure. However, as we saw in our discussion of linear regression in Chapter 18, the more complicated the model, the higher the probability that it has been overfit to the training data. The right-hand plot in Figure 24.3 depicts what happens if we apply the complex model to the holdout set—the accuracy drops to 0.6.

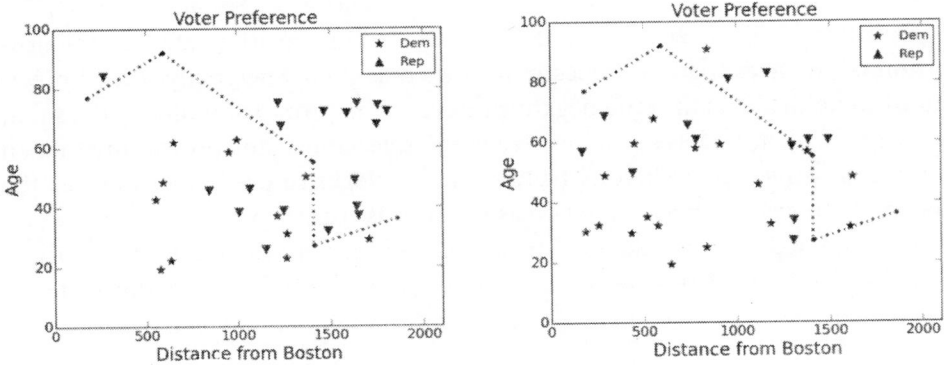

Figure 24.3 A more complex model

Accuracy is a reasonable way to evaluate a classifier when the two classes are of roughly equal size. It is a terrible way to evaluate a classifier when there is a large **class imbalance**. Imagine that you are charged with evaluating a classifier that predicts whether a person has a potentially fatal disease that occurs in about 0.1% of the population to be tested. Accuracy is not a particularly useful statistic, since 99.9% accuracy can be attained by merely declaring all patients disease-free. That classifier might seem great to those charged with paying for the treatment (nobody would get treated!), but it might not seem so great to those worried that they might have the disease.

Fortunately, there are statistics about classifiers that shed light when classes are imbalanced:

$$sensitivity = \frac{true\ positive}{true\ positive + false\ negative}$$

$$specificity = \frac{true\ negative}{true\ negative + false\ positive}$$

$$positive\ predictive\ value = \frac{true\ positive}{true\ positive + false\ positive}$$

$$negative\ predictive\ value = \frac{true\ negative}{true\ negative + false\ negative}$$

Sensitivity (called **recall** in some fields) is the true positive rate, i.e., the proportion of positives that are correctly identified as such. **Specificity** (called **precision** in some fields) is the true negative rate, i.e., the proportion of negatives that are correctly identified as such. **Positive predictive** value is the probability that an example classified as positive is truly positive. **Negative predictive** value is the probability that an example classified as negative is truly negative.

Implementations of these statistical measures and a function that uses them to generate some statistics are in Figure 24.4. We will use these functions later in this chapter.

```
def accuracy(truePos, falsePos, trueNeg, falseNeg):
    numerator = truePos + trueNeg
    denominator = truePos + trueNeg + falsePos + falseNeg
    return numerator/denominator

def sensitivity(truePos, falseNeg):
    try:
        return truePos/(truePos + falseNeg)
    except ZeroDivisionError:
        return float('nan')

def specificity(trueNeg, falsePos):
    try:
        return trueNeg/(trueNeg + falsePos)
    except ZeroDivisionError:
        return float('nan')

def posPredVal(truePos, falsePos):
    try:
        return truePos/(truePos + falsePos)
    except ZeroDivisionError:
        return float('nan')

def negPredVal(trueNeg, falseNeg):
    try:
        return trueNeg/(trueNeg + falseNeg)
    except ZeroDivisionError:
        return float('nan')

def getStats(truePos, falsePos, trueNeg, falseNeg, toPrint = True):
    accur = accuracy(truePos, falsePos, trueNeg, falseNeg)
    sens = sensitivity(truePos, falseNeg)
    spec = specificity(trueNeg, falsePos)
    ppv = posPredVal(truePos, falsePos)
    if toPrint:
        print(' Accuracy =', round(accur, 3))
        print(' Sensitivity =', round(sens, 3))
        print(' Specificity =', round(spec, 3))
        print(' Pos. Pred. Val. =', round(ppv, 3))
    return (accur, sens, spec, ppv)
```

Figure 24.4 Functions for evaluating classifiers

24.2 Predicting the Gender of Runners

Earlier in this book, we used data from the Boston Marathon to illustrate a number of statistical concepts. We will now use the same data to illustrate the application of various classification methods. The task is to predict the gender of a runner given the runner's age and finishing time.

The code in Figure 24.5 reads in the data from a file by calling the function getBMData defined in Figure 17.2, and then builds a set of examples. Each example is an instance of class Runner. Each runner has a label (gender) and a feature vector (age and finishing time). The only interesting method in Runner is featureDist. It returns the Euclidean distance between the feature vectors of two runners.

The next step is to split the examples into a training set and a held-out test set. As is frequently done, we use 80% of the data for training, and test on the remaining 20%. This is done using the function divide80_20 at the bottom of Figure 24.5. Notice that we select the training data at random. It would have taken less code to simply select the first 80% of the data, but that runs the risk of not being representative of the set as a whole. If the file had been sorted by finishing time, for example, we would get a training set biased towards the better runners.

We are now ready to look at different ways of using the training set to build a classifier that predicts the gender of a runner. Inspection reveals that 58% of the runners in the training set are male. So, if we guess male all the time, we should expect an accuracy of 58%. Keep this baseline in mind when looking at the performance of more sophisticated classification algorithms.

24.3 K-nearest Neighbors

K-nearest neighbors (KNN) is probably the simplest of all classification algorithms. The "learned" model is simply the training examples themselves. New examples are assigned a label based on how similar they are to examples in the training data.

CHAPTER 24. CLASSIFICATION METHODS

```python
class Runner(object):
    def __init__(self, gender, age, time):
        self.featureVec = (age, time)
        self.label = gender

    def featureDist(self, other):
        dist = 0.0
        for i in range(len(self.featureVec)):
            dist += abs(self.featureVec[i] - other.featureVec[i])**2
        return dist**0.5

    def getTime(self):
        return self.featureVec[1]
    def getAge(self):
        return self.featureVec[0]
    def getLabel(self):
        return self.label
    def getFeatures(self):
        return self.featureVec

    def __str__(self):
        return str(self.getAge()) + ', ' + str(self.getTime())\
               + ', ' + self.label

def buildMarathonExamples(fileName):
    data = getBMData(fileName)
    examples = []
    for i in range(len(data['age'])):
        a = Runner(data['gender'][i], data['age'][i],
                   data['time'][i])
        examples.append(a)
    return examples

def divide80_20(examples):
    sampleIndices = random.sample(range(len(examples)),
                                  len(examples)//5)
    trainingSet, testSet = [], []
    for i in range(len(examples)):
        if i in sampleIndices:
            testSet.append(examples[i])
        else:
            trainingSet.append(examples[i])
    return trainingSet, testSet
```

Figure 24.5 Build examples and divide data into training and test sets

Imagine that you and a friend are strolling through the park and spot a bird. You believe that it is a yellow-throated woodpecker, but your friend is pretty sure that it is a golden-green woodpecker. You rush home and dig out your cache of bird books (or, if you are under 35, go to your favorite search engine) and start looking at labeled pictures of birds. Think of these labeled pictures as the training set. None of the pictures is an exact match for the bird you saw, so you settle for selecting the five that look the most like the bird you saw (the five "nearest neighbors"). The majority of them are photos of a yellow-throated woodpecker—you declare victory.

A weakness of KNN classifiers is that they often give poor results when there is a large class imbalance. If the frequency of pictures of bird species in the book is the same as the frequency of that species in your neighborhood, KNN will probably work well. Suppose, however, that despite the species being equally common, your books contain 30 pictures of yellow-throated woodpeckers and only one of a golden-green woodpecker. If a simple majority vote is used to determine the classification, the yellow-throated woodpecker will be chosen even if the photos don't look much like the bird you saw. This problem can be mitigated by using a more complicated voting scheme in which the k-nearest neighbors are weighted based on their similarity to the example being classified.

The functions in Figure 24.6 implement a k-nearest neighbors classifier that predicts the gender of a runner based on the runner's age and finishing time. The implementation is brute force. The function findKNearest is linear in the number of examples in exampleSet, since it computes the feature distance between example and each element in exampleSet. The function kNearestClassify uses a simple majority-voting scheme to do the classification. The complexity of kNearestClassify is O(len(training)*len(testSet)), since it calls the function findNearest a total of len(testSet) times.

When the code

```
examples = buildMarathonExamples('bm_results2012.txt')
training, testSet = divide80_20(examples)
truePos, falsePos, trueNeg, falseNeg =\
        kNearestClassify(training, testSet, 'M', 9)
getStats(truePos, falsePos, trueNeg, falseNeg)
```

was run, it printed

```
Accuracy = 0.65
Sensitivity = 0.715
Specificity = 0.563
Pos. Pred. Val. = 0.684
```

```python
def findKNearest(example, exampleSet, k):
    kNearest, distances = [], []
    #Build lists containing first k examples and their distances
    for i in range(k):
        kNearest.append(exampleSet[i])
        distances.append(example.featureDist(exampleSet[i]))
    maxDist = max(distances) #Get maximum distance
    #Look at examples not yet considered
    for e in exampleSet[k:]:
        dist = example.featureDist(e)
        if dist < maxDist:
            #replace farther neighbor by this one
            maxIndex = distances.index(maxDist)
            kNearest[maxIndex] = e
            distances[maxIndex] = dist
            maxDist = max(distances)
    return kNearest, distances

def KNearestClassify(training, testSet, label, k):
    """Assumes training and testSet lists of examples, k an int
       Uses a k-nearest neighbor classifier to predict
          whether each example in testSet has the given label
       Returns number of true positives, false positives,
          true negatives, and false negatives"""
    truePos, falsePos, trueNeg, falseNeg = 0, 0, 0, 0
    for e in testSet:
        nearest, distances = findKNearest(e, training, k)
        #conduct vote
        numMatch = 0
        for i in range(len(nearest)):
            if nearest[i].getLabel() == label:
                numMatch += 1
        if numMatch > k//2: #guess label
            if e.getLabel() == label:
                truePos += 1
            else:
                falsePos += 1
        else: #guess not label
            if e.getLabel() != label:
                trueNeg += 1
            else:
                falseNeg += 1
    return truePos, falsePos, trueNeg, falseNeg
```

Figure 24.6 Finding the k-nearest neighbors

Should we be pleased that we can predict gender with 65% accuracy given age and finishing time? One way to evaluate a classifier is to compare it to a classifier that doesn't even look at age and finishing time. The classifier in Figure 24.7 first uses the examples in training to estimate the probability of a randomly chosen example in testSet being from class label. Using this prior probability, it then randomly assigns a label to each example in testSet.

When we test prevalenceClassify on the same Boston Marathon data on which we tested KNN, it prints

```
Accuracy = 0.514
Sensitivity = 0.593
Specificity = 0.41
Pos. Pred. Val. = 0.57
```

indicating that we are reaping a considerable advantage from considering age and finishing time.

That advantage has a cost. If you run the code in Figure 24.6, you will notice that it takes a rather long time to finish. There are 17,233 training examples and 4,308 test examples, so there are nearly 75 million distances calculated. This raises the question of whether we really need to use all of the training examples. Let's see what happens if we simply **down sample** the training data by a factor of 10. If we run

```
reducedTraining = random.sample(training, len(training)//10)
truePos, falsePos, trueNeg, falseNeg =\
        KNearestClassify(reducedTraining, testSet, 'M', 9)
getStats(truePos, falsePos, trueNeg, falseNeg)
```

it completes in one-tenth the time, with little change in classification performance:

```
Accuracy = 0.643
Sensitivity = 0.726
Specificity = 0.534
Pos. Pred. Val. = 0.673
```

In practice, when people apply KNN to large data sets they do down sample the training data.[172]

---

[172] They often use more sophisticated methods than random choice in constructing the sample.

```
def prevalenceClassify(training, testSet, label):
    """Assumes training and testSet lists of examples
       Uses a prevalence-based classifier to predict
          whether each example in testSet is of class label
       Returns number of true positives, false positives,
          true negatives, and false negatives"""
    numWithLabel = 0
    for e in training:
        if e.getLabel()== label:
            numWithLabel += 1
    probLabel = numWithLabel/len(training)
    truePos, falsePos, trueNeg, falseNeg = 0, 0, 0, 0
    for e in testSet:
        if random.random() < probLabel: #guess label
            if e.getLabel() == label:
                truePos += 1
            else:
                falsePos += 1
        else: #guess not label
            if e.getLabel() != label:
                trueNeg += 1
            else:
                falseNeg += 1
    return truePos, falsePos, trueNeg, falseNeg
```

Figure 24.7 Prevalence-based classifier

In the above experiments, we set k to 9. We did not choose this number for its role in science (the number of planets in our solar system),[173] its religious significance (the number of forms of the Hindu goddess Durga), or its sociological importance (the number of hitters in a baseball lineup). Instead, we learned k from the training data by using the code in Figure 24.8 to search for a good k.

The outer loop tests a sequence of values for k. We test only odd values to ensure that when the vote is taken in kNearestClassify there will always be a majority for one gender or the other.

The inner loop tests each value of k using **n-fold cross validation**. In each of the numFolds iterations of the loop, the original training set is split into a new training set/test set pair. We then compute the accuracy of classifying the new test set using k-nearest neighbors and the new training set. When we exit the inner loop, we calculate the average accuracy of the numFolds folds.

---

[173] Some of us still believe in planet Pluto.

```
def findK(training, minK, maxK, numFolds, label):
    #Find average accuracy for range of odd values of k
    accuracies = []
    for k in range(minK, maxK + 1, 2):
        score = 0.0
        for i in range(numFolds):
            #downsample to reduce computation time
            fold = random.sample(training, min(5000, len(training)))
            examples, testSet = divide80_20(fold)
            truePos, falsePos, trueNeg, falseNeg =\
                 KNearestClassify(examples, testSet, label, k)
            score += accuracy(truePos, falsePos, trueNeg, falseNeg)
        accuracies.append(score/numFolds)
    pylab.plot(range(minK, maxK + 1, 2), accuracies)
    pylab.title('Average Accuracy vs k (' + str(numFolds)\
               + ' folds)')
    pylab.xlabel('k')
    pylab.ylabel('Accuracy')

findK(training, 1, 21, 1, 'M')
```

Figure 24.8 Searching for a good k

When we ran the code, it produced the plot in Figure 24.9. As we can see, 17 was the value of k that led to the best accuracy across 5 folds. Of course, there is no guarantee that some value larger than 21 might not have been even better. However, once k reached 9, the accuracy fluctuated over a reasonably narrow range, so we chose to use 9.

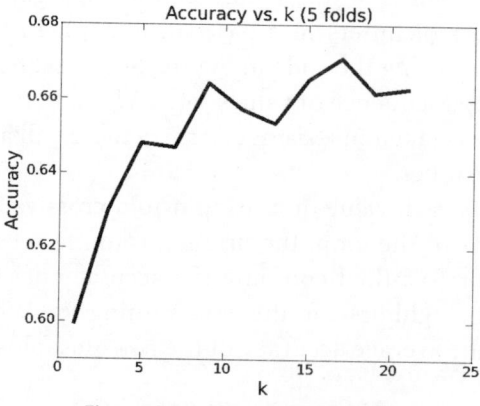

Figure 24.9 Choosing a value for k

24.4 Regression-based Classifiers

In Chapter 18 we used linear regression to build models of data. We do the same thing here, and use the training data to build separate models for the men and the women. The plot in Figure 24.11 was produced by the code in Figure 24.10.

```
#Build training sets for men and women
ageM, ageW, timeM, timeW = [], [], [], []
for e in training:
    if e.getLabel() == 'M':
        ageM.append(e.getAge())
        timeM.append(e.getTime())
    else:
        ageW.append(e.getAge())
        timeW.append(e.getTime())
#downsample to make plot of examples readable
ages, times = [], []
for i in random.sample(range(len(ageM)), 300):
    ages.append(ageM[i])
    times.append(timeM[i])
#Produce scatter plot of examples
pylab.plot(ages, times, 'yo', markersize = 6, label = 'Men')
ages, times = [], []
for i in random.sample(range(len(ageW)), 300):
    ages.append(ageW[i])
    times.append(timeW[i])
pylab.plot(ages, times, 'k^', markersize = 6, label = 'Women')
#Learn two first-degree linear regression models
mModel = pylab.polyfit(ageM, timeM, 1)
fModel = pylab.polyfit(ageW, timeW, 1)
#Plot lines corresponding to models
xmin, xmax = 15, 85
pylab.plot((xmin, xmax), (pylab.polyval(mModel,(xmin, xmax))),
           'k', label = 'Men')
pylab.plot((xmin, xmax), (pylab.polyval(fModel,(xmin, xmax))),
           'k--', label = 'Women')
pylab.title('Linear Regression Models')
pylab.xlabel('Age')
pylab.ylabel('Finishing time (minutes)')
pylab.legend()
```

Figure 24.10 Produce and plot linear regression models

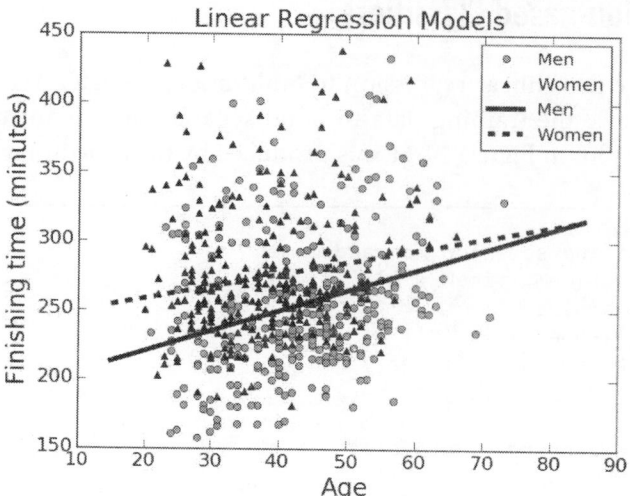

Figure 24.11 Linear regression models for men and women

A quick glance at Figure 24.11 is enough to see that the linear regression models explain only a small amount of the variance in the data.[174] Nevertheless, it is possible to use these models to build a classifier. Each model attempts to capture the relationship between age and finishing time. This relationship is different for men and women, a fact we can exploit in building a classifier. Given an example, we ask whether the relationship between age and finishing time is closer to the relationship predicted by the model for male runners (the solid line) or to the model for female runners (the dashed line). This idea is implemented in Figure 24.12.

When the code is run, it prints

```
Accuracy = 0.616
Sensitivity = 0.682
Specificity = 0.529
Pos. Pred. Val. = 0.657
```

The results are better than random, but a bit worse than for KNN.

---

[174] Though we fit the models to the entire training set, we choose to plot only a small subset of the training points. When we plotted all of them, the result was a blob in which it was hard to see any useful detail.

CHAPTER 24. CLASSIFICATION METHODS

```
truePos, falsePos, trueNeg, falseNeg = 0, 0, 0, 0
for e in testSet:
    age = e.getAge()
    time = e.getTime()
    if abs(time - pylab.polyval(mModel,age)) <\
       abs(time - pylab.polyval(fModel, age)):
        if e.getLabel() == 'M':
            truePos += 1
        else:
            falsePos += 1
    else:
        if e.getLabel() == 'F':
            trueNeg += 1
        else:
            falseNeg += 1
getStats(truePos, falsePos, trueNeg, falseNeg)
```

Figure 24.12 Using linear regression to build a classifier

You might be wondering why we took this indirect approach to using linear regression, rather than explicitly building a model using some function of age and time as the dependent variable and real numbers (say 0 for female and 1 for male) as the dependent variable.

We could easily build such a model using polyfit to map a function of age and time to a real number. However, what would it mean to predict that some runner is halfway between male and female? Were there some hermaphrodites in the race? Perhaps we can interpret the y-axis as the probability that a runner is male. Not really. There is not even a guarantee that applying polyval to the model will return a value between 0 and 1.

Fortunately, there is a form of regression, **logistic regression**,[175] designed explicitly for predicting the probability of an event. The Python library sklearn[176] provides a good implementation of logistic regression and of many other useful functions and classes related to machine learning.

The module sklearn.linear_model contains the class LogisticRegression. The __init__ method of this class has a large number of parameters that control

---

[175] It's called logistic regression because the optimization problem being solved involves an objective function based on the log of an odds ratio. Such functions are called logit functions, and their inverses are call logistic functions.
[176] This toolkit comes preinstalled with some Python IDE's, e.g., Anaconda. To learn more about this library and find out out how to install it, go to http://scikit-learn.org.

things such as the optimization algorithm used to solve the regression equation. They all have default values, and on most occasions it is fine to stick with those.

The central method of class `LogisticRegression` is `fit`. The method takes as arguments two sequences (tuples, lists, or arrays) of the same length. The first is a sequence of feature vectors and the second a sequence of the corresponding labels. In the literature, these labels are typically called **outcomes**.

The `fit` method returns an object of type `LogisticRegression` for which coefficients have been learned for each feature in the feature vector. These coefficients, often called **feature weights**, capture the relationship between the feature and the outcome. A positive feature weight implies that there is a positive correlation between the feature and the outcome, and a negative feature weight implies a negative correlation. The absolute magnitude of the weight is related to the strength of the correlation.[177] The values of these weights can be accessed using the `coef_` attribute of `LogisticRegression`. Since it is possible to train a `LogisticRegression` object on multiple outcomes (called classes in the documentation for the package), the value of `coef_` is a sequence in which each element contains the sequence of weights associated with a single outcome. So, for example, the expression `model.coef[1][0]` denotes the value of the coefficient of the first feature for the second outcome.

Once the coefficients have been learned, the method `predict_proba` of the `LogisticRegression` class can be used to predict the outcome associated with a feature vector. The method `predict_proba` takes a single argument (in addition to `self`), a sequence of feature vectors. It returns an array of arrays, one per feature vector. Each element in the returned array contains a prediction for the corresponding feature vector. The reason that the prediction is an array is that it contains a probability for each label used in building `model`.

The code in Figure 24.13 contains a simple illustration of how this all works. It first creates a list of 100,000 examples, each of which has a feature vector of length 2 and is labeled either 'A', 'B', 'C', or 'D'. The first two feature values for each example are drawn from a Gaussian with a standard deviation of 0.5, but the means vary depending upon the label. The value of third feature is chosen at random, and therefore should not be useful in predicting the label. After creating the examples, the code generates a logistic regression model, prints the feature weights, and finally the probabilities associated with four examples.

---

[177] This relationship is complcated by the fact that features are often correlated with each other. For example, age and finishing time are positively correlated. When features are correlated, the magnitudes of the weights are not independent of each other.

CHAPTER 24. CLASSIFICATION METHODS

```
import sklearn.linear_model

featureVecs, labels = [], []
for i in range(25000): #create 4 examples in each iteration
    featureVecs.append([random.gauss(0, 0.5), random.gauss(0, 0.5),
                        random.random()])
    labels.append('A')
    featureVecs.append([random.gauss(0, 0.5), random.gauss(2, 0.),
                        random.random()])
    labels.append('B')
    featureVecs.append([random.gauss(2, 0.5), random.gauss(0, 0.5),
                        random.random()])
    labels.append('C')
    featureVecs.append([random.gauss(2, 0.5), random.gauss(2, 0.5),
                        random.random()])
    labels.append('D')
model = sklearn.linear_model.LogisticRegression().fit(featureVecs,
                                                      labels)
print('model.classes_ =', model.classes_)
for i in range(len(model.coef_)):
    print('For label', model.classes_[i],
          'feature weights =', model.coef_[i])
print('[0, 0] probs =', model.predict_proba([[0, 0, 1]])[0])
print('[0, 2] probs =', model.predict_proba([[0, 2, 2]])[0])
print('[2, 0] probs =', model.predict_proba([[2, 0, 3]])[0])
print('[2, 2] probs =', model.predict_proba([[2, 2, 4]])[0])
```

Figure 24.13 Using sklearn to do multi-class logistic regression

When the code in Figure 24.13 was run, it printed

```
model.classes_ = ['A' 'B' 'C' 'D']
For label A feature weights =  [-4.65720783 -4.38351299 -0.00722845]
For label B feature weights =  [-5.17036683  5.82391837  0.04706108]
For label C feature weights =  [ 3.95940539 -3.97854738 -0.04480206]
For label D feature weights =  [ 4.37529465  5.40639909 -0.09434664]
[0, 0] probs = [  9.90019074e-01   4.66294343e-04   9.51434182e-03
   2.90294956e-07]
[0, 2] probs = [  8.72562747e-03   9.78468475e-01   3.18006160e-06
   1.28027180e-02]
[2, 0] probs = [  5.22466887e-03   1.69995686e-08   9.93218655e-01
   1.55665885e-03]
[2, 2] probs = [  7.88542473e-07   1.97601741e-03   7.99527347e-03
   9.90027921e-01]
```

Let's look first at the feature weights. The first line tells us that the first two features have roughly the same weight and are negatively correlated with the probability of an example having label 'A'.[178] I.e., the larger the value of the first two features, the less likely that the example is of type 'A'. The third feature, which we expect to have little value in predicting the label, has a small value relative to the other two values, indicating that it is relatively unimportant. The second line tells us that the probability of an example having the label 'B' is negatively correlated with value of the first feature, but positively with the second feature. Again, the third feature has a relatively small value. The third and four lines are mirror images of the first two lines.

Now, let's look at the probabilities associated with the four examples. The order of the probabilities corresponds to the order of the outcomes in the attribute model.classes_. As you would hope, when we predict the label associated with the feature vector [0, 0], 'A' has a very high probability and 'D' a very low probability. Similarly, [2, 2] has a very high probability for 'D' and a very low one for 'A'. The probabilities associated with the middle two examples are also as expected.

The example in Figure 24.14 is similar to the one in Figure 24.13, except that we create examples of only two classes, 'A' and 'D', and don't include the irrelevant third feature.

```
featureVecs, labels = [], []
for i in range(20000):
    featureVecs.append([random.gauss(0, 0.5), random.gauss(0, 0.5)])
    labels.append('A')
    featureVecs.append([random.gauss(2, 0.5), random.gauss(2, 0.5)])
    labels.append('D')
model = sklearn.linear_model.LogisticRegression().fit(featureVecs,
                                                      labels)
print('model.coef =', model.coef_)
print('[0, 0] probs =', model.predict_proba([[0, 0]])[0])
print('[0, 2] probs =', model.predict_proba([[0, 2]])[0])
print('[2, 0] probs =', model.predict_proba([[2, 0]])[0])
print('[2, 2] probs =', model.predict_proba([[2, 2]])[0])
```

Figure 24.14 Example of two-class logistic regression

---

[178] The slight difference in the absolute values of the weights is attributable to the fact that our sample size is finite.

CHAPTER 24. CLASSIFICATION METHODS

When we run the code in Figure 24.14 it printed

```
model.coef = [[ 5.79284554  5.68893473]]
[0, 0] probs = [  9.99988836e-01   1.11643397e-05]
[0, 2] probs = [  0.50622598   0.49377402]
[2, 0] probs = [  0.45439797   0.54560203]
[2, 2] probs = [  9.53257749e-06   9.99990467e-01]
```

Notice that there is only one set of weights in coef_. When fit is used to produce a model for a binary classifier, it only produces weights for one label. This is sufficient because once proba has calculated the probability of an example being in either of the classes, the probability of it being in the other class is determined—since the probabilities must add up to 1. To which of the two labels do the weights in coef_ correspond? Since the weights are negative, they must correspond to 'D', since we know that the larger the values in the feature vector, the more likely the example is of class 'D'. Traditionally, binary classification uses the labels 0 and 1, and the classifier uses the weights for 1. In this case, coef_ contains the weights associated with largest label, as defined by the > operator for type str.

Let's return to the Boston Marathon example. The code in Figure 24.15 uses the LogisticRegression class to build and test a model for our Boston Marathon data. The function applyModel takes four arguments:

- model: an object of type LogisticRegression for which a fit has been constructed
- testSet: a sequence of examples. The examples have the same kinds of features and labels used in constructing the fit for model.
- label: The label of the positive class. The confusion matrix information returned by applyModel is relative to this label.
- prob: the probability threshold to be used in deciding which label to assign to an example in testSet. The default value is 0.5. Because it is not a constant, applyModel can be used to investigate the tradeoff between false positives and false negatives.

The implementation of applyModel first uses list comprehension (Section 5.3.2) to build a list whose elements are the feature vectors of the examples in testSet. It then calls model.predict_proba to get an array of pairs corresponding to the prediction for each feature vector. Finally, it compares the prediction against the label associated with the example with that feature vector, and keeps track of and returns the number of true positives, false positives, true negatives, and false negatives.

```
def applyModel(model, testSet, label, prob = 0.5):
    #Create vector containing feature vectors for all test examples
    testFeatureVecs = [e.getFeatures() for e in testSet]
    probs = model.predict_proba(testFeatureVecs)
    truePos, falsePos, trueNeg, falseNeg = 0, 0, 0, 0
    for i in range(len(probs)):
        if probs[i][1] > prob:
            if testSet[i].getLabel() == label:
                truePos += 1
            else:
                falsePos += 1
        else:
            if testSet[i].getLabel() != label:
                trueNeg += 1
            else:
                falseNeg += 1
    return truePos, falsePos, trueNeg, falseNeg

examples = buildMarathonExamples('bm_results2012.txt')
training, test = divide80_20(examples)

featureVecs, labels = [], []
for e in training:
    featureVecs.append([e.getAge(), e.getTime()])
    labels.append(e.getLabel())
model = sklearn.linear_model.LogisticRegression().fit(featureVecs,
                                                      labels)
print('Feature weights for label M:',
      'age =', str(round(model.coef_[0][0], 3)) + ',',
      'time =', round(model.coef_[0][1], 3))
truePos, falsePos, trueNeg, falseNeg = \
                    applyModel(model, test, 'M', 0.5)
getStats(truePos, falsePos, trueNeg, falseNeg)
```

Figure 24.15 Use logistic regression to predict Gender

When the code is run, it prints

```
Feature weights for label M: age = 0.055, time = -0.011
 Accuracy = 0.635
 Sensitivity = 0.831
 Specificity = 0.377
 Pos. Pred. Val. = 0.638
```

CHAPTER 24. CLASSIFICATION METHODS

Let's compare these results to what we got when we used KNN:

```
Accuracy = 0.65
Sensitivity = 0.715
Specificity = 0.563
Pos. Pred. Val. = 0.684
```

The accuracies and positive predictive values are similar, but logistic regression has a much higher sensitivity and a much lower specificity. That makes the two methods hard to compare. We can address this problem by adjusting the probability threshold used by applyModel so that it has approximately the same sensitivity as KNN. We can find that probability by iterating over values of prob until we get a sensitivity close to that we got using KNN.

If we call applyModel with prob = 0.578 instead of 0.5, we get the results

```
Accuracy = 0.659
Sensitivity = 0.714
Specificity = 0.586
Pos. Pred. Val. = 0.695
```

I.e., the models have similar performance.

Since it is easy to explore the ramifications of changing the decision threshold for a linear regression model, people often use something called the **receiver operating characteristic curve**,[179] or **ROC curve** to visualize the tradeoff between sensitivity and specificity. The curve plots the true positive rate (sensitivity) against the false positive rate (1 − specificity) for multiple decision thresholds.

ROC curves are often compared to one another by computing the area under the curve (**AUROC**). This area is equal to the probability that the model will assign a higher probability of being positive to a randomly chosen positive example than to a randomly chosen negative example. This is known as the **discrimination** of the model. It is important to keep in mind that discrimination says nothing about the accuracy, often called the **calibration**, of the probabilities. One could, for example, divide all of the estimated probabilities by 2 without changing the discrimination—but it would certainly change the accuracy of the estimates.

The code in Figure 24.16 plots the ROC curve for the logistic regression classifier as a solid line, Figure 24.17. The dotted line is the ROC for a random classifier—a classifier that chooses the label randomly. We could have computed the AUROC by first interpolating (because we have only a discrete number of points)

---

[179] It is called the "receiver operating characteristic" for historical reasons. It was first developed during World War II as way to evaluate the operating characteristics of devices receiving radar signals.

and then integrating the ROC curve, but we got lazy and simply called the function `sklearn.metrics.auc`.

```
def buildROC(model, testSet, label, title, plot = True):
    xVals, yVals = [], []
    p = 0.0
    while p <= 1.0:
        truePos, falsePos, trueNeg, falseNeg =\
                            applyModel(model, testSet, label, p)
        xVals.append(1.0 - specificity(trueNeg, falsePos))
        yVals.append(sensitivity(truePos, falseNeg))
        p += 0.01
    auroc = sklearn.metrics.auc(xVals, yVals, True)
    if plot:
        pylab.plot(xVals, yVals)
        pylab.plot([0,1], [0,1,], '--')
        pylab.title(title + ' (AUROC = '\
                    + str(round(auroc, 3)) + ')')
        pylab.xlabel('1 - Specificity')
        pylab.ylabel('Sensitivity')
    return auroc

buildROC(model, test, 'M', 'ROC for Predicting Gender')
```

Figure 24.16 Construct ROC curve and find AUROC

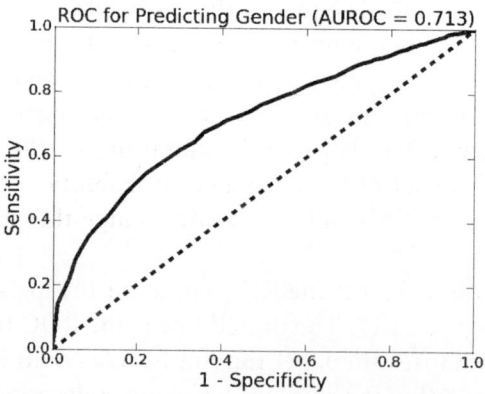

Figure 24.17 ROC curve and AUROC

Finger exercise: Write code to plot the ROC curve and compute the AUROC when the model built in Figure 24.15 is tested on 200 randomly chosen competi-

CHAPTER 24. CLASSIFICATION METHODS

tors. Use that code to investigate the impact of the number of training examples (try varying it from 10 to 1010 in increments of 50) on the AUROC.

24.5 Surviving the Titanic

On the morning of April 15, 1912, the RMS Titanic hit an iceberg and sank in the North Atlantic. Of the roughly 1,300 passengers on board, 832 perished in the disaster. There were many factors contributing to the disaster, including navigational error, inadequate lifeboats, and the slow response of a nearby ship. Whether or not individual passengers survived had an element of randomness, but was far from completely random. In fact, it is possible to make a reasonably good model for predicting survival using information from the ship's passenger manifest.

In this section, we build a classification model from a data set containing information for 1046 passengers.[180] Each line of the file contains information about a single passenger: cabin class (1st, 2nd, or 3rd), age, gender, whether the passenger survived the disaster, and the passenger's name.

We build the model using logistic regression. We chose to use logistic regression because

- It is the most commonly used classification method.
- By examining the weights produced by logistic regression we can gain some insight into why some passengers were more likely to have survived than others.

Figure 24.18 defines class `Passenger`. The only thing of interest in this code is the encoding of cabin class. Though the file encodes the cabin class as a integer, it is really shorthand for a category. Cabin classes do not behave like numbers, e.g., a first class cabin plus a second class cabin does not equal a third class cabin. We encode cabin class using three binary features (one per possible cabin class). For each passenger, exactly one of these variables is set to 1, and the other two are set to 0.

This is an example of an issue that frequently arises in machine learning. Categorical (sometimes called nominal) features are the natural way to describe many things, e.g., the home country of a runner. It's easy to replace these by integers, e.g., we could choose a representation for countries based on their ISO

---

[180] The data was extracted from a data set constructed by R.J. Dawson, and used in "The 'Unusual Episode' Data Revisted," *Journal of Statistics Education*, v. 3, n. 3, 1995.

3166-1 numeric code,[181] e.g., 076 for Brazil, 826 for the United Kingdom, and 862 for Venezuela. The problem with doing this is that the regression will treat these as numerical variables, thus using a nonsensical ordering on the countries in which Venezuela would be closer to the UK than it is to Brazil.

This problem can be avoided by converting categorical variables to binary variables, as we did with cabin class. One potential problem with doing this is that it can lead to very long and sparse feature vectors. For example, if a hospital dispenses 2000 different drugs, we would convert one categorical variable into 2000 binary variables, one for each drug.

```
class Passenger(object):
    features = ('C1', 'C2', 'C3', 'age', 'male gender')
    def __init__(self, pClass, age, gender, survived, name):
        self.name = name
        self.featureVec = [0, 0, 0, age, gender]
        self.featureVec[pClass - 1] = 1
        self.label = survived
        self.cabinClass = pClass
    def distance(self, other):
        return minkowskiDist(self.veatureVec, other.featureVec, 2)
    def getClass(self):
        return self.cabinClass
    def getAge(self):
        return self.featureVec[3]
    def getGender(self):
        return self.featureVec[4]
    def getName(self):
        return self.name
    def getFeatures(self):
        return self.featureVec[:]
    def getLabel(self):
        return self.label
```

Figure 24.18 Class Passenger

Figure 24.19 contains code that reads the data from a file and builds a set of examples from the data about the Titanic.

---

[181] ISO 3166-1 numeric is part of the ISO 3166 standard published by the International Organization for Standardization.

CHAPTER 24. CLASSIFICATION METHODS

```python
def testModels(examples, numTrials, printStats, printWeights):
    survived = 1 #value of label indicating survived
    stats, weights = [], [[], [], [], [], []]
    for i in range(numTrials):
        training, testSet = divide80_20(examples)
        featureVecs, labels = [], []
        for e in training:
            featureVecs.append(e.getFeatures())
            labels.append(e.getLabel())
        featureVecs = pylab.array(featureVecs)
        labels = pylab.array(labels)
        model =\
           sklearn.linear_model.LogisticRegression().fit(featureVecs,
                                                         labels)
        for i in range(len(Passenger.features)):
            weights[i].append(model.coef_[0][i])
        truePos, falsePos, trueNeg, falseNeg =\
                    applyModel(model, testSet, survived, 0.5)
        auroc = buildROC(model, testSet, survived, None, False)
        tmp = getStats(truePos, falsePos, trueNeg, falseNeg, False)
        stats.append(tmp + (auroc,))
    print('Averages for', numTrials, 'trials')
    if printWeights:
        for feature in range(len(weights)):
            featureMean = sum(weights[feature])/numTrials
            featureStd = stdDev(weights[feature])
            print(' Mean weight of', Passenger.features[feature],
                '=', str(round(featureMean, 3)) + ',',
                '95% confidence interval =', round(1.96*featureStd, 3))
    if printStats:
        summarizeStats(stats)
```

Figure 24.19 Read Titanic data and build list of example

Now that we have the data, we can build a logistic regression model using the same code we used to build a model of the Boston Marathon data. However, because the data set has a relatively small number of examples, we need to be concerned about using the evaluation method we employed earlier. It is entirely possible to get an unrepresentative 80-20 split of the data, and then generate misleading results.

To ameliorate the risk, we create many different 80-20 splits (each split is created using the divide80_20 function defined in Figure 24.5), build and evaluate a classifier for each, and then report mean values and 95% confidence intervals, using the code in Figure 24.20 and Figure 24.21.

```python
def testModels(examples, numTrials, printStats, printWeights):
    stats, weights = [], [[], [], [], [], []]
    for i in range(numTrials):
        training, testSet = divide80_20(examples)
        xVals, yVals = [], []
        for e in training:
            xVals.append(e.getFeatures())
            yVals.append(e.getLabel())
        xVals = pylab.array(xVals)
        yVals = pylab.array(yVals)
        model = sklearn.linear_model.LogisticRegression().fit(xVals,
                                                              yVals)
        for i in range(len(Passenger.features)):
            weights[i].append(model.coef_[0][i])
        truePos, falsePos, trueNeg, falseNeg =\
                      applyModel(model, testSet, 1, 0.5)
        auroc = buildROC(model, testSet, 1, None, False)
        tmp = getStats(truePos, falsePos, trueNeg, falseNeg, False)
        stats.append(tmp + (auroc,))
    print('Averages for', numTrials, 'trials')
    if printWeights:
        for feature in range(len(weights)):
            featureMean = sum(weights[feature])/numTrials
            featureStd = stdDev(weights[feature])
            print(' Mean weight of', Passenger.features[feature],
                '=', str(round(featureMean, 3)) + ',',
                '95% confidence interval =', round(1.96*featureStd, 3))
    if printStats:
        summarizeStats(stats)
```

Figure 24.20 Test models for Titanic Survival

CHAPTER 24. CLASSIFICATION METHODS

```
def summarizeStats(stats):
    """assumes stats a list of 5 floats: accuracy, sensitivity,
        specificity, pos. pred. val, ROC"""
    def printStat(X, name):
        mean = round(sum(X)/len(X), 3)
        std = stdDev(X)
        print(' Mean', name, '=', str(mean) + ',',
              '95% confidence interval =', round(1.96*std, 3))
    accs, sens, specs, ppvs, aurocs = [], [], [], [], []
    for stat in stats:
        accs.append(stat[0])
        sens.append(stat[1])
        specs.append(stat[2])
        ppvs.append(stat[3])
        aurocs.append(stat[4])
    printStat(accs, 'accuracy')
    printStat(sens, 'sensitivity')
    printStat(accs, 'specificity')
    printStat(sens, 'pos. pred. val.')
    printStat(aurocs, 'AUROC')
```

Figure 24.21 Print statistics about classifiers

The call testModels(examples, 100, True, False) printed

```
Averages for 100 trials
 Mean accuracy = 0.783, 95% confidence interval = 0.046
 Mean sensitivity = 0.699, 95% confidence interval = 0.099
 Mean specificity = 0.783, 95% confidence interval = 0.046
 Mean pos. pred. val. = 0.699, 95% confidence interval = 0.099
 Mean AUROC = 0.839, 95% confidence interval = 0.051
```

It appears that this small set of features is sufficient to do a reasonably good job of predicting survival. To see why, let's take a look at the weights of the various features. We can do that with the call

```
testModels(examples, 100, False, True)
```

which printed

```
Averages for 100 trials
 Mean weight of C1 = 1.648, 95% confidence interval = 0.156
 Mean weight of C2 = 0.449, 95% confidence interval = 0.095
 Mean weight of C3 = -0.499, 95% confidence interval = 0.112
 Mean weight of age = -0.031, 95% confidence interval = 0.006
 Mean weight of male gender = -2.367, 95% confidence interval = 0.144
```

When it comes to surviving a shipwreck, it seems useful to be rich,[182] young, and female.

24.6 Wrapping Up

In the last three chapters, we've barely scratched the surface of machine learning.

The same could be said about many of the other topics presented in the second half of this book. We've tried to give you a taste of the kind of thinking involved in using computation to better understand the world—in the hope that you will find ways to pursue the topic on your own. You probably found some topics less interesting than others. But we do hope that you encountered at least a few topics you are looking forward to learning more about.

---

[182] A first class cabin on the Titanic cost the equivalent of about $70,000 in today's U.S. dollars.

PYTHON 3.5 QUICK REFERENCE

Common operations on numerical types
  i+j is the sum of i and j.
  i-j is i minus j.
  i*j is the product of i and j.
  i//j is integer division.
  i/j is floating point division.
  i%j is the remainder when the int i is divided by the int j.
  ij** is i raised to the power j.
  x += y is equivalent to x = x + y. *= and -= work the same way.

Comparison and Boolean operators
  x == y returns True if x and y are equal.
  x != y returns True if x and y are not equal.
  <, >, <=, >= have their usual meanings.
  a and b is True if both a and b are True, and False otherwise.
  a or b is True if at least one of a or b is True, and False otherwise.
  not a is True if a is False, and False if a is True.

Common operations on sequence types
  seq[i] returns the ith element in the sequence.
  len(seq) returns the length of the sequence.
  seq1 + seq2 concatenates the two sequences. (Not available for ranges.)
  n*seq returns a sequence that repeats seq n times. (Not available for ranges.)
  seq[start:end] returns a slice of the sequence.
  e in seq tests whether e is contained in the sequence.
  e not in seq tests whether e is not contained in the sequence.
  for e in seq iterates over the elements of the sequence.

Common string methods
   s.count(s1) counts how many times the string s1 occurs in s.
   s.find(s1) returns the index of the first occurrence of the substring s1 in s; returns -1 if s1 is not in s.
   s.rfind(s1) same as find, but starts from the end of s.
   s.index(s1) same as find, but raises an exception if s1 is not in s.
   s.rindex(s1) same as index, but starts from the end of s.
   s.lower() converts all uppercase letters to lowercase.
   s.replace(old, new) replaces all occurrences of string old with string new.
   s.rstrip() removes trailing white space.
   s.split(d) Splits s using d as a delimiter. Returns a list of substrings of s.

Common list methods
   L.append(e) adds the object e to the end of L.
   L.count(e) returns the number of times that e occurs in L.
   L.insert(i, e) inserts the object e into L at index i.
   L.extend(L1) appends the items in list L1 to the end of L.
   L.remove(e) deletes the first occurrence of e from L.
   L.index(e) returns the index of the first occurrence of e in L. Raises ValueError if e not in L.
   L.pop(i) removes and returns the item at index i; i defaults to -1. Raises IndexError if L is empty.
   L.sort() has the side effect of sorting the elements of L.
   L.reverse() has the side effect of reversing the order of the elements in L.

Common operations on dictionaries
   len(d) returns the number of items in d.
   d.keys() returns a view of the keys in d.
   d.values() returns a view of the values in d.
   k in d returns True if key k is in d.
   d[k] returns the item in d with key k. Raises KeyError if k is not in d.
   d.get(k, v) returns d[k] if k in d, and v otherwise.
   d[k] = v associates the value v with the key k. If there is already a value associated with k, that value is replaced.
   del d[k] removes element with key k from d. Raises KeyError if k is not in d.
   for k in d iterates over the keys in d.

Common input/output mechanisms

`input(msg)` prints `msg` and then returns the value entered as a string.

`print(s1, ..., sn)` prints strings `s1, ..., sn` separated by spaces.

`open('fileName', 'w')` creates a file for writing.

`open('fileName', 'r')` opens an existing file for reading.

`open('fileName', 'a')` opens an existing file for appending.

`fileHandle.read()` returns a string containing contents of the file.

`fileHandle.readline()` returns the next line in the file.

`fileHandle.readlines()` returns a list containing lines of the file.

`fileHandle.write(s)` write the string `s` to the end of the file.

`fileHandle.writelines(L)` writes each element of `L` to the file as a separate line.

`fileHandle.close()` closes the file.

INDEX

__init__, 112
__lt__, 117
__name__, 221
__str__, 114

: slicing operator, 19, 77

α (alpha), threshold for significance, 329
μ (mu), mean, 259
σ (sigma), (standard deviation), 259

""" (docstring delimiter), 48

* repetition operator, 77

\ continuation character for lines, 80
\n, newline character, 61

start comment character, 13

+ concatenation operator, 18
+ sequence method, 77

68-95-99.7 rule (empirical rule), 259

abs built-in function, 24
abstract data type. *See* data abstraction
abstraction, 49
abstraction barrier, 110
acceleration due to gravity, 306
accuracy, of a classifier, 405
algorithm, 2
aliasing, 71, 78
    testing for, 88
al-Khwarizmi, Muhammad ibn Musa, 2
alpha (α), threshold for significance, 329
alternative hypothesis, 329
Anaconda IDE, 14
annotate, PyLab plotting, 390
Anscombe, F.J., 361
append, list method, 71, 72, 432
approximate solution, 30
arange function, 320

arc of graph, 191
Archimedes, 284
arguments of function, 41
arm of a study, 341
array type, 177
    operators on, 318
ASCII, 21
assert statement, 108
assertions, 108
assignment statement, 12
    multiple, 14, 67
    mutation versus, 68
    unpacking multiple returned values, 67
AUROC, 423
axhline, PyLab plotting, 242

Babbage, Charles, 355
Bachelier, Louis, 216
backtracking, 197, 198
bar chart, 358
baseball, 272
Bayes' Theorem, 349
Bayesian statistics, 345
bell curve, 258
Bellman, Richard, 203
Benford's law, 269
Bernoulli, Jacob, 241
Bernoulli's theorem, 241
BFS (breadth-first search), 199
Bible, 284
big O notation. *See* computational
    complexity
binary classification, 403
binary feature, 382
binary number, 34, 147, 237
binary search, 155
binary tree, 206
binding, of names to objects, 12
binomial coefficient, 264
binomial distribution, 264
bisection search algorithm, 32, 33
bisection search debugging technique, 96
bit, 35
black-box testing, 87–88
block of code, 17
Boesky, Ivan, 190

Bonferroni correction, 344, 366
bool type, 10
Boolean expression, 12
    compound, 17
        short-circuit evaluation, 55
boolean operators quick reference, 431
Boston Marathon, 292, 342, 344, 408
Box, George E.P., 215
branching program, 15
breadth-first search (BFS), 199
break statement, 24, 27
Brown, Rita Mae, 95
Brown, Robert, 216
Brownian motion, 216
Buffon, Comte de, 284
bug, 92
    covert, 93
    intermittent, 93
    origin of word, 92
    overt, 93
    persistent, 93
built-in functions
    abs, 24
    help, 48
    id, 70
    input, 20
    isinstance, 122
    len, 19
    list, 74
    map, 76
    max, 40
    range, 27
    raw_input, 20
    round, 36
    sorted, 158, 163, 186
    sum, 132
    type, 11
byte, 1

C++, 109
calibration of a model, 423
Canopy IDE, 14
Cartesian coordinates, 217, 378
case sensitivity in Python, 13
categorical variable, 264, 425
causal nondeterminism, 235
Central Limit Theorem, 298–301, 304
centroid, 385
character, 18
character encoding, 21
child node, 191
Church, Alonzo, 41
Church-Turing thesis, 4
Chutes and Ladders, 231
class variable, 119
class, machine learning, 403, 418
    class imbalance, 406
classes in Python, 109–34
    __init__ method, 112
    __lt__ method, 117
    __name__ method, 221
    __str__ method, 114
    abstract, 131
    attribute, 113
    attribute reference, 112
    class variable, 113, 119
    data attribute, 112, 113
    defining, 112
    definition, 110
    dot notation, 113
    inheritance, 118
    instance, 113
    instance variable, 113
    instantiation, 112
    isinstance function, 122
    isinstance vs. type, 122
    method attribute, 112
    overriding attributes, 118
    printing instances, 114
    self, 113
    subclass, 118
    superclass, 118
    type hierarchy, 118
    type vs. isinstance, 122
classification model, machine learning, 373, 403
classifier, machine learning, 403
client, of class or function, 48, 126
clique in graph theory, 196
cloning, 74
cloning a list, 74
close method for files, 61
CLT. *See* Central Limit Theorem
CLU, 109
clustering, 374, 383–402
coefficient of determination (R^2), 317–19

INDEX

coefficient of polynomial, 37
coefficient of variation, 250–53
command. *See* statement
comment in program, 13
compiler, 7
complexity. *See* computational complexity
complexity classes, 141
comprehension, list, 74, 421
computation, 2
computational complexity, 18, 135–49
    amortized analysis, 158
    asymptotic notation, 139
    average-case, 137
    best-case, 136
    big O notation, 140
    Big Theta notation, 141
    constant, 17, 141
    expected-case, 137
    exponential, 141, 145
    inherently exponential, 189
    linear, 141, 142
    logarithmic, 141
    log-linear, 141, 144
    lower bound, 141
    polynomial, 141, 144
    pseudo-polynomial, 212
    quadratic, 144
    rules of thumb for expressing, 140
    tight bound, 141
    time-space tradeoff, 168, 282
    upper bound, 137, 140
    worst-case, 137
concatenation (+)
    append vs., 72
    lists, 72
    sequence types, 18
    tuples, 66
conceptual complexity, 135
conditional probability, 346–48
confidence interval, 253, 261, 280, 295, 300
confidence level, 295, 300
confusion matrix, 404
conjunct, 55
continuation character for lines (\\), 80
continuous probability distribution, 256, 257
continuous random variable, 256
control group, 327

convenience sampling, 363
Copenhagen Doctrine, 235
copy standard library module, 74
    copy.deepcopy, 74
correlation, 359, 375
cosine similarity, 377
count, list method, 72, 432
count, str method, 79, 432
craps (dice game), 277
cross validation, 325
curve fitting, 309

data abstraction, 110, 113–15, 216
datetime standard library module, 115
debugging, 48, 61, 85, 92–100, 108
    stochastic programs, 243
decision tree, 206–7
declarative knowledge, 1
decomposition, 49
decrementing function, 25, 157
deepcopy function, 74
default parameter values, 42
defensive programming, 93, 106, 108
degree of belief, 349
degree of polynomial, 37
degrees of freedom, 331
del, dict method, 432
dental formula, 395
depth-first search (DFS), 197
destination node, 191
deterministic program, 215, 236
DFS (depth-first search), 197
dict methods quick reference, 432
dict type, 79–81
    deleting an element, 83
    iterating over, 82
    keys method, 82, 83
    values method, 83
    view, 82
dictionary. *See* dict type
Dijkstra, Edsger, 86
dimensionality, of data, 375
discrete probability distribution, 256, 257
discrete random variable, 256
discrete uniform distribution, 264, *See also* distributions, uniform
discrimination of a model, 423
disjunct, 55

dispersion, 252
dissimilarity metric, 384
distributions, 246
    Benford's, 269
    empirical rule for normal, 300
    exponential, 265
    Gaussian (normal), 259
    geometric, 267
    normal, 286, *See also* normal distribution
    rectangular, 263
    uniform, 165, 166, 264
divide-and-conquer algorithms, 159, 213
divide-and-conquer problem solving, 55
docstring, 48
don't pass line, craps, 277
dot notation, 54, 60, 112
downsample, 412
Dr. Pangloss, 85
driver, in testing, 91
dynamic programming, 203–12, 282
dynamic-time-warping distance, 387

e (Euler's number), 258
earth-movers distance, 387
edge of a graph, 191
efficient programs. *See also* computational complexity
Einstein, Albert, 86, 216
elastic limit of springs, 313
elif, 17
else, 16
empirical rule, 259
encapsulation, 126
ENIAC, 275
equality test
    for objects, 70
    value vs. object, 98
error bars, 262
escape character (\), 61
Euclid, 267
Euclidean distance, 378
Euclidean mean, 384
Euler, Leonhard, 191
Euler's number (*e*), 258
exceptions, 101–8
    built-in
        AssertionError, 108
        IndexError, 101

        NameError, 101
        TypeError, 101
        ValueError, 101
    built-in class, 105
    except block, 102
    handling, 101–5
    Python 2, 106
    raising, 101
    try–except, 102
    unhandled, 101
exhaustive enumeration algorithms, 25, 26, 31, 183, 205
    square root algorithm, 31, 138
exponential decay, 266
Exponential distribution, 265
exponential growth, 267
expression, 10
extend, list method, 72, 432

factorial, 51, 137, 143
    iterative implementation, 51, 137
    recursive implementation, 51
false negative, 356, 377
false positive, 348, 349, 356, 377
family of hypotheses, 344
family-wise error rate, 344
feature vector, machine learning, 372
feature, machine learning
    elimination, 375
    engineering, 375
    scaling, 400
    weight, 418
Fibonacci sequence, 52, 203–5
    dynamic programming implementation, 204
    recursive implementation, 53
file system, 61
files, 61–63, 62
    appending, 62
    close method, 61
    file handle, 61
    open function, 61
    reading, 61
    write method, 61
    writing, 61
find, str method, 79, 432
first-class values, 75, 104
Fisher, Ronald, 328

INDEX

fit method, logistic regression, 418
fitting a curve to data, 309–14, 315
    coefficient of determination (R^2), 317–19
    exponential with polyfit, 320
    least-squares objective function, 309
    linear regression, 310
    objective function,, 309
    overfitting, 313
    polyfit, 309
fixed-program computers, 3
float type. *See* floating point
floating point, 10, 11, 35, 34–37
    conversion to int, 21
    exponent, 35
    internal representation, 34
    precision, 35
    reals vs., 34
    rounded value, 35
    rounding errors, 37
    significant digits, 35
    test for equality (==), 37
    truncation of, 21
floppy disk, 171
flow of control, 3
for loop, 27, 61
Franklin, Benjamin, 56
frequency distribution, 256
frequentist statistics, 345
function, 40, *See also* built-in functions
    actual parameter, 41
    argument, 41
    as parameter, 162
    call, 41
    class as parameter, 220
    default parameter values, 42
    defining, 40
    invocation, 41
    keyword argument, 42
    positional parameter binding, 42

gambler's fallacy, 241
Gaussian distribution. *See* distributions, normal
generalization, 371, 372
generators, 128
geometric distribution, 267
geometric progression, 267
get, dict method, 432

glass-box testing, 88–90
global optimum, 190
global statement, 57
global variable, 57, 91
Gosset, William, 330
graph, 191
    adjacency list representation, 194
    adjacency matrix representation, 194
    breadth-first search (BFS), 199
    depth-first search (DFS), 197
    directed graph (digraph), 191
    edge, 191
    graph theory, 191
    node, 191
    problems
        cliques, 196
        maximum clique, 196
        min cut, 196
        shortest path, 195
        shortest weighted path, 195
    weighted, 192
Graunt, John, 355
gravity, acceleration due to, 306
greedy algorithm, 184–87
guess-and-check algorithms, 2, 26
Guinness, 330

halting problem, 4
hand simulation, 23
hand, in craps, 278
hashable type, 82, 114
hashing, 80, 164–68, 282
    collision, 165, 166
    hash buckets, 165
    hash function, 165
    hash tables, 164
    probability of collisions, 269
help built-in function, 48
helper functions, 54, 156
Heron of Alexandria, 1
higher-order functions, 75
higher-order programming, 75
histogram, 254
Hoare, C.A.R., 162
holdout set, 325, *See also* test set
Holmes, Sherlock, 99
Hooke's law, 305, 313
Hopper, Grace Murray, 92

hormone replacement therapy, 360
housing prices, 357
Huff, Darrell, 355, 370
hypothesis testing, 328
    multiple hypotheses, 342–44

id built-in function, 70
IDE (integrated development environment), 14
identity function, 400
IDLE IDE, 14
if statement, 17
image processing, 259
immutable type, 68
imperative knowledge, 1
import *, 60
import statement, 59
in operator, 77
in, dict method, 432
in, operator, 29
indentation of code, 16
independent events, 237
index, list method, 72, 432
index, str method, 79, 432
indexing for sequence types, 19
indirection, 154
induction, loop invariants, 158
inductive definition, 51
inferential statistics, 291
information hiding, 126, 128
    leading __ in Python, 126
input built-in function, 20
    raw_input vs., 20
input/output
    quick reference, 433
insert, list method, 72, 432
instance, of a class, 112
int type, 11
integrated development environment (IDE), 14
integration, numeric, 259
interface, 110
interpreter, 3, 7
Introduction to Algorithms, 151
isinstance built-in function, 122
iteration, 22
    for loop, 27, 61
    generators, 128

    over dicts, 82
    over files, 61
    over integers, 27
    over lists, 72
    tuples, 66
    while loop, 22

Java, 109
Julius Caesar, 56

Kahneman, Daniel, 369
Kennedy, Joseph, 98
key, in dict, 79
keys, dict method, 432
    in Python 2, 82
keyword (reserved words) in Python, 13
keyword argument, 42
k-means clustering, 387–402
knapsack problem, 184–90
    0/1, 188
    brute-force solution, 188
    dynamic programming solution, 205–12
    fractional (or continuous), 190
k-nearest neighbors (KNN), 410–14
Knight Capital Group, 94
KNN (k-nearest neighbors), 410–14
knowledge, declarative vs. imperative, 1
Knuth, Donald, 140
Königsberg bridges problem, 191

label, machine learning, 403
lambda abstraction, 41
lambda expression, 77, 161
Lampson, Butler, 154
Laplace, Pierre-Simon, 284
latent variable, 374
law of large numbers, 241, 243, 295
leaf, of tree, 206
least squares fit, 309, 311
legend on plot, 180
len built-in function, 77
len, dict method, 432
length (len), for sequence types, 19
Leonardo of Pisa, 52
lexical scoping, 44
library, standard Python, 61

INDEX

library, standard Python, *See also* standard library modules, 61
linear interpolation, 400
linear regression, 310, 371
linear scaling, 400
Liskov, Barbara, 123
list built-in function, 74
list comprehension, 74, 421
list methods quick reference, 432
list type, 68–73
    + (concatenation) operator, 72
    cloning, 74
    comprehension, 74
    copying, 74
    indexing, 153
    internal representation, 153
literal, in Python, 5, 10
local optimum, 190
local variable, 43
log function, 322
logarithm, base of, 141
logarithmic axis, 149
logarithmic scaling, 226
logistic regression, 417–25, 427
LogisticRegression class, 417
loop invariant, 158
lower, str method, 79, 432
lurking variable, 360

machine code, 7
machine learning
    binary classification, 403
    definition, 371
    multi-class learning, 403
    one-class learning, 403
    supervised, 373
    two-class learning, 403
    unsupervised, 373
Manhattan distance, 378
Manhattan Project, 275
many-to-one mapping, 165
map built-in function, 76
    in Python 2, 76
markeredgewidth, 320
math standard library module, 322
MATLAB, 169, 388
max built-in function, 40
maximum clique, 196

memoization, 204
merge sort, 144, 159–62, 203
method invocation, 54, 112
min cut, 196
Minkowski distance, 377, 382, 387
model, 215
modules, 59–61, 59, 90, 109
modulus, 11
Moksha-patamu, 231
Molière, 110
Monte Carlo simulation, 275–88, 275
Monty Python, 14
mortgages, 130, 175
multi-class learning, 403
multiple assignment, 14, 67
    return values from functions, 67
multiple hypotheses, 342–44
multiple hypothesis, 366
multiplicative law for probabilities, 238
mutable type, 68
mutation versus assignment, 68

n choose k, 264
name space, 43
names in Python, 13
nan (not a number), 106
nanosecond, 27
National Rifle Association, 363
natural number, 51
negative predictive value, 406
nested statements, 17
newline character (\n), 61
Newton's method. *See* Newton-Raphson method
Newtonian mechanics, 235
Newton-Raphson method, 37, 38, 152, 309
n-fold cross validation, 413
Nixon, Richard, 65
node, of a graph, 191
nominal variable. *See* categorical variable
nondeterminism, causal vs. predictive, 235
None, 10, 41, 104, 131
non-scalar type, 9, 65
normal distribution, 258–63, 286
    standard, 400
not in, operator, 77
null hypothesis, 329
numeric operators, 11

quick reference, 431
numeric types, 10
numpy module, 177

O notation. *See* computational complexity
O(1). *See* computational complexity, constant
Obama, Barack, 51
object, 9–12
    class, 118
    equality, 70
    equality, vs. value equality, 98
    first-class, 75
    mutation, 68
objective function, 309, 372, 383
object-oriented programming, 109
one-class learning, 403
one-sample t-test, 336
one-tailed t-test, 336
open function, for files, 61
operator precedence, 11
operators, 10
    -, on arrays, 177
    -, on numbers, 11
    : slicing sequences, 20
    *, on arrays, 177
    *, on numbers, 11
    *, on sequences, 77
    **, on numbers, 11
    *=, 30
    /, on numbers, 11
    //, on numbers, 11
    %, on numbers, 11
    +, on numbers, 11
    +, on sequences, 77
    +=, 30
    -=, 30
    Boolean, 12
    floating point, 11
    in, on sequences, 77
    infix, 5
    integer, 11
    not in, on sequences, 77
    overloading, 18
optimal solution, 188
optimal substructure, 203, 209
optimization problem, 183, 309, 372, 383
    constraints, 183

objective function, 183
order of growth, 140
outcomes, 418
overfitting, 313, 395, 405
overlapping subproblems, 203, 210
overloading of operators, 18
overriding, 118, *See also* classes in Python: class attributes

palindrome, 54
parallel random access machine, 136
parent node, 191
Pascal, Blaise, 276
pass line, craps, 277
pass statement, 121
paths through specification, 87
PDF (probability density function), 257, 258
Peters, Tim, 162
Pingala, 52
Pirandello, 49
plotting in PyLab, 169, 229, 254–57
    annotate, 254, 390
    axhline function, 242
    bar chart, 358
    current figure, 171
    default settings, 174
    figure function, 169
    format string, 173
    hatch keyword argument, 298
    hist function, 254
    histogram, 254
    histogram scaling, 298
    keyword arguments, 174
    legend function, 180
    markeredgewidth, 320
    markers, 229
    plot function, 169
    rc settings, 174
    savefig function, 171
    semilogx function, 226
    semilogy function, 226
    show function, 170
    style, 226
    table function, 379
    tables, 379
    title function, 173
    weights keyword argument, 298
    windows, 169

INDEX

xlabel function, 173
xlim function, 242
xticks function, 358
ylabel function, 173
ylim function, 242
yticks function, 358
png file extension, 171
point of execution, 41
point, in typography, 174
pointer, 154
polyfit, 309
    fitting an exponential, 320
polymorphic functions and methods, 104, 117
polynomial, 37
    coefficient of, 37, 311
    degree of, 37, 309
polynomial regression, 310
polyval, 311
pop, list method, 72, 432
popping a stack, 45
population mean, 291
portable network graphics format (PNG), 171
positive predictive value, 406
posterior, Bayesian, 349
power set, 188
precision (specificity), 406
predictive nondeterminism, 235
print function, 9, 20
print statement in Python 2, 9
prior probability, 348, 412
prior, Bayesian, 349
private attributes of a class, 126
probability density function (PDF), 257, 258
probability distribution, 256
probability sampling, 291
probability, calculating, 238
probability, conditional, 346–48
program, 9
programming language, 4, 7
    compiled, 7
    high-level, 7
    interpreted, 7
    low-level, 7
    semantics, 5
    static semantics, 5
    syntax, 5

prompt, shell, 10
prospective study, 367
pseudocode, 387
pseudorandom number generator, 243
push, in gambling, 277
p-value, 333–36, 333
    misinterpretation of, 334
PyLab, 169, *See also* Plotting
Pythagorean theorem, 217, 285
Python, 8, 40
Python 3, versus 2.7, 9, 20, 28, 36, 65, 76, 82, 83, 106, 243

quad function, 259
quantum mechanics, 235
quicksort, 162

R^2 (coefficient of determination), 317–19
rabbits, 52
raise statement, 105
random access machine, 136
random module, 237
random sampling, 363
random standard library module
    random.choice, 220
    random.expovariate, 267
    random.gauss, 259
    random.random, 212, 237
    random.sample, 294
    random.seed, 243
    random.uniform, 264
random variable, 256
random walk, 216, 215–33
    biased, 224
randomized trial, 327
range built-in function, 27, 67
    Python 2, 28
range type, 67
    not a type in Python 2, 65
rate of decay, 267
raw_input built-in function, 20
    input vs., 20
recall (sensitivity), 406
receiver operating characteristic curve (ROC), 423
recurrence, 53
recursion, 50–57
    base case, 51

recursive (inductive) case, 51
regression model, 373
regression testing, 92
regression to the mean, 241, 369
regressive fallacy, 369
rejection, of null hypothesis, 329
remove, list method, 72, 432
repetition operator (*), 18, 66
replace, str method, 79, 432
representation invariant, 113
representation-independence, 113
reserved words in Python, 13
retrospective study, 367
return on investment (ROI), 279
return statement, 41
reverse argument for sort and sorted, 186
reverse method, 72
rfind, str method, 79, 432
Rhind Papyrus, 283
rindex, str method, 79, 432
ROC curve (receiver operating characteristic curve), 423
ROI (return on investment), 279
root of polynomial, 37
root of tree, 206
round built-in function, 36
R-squared (coefficient of determination), 317–19
rstrip, str method, 79, 432

sample, 291
sample function, 294
sample mean, 291, 298
sample standard deviation, 303
sampling
    accuracy, 246
    bias, 362
    confidence in, 247, 249
    convenience sampling, 363
    simple random, 291
    stratified, 291
Samuel, Arthur, 371
scalar type, 9
scaling features, 400
scientific method, 333
SciPy library, 259
    scipy.integrate.quad, 259
    scipy.random.standard_t, 331

scipy.stats.ttest_1samp, 337
scipy.stats.ttest_ind, 343
scoping, 43
    assignment to variable, impact of, 46
    lexical, 44
    static, 44
script, 9
SE. *See* standard error of the mean
search algorithms, 152–57
    binary search, 155, 156
    bisection search, 33
    breadth-first search (BFS), 199
    depth-first search (DFS), 197
    linear search, 136, 153
search space, 152
self, 113
SEM. *See* standard error of the mean
semantics, 5
semilogx, 226
semilogy, 226
sensitivity (recall), 406
seq, sequence method, 77
sequence methods quick reference, 431
sequence types, 19, *See also* str, tuple, list
shell, 9
shell prompt, 10
short-circuit evaluation of Boolean expressions, 55
shortest path, 195
shortest weighted path, 195
side effect, 71, 72
signal processing, 259
signal-to-noise ratio (SNR), 374
significant digits, 35
simple random sample, 291
simulation, 215, 237
    coin flipping, 239–53
    continuous, 289
    deterministic, 289
    discrete, 289
    dynamic, 289
    Monte Carlo, 275–88
    multiple trials, 240
    random walks, 215–33
    smoke test, 223
    static, 289
    stochastic, 289
    typical structure, 279

INDEX

simulation model, 215, *See* simulation
sklearn, 417
    sklearn.metrics.auc, 424
slicing for sequence types, 19
SmallTalk, 109
smoke test, 223
snake oil, 369
Snakes and Ladders, 231
SNR (signal to noise ratio), 374
social networks, 196
software quality assurance (SQA), 91
sort built-in method, 72, 432
    key parameter, 164
    mutates argument, 163
    mutates list, 158
    polymorphic, 117
    reverse parameter, 164
sorted built-in function, 186
    does not mutate argument, 163
    key parameter, 164
    returns a list, 158
    reverse parameter, 164
sorting algorithms, 158–64
    in-place, 162
    merge sort, 144, 159–62, 203
    quicksort, 162
    stable, 164
    timsort, 162
source code, 7
source node, 191
space complexity, 143, 162
specification, 47–50
    assumptions, 48, 155
    docstring, 48
    guarantees, 48
specificity (precision), 406
split, str method, 79, 162, 432
spring constant, 305
SQA (software quality assurance, 91
square root, 30, 31, 32, 38
stable sort, 164
stack, 45
stack frame, 44
standard deviation, 247, 280
    relative to mean, 250
standard error. *See* standard error of the mean

standard error of the mean (SE, SEM), 302–4, 330
standard library modules
    copy, 74
    datetime, 115
    math, 322
    random, 237
standard normal distribution, 400
statement, 9
statements
    *=, 30
    +=, 30
    -=, 30
    = (assignment), 12
    assert, 108
    break, 27, 29
    conditional, 15
    for loop, 27, 61
    global, 57
    if, 17
    import, 59
    import *, 60
    pass, 121
    raise, 105
    return, 41
    try–except, 102
    while loop, 22
    yield, 128
static scoping, 44, *See also* scoping
static semantic checking, 5, 128
statistical machine learning. *See* machine learning
statistical significance, 328–44, 328, 366
    correctness versus, 288
statistical sin
    assuming independence, 356
    confusing correlation and causation, 360
    convenience (accidental) sampling, 363
    Cum Hoc Ergo Propter Hoc, 359
    extrapolation, 364
    Garbage In Garbage Out (GIGO), 356
    non-response bias, 362
    reliance on measures, 361
    Texas sharpshooter fallacy, 364
statistics
    alternative hypothesis, 329
    coefficient of variation, 250–53
    confidence interval, 253, 261, 300

confidence interval, overlapping, 281
confidence level, 261
correctness vs. statistical validity, 287
correlation, 359
error bars, 262
frequentist approach, 336
null hypothesis, 329
sample standard deviation, 303
significance, 328–44
standard error of the mean, 302
t-distribution, 304, 330
test statistic, 329
α (alpha), 329
stats module
    stats.ttest_1samp, 368
    stats.ttest_ind, 333
step (of a computation), 136
stochastic process, 215
stochastic programs, 236
stored-program computer, 3
str
    built-in methods, 78
    character as, 18
    concatenation (+), 18
    escape character, \, 120
    indexing, 19
    len, 19
    newline character (\n), 61
    slicing, 19
    split method, 162, 432
    substring, 19
str methods quick reference, 432
straight-line programs, 15
stratified sampling, 291
string type. *See* str
stub, in testing, 91
Student's t-distribution, 330
study power, 336
substitution principle, 123, 195
substring, 19
successive approximation, 38, 309
sum built-in function, 132
supervised learning, 373, 403
support, Bayesian, 349
symbol table, 44, 60
syntax, 5

table function, PyLab, 379

table lookup, 204
tables, in PyLab, 379
t-distribution, 304, 330
tea test, 328
termination
    of loop, 23, 25
    of recursion, 157
test set, 325, 367, 403
test statistic, 329
testing, 85, 86–92
    black-box, 87–88
    boundary conditions, 87
    driver, 91
    glass-box, 88–90, 88–90
    integration testing, 90
    partitioning inputs, 86
    path-complete, 89
    regression testing, 92
    stub, 91
    test functions, 48
    test suite, 86
    unit testing, 90
Texas sharpshooter fallacy, 364
timsort, 162
Titanic, 425
total ordering, 32
training error, 403
training set (training data), 325, 367, 372, 403, 408
translating text, 80
treatment effect, 369
treatment group, 327
tree, 205
    decision tree, 206–7
    enumeration, left-first depth-first, 207
    leaf node, 206
    root, 206
    rooted binary tree, 206
triangle inequality, 378
true negative, 404
true positive, 348
try block, 102
try-except statement, 102
t-statistic, 330
t-test, 333
tuple type, 65
Turing completeness, 4
Turing machine, universal, 4

INDEX

two-class learning, 403
type, 9, 109
    hashable, 82
    immutable, 68
    mutable, 68
type built-in function, 11
type cast, 21
type checking, 19
type conversion, 21
    list to array, 177
type I error, 330
type II error, 330
type type, 110
types
    array, 177
    bool, 10
    dict. *See* dict type
    float, 10, *See also* floating point
    instancemethod, 110
    int, 10
    list. *See* list type
    None, 10
    range, 67
    str. *See* str
    tuple, 65
    type, 82, 110

U.S. citizen, definition of natural-born, 50
Ulam, Stanislaw, 275
unary function, 76
Unicode, 21
uniform distribution, 166, 263, 264
unsupervised learning, 373
utf-8, 21

value, 10
value equality vs. object equality, 98
values, dict method, 432
variability, of a cluster, 384
variable, 12
    choosing a name, 13
variance, 246, 384
versions of Python, 8
vertex of a graph, 191
view type, 82
von Neumann, John, 160
von Rossum, Guido, 8

while loop, 22
whitespace characters, 78
Wing, Jeannette, 123
word size, 153
Words with Friends game, 338
World Series, 272
wrapper functions, 156
write method for files, 61

xlim, 242
xrange, in Python 2, 28
xticks, 358

yield statement, 128
ylim, 242
yticks, 358

zero-based indexing, 19
z-scaling, 400